D0945498

LORD
READING

LORD READING

Rufus Isaacs, First Marquess of Reading,
Lord Chief Justice and Viceroy of India,
1860–1935

Denis Judd

Weidenfeld and Nicolson
London

First published in Great Britain by
George Weidenfeld and Nicolson Limited
91 Clapham High Street, London SW4

Designed by Kevin Shenton

ISBN 0 297 78014 X

Printed by Butler & Tanner Ltd, Frome and London

Contents

Illustrations

Joseph and Sarah Isaacs, Rufus's parents, on their Golden Wedding day, 25 July 1905 (*by permission of Lady Joan Zuckerman*)

Rufus aged eleven and a half standing by the side of his brother Godfrey (*Lady Zuckerman*)

Rufus Isaacs, aged twenty-six, the rake of Belsize Park (*Lady Zuckerman*)

Rufus Isaacs, QC (*BBC Hulton Picture Library*)

Liberal lawyers: Isaacs, Attorney-General, with John Simon, the Solicitor-General, at a levée at St James's Palace in 1911 (*BBC Hulton Picture Library*)

Sir Rufus and Lady Isaacs walking to St Paul's to attend a thanksgiving service in February 1912 for George v's safe return from India(*BBC Hulton Picture Library*)

Asquith, Prime Minister 1908–16 (*BBC Hulton Picture Library*)

Godfrey Isaacs, October 1912 (*BBC Hulton Picture Library*)

Max Beerbohm's ironic view of the Marconi scandal (*the Beerbohm Estate*)

Max Beerbohm's cartoon of Lloyd George flanked by his two 'Guardians' (*the Beerbohm Estate*)

Lloyd George stepping out at Cannes in February 1913 with Sir Rufus and Lady Isaacs (*BBC Hulton Picture Library*)

Lord Reading leads the procession to the Lord Chancellor's breakfast, 1913 (*Central Press*)

Wartime associates: Colonel House and President Woodrow Wilson, 1918 (*BBC Hulton Picture Library*)

Lord and Lady Reading in Viceregal poses (*Lady Zuckerman*)

The Viceroy and Vicereine are welcomed at Victoria Station by Lord Birkenhead, April 1925 (*BBC Hulton Picture Library*)

The Viceroy about to shoot a tiger in the line of duty (*BBC Hulton Picture Library*)

Old friends: Margot Asquith bids Reading farewell before his return to India, July 1925 (*BBC Hulton Picture Library*)

The human touch: the Viceroy doffs his sun hat to respectful subjects at Calcutta, February 1926 (*BBC Hulton Picture Library*)

Reading as Foreign Secretary in the first National government in 1931 (*BBC Hulton Picture Library*)

Reading with his second wife after their wedding in 1931 (*Popperfoto*)

Reading, the newly installed Lord Warden and Admiral of the Cinque Ports, inspects the Silver Oar, June 1934 (*BBC Hulton Picture Library*)

Preface

This is the first biography of Lord Reading to be written with full access to his private papers since his son Gerald's predictably loyal two-volume *Life* was published during the Second World War. Even though Gerald Reading was able to make interesting use of his father's papers, he seems to have ignored, or to have been unaware of, a considerable number of them. This is especially true of the last ten years of Lord Reading's life, to which his son devotes a mere thirty-three pages out of a total of six hundred and fifty-seven. I have tried to set this to rights. Also, my biography, perhaps inevitably, is a far more critical, though I hope fair, appraisal of Lord Reading's life and career.

I have received the most generous help from the Reading family during my work on the book. At the beginning of my researches the Third Marquess, Rufus Isaacs's grandson, provided me with some documents not in the official collection at the India Office Library; he was also a kindly and courteous source of much useful information. I was greatly saddened by his death in 1980, not least because I had hoped to present him with a finished copy of the book. The Fourth Marquess and his brothers have continued their father's tradition of interested involvement. Lady Zuckerman, Rufus Isaacs's granddaughter, has been most helpful, not least in providing family photographs. I must, however, stress that no member of the Reading family has tried in any way to influence my professional judgement or to press a particular interpretation of events upon me. The views expressed in the book are, for better or worse, entirely my own.

I owe thanks to a good many others: to Christine Turnbull for her invaluable researches on my behalf; to the Polytechnic of North London for granting me sabbatical leave to complete the book; to my friend and colleague Dr Chris Cook for reading and criticizing parts of the text; to a variety of librarians and keepers of archives; to my friend John Curtis, Deputy Chairman of Weidenfeld and Nicolson, for his support and encouragement; to my editor Linda Osband for her enthusiasm and efficiency; to my mother for typing an impeccable typescript, and to my father for helping her to do so. My family were both a hindrance and a help, and I love them anyway.

Denis Judd
London, 1981

Introduction:
Rufus Isaacs and Lord Reading

Reading had a pleasing countenance. In conversation he had little to say, but when he spoke it was with authority. He did most of his talking and much of his public speaking with his hands on the lapels of his coat.... He could sleep anywhere at any time.
Lord Beaverbrook

Not go for the carry? I have gone for the carry all my life!
Lord Reading, in old age, to his caddie

If the events of Rufus Isaacs's life were to be presented in the form of a novel, any reader might pardonably claim that the book was the product of a feverish and unstable imagination. Lord Birkenhead indeed asserted that the story of Dick Whittington 'compared with the romance of Lord Reading ... fades into pale ineffectiveness'.[1]

Certainly the bare facts of Reading's career are eloquent enough: born the son of a Jewish fruit merchant, he was eventually made a Marquess, the first citizen since the Duke of Wellington to rise so high so fast; he became a brilliant QC, a Liberal MP and Cabinet minister, Lord Chief Justice, special wartime Ambassador to the United States, Viceroy of India, Foreign Secretary and a respected and influential elder statesman.

His life abounds with apparent paradox: leaving school after a piece-meal education at the age of fourteen, he was later more than able to hold his own with the best minds in international politics and diplomacy; as a rebellious, even disturbed, child, he came to personify the grave and sober majesty of the law; once a ship's boy, he ruled successfully over the Indian Empire; the youthful rake of Belsize Park, he was later a faithful husband and a prudish and somewhat inhibited adult; humiliatingly 'hammered' on the Stock Exchange, he became a widely

respected public figure; smeared during the Marconi scandal and subjected to anti-semitic attack, he was promptly appointed Lord Chief
Justice; he joined the Liberal party at its height and saw it disintegrate
into squabbling factions before his death; he rose to wealth and power
through the law, yet found the Lord Chief Justiceship an unstimulating
drudgery; unenthusiastic for Zionism, he was quick to defend his fellow
Jews from belittlement and slight.

For one who became so commanding a figure in Edwardian politics
and the law, Reading was a complete outsider. He was a Jew and the
son of a tradesman; he had attended no university, let alone Oxford or
Cambridge. It is perhaps this triumph over modest antecedents which
enabled him to form so close a relationship with Lloyd George, the
other great outsider of the Edwardian age, but a Welshman where
Reading was a Jew, and a solicitor where Reading was a barrister.

That his friendship with Lloyd George was the making of Reading's
later public career there is no doubt. Both men complemented each
other's virtues and deficiencies: where Lloyd George was passionate and
decisive, Reading was restrained and judicial; the Welshman struggled
to bring about radical change, his friend merely wanted to make things,
even if reformed, work more smoothly; Lloyd George pursued, and
generally caught, women, Reading even found ribald tales highly offensive; Lloyd George was naïve and careless in money matters, where
Reading was experienced and generally successful.

Their friendship toughened in the fierce fires of the Marconi controversy, both men went on to high office; Reading almost immediately to
the Lord Chief Justiceship, and Lloyd George, three years later, to the
Prime Ministership. From 1916 Reading enjoyed a Prime Minister's
preferment, which enabled him to shake off the dead weight of his high
judicial post and to play an important part in war politics, especially in
co-ordinating the war efforts of the United States and the Allied powers.
In 1921 Lloyd George appointed him to his greatest office of state, the
Viceroyalty of India. While Reading was in India, it seemed to some
that Lloyd George missed his advice and 'balance'.

Despite his intimate association with Lloyd George, Reading remained, with one awkward interlude, close to, and trusted by, Asquith.
To retain the good opinions of the two last Liberal Prime Ministers is
some indication of Reading's celebrated tact and reputation for fair
dealing. Asquith went out of his way to protect Reading and Lloyd
George during the Marconi scandal, and his wife Margot was later to
assert that he did it only because of his high regard for Reading.[2] When
in the 1920s the Lloyd George and Asquithian Liberals strove for

dominance in the party, it was Reading, particularly after his return from India in 1926, who was charged with attempting a reconciliation of the irreconcilable.

Reading's public career, even in his seventies, did not subside into a mumbling and contemplative retirement. He served as Foreign Secretary in Ramsay MacDonald's first National government, and might have had office again in 1932 – three years before his death. The lavish tributes paid to his memory when he died are further indications of the widespread regard and affection felt for him.

Why did Reading achieve so much? Was the extrovert and attention-seeking youth still there, lurking behind the sober purpose of the man of state, longing for affirmation? Asquith's wife believed that Reading was one of the four most ambitious men she had known,[3] and Frances Donaldson has suggested in *The Marconi Scandal* that 'at those moments when some great future opening out before him had yet to be secured ... his desire for self-advancement became a passion which drove this reserved and disciplined man'.[4] Clearly no man could have achieved so much if he had been devoid of ambition, and his son's judgement that the diversity of his offices 'almost excluded design' has a hollow ring. Of course, Reading also worked prodigiously hard and made very few enemies, all of which helped him to succeed. No one can doubt, however, that it was success he sought.

Not that he was uncritically admired. His parliamentary career was disappointing set beside his meteoric rise at the Bar, and his connections with the worlds of high finance and business enabled his Tory critics to taunt him in Parliament with cries of 'sticky fingers' during the Marconi controversy. Maynard Keynes found him maddeningly indecisive, and 'terrified of identifying himself with anything controversial', shortly after the armistice of 1918. Lady Oxford and Asquith described him, not altogether flatteringly, as being 'provokingly conciliatory'.[5] Walter Hines told President Wilson that the 'very general Conservative view of him is that he cannot be trusted';[6] Lord Beaverbrook considered his speeches to be 'dignified and dull', adding 'He was cautious, so cautious that he never gave an opinion unless he was forced to do so.'[7]

Despite his tact, patience and consideration, his personal charm and his capacity to cajole and persuade, Reading's public persona was stiff and lacking in charisma. He became particularly wary of giving more hostages to fortune after his battering at the hands of the press and Parliament during the Marconi scandal, and his speechmaking reflected that caution. Yet even earlier in his career his personality seemed curiously muted, with many defences; he was both elusive and

3

unfathomable to all but a few intimates, and showed a positive dread of emotional display. What was hidden behind his public mask? There was, perhaps, an element of anxious mutual reassurance in the slogan of the Reading Liberal party for his election campaign of January 1910: 'What's the matter with Rufus? He's all right!'

Reading was not a great reformer with the traditional 'fire in his belly', though he was happy to serve those, particularly Lloyd George, who were. His Liberalism was essentially ameliorative and he belonged by temperament to the right of the party. Although he never forsook the party which had, after all, provided him with a vehicle for promotion, he fitted hand in glove into MacDonald's first National government of 1931 and a year later barely tolerated Herbert Samuel's break with the second National administration over the tariff issue. Although not a National Liberal in name, he was one by instinct – an instinct that put his country above his race, and ensured that 'he loved and served England with all the silent passion of his heart'.

It was not surprising that Reading made no great impact upon the House of Commons during his five and a half years as a back-bencher. The law, particularly the Bar, had lifted him from obscurity, and he saw little reason to drop the techniques that had made him famous. His Commons' speeches tended to be forensic in style: lucid and subtle, showing a quiet mastery of detail, and an unwavering attachment to the central issues under discussion. He also believed, wrongly as it happened, that 'two men cannot exchange ideas and discuss problems without deriving some benefit to either side'. Both in Parliament and on the public platform he made less impact upon his audiences than those who scorned detail and reasoned argument, and instead presented great themes in bold and colourful imagery.

By temperament and training Reading was not a leader of men. Rather he was a ruler, an administrator, a born diplomat and conciliator. Though a Liberal for the whole of his political career, he remained somewhat detached from the fierce controversies that beset his party, sometimes adopting a positively non-partisan approach to great issues. These qualities won him wide respect, but they did not inspire either a passionate following or a host of bitter enemies.

Reading's political career, after he left the Bar, could be considered a failure, if judged by the highest standards. He scraped into Asquith's Cabinet as Attorney-General, and rose no higher in the hierarchy of the Liberal government; his appointment as Foreign Secretary in 1931 arose out of a national emergency and was essentially a stopgap appointment. His wartime appointments were temporary and diplomatic in nature, and the Viceroyalty of India was an office to which relatively few aspired.

Nor was his time as Lord Chief Justice a great success: he came heartily to dislike his duties on the Bench, and contrived to escape from them whenever he could. He left very little permanent impression behind, and it is clear that but for the moral obligation on him to accept the post in 1913 he would have preferred to seek preferment in other fields.

Yet Reading was undoubtedly one of the great figures of his time, and honours and high office were showered on him, often in erratic sequence. He was also an opportunist, in the best sense of the word: making unexpected changes in his public life according to circumstantial, though not dishonourable, pressures, and finding it easier to work towards an end than to devise the end itself. In some respects, he was a fixer: discreet, skilful and inventive, but a fixer all the same.

At this death there were inevitable comparisons with Disraeli, but apart from their Jewishness the two men had little in common. As the New York *Herald Tribune* pointed out, 'Lord Reading's intellectual abilities were not those of Britain's great Jewish Premier. Rather did he win by his industry and his charm, albeit he was a man of exceptional intelligence. Where Disraeli was brilliant, Lord Reading was cautious. Where Disraeli was witty, Lord Reading was suave.'[8] Reading would have been content with that assessment.

1 Origins and Schooldays, 1860–75

If your mother says it is so, it is so, even if it isn't so.
Joseph Isaacs, father of Rufus, to his children

Lessons he left unlearnt, class work he shirked, and mischief was his only devotion.
A schoolboy contemporary describing Rufus Isaacs

Rufus Daniel Isaacs was born on 10 October 1860, at 3 Bury Street, St Mary Axe, within the sound of Bow Bells. He was the fourth child, and the second son, of Joseph and Sarah Isaacs; five children were later born to Joseph and Sarah, and Rufus thus enjoyed a comfortable middle position among his siblings.

To be born into a Jewish family in mid-Victorian Britain, however, by no means guaranteed a comfortable life, free of slights and indignities. Nor did it promise an effortless advancement in public affairs. On the contrary, Rufus Isaacs's Jewish origins at various times provided his critics and enemies with an easy, and mostly cheap, source of ammunition to use against him. This was ironical in the case of a man who set little store by formal religion, and who eventually fitted so painlessly into the highest social and official positions offered by his country.

Isaacs's ancestors had first come to England from central Europe at the turn of the seventeenth century when Michael, son of Isaac, had settled in Chelmsford from where he peddled his merchandise. Michael Isaacs had a son, Israel, born about 1735. Israel Isaacs married Katherine Judah: two sons were born to them, Samuel in 1759 and Isaac in 1767, at a time when Britain was triumphantly asserting her claims to naval and colonial supremacy at the expense of Spain and France.

Samuel Isaacs lived to the awesome age of one hundred and six years. He died in 1865, the year in which the death of Lord Palmerston cleared the way for the supremacy of Gladstone and the creation of a new Liberal party. Five years before Samuel Isaacs's death was born the great-grandson who was destined to sustain the Liberal party in the more taxing conditions of the twentieth century, and the subject of this biography.

Rufus Isaacs's extended family, with the patriarch Samuel at its head, was both varied and interesting. His great-grandmother Sarah, wife of the centenarian, herself lived to be one hundred and three, and various of her and Samuel's descendants lived well into their eighties and nineties. One of Rufus's great-uncles was the celebrated prize-fighter Daniel Mendoza (1765–1836) whose success with his fists provided the British public with an image very different from the contemporary stereotype of the cringing, peddling, money-lending Jew. Before he retired to a pub in Whitechapel, Daniel Mendoza had helped to revolutionize pugilism with his skill and dexterity, and had written his classic *Art of Boxing*, first published in 1789, the year of the French Revolution. Although Rufus Isaacs never knew this fighting great-uncle, he admired his achievements greatly, and was for a time an enthusiastic amateur boxer himself.

Daniel Mendoza's Spanish name is an indication that the Isaacs had already married into the Sephardic branch of the Jewish faith. Michael Isaacs, son of the redoubtable Samuel, had married Sarah, daughter of Aaron Mendoza, and the niece of the prize-fighter. It was later rumoured that the Mendozas were somehow related to Benjamin Disraeli, though there is no clear proof of this, and when a subsequent generation of the Isaacs family referred to 'Uncle Ben' it was somewhat tongue-in-cheek. Despite this tenuous connection with Disraeli, the Mendozas had a forbear to be proud of in his own right: in 1732 an earlier Aaron Mendoza had published one of the first books produced by a Jew in England – a manual of the laws governing ritual slaughter, with illustrations in his own hand.

As well as marrying Sarah Mendoza, Michael Isaacs launched the family into the fruit business on a considerable scale. Whereas his father Samuel had held a stall in the fruit market in Duke's Place, Aldgate, Michael Isaacs set up a company devoted to the importing of foreign fruit – mostly from Italy and Spain – at Mitre Street, in Aldgate. The business was still thriving in the immediate post-Second World War era.

Michael and Sarah Isaacs had two sons: Henry Aaron and Joseph Michael. The career of the former exemplifies the new freedom from civil disabilities which Jews, and other religious dissenters, were able to enjoy fully by the middle of the nineteenth century. Henry, or 'Harry', Isaacs became a member of the Corporation of London in 1882, then Alderman and later Sheriff. He was knighted in 1887 and two years afterwards was elected Lord Mayor of London.

His younger brother Joseph met, as a small boy, his future wife Sarah Davis at a dancing class. He fell instantly in love with her and determined to marry her as soon as it became practical. In 1855 the wedding took place, when Joseph was twenty-three years old and Sarah was twenty. The marriage was to last for fifty-two years.

After their wedding Joseph and Sarah moved to the Bury Street address where Rufus was born in 1860. Why he was given the unlikely name of Rufus is quite clear: he was named after the eldest of his mother's six brothers. There was, however, doubt in the family as to whether this uncle Rufus had formally been given this name; it seems most likely that he had originally been called Abraham but had later adopted the name of Rufus as more striking and original. The properly named Rufus Isaacs certainly had no cause to regret his uncle's eccentricity, and his own son later wrote, 'the name ... was so invaluable an asset to him throughout life. "Rufus Isaacs": it was always a distinguishing mark, a proclamation, at once arresting and euphonious, of his identity, which reached its zenith in the inevitable and invincible slogan of later electioneering days: "Rufus for Reading" in huge letters of the Liberal red.'[1]

Not long after Rufus's birth, Joseph and Sarah Isaacs moved to Finsbury Square, into a larger house which in due course provided a home for their nine children. Finsbury Square was still within the City of London and thus conveniently close to the family fruit business, M. Isaacs and Sons Limited. A few years later the family moved again, this time to the more bracing air of Hampstead, where they settled at 21 Belsize Avenue, next door to Sarah Isaacs's parents. The Isaacs were to live there for the next quarter century.

The migration from the City to Hampstead represented more than a proof of Joseph Isaacs's prosperity, and was not merely a predictable drift from an inner city area that was becoming less residential in nature to an attractive suburb well-served by public transport. In part, at least, the move to Belsize Avenue was a step towards emancipation – a break away from the close embrace of orthodox City Jewry to the more cosmopolitan environment of Hampstead where the Isaacs made new friends among neighbours that were predominantly either gentile or loosely attached to Jewish religious ritual.

Rufus's mother, Sarah, flourished in this new setting. Unlike her husband, Joseph, she set no great store by orthodox religion. Even her appearance belied her ethnic origins and her grandson has described her as, 'Rather above average height and strongly built, with brown hair, grey eyes, firm chin and her father's short, straight nose, she gave little outward indication of being a Jewess.' [2] Joseph Isaacs, called 'the Guv'nor' by his children, was of medium height, sturdily built, 'brown eyed, with a heavy moustache, short side whiskers and an expression of great kindliness which was not belied by his real nature in spite of occasional explosions into wrath'.[3]

Joseph Isaacs fought a losing, and sometimes noisy, battle to keep his family in the ways of the old religion. Until after the move to Belsize Park, Joseph insisted upon the ritual of daily family prayers. An incident not long after the move, however, shook his determination in this respect. He and his wife went on a few weeks' holiday. Before leaving, Joseph had summoned his elder sons Harry and Rufus, and, urging upon them the desirability of daily prayer in his absence, had secretly put a small onion into each boy's prayer bag. On his return, he inquired if they had prayed daily, and was assured that this had indeed been the case. On opening their prayer bags, however, Joseph found that each young onion had sprouted undisturbed in the dark. Although he thrashed his sons as punishment, the sprouting onions symbolized a defiant and independent filial outlook that could not be curbed. Indeed, Rufus Isaacs grew up to hold no religious beliefs, took a gentile as his second wife, and viewed his grandson's Anglican baptism with equanimity, even encouragement.

Perhaps the prime reason why Joseph Isaacs lost the battle to maintain religious orthodoxy lay in the fact that 'in the home Mrs Isaacs, always called by her family "the Mater", exercised unchallenged sway'. Dominated in business by his elder brother Harry, he was equally submissive at home, telling his children, 'If your mother says it is so, it is so, even if it isn't so.'[4] Occasionally Joseph's frustrated aggression would explode in violent displays of temper and he would pursue his delinquent sons round the garden, cracking a horse whip and roaring revenge. Even these demonstrations of paternal authority tended to be cut short by his wife, who prided herself on her French, interceding with a commanding '*Assez*, Joe!' Meted out more discreetly, however, physical punishment was part and parcel of Rufus Isaacs's childhood – though it seems to have had little deterrent effect on his boyhood escapades.

In general, family life was warm, close and lively. Despite his whipcracking tendencies, Joseph Isaacs was fundamentally a kindly man,

'Simple almost to guilelessness, generous to a fault, jovial and hospitable, he had something of the manner and appearance of a sea captain of the old school. . . . Wherever he went, he was greatly liked, for he had about him a warm and genial humanity which was prepared to welcome and retain each new acquaintance as a friend.'[5] His son Rufus was also to display the same geniality and courtesy in his adult life.

Joseph Isaacs liked a gamble, whether at cards or, more dangerously, at the Stock Exchange. Although it would be absurd to lay even part of the responsibility for Rufus Isaacs's involvement in the Marconi scandal at Joseph's door, the family were certainly no strangers to financial speculation. Indeed, according to Joseph Isaacs's grandson, the Second Marquess of Reading:

> The scale of living fluctuated with remarkable frequency. Mr Isaacs could make money but not keep it. When things were good, there would be horses and carriages in the stables; when things were bad, they would vanish. So accurate a test of the family fortunes were the stables that the children's first question on arriving at the station from school came by long experience to be: 'Is the carriage up or down?' If up, their holidays were likely to be gay, carefree affairs; if down, strict economy was the order of the day.[6]

Rufus's mother, Sarah, though insisting that she was of delicate health, none the less bore nine children and lived until she was eighty-eight. She conserved her energies, and at the same time gave proof of her alleged frailty, by lying in bed regularly until lunch-time, from where she issued orders for the running of the household and summoned into her presence those of the family whom she needed to encourage or warn. She has been described, not altogether accurately, as being, 'Very downright, very just and very undemonstrative, she viewed the children with a real and deep affection but equally with complete detachment.' Sarah Isaacs was no bluestocking: 'She had no intellectual interests, read great quantities of worthless novels, adored a game of whist or nap, took no exercise and had no women friends, holding that women were not to be trusted and that it was a mistake to indulge in intimacy with such unstable creatures.' She was clearly more interested in her sons than in her daughters.

Despite Sarah's misgivings as to the qualities of womankind, one of her daughters, Esther, went on to study art and became a reasonably well-known painter, marrying Alfred Sutro, the playwright. Apart from Rufus, whose achievements were to exceed even the most extravagant of maternal dreams, one other child, Godfrey, the fourth son, made his mark, becoming managing director of the Marconi Wireless Telegraph

Company Limited and one of the personalities at the centre of the scandal that came close to wrecking his brother's career.

Although as a man Rufus was to display great calm and dignity in his official career, as a boy he was ebullient to the point of wildness, and provocative to the point of anarchy. His son wrote:

> His is not the epic of the hungry boy poring over his books in a garret by the light of a flickering candle in order that he might equip himself for ultimate dominion over the vast concern of which he was then the smallest and least considered unit. He was wild; he was idle; he was volatile alike in his occupations and his affections. He was the terror of his schoolmasters, the scandal of the neighbourhood, the despair of his father. But he had vitality in super abundance and the courage never to submit for long to the uncongenial.... If Nature had made him a square peg, he was determined ultimately to find for himself a square hole, however long the search, rather than to suffer himself by a wearisome process of attrition to be forced into a round one.[7]

Perhaps Rufus's wildness was in part due to the fact that, at the age of four, together with his elder brother Harry, he was packed off to a kindergarten at Gravesend run by a Polish Jew named Barczyusky. After a year, their mother, distressed with their lack of progress with foreign languages, insisted that they be sent abroad to learn French – which she had somehow, though not without difficulty, managed to teach herself.

Rufus and Harry were accordingly placed in a school in Brussels kept by a man called Kahn. Since all the lessons there were conducted in French, the two boys soon mastered the language. It was here that Rufus gave an early demonstration of the intellectual powers that were to carry him to high office in both the law and politics. Monsieur Kahn offered a prize for the boy who, after reading two pages of French prose for ten minutes, could repeat them aloud with the most accuracy. Although Rufus was only five years old in a school where the oldest pupil was eighteen, he proceeded to win the prize. It was a story that he loved to tell later in life, saying that no subsequent success story had been as easy or as sweet. Quite apart from Rufus's legitimate feeling of triumph, the episode was an indication of an unusually retentive memory that would one day enable him, apparently effortlessly, to master complicated briefs and Cabinet papers.

School life in Brussels, however, was not all prize-winning. Out of the classroom, Harry and Rufus were mischievous and often disruptive. Their behaviour, in fact, was sometimes delinquent, and it is difficult to put it all down to 'high jinks' or some similar cliché. The two young boys seem, in certain ways, to have been quite seriously disturbed, something which may have resulted from their being sent away from home at so tender an age. One incident at Brussels shows the extent of their naughtiness, and perhaps illustrates their destructive rage. Once, when they had merited the ultimate punishment of solitary confinement in an upstairs room on bread and water, they threw all the furniture out of the window into the courtyard below!

Monsieur Kahn at last acknowledged defeat. He sent for Joseph Isaacs and gave him an ultimatum: he would keep on either Harry or Rufus, but not both. A humiliated Joseph Isaacs emerged from the interview with tears staining his cheeks. Harry was taken home, and at the beginning of the next term Rufus, then aged six, returned with Albert, a more docile younger brother.

A year later, both Rufus and Albert were sent to an Anglo-Jewish boarding school in London, in Northwick Terrace, Regents Park, run by a Mr A.P. Mendes who already had charge of the disgraced Harry. Rufus hardly distinguished himself at Mr Mendes's academy, although he fell passionately in love with his headmaster's daughter, who was of his own age, and took to passing her sweets and *billets-doux* in class.

He learnt Hebrew and German with Mr Mendes, but not, apparently, the classics so often taught at Christian private schools. He was also, and by now predictably, badly behaved. Though clever, he was mostly idle, and his teachers reproached him with 'Isaacs secundus, you will go to the devil!' According to a contemporary, 'lessons he left unlearnt, class work he shirked, and mischief was his only devotion. Nor was he mischievous only in himself – he delighted in inspiring others in his "wicked ways" ... a demoniacal young mischievous boy with sparkling eyes who was ever in disgrace or being caned, and yet withal was ever merry and deliciously humorous.' Once when a despairing Mr Mendes was caning him before his school fellows he 'screamed and twisted about – well, to the complete satisfaction of the schoolmaster', while at the same time laughing for the benefit of his friends.[8]

By the time Rufus had reached the age of eleven, he seems to have become more reconciled to the constraints of school. At least, a letter written then to a fellow pupil contains (in addition to a good many semicolons) a favourable reference to one of his teachers as well as some frank enjoyment at witnessing a fire in Camden Town:

Dear Delly,

I was very much astonished at not having received a letter from you: it has very much surprised me, but I thought I will write to you and I suppose you will answer me.

The weather here is very bad, at least it has been so for the last two days; it has constantly rained for one whole night.

I suppose you are astonished at not having received all your books. I have most of your books locked up in my desk. Ben Mosely uses your spelling, because he says that you said that if he liked he could use all the books; I will leave them locked up in my desk. The examinations have not yet commenced; they will commence on 1st September and end on the 17th or 18th; and on the glorious 19th, hurrah for the holidays.

I am enjoying myself quite as much as you are; I am looking forward to the holidays, you are in the midst of your holidays. Mind you write to Mr Mendes. I suppose you do not know that Dr Mendes is home, he is awfully clever and kind.

Dr Aronsohn has left, and Dr Mendes takes us in German and Hebrew. He does all doctor's teaching but is not on duty; but does he not give us a lot of German, enough to make us satisfied, I can tell you. But I can see we will get on with him. Dr Mendes takes first division and Mr Mendes the other, dodging like Mr Mendes and Mr Boys used to do.

We have a new boy, whose name is L. – he is an English boy but five years in Germany; he comes from the Jews' College. He is rather a dull fellow to play with; he speaks in such a mournful tone when he asks for a book or any such thing that he nearly makes you cry; but wait till next term to find out for yourself.

Mind next term when I come back, I shall be 12 years old; but I forget; so will you be, I shall come back eldest Isaacs in this school.

Such a sight, 26th August there was a great fire at Camden Town, the boys all put on their trousers, boots and stockings and ran up to the nursery with Mr and Mrs Mendes; then we stood on chairs and the table and we saw the fire blazing up; it was a beautiful sight, really worth seeing. I wish you had been there; your sleepy head would have jumped out of bed pretty quickly, I can tell you.[9]

Rufus's generally happy time at Northwick Terrace was marred by a crippling injury to his younger brother Albert, who so damaged his leg in a fall during a riotous magic lantern show that he never walked again and died at the age of sixteen, the only one of Rufus's siblings not to reach adulthood. At least Rufus had done his best to cope with the situation when, appalled at the school's refusal to tell his parents of Albert's injury and worsening condition, he ran away from school and told them himself. Although Albert was at once taken home, the complications from the accident were too far advanced to reverse.

In September 1873 Rufus entered University College School, then nestling by the side of its parent institution, 'that godless place', University College, in Gower Street. University College School was a natural refuge for non-Anglican pupils and some notable former pupils from dissenting or sceptical Christian backgrounds included Joseph Chamberlain and John Morley; like them Rufus Isaacs went on to become a Liberal Member of Parliament and a major statesman.

The headmaster of University College School, Professor Thomas Hewitt Key (who had been Joseph Chamberlain's headmaster two decades before), was a portly, kindly man of pronounced Liberal views – views which might well have influenced Rufus at the impressionable age of thirteen. Key had pioneered the inclusion of the natural sciences in the school curriculum, and had governed the school with a creative humanity, dispensing with corporal punishment and setting academic endeavour well above athletic prowess.

Although Rufus only attended the school for one academic year, he obviously flourished there and made a very favourable impression upon Professor Key. When Joseph Isaacs informed the school of his intention to remove Rufus and send him into commerce, Key argued against it, proposing, with imaginative foresight, that the boy should stay on into the sixth form, go to university and then study for the Bar. Joseph Isaacs and his immediate relatives were not impressed: trade was their means of livelihood and they felt relatively secure in commerce, arguing that it was foolish to set Rufus's sights on the mirage of Oxford or Cambridge, or to encourage him to aspire to the often unremunerative occupation of barrister-at-law. There is no doubt that Rufus later resented the fact that he had not enjoyed a university education, despite the tremendous professional and political progress he made without such an advantage.

Still, at the age of fourteen he left University College School, destined to become a fruit merchant in the family tradition. Before this, however, his father sent him for six months to Hanover to stay with a Dr Keyserling and to learn German. Early in 1875 he returned to England and was sent as an apprentice to his father's firm of M. Isaacs and Sons Limited, then situated at Moscow House, Eastcheap.

Rufus was still only fourteen years old, and not overjoyed at the prospect of working in Eastcheap. The only consolation, since the family firm now acted as shipping agents, was the possibility of overseas travel.

2 Some False Starts, 1876–85

I remember, as we were drawn from the quay by hauling at the capstan, we sang as we paced the forecastle: 'Hooray, my boys, we're homeward bound!' and 'Goodbye, Calcutta!' I, in my dream said: 'Goodbye, Calcutta, I shall return, but not on the forecastle's head.'

Rufus Isaacs, recalling his days as ship's boy aboard the Blair Athole

The chance of overseas travel did not materialize, and Rufus found his apprenticeship unsatisfying and unstimulating, although he inevitably acquired a basic knowledge of the fruit business in particular and of commercial practice in general. The tedium of his working day, allied with his own taste for adventure, led him to pursue a hectic social life during his leisure hours. His parents disapproved of a good many of his friends, but he refused to give up any of them. At the age of fifteen he even told his father that he wished to marry the sister of one of his least acceptable friends. Mr Isaacs, struggling to maintain his composure, asked him what he proposed to live on. 'Oh, that's your business!' was the reply, and the interview ended abruptly.

This premature suggestion of marriage was a clear sign of Rufus's restlessness and dissatisfaction. His father began to feel that London society was encouraging his son's disaffection with his work, and consequently sought a suitable environment to contain and discipline him. He eventually hit upon the idea of a spell at sea aboard a ship for which his firm acted as agents.

This episode in Rufus Isaacs's life was later suffused with the romantic glow so central to Victorian morality tales: namely, that he had run away to sea and signed on as a cabin boy, and, after a manly spell before the mast, had gone on to brilliant success in the law and politics. The reality was somewhat different.

Rufus was taken by his father to Cardiff to join the *Blair Athole*, an iron-built, full-rigged ship of 1,777 tons gross, on 9 October 1876. When, the next day, the boy was introduced to the *Blair Athole*'s captain, a Scot named Alexander Taylor, there was no smooth arrangement of the business. To begin with, Rufus refused to sign the ship's apprenticeship agreement without having its implications explained first. Having learnt that his signature would bind him for a full two years to an untried occupation, he refused to sign. Captain Taylor assured him, inaccurately, that the three other apprentices aboard were happy; his father raged, saying he was not to be made a fool of by his son.

Eventually Rufus proposed a compromise: he would not sign for two years as an apprentice, but he would sign articles as one of the crew – this meant that he could be paid off when the ship had completed her voyage and returned to the home port. From this decision he refused to budge. At last his father and Captain Taylor agreed, and on his six-teenth birthday he was signed on as a ship's boy at the wage of ten shillings a month.

The voyage of the *Blair Athole* lasted a little over a year. Captain Taylor, aged thirty-three, was a tough skipper with a firm sense of discipline. Apart from Taylor, the crew consisted of four ship's officers and thirty-three hands, among which were two Germans, two Swedes, two Portuguese, a Frenchman, an Italian, an Austrian and a Brazilian. The boatswain was a bully, apt to lay about him with the rope's end. Two men deserted while the *Blair Athole* lay in Cardiff, and two more were to leave at the next port of call. The ship was clearly not the happiest vessel afloat.

As ship's boy, Rufus had the most lowly position among the crew and consequently the dirtiest jobs. Among his daily duties was the cleaning out of the pigsty, which was not the most congenial task for someone from a Jewish background. Shortly after leaving Cardiff the ship ran into bad weather, and Rufus was violently seasick.

Apart from these trials, he was also completely ignorant of the skills of seamanship. Very soon after setting sail a storm blew up and the crew climbed on to the rigging to take in sail. Captain Taylor, seeing Rufus idle, and doubtless bemused, shouted at him: 'Boy, up there and make fast that mizzen crojick clew garnet!' Not understanding a word of this technical double dutch, Rufus seized hold of the first loose rope end in sight and secured it. By some miracle, it was exactly what the captain wanted and all was well.

Rufus showed great courage and maturity during the *Blair Athole*'s voyage across the Atlantic to Rio de Janeiro. He had to fend for himself among the crew, but was able to hold his own in physical confrontation – perhaps the example of fighting Daniel Mendoza was an inspiration.

He also gave an early demonstration of his powers of advocacy, if not exactly of leadership. Although Board of Trade regulations stated that each man was entitled to one pound of bread, one and a half pounds of beef or one and a quarter pounds of pork, half a pound of flour or one-eighth of a pint of peas, one-eighth of an ounce of tea, a half ounce of coffee, two ounces of sugar and three quarts of water per day, things were not always so straightforward at sea. Aboard the *Blair Athole* salt pork and weevil-infested ship's biscuits were the staple victuals, and there was nowhere this monotonous diet could be varied in the middle of the North Atlantic.

After semi-mutinous discussions, the crew decided to send a representative to the captain to put their complaints before him. Their choice fell upon Rufus, although whether this was in recognition of his superior education or because, as ship's boy, he was in no position to resist, is unclear. As it happened, Rufus responded well to the challenge, and put the crew's grievances to the captain. After a brief reflection, Captain Taylor sent the ship's boy back with the promise that he would in future have the ship's biscuits baked.

Feeling his mission to have been a failure, Rufus gloomily told his messmates the outcome and was amazed at their triumphant reaction. Baking the biscuits, it transpired, was an old dodge which enabled them to be easily broken up with a belaying pin thus making much easier the task of knocking out the weevils. In later years, at the height of his success, Rufus Isaacs liked to quote the incident 'as an example of the fact that the most spectacular victories were not always the most effective and that it was often well worth while to score a local success even if one could not win a decisive battle'.[1]

On 1 December the ship reached Rio after more than seven weeks at sea. Here was a world rather different from the City of London or Hampstead! While his crewmates headed for bars and brothels, Rufus decided to desert the *Blair Athole*. He made for the open country outside Rio and spent several days in hiding, without money and sorely tried by hunger. At last a hefty Brazilian negress took pity on him, and he stayed for two days in her cabin relieving his hunger on a diet consisting solely of bananas. When his hostess began to make amorous advances, however, he felt unable to pay such a price for her hospitality, and fled.

He now made his way back to Rio, hoping to sign on aboard another ship and thus return home. As a prelude he entered a seaman's lodging house near the docks. Here he was soon apprehended. According to one

17

account the suspicions of officialdom were aroused when he admitted, in response to a casual question, that he could do logarithms and thus revealed himself as an unusual customer. His own version was that he was taken before the harbour master and closely questioned as to his identity. All might have gone well but for the distraction provided by the harbour master's daughter, a girl 'of such ravishing beauty that Rufus, gazing upon her spellbound, paid no heed to answering the questions rained upon him, replied at random, and was swiftly exposed'.[2]

As punishment for his attempted desertion, he was put to the task of shovelling coal from the dockside into ships' bunkers. He laboured for three days under the blazing Brazilian sun, the only white man in a gang that consisted of negroes, South American Indians and men of mixed blood. He made no further attempt to escape, and when the *Blair Athole* sailed for Calcutta on 12 January 1877 he was once more at his post as ship's boy.

As the *Blair Athole* made her way across the South Atlantic under a scorching sun, the crew tended to bicker and fight. Rufus came in for particular attention from the boatswain, a heavy-handed tyrant called Isaac Cribb – shades of Israel Hands and mutiny at sea! Finally, cheered on by his shipmates, Rufus fought his persecutor on the deck and knocked him clean out. He was not troubled by the boatswain again.

Fourteen weeks out of Rio the *Blair Athole* entered the Hooghly river, below Calcutta, and dropped anchor. As the pilot came aboard, dapper in a uniform with bright brass buttons, and wearing white gloves, Rufus was ordered to carry this official's bag. He did so with alacrity, overcome by the pilot's smart uniform, and, as he later recalled, considering it to be 'the proudest day of his life'.

His main recollection of India in those first few hours was 'of the blood-curdling roars of tigers in the Calcutta zoo, echoing through the stillness of the night and causing him to be thankful for the protective strip of water between ship and shore'.[3] When he visited the city itself, he apparently made a favourable impression upon female observers with a spirited display of roller skating.

Towards the end of his life, Rufus Isaacs recalled how he left India:

I have often wished I could have seen ahead. I have often dreamed of that time when I stood at the capstan head and helped to heave my small weight at the capstan bar with the rest of the company on the forecastle, to get our ship into a proper position to be towed by the tug to take us down the Hooghly until we could sail. I remember, as we were drawn from the quay by hauling at the capstan, we sang as we paced the forecastle: 'Hooray, my boys, we're homeward bound!' and 'Goodbye, Calcutta!' I, in my dream said: 'Goodbye Calcutta, I shall return, but not on the forecastle's head.'[4]

Reality was to outstrip by far the sixteen-year-old boy's dream, for when next he entered the Hooghly it was as Viceroy of India, to the thud of a thirty-one gun salute.

On 15 September 1877 the *Blair Athole* docked at London. Rufus was paid off, receiving £3. 11s. as the balance, after expenses, from his wages of ten shillings a month. Delighted at his liberation, he literally leaped ashore, leaving his sea-chest behind him in his impetuosity. The *Blair Athole* was eventually lost at sea sometime during 1893, just as her former ship's boy was beginning to make his mark as a barrister.

Back in London, Rufus grew to cherish his experiences at sea. Although he had no liking for the rough life of a deck-hand, according to his son:

He never lost for the rest of his days his abiding passion for the sea. Never again was he as happy as when on it or beside it. ... In later years he would leave London at the end of a summer of overwhelming work, white and drawn and weary almost to speechlessness, bound for his annual cure at some Continental spa. As soon as he got on board the Channel steamer an almost magical change would come over him. He would pace the deck tirelessly, however stormy the sea, sniffing the brine, watching the sailors, scanning the water for passing ships.... Great was his joy if a sailing ship hove into sight. He would examine her rig with professional eye, and, if it bore any close resemblance to the *Blair Athole*, his happiness was complete.[5]

In September 1877, however, Rufus had put seafaring behind him. He returned reluctantly to his father's fruit business, finding his apprenticeship there as dreary as before. Perhaps to keep a flicker of interest alive, Joseph Isaacs sent him to Magdeburg in Germany to learn the trade with the fruit firm of Junker and Heyremann. After eight months the experiment came to an abrupt end when Rufus, quarrelling violently with a fellow-apprentice from Holland, poured a tureen of hot soup over his enemy's head.

Although he subsequently went on shorter trips, representing M. Isaacs and Sons in Belgium and Holland, for instance, it was plain that he lacked any inclination to work for his father and uncle. In 1879, therefore, he tried another career.

His eldest sister, Frances, had married a Dutch stockbroker, Albert Keyser, of the firm of Keyser and Frederici, and it was she who tried to help Rufus by proposing that he joined his brother-in-law's firm as a clerk. So, towards the end of 1879, Rufus went to work at the office in

Copthall Court, hoping eventually to become a full member of the Stock Exchange.

Here was a career in which Rufus Isaacs might well have spent the rest of his working life – his family connections were a positive advantage and his Jewish origins certainly no handicap. It was, however, to be a chastening and even humiliating episode in his life. To begin with, he began inadvisedly. Shortly after his nineteenth birthday, he applied to be admitted as a member of the Stock Exchange. The rules of the Stock Exchange at that time required all candidates for membership to be over twenty-one years of age. Amazingly, Rufus signed a printed statement to this effect, and was admitted as a member, having provided three sureties of £500 each.

What did he mean by this deception? Was it an early indication of tendencies which, it was later alleged, had helped to bring about the Marconi scandal? Certainly his critics at that time dug up this damaging example of dishonesty, and he was obliged to explain it to Asquith in July 1913: 'I acted in this manner upon private advice and was assured (quite wrongly) and I believed that this statement was only required as a matter of form to prevent the repudiation of obligations on the ground of infancy and that the effect of my signature was to make myself as responsible as a man of full age would be.'[6] A thin explanation, and a serious handicap amid the controversy and vilification of 1913.

On the other hand, there is an alternative explanation. The false statement of age was not inconsistent with the character of the young Rufus Isaacs. Despite his good qualities, he was unpredictable, rash, self-opinionated and essentially conceited. His mother doted on him, his siblings (on the whole) admired him, women found him attractive, he had discovered that he could manipulate and defy his father, he set little store by religious orthodoxy and social convention, he had refused to sign Captain Taylor's apprenticeship agreement, and he had shaken off all attempts to fit him into the family business. Perhaps he subsequently felt that the rules of the Stock Exchange could be treated in an equally cavalier fashion: that he could get away with it.

Indeed, he did get away with it, at least for a time, and in the middle of November 1879 his application was passed by the Committee for General Purposes. As a member of the Stock Exchange, Rufus entered into partnership with a Gerald Phipps as a jobber in the foreign exchange market. The partnership was to be dissolved three years later, though the reasons for this are not entirely clear.

For nearly five years Isaacs dealt chiefly in foreign bonds and securities, achieving sufficient success to live the life of a London 'swell'. He was now a very good-looking young man, taking after his mother's side of the family in appearance. He dressed in immaculate, even dandyish, style, and on Sundays rode on a thoroughbred mare into the countryside beyond Belsize Park at the centre of a squadron of admiring contemporaries. He was quick, agile, strong far beyond his eleven stones in weight, and expert with his fists.

His Stock Exchange colleagues included Jack Angle, a well-known amateur boxer who was pleased to make the acquaintance of fighting Daniel Mendoza's grand-nephew. Angle suggested that Isaacs should take boxing lessons to improve his technique which, though more than adequate aboard the *Blair Athole*, was not a classical example of the art. So on many afternoons, after the Stock Exchange had closed, Rufus sparred at a boxing school run by the ex-prize fighter Ned Donnelly, and conveniently tucked behind the Café Royal. His amateur boxing career, however, ended after an unfortunate encounter with Ned Donnelly. On one occasion Donnelly had told Isaacs to hit him as hard as he could and was soon gasping from a flurry of blows that drew blood. Enraged, Donnelly pursued Rufus round the ring, eventually breaking his nose, which thereafter retained a distinctive Roman bridge. Joseph Isaacs was horrified by the damage to Rufus's nose and made him withdraw from the amateur championship that he planned to enter. Despite the curtailment of his amateur boxing career, Isaacs occasionally found his skills useful outside the ring, as on the occasion when he knocked out a thug who was pestering him and his brother Harry at a coffee stall in Trafalgar Square.

Rufus had other skills in plenty: he 'had a light baritone voice of great purity' and joined in family renderings of the new, popular comic operas of Gilbert and Sullivan. He also danced well, and was still inclined to acts of self-advertisement like standing on his head in a box at the Empire Music Hall and applauding with his feet. He talked well, read little of any consequence, had a nice, and none too gentle, line in wit, and was, in short, very lively company.

It is no surprise that women found him very attractive; in addition to his good looks and athletic prowess, he had an irresistible, worldly-wise charm which fluttered hearts within a wide radius of Belsize Park. So successful was he with women, that he took to escorting one of his younger sisters to every dance so that she could act as a protective shield between himself and some female to whom, in a rash moment, he might have proposed marriage. Despite, or because of, his rakish reputation, young women flocked round him, and one of them once spoke for all when she told Rufus's sister Florrie, 'I know he's a very bad man, but if he asked me to marry him tomorrow, I could not possibly say no.'

By 1884 Rufus Isaacs seemed to have found a career that provided him with enough money to indulge his taste for pleasure and diversion. There the story might have ended. He might have gone from strength to strength in the Stock Exchange; become the head of a prosperous and lively household within London's financial and commercial inner circle; ending his days as a respected, but obscure, man of substance, his career of no interest to the nation at large.

Instead he was set on the path to extraordinary success by a humiliating failure. In the spring of 1884 there was a slump in the foreign market. His working capital had been diminished as a result of the break-up of his partnership with Gerald Phipps, and no doubt his relative inexperience told against him. There was subsequently a rumour that J.B. Joel, the South African magnate, had caused his financial problems by 'some stockbroker's trick'. At any rate, he was suddenly unable to cover his debts, to the tune of £8,000. On 14 August 1884 he was 'hammered', two Stock Exchange waiters striking the rostrum with their hammers prior to the public announcement that Rufus Isaacs was unable to meet his financial obligations.[7]

It was ironical that, having at last found a career to his liking, he should have been cast out of his membership of the Stock Exchange. Still, he was twenty-four years old, as yet unmarried, and with good family connections. His first concern was to earn sufficient money to repay his Stock Exchange creditors. Panama seemed a likely place where he could retrieve his fortunes: a French company, with which he had had some dealings, was planning to cut a canal through the isthmus; gold and other mineral deposits there were tempting; above all, Panama might become a 'boom' state, with many opportunities for an enterprising young businessman. His father agreed to the plan, though not without misgivings, and Rufus's passage was booked from Liverpool to Panama.

But as soon as he had left Belsize Park for Euston Station, his mother threw an hysterical fit of such intensity that the family became seriously alarmed. Mrs Isaacs, it was clear, was not prepared to see her favourite son set off for some fly-blown Central American state. In fact she still clung to the idea, first expounded by Professor Key at University College School, that Rufus should be encouraged to read for the Bar, and her hysterics were part of her campaign to bring that about.

Mrs Isaacs was not easily ignored by her family, and on this occasion her son Harry was soon dashing off to Euston in a hansom cab to bring

Rufus back. He hauled him from his compartment just as the train was about to steam out of the station.

Back in Belsize Park Mrs Isaacs calmed down and, with her son restored to her, reopened the debate over his potential legal career. This time she won, and it was decided that Rufus should at least find out if the law suited him.

To this end, it was arranged that he should be attached for six months to the firm of the family's solicitor, Algernon Sydney, at 46 Finsbury Circus in north London. If all went well, steps could be taken to advance his career along the lines proposed by Professor Key. Given Rufus's erratic progress so far, however, it was by no means certain that all would go well.

3 Barrister: Called to the Bar, 1886–97

> The Bar is never a bed of roses. It is either all bed and no roses, or all roses and no bed.
>
> *Rufus Isaacs*

Rufus Isaacs was twenty-five years old when he first went to work at the offices of the family solicitor Algernon Sydney. Given Rufus's reputation for dandyism compounded with obstinacy, this experiment might well have been as short-lived and disastrous as earlier attempts to find him a means of livelihood. There were many reasons why the experiment might be expected to fail: his formal education had been patchy, and he might not have the will to study for the three years before he could even begin to earn money to pay back the £8,000 owed to his creditors; he had earlier shown no liking for the state of apprenticeship either in the fruit trade or at sea; moreover, as a Jew, he was aspiring to a profession where few Jews had so far gone to the Bar. Weighing the odds, a betting man might well have waged against his making a success of his new venture.

As it turned out, Isaacs took immediately to the law, especially to the art of advocacy. Well before he had completed his six months' period with Algernon Sydney, he had made up his mind to become a barrister. Certainly advocacy would enable him to exercise both his intelligence and his love of being at the centre of the stage; it might also provide him with a level of income that would enable him to live in great style.

So badly did he want to succeed in his new profession that he quite dramatically changed his life-style. The frivolous youth was replaced by a serious young man, the seeker after ephemeral pleasures became a hard-working student. According to his son 'he suddenly vowed that he would go to no more theatres or dances until his Bar examinations were passed. His resolve was greeted with mingled incredulity and derision, but he kept to it.'[1] He hardly went to Ned Donnelly's boxing gymnasium, and instead got his exercise on his one free day, Sunday, when, with a couple of friends, he would walk as far as St Albans and back.

On 10 January 1885 he was admitted as a student to the Honourable Society of the Middle Temple. He now entered into the arcane ritual of 'eating dinners', as well as into the more comprehensible work of preparing himself for his examinations. He most dreaded Roman Law, for which he had to learn far more Latin than the minimal amount he had acquired at school.

The knowledge that he was studying for examinations in competition with young men just down from university, made him keenly aware of his own academic deficiencies. Like Joseph Chamberlain and Lloyd George, he sometimes felt at a disadvantage over his lack of a university education: 'Time and again in later years he would express ... his unqualified regret that he had never been to a university. ... He felt always that he had missed something for which no substitute can compensate and that, if he had had the benefit of a university education, he would have been able to take in his stride difficulties over which he had been compelled in afterlife to waste precious time.'[2]

As well as now struggling with feelings of academic inadequacy, Isaacs, for the first time, also seriously took stock of his lack of religious faith. While many leading Victorians merely paid lip service to religion, they at least knew at which altar they feigned worship: Anglican, Catholic, Presbyterian, Methodist, Unitarian and so on. Isaacs's trouble was that his mother had uprooted Jewish orthodoxy and put nothing in its place. He found liberal Judaism unsatisfying, and could not turn to Christianity. He 'never made any pretence of observing even the most solemn occasions of the Jewish year, and never entered a synagogue save for a wedding or memorial service'.

In October 1886 he expressed his dilemma in a letter to the daughter of an Anglican clergyman whom he had met while staying in Yorkshire: 'I still envy all believers, and can only continue to regret that I have ceased to be of their number. Had I seen more *true* religion, be it Christianity or anything else you like, I should possibly never have seceded.'[3] He claimed later in life that, if he could be allowed a fresh start, free from environmental influences, he would have become a Unitarian, worshipping one god in straightforward fashion.

Isaacs's religious doubts remained with him to the end of his life; more pressing was the need to pass his Bar examinations. Initially he worked under the supervision of a celebrated 'crammer', a Mr Hinde, but for his last year of study he entered the chambers of John Lawson

Walton as a pupil. Lawson Walton was a high-minded Wesleyan who proved to be an inspiring instructor with a particular flair for advocacy. Both men were to become Attorney-Generals in Liberal governments.

In the same chambers was Harry Poland, a barrister with an extensive criminal practice, who took Rufus under his wing and gave him some much cherished advice: 'Never come to the Temple later than ten o'clock in the morning and never leave it before six o'clock in the evening. What chance of success has a barrister who strolls into chambers about 11.00 a.m., with a great cigar in his mouth, lounges about till lunch-time, and then takes himself off to a club, or what he calls "home".'

As a result of hard work and good teaching, Isaacs passed all his examinations at the first attempt. Before he could formally be called to the Bar, he showed considerable self-confidence in moving into a set of his own chambers at 1 Garden Court, round the corner from Crown Office Row. He was next 'called', certified as a fit and proper person by the Recorder of London, Sir Thomas Chambers, a friend of his uncle Harry Isaacs, now knighted and a City Alderman. On 17 November 1887, the year of Queen Victoria's Golden Jubilee, Rufus Isaacs first wore his barrister's gown and wig at a ceremony in the beautiful hall of the Middle Temple.

Within two days of being 'called' he received his first brief – to represent his family's firm M. Isaacs and Sons Limited, who were being sued for breach of contract over a consignment of fruit from Spain. The fee was two guineas with half-a-crown for the barrister's clerk. Two weeks later he received a more substantial brief, again from M. Isaacs and Sons, to pursue the case further and go out to Spain to collect statements from various witnesses. This time the brief was worth seventy-five guineas, and it enabled the fledgeling barrister to conduct some family business of his own, namely to get married.

Rufus had first met his future wife at a dancing class, in exactly the same way that his parents had met. Alice Cohen was 'a young woman of rather more than middle height ... with hazel eyes and a mass of fair hair in naturally close waves. ... she painted creditably in oils, danced well and possessed an abounding vitality unquenched by the slightly petrifying atmosphere of her home.'[4]

The atmosphere was 'petrified' by her father Albert, a prosperous and self-made cotton merchant of German-Jewish extraction. Although not loud or violent, Albert Cohen was the absolute ruler in his home, allowing his wife and children very little social contact with the outside world. His obsessional personality made ritual and regularity the highest virtues known to mankind. He left for, and returned from, work at exactly the same times each day; on his return, his slippers had to be ready, his chair and lamp in their appointed places, and the household must be attentively silent; on Saturday night he took a weekly bath before dinner and, before he descended to dine, the family and the servants had to ensure that every draught had been excluded from the house. His 'wildest dissipation consisted in taking his favourite daughter Alice on each anniversary of her birthday to see Irving at the Lyceum'.

Determined to exclude all draughts and generally keep the outside world at bay, Albert Cohen was scandalized to find that Rufus Isaacs, the rake of Belsize Park and recently 'hammered' stockjobber, was paying serious court to his third daughter. For Alice, Rufus, with his worldly ways, his conviviality and his very different, infinitely more liberated, home background, must have appeared an armoured knight able to snatch her from the dragon's lair.

The dragon, however, was not willing to surrender his treasure. Alice was forbidden to have contact with Rufus, although her younger sister Rosie acted as a go-between, bearing letters to and fro. When Albert Cohen discovered that letters were being exchanged, the whole family was blasted by his wrath and he refused to speak to Rosie for six months.

At last Alice brought matters to a head by falling ill and taking to her bed. The malady was almost certainly psychosomatic; she was expressing very clearly both her anger and her helplessness. The family doctor could diagnose nothing wrong. Eventually an eminent physician, Sir William Gull, was summoned, and gave Albert Cohen his verdict: 'Give her the young man, and I promise you she will soon recover. Otherwise she will die.' Faced with this choice Mr Cohen surrendered with good grace, and on 8 December 1887 Rufus married Alice at the West London Synagogue, Upper Berkeley Street.

The marriage lasted for forty-two years, until Alice's death from cancer in 1930. They had only one child, a son, Gerald – the Second Marquess and his father's biographer. What sort of marriage was it? Lloyd George once told Rufus that 'I am always convinced that [Alice's] wise and affectionate guidance and care accounts largely for your brilliant career.'[5] Lady Cynthia Asquith, on the other hand, having met her at dinner in 1916, dismissed her as 'poor trumpeting Lady Reading', which hardly gives the impression of a valuable political asset.[6] Certainly Rufus Isaacs valued his wife's contribution to his career and in May 1919 wrote to Lloyd George urging him to grant her some sort of honour for her recent services as ambassadress in the United States.[7]

Rufus's and Alice's only child, Gerald, has left an affectionate account of their marriage, describing 'a mutual happiness and trust ... singularly free from even the most minor and casual domestic explosions. ... Though she was almost always at least a semi-invalid and he was habitually overworked, the nervous strain which their respective states imposed upon each of them never found relaxation in bickerings or reproaches.' According to her son, Alice's poor health was the sole reason for the restricted life she led, even in the first years of her marriage. We learn that moving house 'imposed a considerable strain on her health'; that 'given better health, she would have liked nothing better than to entertain frequently'; that 'unfortunately she was so much of an invalid as to be able to undertake only very occasional dinners at home, and for her to dine out was a first class event', and so on.

No one can doubt that Alice Isaacs had poor health, especially in the latter part of her life. As early as 1891 she underwent surgery, and in June 1919 she endured a serious operation for gall bladder trouble, causing her husband to write, 'She has had great pain during the whole of last year but carried on ... then came acute inflammation and an immediate operation was imperative. Thank God it was not delayed.'[8] She was finally stricken by cancer early in 1929 and suffered considerable pain for nearly two years before her death.

On the other hand it is possible, especially in the early part of her marriage, that she sometimes chose to see herself as more of an invalid than she was. Perhaps it would have been too daunting, threatening even, simply to have exchanged the restricted home life of her father's house for the free and varied social activities of her husband and his family. As Rufus rose to fame at the Bar, and then in politics, the social demands placed upon the wife of so successful a man would have seemed intolerable to a shy and indifferently educated young woman, recently plucked from a home where draughts and the outside world in general were seen as unwholesome intruders. Her invalid status perhaps provided her with an excuse for staying within the refuge of her home.

Alice's confinement to the house did not restrict her husband's activities outside of it. As his professional reputation increased, 'She constantly urged him to accept as many as possible of the numerous invitations that now began to arrive, holding that it was essential for his career that he should meet as many people as possible.'[9] Alice did not entirely miss out on the excitement and interest provided by these contacts: 'She was a poor sleeper and was almost always awake on his return, and it was his cherished habit to come in and tell her all that had happened so that she might enjoy his evening at least at second hand.'

Within her domestic fastness, Alice, perhaps surprisingly, was stronger and more decisive than Rufus:

Her view prevailed in this as in other fields of their domestic life, not entirely because he gave way to her wishes but because he was only too thankful to have his mind made up for him. Swift and sure as was his power of decision in his work and in the major crises of his life, in small things he was hopelessly undecided and would hover endlessly about the most insignificant problem until she firmly took the matter out of his hands.[10]

What did she do during her long hours alone? She 'was an indefatigable letter writer, she read innumerable novels of varying type and quality and was engrossed in many friendships, among which the newly acquired blended happily with, but never ousted, the old established – indeed her closest friend at the end of her life was a neighbour and schoolfellow of her girlhood'. She enjoyed collecting antiques and soon became something of an expert, acquiring some good examples of eighteenth-century satinwood and of old Chelsea porcelain. When she did entertain, she apparently enjoyed 'the ordering of the dinner, the selection and arranging of the flowers, the regulation of every detail of the proceedings'.

Alice also got considerable pleasure from furnishing and decorating her homes, even, towards the end of her life, the viceregal apartments that she and her husband occupied. The several moves of her married life at least enabled her to give full expression to this interest. When newly married she and Rufus lived in Broadhurst Gardens near Finchley Road railway station, when he was first called to the Bar. They later moved to Palace Court in Bayswater, as Rufus was applying for silk. In 1903, shortly before he entered the House of Commons, they moved to Park Lane, to a small Georgian house with a lovely view over Hyde Park. In 1910 the ever increasing petrol fumes from the traffic of Park Lane drove them to the quieter but equally prestigious confines of Curzon Street where they occupied number 32, an early Georgian house of considerably larger proportions than their Park Lane home. Number 32 Curzon Street was the family home until after Rufus's death in 1935.

Despite his rapidly rising income after he had established himself at the Bar, neither Isaacs nor his wife lived extravagantly. On the contrary, their tastes remained essentially simple – despite the moves to Park Lane and Curzon Street, and Alice's love of the antique market. She did not drink or smoke, and her indifferent health required a plain, light diet. Isaacs smoked cigarettes, but disliked a pipe and was both

intrigued and slightly repelled by the capacity of colleagues like Asquith, Haldane and Churchill for smoking large cigars.

The lavish courses of a City dinner gave Isaacs no real pleasure, and
he preferred to eat simply and sparingly at home. His son recalled
receiving his father's enthusiastic invitation to a dinner consisting of
bacon and eggs, baked apples and huge cups of tea: 'Left to himself, he
would probably always have ordered for choice a roast chicken and a
rice pudding.' Nor was he by any means a slave to alcohol. For some
time he enjoyed an occasional glass of champagne, until he discovered
that it brought on bouts of faintness. Afterwards he preferred to
drink a small whisky and soda at dinner, sometimes taking a second
before going to bed. On very rare occasions he enjoyed a glass of good
brandy.

Compatible in background and in their basic attitudes towards life
and living, the Isaacs's marriage seems to have been a happy one.
Certainly they offered each other steadfast mutual support. She 'never
missed an opportunity to further his interests', and for his part, 'though
his innate fastidiousness was sorely tried by the atmosphere of the sick
room, he watched over her in her illnesses with a tender consideration
rare in any man and especially remarkable in one who was as austere in
the outward expression of his emotions as he was inwardly warm-
hearted and sensitive'.[11]

Rufus and Alice began their married life on a private income of £200.
They spent their honeymoon in Valencia where, it must be confessed,
Rufus spent part of the time collecting statements to be used in evidence
in the impending case of Young v. Isaacs; at least business was mingled
with pleasure.

Isaacs's first appearance in court, however, was in a London county
court case. It was not the sort of legal confrontation to make Rufus's
name overnight; indeed he lost the case, though the fault was hardly
his. A fruit merchant was being sued by a costermonger who claimed
that he had been sold some boxes of fruit that were rotten. Under
Isaacs's cross-examination the plaintiff grew irritated, and brought
matters to a head by saying, 'Look 'ere, Guv'nor, some of these 'ere figs
are in court, and if you eat three of them and aren't ill in five minutes,
I'll give up the bloomin' case!'

Declining the challenge, Rufus proposed that his client should submit
to the test himself.

The fruit merchant whispered, 'What will happen if I don't eat those
figs?'

Isaacs replied that probably the judgment would go against him.

'Very well, then, I'll lose the case,' said the defendant without a moment's hesitation, and the costermonger triumphed.

Rufus Isaacs's fee for this first court case was one guinea and was mainly composed of one gold sovereign. Rufus had the sovereign set in a brooch and presented it to his wife. Alice was delighted, though neither her family nor Rufus's shared her pleasure, believing that the coin should have been put into his bank account.

The young couple's families need not have fretted so much over the sovereign. The fees from Isaacs's first year of practice were £519 and for the second £750. But, though far from penniless, Rufus and Alice were hardly rolling in riches, and it is recorded that Mrs Cohen and her youngest daughter sometimes popped round from nearby Adamson Gardens with items of food to help the housekeeping.

One reason why Isaacs's very fair beginner's income was barely adequate was that he had still not repaid the debts incurred at the Stock Exchange. Another reason can be found in the birth of the couple's only child, Gerald, on 10 January 1889. Both the baby and Mrs Isaacs were ill after the birth; indeed, Gerald's life was despaired of and it was only after his father, against all medical advice, gave him large doses of brandy that he began to thrive. Alice, however, could not be cured so easily, and the doctor's bills provided a heavy additional strain on the family's finances.

Isaacs's task in establishing himself as a successful barrister was given a boost by his being briefed to appear in a case of some public interest in June 1889. The case had some of the basic ingredients so apt to cause a stir in Victorian society, involving a writ of libel issued by Sir George Chetwynd, a racing baronet, against Lord Durham, a Steward of the Jockey Club: the aristocracy, the turf and imputations of dishonour were a heady brew.

In essence Lord Durham had accused Sir George Chetwynd of certain racing malpractices such as 'pulling' his horses, or ensuring that they performed badly in some races so as to lower their handicap. Sir George claimed £20,000 damages. Rufus was retained for the plaintiff, whose chief advocate was Sir Henry James QC, later Lord James of Hereford. Another junior counsel for the plaintiff was A.T. Lawrence, who, as Lord Trevethin over thirty years later, succeeded Isaacs as Lord Chief Justice.

Rufus Isaacs played no dramatic part in the hearing; he put no penetrating questions, constructed no brilliant interpretations of motives. Instead he spent long hours on the preliminary paperwork, setting out the plaintiff's refutation of the charges made against him. The paperwork was apparently done well enough. The court found for Chetwynd on the more serious charge of 'pulling' his horses, and against him on the lesser malpractices. No large sums of money changed hands: both sides paid their own costs, and Chetwynd was awarded the derisory sum of one farthing on the charge of 'pulling'. The result was thus a dishonourable draw.

As a junior barrister Isaacs joined the Northern Bar circuit in order to supplement his income, and also because his sister Florrie was now married and living in Birkenhead. He never travelled the circuit regularly as a junior, though he made some appearances at both the Liverpool and Manchester assizes.

He also received during these early days of practice a few briefs for cases in the High Court. As a junior his task in such cases was to draft the pleadings on behalf of his clients, that is, to set out the disputes over fact and circumstance. His work completed, the senior barrister would appear to conduct the case in court along the lines set out by his junior's researches. It was during one of Isaacs's appearances as a junior in the High Court that the celebrated solicitor Sir George Lewis noticed him and enquired of a colleague: 'Who's that young man? He knows what he is talking about and I like his style.' On being told that the impressive junior was 'young Rufus Isaacs', Lewis nodded and made a note of the name.

One of the established barristers who often engaged Isaacs as his junior was his old master Lawson Walton who had 'taken silk' in 1890 and who was thus a Queen's Counsel. So valuable did Walton find his former pupil's work that on 7 May 1891 he decided to award Isaacs the 'red bag' that symbolizes a barrister's progress from the rank and file to a position of some prominence. When a barrister is first called, his wig and gown are supplied to him in a blue damask bag. The red bag can only be presented as an affirmation of progress by a leading barrister.

Lawson Walton's letter of 7 May simply said:

My Dear Isaacs,

I have taken great pleasure in observing your early and rapid success in our profession and the promise which it gives of achievement in the future. As your old master in the art and mystery of the law I should like to show my recognition of the position which you have achieved and my interest in your future career by offering for your acceptance a red bag. *Sic itur ad astra.*[12]

It should not be supposed that at this stage in his career Rufus Isaacs was overwhelmed by a flood of briefs. There were spells of inactivity during which he seized the opportunity to extend his education through a wide reading of the English classics. He turned for a time to the study of philosophy, and came greatly to admire the works of Spinoza. He also joined a small debating society known as the Ravenswood, which held its meetings at the house of each member in turn, and which gave him a wider platform than the law courts upon which to shine up his eloquence.

At about this time, in 1892, he gave the first signs of an active interest in politics. S.H. Emanuel, a colleague at the Bar, introduced him to the 'Hampstead Parliament', a mock parliamentary assembly which enabled amateur politicians to cut their teeth in debate. Equipped with all the paraphernalia of Mr Speaker, government, opposition and proper rules of procedure, the 'Hampstead Parliament' saw Isaacs join its Liberal ranks.

This was an important step for the young barrister. Both Jews and Christian Nonconformists tended, in the late nineteenth century, to support Liberalism as opposed to Toryism. Rufus had hitherto vaguely subscribed to the general principles of Liberalism. His activities as a Liberal in the 'Hampstead Parliament', however, helped to focus his views and to make him identify far more closely with the Liberal party. It also stirred thoughts of an active participation in politics, and within eight years of his joining Hampstead's version of Parliament he was a candidate for the more august body at Westminster.

While his political career was in this embryonic phase, Isaacs's legal standing improved further. This was largely due to his success in building up a practice in a newly established division of the High Court. In 1892, following complaints from the business community that some High Court judges were quite unfitted to try commercial cases of any complexity, a Commercial Court was established. Isaacs, with his business background and his useful experience of the Stock Exchange, quickly decided to specialize in the work of the Commercial Court, thus causing Lawson Walton later to say, with some exaggeration, that he was the only successful barrister he knew who had 'not had to go through the grind of Quarter Session and the County Court like the rest of us'.

Within a few years of his growing involvement with the Commercial Court, Isaacs played an important part in a case which, from the legal point of view, was one of the most important of his career and which went before the Court of Appeal and twice before the House of Lords. Allen v. Flood was a case that made legal history in the affairs of trade unions and industrial relations. The conflict was essentially a demarcation dispute. Two shipwrights, Flood and Taylor, sued leading

33

members of the Boilermakers' Union, including Allen, the Union's London delegate, for maliciously inducing the Glengall Iron Company to break their contract with them, and also for intimidation and conspiracy.

The conflict arose out of objections raised by members of the Boilermakers' Union to the employment of Flood and Taylor in repair work upon the ship *Sam Weller* lying in Regent's Dock. The ironworkers claimed that, although Flood and Taylor were engaged to repair the *Sam Weller*'s woodwork, they had previously repaired ironwork on other ships. Allen, the Boilermakers' representative, had eventually issued an ultimatum to the Glengall Iron Company: either they discharged Flood and Taylor or the Boilermakers working on the ship would come out on strike. The company proceeded to discharge the two shipwrights. Backed by their own union, Flood and Taylor decided to sue.

It was a case of a sort that has bedevilled Britain's industrial relations down to the present day, in the form of trade unions competing for the same sort of work. It was heard before Mr Justice Kennedy and a common jury in February 1895. Rufus Isaacs appeared in support of his mentor Lawson Walton, and for the plaintiffs Flood and Taylor.

The trial went well for Isaacs's clients. The jury found that Allen had, as alleged, maliciously induced the company to discharge the plaintiffs, who were awarded £20 in damages. It was next the duty of the court to decide whether Allen was liable in law.

Isaacs made the opening speech, contending that there was no material difference between inducement to break a contract and inducement not to enter into a contract, and that when the inducer was acting out of malice he was liable. Lawson Walton followed him and argued that there had been a wrongful interference with the plaintiffs' legal rights and their freedom of action. The judge agreed with these pleadings and gave judgment for Flood and Taylor with damages of £40.

Allen proceeded to make an appeal applying for a new trial on the basis of the misdirection of the jury; at the same time there was a cross-appeal against the judge's ruling that only Allen, not the chairman and secretary of the Boilermakers' Union, was liable. The Court of Appeal dismissed both of these appeals.

Undeterred, Allen took his case to the House of Lords, thus providing Isaacs with the challenging opportunity of addressing the highest tribunal in the country. In December 1895 the appeal was heard by seven Law Lords presided over by Lord Halsbury, the Lord Chancellor. On the fourth day of the hearing, however, their lordships decided that the point at issue was of such difficulty and significance that they wished to take the opinion of the High Court before delivering their judgment.

The hearing did not therefore resume until 25 March 1897 when the earlier court met, strengthened by the addition of Lord Ashbourne and Lord James of Hereford. Late on the afternoon of the fourth day, Isaacs rose to speak for the first time. He was, with some cause, anxious – their lordships had listened at length to Lawson Walton and were in a noticeably drowsy state. His opening remarks seemed to have no impact whatsoever, but after a while first Lord Morris, then the rest of the court, began to perk up and pay serious attention. When the hearing resumed the next morning, Isaacs made a ritual apology for taking up more of their lordships' time and was briskly reassured by the Lord Chancellor that he should in no way cut short his argument. Thus encouraged he launched once more into the complexities of the case. After counsel for Allen had replied, the Lord Chancellor stated that he proposed to submit to the High Court judges the matter of whether there was evidence of a cause of action fit to be left to a jury.

On 4 June 1897 the High Court judges decided by a majority of six to two that there was evidence of a cause of action fit to be left to a jury: in short, that Flood and Taylor could take their alleged grievances further. Isaacs and Walton seemed to have won.

Six months later, however, as is so often the way in contentious legal matters, the Law Lords decided that there was *no* evidence fit for a jury and that thus no further action could be taken against Allen. It was a decision which gave encouragement to the growing trade union movement.

Although the final judgment in this drawn out legal saga had gone against him, Rufus Isaacs was delighted with his involvement in the case. His prestige at the Bar was dramatically increased, as well as his earnings, and he had acquitted himself well before the nation's leading legal authorities. Indeed his reaction to his successful appearance before the High Court in March 1897 had been to rush back to his chambers with his pupil, Francis Oppenheimer, and drink champagne.

The fact that he now had a pupil, though he had initially considered himself insufficiently established to take one on, spoke for his growing success. Oppenheimer was later to recall his memory of Isaacs's impressive pleading: 'I heard his suave and confident voice which had flowed, even and imperturbable, throughout the ordeal. I heard again the Lord Chancellor's words of encouragement at the beginning of the second day and at the end of the proceedings. I knew then that I could never achieve what that day Rufus Isaacs had achieved.'[13]

Oppenheimer has left a striking pen portrait of Rufus and Alice Isaacs at this stage of their lives. Alice (whose sister he was later to marry) is described as 'a striking young woman, tall and erect with an excellent figure and an impressive gait, her head crowned by masses of blonde hair. She and her husband formed a remarkably good-looking couple, their physical attractions enhanced by their *joie de vivre* and their radiant devotion to each other.' [14]

Like Lloyd George, Oppenheimer believed that Alice had been instrumental in promoting Rufus's rise to fame, pointing out, for instance, that 'it was she who had induced him to continue his early struggles at the Bar when as a young married man he played with the idea of returning to the City with its brighter immediate prospects'. Oppenheimer, somewhat surprisingly, was also 'convinced that, however great his gifts, she was the more gifted of the two'. [15]

So, happy in his marriage, Rufus Isaacs could also take pleasure from an enhanced reputation and a gratifying increase in his legal work. Although he had not yet repaid all his Stock Exchange debts, his growing prosperity enabled him to move in 1897 to a spacious flat at 24 Palace Court, Bayswater, where he at last had a study of his own.

Accompanying the Isaacs on their move to Bayswater was Emma Squires, originally engaged as their son's nurse six months after his birth. Emma, described as 'a short, sandy-haired, chubby little Devonshire woman ... with a face like a cider apple and a heart of pure gold', remained with the Isaacs, first as a nurse then as Alice's maid, for thirty-seven years.

Emma was a tower of strength during these years. Her duties varied from waking Rufus at four or five o'clock in the morning to start work with a cup of hot milk into which an egg had been beaten (though he would have preferred a cup of tea), to caring for Alice during her illnesses, often denying access to a trained nurse. She adopted the Isaacs as her family, ruling the household 'with despotic benevolence and, rarely surprised and never disconcerted, followed [them] from Broadhurst Gardens to Delhi, taking Washington in her stride on the way'. [16] In fact, in 1921, before Isaacs left Britain for India and his viceregal duties, he summoned Emma and tried tactfully to tell her that perhaps she should stay at home with a comfortable pension. Before he could say more than they had decided to go to India, she interrupted with 'Oh, have you, my Lord? That will be very nice. I have always wanted to see India.'

The unfailing punctuality with which Emma awoke Isaacs on his working mornings at least provided a solution as to when to carry out his rapidly increasing work at home. He soon discovered he was unable to take on the extra work in the evenings when, in any case, he preferred to spend time with his family. So a very early morning start, after about five hours' sleep, was found to be the answer. Emma's egg-laced cup of hot milk also solved another problem for, according to his son, he could not have made his own cup of tea with a kettle and a spirit lamp:

> they would have conspired together to upset, catch fire, boil over, or blow up, for he was always a prey to the malice of inanimate things. No knot would untie, no latch lift, no gadget work under his hands. Thin and fine and sensitive as they were ... they were singularly lacking in suppleness and dexterity and would fumble helplessly over a task which coarser and heavier hands performed without pause or effort.[17]

Fortunately Rufus Isaacs's mind lacked nothing in suppleness and dexterity. His success, however, placed an enormous amount of work in his hands. His industry became a legend, and in the Temple his colleagues said he only went to bed during the long vacation. In 1897, soon after the family's move to Bayswater, he developed unpleasant symptoms of overwork, particularly attacks of bleeding from the nose and eyes. His doctor and his wife urged him to work less hard.

One solution was to 'take silk', to become a Queen's Counsel, and thus to relieve himself of the labour of drafting pleadings and undertaking the often dreary preliminary work of a junior barrister. Isaacs hesitated: no junior of a mere ten years' standing had ever made the transition.

He did consult J.C. Bingham, however, a leader in the Commercial Court who had recently been made a judge. Bingham was unhesitating: 'Sit down and write the letter of application now.' Isaacs still hesitated. He spoke to Mr Justice Mathew, another Commercial Court judge, who was equally encouraging, saying, 'I should take silk. Don't make the mistake I made of postponing your application until you are old and have lost your energy. If you do, you will never apply.'[18]

Though still unsure, Isaacs wrote his letter of application to the Lord Chancellor, Lord Halsbury. Doubtless remembering Rufus's impressive performance in the case of Allen v. Flood, Halsbury put his name on the next list of 'silks'.

Isaacs was only thirty-seven years old, and had been barely ten years at the Bar. To have become a Queen's Counsel so quickly was without precedent, and a most striking confirmation of his ability. The former ship's boy had travelled far and fast in his chosen profession.

4 Rufus Isaacs, QC, 1897–1904

With Rufus Isaacs it was in the Courts as in his conduct of life: he did not challenge; he charmed. And, as a result, opposition did not yield – it did not have to; it simply dissolved.

Sir Derek Walker-Smith

Shortly before Rufus Isaacs was formally admitted to the front row of barristers as Queen's Counsel, he wrote a ruminative, and in some ways pessimistic, letter to his family's solicitor, and his own friend and patron, Algernon Sydney. After explaining why he had decided to apply for silk so early in his career, he ended by saying: 'Of course my people are highly delighted and are much more confident of my future than I am. Were the world composed of partial relations, I might feel more confidence. However, industry and zeal always tell and I can take credit for both.'[1]

As it happened, his first year as Queen's Counsel was more profitable than his last year as a junior, which was by no means a common experience for rising barristers. One of the reasons for this financial success lay in his carrying over a large amount of work from his pre-silk days, and even augmenting it as his reputation expanded further. Another reason lay in his continuing capacity for extraordinarily hard work.

His labours were, admittedly, lightened by the recruitment of two young barristers to his chambers. These juniors had been engaged while Isaacs was himself still a junior; both were to remain closely associated with him during his remaining years at the Bar. One was Walter Schwabe, later knighted, and for a time Chief Justice of Madras; the other was G.A.H. Branson, who retired as senior puisne judge in 1939. Of the two, Branson became in time the more highly valued by Isaacs, and the latter was eventually afforded the pleasure, as Attorney-

General, of appointing him a Junior Treasury Counsel; Branson went on to become a High Court judge for eighteen years.

With the laborious task of drawing up pleadings and equivalent paperwork now in the hands of his two 'devils', Isaacs was free to flourish in the limelight of front bench activity.

Looking back on his early years as Queen's Counsel, he always chose them as the time of his greatest personal happiness, when the increasing success of his professional life went hand in hand with private contentment. Not only was he head and shoulders above nearly all of his legal contemporaries in promise and achievement, he had also been able to pay off the crippling debts from his Stock Exchange débâcle. He now lived in a spacious flat in Bayswater, with a brougham and a pair of handsome black horses in the mews below. His wife's health seemed, for the moment, to be markedly improved, and he could take pride and pleasure in his young son's development.

His financial success also led him to sample the mixed delights of fashionable European holiday places. Although he retained an affection for Brighton, and continued to spend his short Christmas breaks there, often with his brother Harry and his parents, he sought the summer sun elsewhere. In 1897, troubled by gout, he went with his wife to take the cure at the fashionable spa of Aix-les-Bains.

His son has described his activities there:

He would spend the mornings in the gentle toils of the cure, borne to and from the baths in one of the carrying chairs with their red-and-white striped awnings, then so characteristic a feature of the place. The afternoons would be dedicated to some mild expedition, the whole party mounted on the newly fashionable bicycle, and the evenings to dining with friends, followed by a visit to the Villa des Fleurs, where he found in baccarat a constant source of amusement. He particularly enjoyed taking a bank and, though he never played high, he was not averse to what he himself would describe as 'a little flutter', which always meant that he had hazarded just a little more than he could properly afford![2]

Isaacs was no great sightseer: 'If there were places of interest in the not too distant or inaccessible neighbourhood, he would visit them, dutifully and appreciatively and with slightly exhausting thoroughness.' His fastidiousness, however, limited what he was prepared to see: 'he detested dirt and smells and nothing would induce him to plunge into squalid alleys in pursuit of the historic or the picturesque.'

The hotel and the casino at Aix-les-Bains provided him with some useful social and professional contacts. Here he met Lord Russell of Killowen, then Lord Chief Justice, Lord Esher, Master of the Rolls, and another aspiring QC, Henry Dickens, the son of the great novelist and later to be knighted. Lord Esher, in particular, found Isaacs a ready listener and 'would sit by the hour in the shady hotel garden discoursing to the younger man of great legal battles and figures of the past, emphasizing his words by movements of his beautifully shaped, exquisitely kept and heavily ringed hands'.

In the widening circle of his acquaintances, Isaacs was undeniably well liked. He was not aggressive or offensive and had an attractive personality which included 'good looks, vitality, amiability, a faculty, very gratifying to the other person, of apparent absorption in his companion of the moment, a reputation as a coming man at the Bar, and a fund of entertaining reminiscences of his earlier years in very different surroundings'.

Rufus Isaacs's spectacular advancement during these years, however, owed nothing to good looks or similar fortuitous advantages. He established himself as a leading counsel, earning the magnificent sum of £15,000 a year within five years of taking silk, through his application and through his supreme forensic talents.

What made him such a successful counsel? In his book *Lord Reading and His Cases* Sir Derek Walker-Smith says succinctly, 'With Rufus Isaacs it was in the Courts as in his conduct of life: he did not challenge; he charmed. And, as a result, opposition did not yield – it did not have to; it simply dissolved.'[3]

It was, of course, not quite as simple as that. Walker-Smith, indeed, calls Isaacs, 'Learned in law, quick and resourceful in argument, penetrative in cross-examination. . . . he was possessed of a memory quite out of the ordinary and a capacity to unravel and elucidate the intricate mystery of figures, which was unrivalled.' Walker-Smith also pays tribute to Isaacs's 'invarying self-discipline' which 'enabled him to husband his resources, and at the same time diminished the call upon them'.[4]

He never made the mistake of putting his own case too high. 'He would admit its defects and acknowledge the strong points of his adversary's with disarming frankness.' He did not bully or bait or overawe. He also had 'an almost instinctive faculty for foretelling the outcome of a case, and he never hesitated to advise a settlement if he considered it in the best interests of his client. In negotiating a compromise he was at his most formidable, for his air of reasonableness and impartiality was almost as effective with his opponents as with juries.' He was never a great 'case lawyer', and indeed felt little interest in the academic aspect of the law. He always approached the facts of a case in strict chronological order, and appeared 'to have no difficulty in keeping any number of threads separate in his mind and would follow each to its end, while at the same time he watched the pattern of the general situation taking shape'.

Rufus Isaacs, admittedly, 'had not the dominating personality of a Carson, the soaring eloquence of a Marshall Hall, the profound learning of a Sumner, nor the masterly invective of an F.E. Smith'. But 'he had all the quieter attributes of success'. F.E. Smith, indeed, admired Isaacs greatly, introducing him to his wife with the words, 'I may say that I consider this man quite as clever as I am myself.'[5] Lewis Broad, in his *Advocates of the Golden Age*, considered that Isaacs's success was 'founded on an all-round excellence' and, though judging him less eloquent and powerful than Carson and F.E. Smith, argued that 'He had no equal at the Bar for persuasive reasoning, for presenting a case to the commonsense judgement of a jury. There was something disarming about the methods of this man who went about his business with the minimum fuss, so quiet and so courteous. He was the mildest mannered man who held a thousand-guinea brief and one of the most effective.'[6]

Contemporary press comment was equally complimentary. In 1902 after his successful defence of Dr Krause, in Rex v. Krause, the *Daily Graphic* praised Isaacs's 'brilliant handling' of the case, remarking that he had 'covered himself with honour and shown that both as lawyer and as advocate he has few equals and certainly no superiors'.[7] Two years later the *Illustrated News* described him as 'A man who never loses his temper.'[8] In 1910, on his appointment as Solicitor-General in Asquith's Liberal government, the *Daily Mirror* commented that 'In court Mr Isaacs' manner is, as a rule, quiet and restrained, but it is a deadly sort of quietness, only lightened now and then by a flash of humour.'[9] A few days later the *Lancashire Post* spoke warmly of his 'dynamic quality' and of the 'great abilities' that had 'done so much to raise him rapidly to a leading position at the Bar'.[10]

What were the cases that won such golden opinions of Rufus Isaacs, and how were his qualities revealed by his conduct in court?

Two such cases arose out of the Boer War of 1899-1902, which aroused political passions at home, while providing Britain's enemies abroad with a gratifying display of military incompetence compounded by the controversial tactics of farm-burning and the establishment of concentration camps in South Africa. The war also gave the Unionist government the chance to appeal successfully to the country in the 'Khaki' election of October 1900, during which campaign Rufus Isaacs stood as a Liberal candidate for North Kensington and, though losing, reduced the Conservative majority by over 20 per cent.

At the centre of the controversy over the legitimacy of the Boer War stood the commanding figure of Joseph Chamberlain, the Liberal Unionist Colonial Secretary in a predominantly Tory government. Radicals and Liberals reviled Chamberlain, their erstwhile colleague, as a traitor to their cause, and raised the outcry that the unsavoury conflict in South Africa was really 'Chamberlain's War'. Chamberlain, moreover, was wealthy; a self-made Birmingham businessman, retaining close connections with industrialists and financiers.

Within the first year of the war, the Liberal evening newspaper, the *Star*, came across a heaven-sent opportunity to vilify the Colonial Secretary. In a series of articles the *Star* alleged that improper political pressure had been brought upon the government to secure contracts for the supply of cordite to the armed forces. Among those firms that had won government contracts for the supply of cordite was Kynoch's, the Midlands firm of which Arthur Chamberlain, Joseph's younger brother, was chairman.

After a furore in the House of Commons, the government had referred the matter to a select committee, which, in August 1900, had declared itself satisfied, though admitting that on several occasions Kynoch's had put in a tender higher than its competitors and had subsequently been given the chance of revising its tender to a figure acceptable to the War Office or the Admiralty. The select committee justified this questionable practice on the grounds of its being 'in the public interest'. In the same month as the committee's report, the Colonial Secretary had stated in the Commons: 'I have no interest, direct or indirect, in Kynoch's or in any other firm manufacturing ammunition or war materials.'

Not satisfied, the *Star* had made further enquiries which revealed that Joseph Chamberlain had shares in the Birmingham Trust Company which had invested 10 per cent of its capital in Kynoch's. The *Star* therefore claimed that the Colonial Secretary did indeed have an interest, albeit indirect, in Kynoch's and that the firm had in fact received preferential treatment. The *Star*'s attacks encompassed not only Joseph Chamberlain, but also his elder son Austen, Civil Lord of the Admiralty.

Here was a confrontation of enormous public interest, centring on a highly controversial politician in the midst of prosecuting an equally controversial war, the whole affair apparently reeking of corruption in high places. Joseph and Austen Chamberlain were, however, advised that they would be mistaken to commence libel proceedings against the *Star*. Instead Arthur Chamberlain brought an action, alleging libel on himself. The *Star* contended that, since the remarks objected to were statements of fact, they were not defamatory, and that, in all other respects, the articles were fair comment on matters of public interest.

The trial was held at the end of March 1901 before Lord Alverstone, the Lord Chief Justice, and a special jury in the King's Bench division of the High Court. Sir Edward Clarke, a former Solicitor-General and a most illustrious advocate, led for the plaintiff, Arthur Chamberlain. Rufus Isaacs led for the *Star*, supported by Eldon Banks.

Clarke's opening speech described Arthur Chamberlain as a man of great commercial integrity, and the plaintiff himself presented an apparently unassailable character during Clarke's questioning of him. When it came to Isaacs's turn to cross-examine Chamberlain, there seemed little chance of seriously damaging his defences. However, through a series of shrewd questions, Isaacs did manage to rattle the plaintiff's confidence. The jury were impressed by exchanges such as these:

Isaacs: In your opinion would it be legitimate to use political influence to get contracts for Kynoch's?
Chamberlain: No.
Isaacs: Do you consider it would be legitimate to make use of the name of the Secretary of State for the Colonies to advance the interests of Kynoch's or any other company in which you are interested?
Chamberlain: There are circumstances under which it would be perfectly legitimate.
Isaacs: Have you ever done it?
Chamberlain: No.
Isaacs: Have any of your subordinates?
Chamberlain: One did so without my knowledge. A gentleman of the name of Cullen has done so. He was the manager of the London office of Kynoch's till about six months ago.
Isaacs: How did he do it?
Chamberlain: By writing letters to the Agents-General for the Colonies.

The witness added that Mr Cullen had dictated and Mr Cocking, the London director, had signed a letter to the Foreign Office asking for letters of introduction.

This was a difficult moment for Arthur Chamberlain, who had earlier denied all knowledge of such letters until a question had been asked about them in the House of Commons. Stonewalling, Chamberlain now replied that he had formed no opinion as to why such letters had been written.

Isaacs: Is your mind a blank on the subject?
Chamberlain: Quite a blank.

This was an effective point for the defence, and one which Isaacs let sink into the jurymen's minds rather than elaborate upon it.

He soon had Chamberlain in further difficulties on the point of the reduction of tenders to secure an order.

Isaacs: Do you say it would be wrong to describe it as a highly unusual process to be allowed to reduce your tender?
Chamberlain: It is not 'highly' unusual.
Isaacs: Is it unusual without the 'highly'?
Chamberlain: I cannot argue about it.
The Lord Chief Justice: I suppose it is not a common thing?
Chamberlain: No, it is not common.
The Lord Chief Justice: Then it is unusual.

When Rufus Isaacs made his speech to the jury, he avoided hyperbole and false passion, quietly presented his client's case, and told the jurymen: 'You must deal with the whole question broadly and in a public spirit, and I look to you to vindicate the position the defendants have taken up in fearlessly commenting on matters of great public importance.'

Although there was little doubt that Arthur Chamberlain had been libelled, and the jury recorded their verdict accordingly, only £200 were awarded in damages. The *Star* rejoiced in the outcome, and the next day spoke warmly of 'the vast skill and the perfect discretion with which the defence in the Chamberlain case was conducted ... in the face of ... adverse circumstances and against such redoubtable opponents as Sir Edward Clarke – the unquestioned head of his profession'.[11]

To have fought so skilful a campaign against Sir Edward Clarke, and on behalf of a newspaper with pronounced and widely unpopular 'pro-Boer' views, was a triumph for Isaacs, and brought him welcome and beneficial publicity. He now turned back for a while to his heavy and lucrative practice in commercial and Stock Exchange cases.

By January 1902, however, he was back at the centre of the stage in another case arising from the Boer War. Rex v. Krause centred on whether Dr Frederick Krause, a young Afrikaner advocate, was guilty of incitement to murder and of attempted soliciting to commit murder.

Krause was a Transvaal citizen, working in the Public Prosecutor's office in Johannesburg before and during part of the Boer War. After the British occupation of Johannesburg in June 1900, Krause, who had fought as a Boer commandant in the Witwatersrand district, refused to take the oath of allegiance to the Crown, was deprived of his right to practise and eventually arrived in London. Krause blamed his loss of professional status upon the influence of John Douglas Foster, a fellow barrister and an ardent supporter of the British side in the Boer War. Foster had for a time been legal adviser to the military governor of Johannesburg, Field Marshal Lord Roberts, and had been instrumental in getting Krause and other Afrikaner advocates deprived of their certificates to practise.

In London Krause had consequently written, in August 1901, two letters to a former colleague in the Johannesburg Public Prosecutor's Office, Cornelius Broeksma, in which he said of Foster: 'This man must be got out of the way, cost what it may. His influence is very damaging.' And again, suggesting that Foster should 'be shot dead in some lawful way, or otherwise put out of the way. This is absolutely necessary and the sooner the better for our cause.' [12]

In South Africa Broeksma never received these letters, which were intercepted by the military authorities. He was subsequently tried before a military tribunal on a charge of high treason, found guilty and shot. Dr Krause was arrested in Britain and faced with a similar charge, though it was decided to try him at the Old Bailey rather than ship him back to South Africa and put him before a military tribunal.

The prosecution for the Crown was led by the Solicitor-General, Sir Edward Carson, with Rufus Isaacs as the leading counsel for the defence. It was a fascinating confrontation between one of the most renowned and powerful barristers in the United Kingdom and one of the profession's rising stars.

Carson argued that the jury must decide whether Krause had written the letters, whether the letters indeed incited to murder, and whether the accused had intended that Broeksma should receive them.

For this part Isaacs submitted that, on a point of law, there was no evidence that Broeksma had ever received the letters, and that therefore there could be no offence. As to Carson's argument, Isaacs contended that mere intention was no offence under the law, nor was intention, plus an act to communicate intention, enough to convict in a case where the person to be influenced had not been reached.

The Lord Chief Justice upheld Isaacs's view, and Carson was obliged to argue for a conviction on the lesser charge of attempting to solicit a person to commit murder. With little hesitation, the jury agreed with Carson and Krause was sentenced to two years' imprisonment.

Once more Isaacs could feel well satisfied with the outcome of the case. He had enabled his client to avoid a possible life sentence, and he had established an important precedent in law regarding incitement to murder by letter. He had, moreover, got the better of the great Carson, a man of enormous legal and political standing and soon to emerge as one of the leaders of Ulster's Protestant Unionists. He had also been briefed for the first time by the well-established solicitors Lewis and Lewis, and could now expect more work from them.

Rufus Isaacs's success at this point in his career was in marked contrast to some of his contemporaries including Marshall Hall, destined for an illustrious legal career. In fact six months after the hearing of Rex v. Krause, Isaacs offered Marshall Hall in effect an interest-free, one-year loan of £500 to help him weather a particularly bad patch in his profession. Marshall Hall refused the offer, and on 12 August 1902 Isaacs wrote a letter of warm encouragement in return, ending:

Good-bye, my dear friend, for the present. Your dash and courage will stand you in good stead now, as always in fighting the battle of life, and when we return to these haunts [the courts after the summer vacation] I hope you will be quite restored to health and spirits – professionally I am quite sure you have *had* your bad times.
Yours very sincerely,
Rufus D. Isaacs.

Isaacs spent the long vacation of 1902 at Homburg at the suggestion of his former pupil Francis Oppenheimer. The spa had recently become fashionable due to the patronage of King Edward VII, who had at last succeeded to the throne in 1901. Other patrons of Homburg included Lord Halsbury, the Lord Chancellor, and Sir George Lewis, the senior partner in Lewis and Lewis, the firm of solicitors that had instructed Isaacs in the Krause case.

Such contacts could hardly hinder Isaacs's career, and Lewis, indeed, was eager to introduce him to the King. Rufus was duly presented to Edward VII while carrying a large glass of spa water and was obliged to balance this while dropping on to a knee in order to kiss his sovereign's hand. This delicate task accomplished, he proceeded to make such a good impression on the King that he and his wife were often invited into the royal presence during their stay. Among other influential men Isaacs met at Homburg were the proprietors of the *Daily Telegraph*, Sir Edward Lawson, and of the *Morning Post*, Lord Glenesk.

Back in Britain, Isaacs was briefed in the fashionable society divorce case of Hartopp v. Hartopp, when he represented a Mrs Sands, a beautiful woman of reputedly easy virtue, named as co-respondent and the mistress of Sir Charles Hartopp. Isaacs succeeded in convincing the jury that Mrs Sands had not committed adultery with Sir Charles, despite her 'history and her past', and spontaneous applause broke out in court after his speech in her defence. The Hartopp divorce case ended in the dismissal of petition and counter-petition, but not before the public had been able to gorge itself upon the detailed press reports of the proceedings.

At the end of 1902 Rufus Isaacs was involved in a hearing of great significance in trade union history – the Taff Vale case. Briefly, the Taff Vale dispute turned on the vexed question of union liability for losses incurred by a company against which industrial action had been taken. A strike by railwaymen working for the Taff Vale Railway Company in South Wales, and involving violence by pickets, had led to a legal wrangle between the Company and the railwaymen's union, the Amalgamated Society of Railway Servants. Finally, the House of Lords had confirmed that a trade union could be sued, or sue, in its registered name under statute law.

The Company's claim for financial loss thus came before court in the King's Bench Division on 2 December 1902. Leading for the union, Isaacs argued that, in the final settlement of the dispute, it had been agreed that the Company should discontinue all legal proceedings against the men involved. This argument was, alas, punctured by the point that the Company had made its agreement with the men, *not* with the union, and that the union could not therefore benefit from the agreement. The judge also rejected Isaacs's contention that neither the union nor its general secretary were liable for acts of violence carried out by the pickets, and accepted that there was evidence of conspiracy to injure the Company.

The Taff Vale judgment cost the Amalgamated Society of Railway Servants £50,000 in costs and damages, and cast a long shadow over the aspirations of trade unions. It was a judgment which the new Liberal government hastened to neutralize in 1906 with their Trade Disputes Act, and which was an issue of bitter national controversy.

Although Rufus Isaacs had unsuccessfully represented his clients in the Taff Vale case, the dispute did wonders for his standing with trade unionists and the Liberal party. Having defended the pro-Boer *Star*, and now the Amalgamated Society of Railway Servants, he was well on course for a seat in the Commons and perhaps a part in government. Certainly he was seen as a friend of the working class in Wales, and on subsequent visits to appear on Liberal platforms in the principality he was often hauled about in his carriage by enthusiastic supporters.

In January 1904 Isaacs was the leading prosecuting counsel in a trial that firmly fixed him at the pinnacle of his profession. This was the trial of Whitaker Wright, a self-made man of business, company promoter and, for a time, a millionaire. Wright was accused of publishing false accounts of various companies, and the City and the public in general paid close attention to his trial.

Wright's fortune had first been made in the United States in mining, and then greatly increased through the formation of 'promoting companies' – companies that used shareholders' money to acquire subsidiary companies and other properties rather than develop and run them. By the late 1890s he had established several such 'promoting companies' in London, notably the London and Globe Finance Corporation. Wright enticed a respectable public figure, the Marquess of Dufferin and Ava, a former Viceroy of India, into the chairmanship of the London and Globe. For his part, he lived a life of vulgar and unashamed luxury with palatial town and country houses; he instigated massive schemes of landscaping at his country seat, had a billiard saloon with a glass ceiling constructed under one of the lakes there, and bought an ostentatiously large yacht, the *Sybarita*, which defeated Kaiser Wilhelm II's *Meteor* in the Solent.

Whitaker Wright's ruin came precipitately. On 17 December 1900, after the company's report on 5 December, the London and Globe held a shareholders' meeting and showed a handsome profit of £463,672 on the balance sheet. The credit side of the balance sheet totalled £2,332,632. 0s. 1d. When a shareholder enquired how much of that had been written off during the past year, Wright replied that over a million pounds had been written off and remarked that the shares so disposed of had been marked down as low as possible.

Eleven days later came the staggering announcement that the London and Globe was insolvent, and the company went into voluntary liquidation. Its creditors were eventually paid a shilling in the pound which was a pitiful proportion of the £2,296,000 that was owed them.

Amid the uproar that resulted from the crash, the Official Receiver struggled to make sense of the London and Globe's labyrinthine accounts. In February 1903 in the Commons a Liberal MP, George Lambert, called for the Public Prosecutor to take action, pointing out that 'Here is a Company which issued a report [on 5 December 1900] showing a profit for the year of £463,000, and twenty-three days afterwards they collapsed and were unable to meet their liabilities.'

No action was taken to bring Wright to justice, however, until March 1903 when a warrant for his arrest was issued describing him, not inaccurately, in terms reminiscent of the 'wicked capitalist' so beloved of cartoonists: 'aged about 50, height about 5ft. 9 or 10 inches, stout build, large head, dark hair and moustache, florid complexion, small eyes, receding forehead, small chin with large fat roll beneath. Wears gold pince-nez with gold chain attached. Speaks with slight American accent. Usually dressed in frock-coat suit and silk hat.' [13]

Wright was eventually arrested in New York and extradited. His trial was held at the Law Courts in the Strand before a special jury of householders. Rufus Isaacs led for the prosecution, which claimed, in essence, that the reports and balance sheets for the London and Globe Corporation were false in important particulars, and that these false reports and accounts had been published for the purpose of deceiving shareholders, defrauding creditors and inducing others to become shareholders.

Isaacs opened the case for the prosecution, although Wright had earlier been very anxious to engage him for the defence. He spoke for five hours, threading his way with outstanding skill through the complexities of the corporation's finances, and being sometimes asked for clarification by Mr Justice Bingham, a distinguished commercial judge, who freely confessed his difficulties in coping with the tangled accounts. Though serious and restrained, Isaacs raised an occasional laugh in court, saying, for instance, that an item of a mere £10,000 was hardly worthy of note, and, again, when referring to the 1900 balance sheet showing credit of £2,332,632. 0s. 1d., remarking that the penny was there as 'an artistic touch'.

The case turned on Rufus Isaacs's cross-examination of Wright, which began on the seventh day of the trial. The two protagonists provided an almost ludicrous contrast: Isaacs, 'pale, slender, fine drawn, with quick movements of head and hand, calm and dispassionate'; Wright, bull-like, florid and heavy, 'with a head disproportionately large even for his massive body', but still commanding and self-confident.

Isaacs's cross-examination of Wright on the subject of the London and Globe's 1900 balance sheet deflated the defendant as surely as a pin pricking an over-blown balloon:

Isaacs: You made a speech at the shareholders' meeting. You knew there were rumours as to the state of the Globe's affairs?
Wright: No doubt.
Isaacs: You were anxious to put the best face on affairs you could?
Wright: No doubt.
Isaacs: You knew that the important matter to the shareholders was the item of £2,332,000 'value of shares held in sundry companies'?

Wright: The state of the company was the important thing.
Isaacs: The company owed to sundry creditors £570,000?
Wright: Yes.
Isaacs: Your assets were about £2,700,000?
Wright: Yes.
Isaacs: The largest item in the £2,700,000 was the £2,332,000?
Wright: Yes.
Isaacs: It was important to know how much had been written off?
Wright: Yes.
Isaacs: You dealt with that in your speech?
Wright: I answered questions.
Isaacs: You said over a million sterling had been written off for depreciation. That was untrue?
Wright: I do not admit it. You must take the whole report together.
Isaacs: You said 'over a million sterling'?
Wright: I should have said 'for loss and depreciation'.
Isaacs: Have you any doubt that this statement is absolutely untrue?
Wright: In its connection it is true. But I ought to have said 'loss and depreciation'. It was an extempore utterance.
Isaacs: That is, as it stands, the statement is untrue?

And a little later:

Isaacs: You said you had marked [the Lake Views] as low as possible. Had you in the list of assets – the £2,332,000 – marked them down a penny?
Wright: The sum of £500,000 was not taken into account.
Isaacs: Then you had not marked them down as low as possible. Would you like to say it was a slip of the tongue?
Wright: Yes, if you like.

And again:

Isaacs: You edited the report, put in the 'hear hears' and so on?
Wright: Yes, and rightly.
Isaacs: But the slip of the tongue was left uncorrected. The sentence before the sentence which spoke of 'marking off.' was corrected, but not the 'marking off.' sentence?
Wright: My time was absorbed. The manager or secretary ought to have looked at it. In this company I had to do everybody's work.[14]

Wright left the witness box, according to one observer, 'not only a weary but a beaten man. His great frame seemed to have shrunk and his face was grey and drawn.' He was duly convicted and a sentence of seven years' penal servitude passed against him.

Rufus Isaacs's pleasure at securing a conviction after such a masterly forensic display was marred by a dramatic epilogue to the trial. In a toilet near the court where he had just been sentenced, Wright swallowed a capsule of potassium cyanide and, back in the consultation room, collapsed and died in the presence of his solicitor Sir George Lewis and other supporters. Isaacs's first reaction was to believe that Wright had collapsed and died as a result of the strain put upon him, and he was somewhat relieved to learn that in fact the financier had taken his own life.

What more awaited Rufus Isaacs after the triumph of the Whitaker Wright case? His income for 1904 was to be over £28,000, a fabulous sum for the Edwardian age, and an almost unbelievable improvement on the £200 a year on which he had begun married life. He was only in his early forties and could look forward to an equally illustrious and lucrative future at the Bar. But 1904 was to prove another turning-point in his career, for in August of that year he was returned to Parliament as the Liberal member for Reading.

5 Member of Parliament and King's Counsel, 1904-10

Never have the Liberals of Reading had so brilliant and popular a candidate as Mr Isaacs.
Reading Standard, 20 January 1906

Mr Isaacs is ... not a great Parliamentary figure. The impression he creates is one of a light skirmisher on the fringe of the battle.
Saturday News, 15 February 1908

On 4 August 1904 Rufus Isaacs became MP for Reading after a by-election victory that gave the Liberals a majority of 230 votes in the seat. He sat as the member for Reading until his appointment as Lord Chief Justice in 1913, holding two ministerial posts in the process, those of Solicitor-General and Attorney-General. When he was elevated to the peerage on New Year's Day 1914 he took the title of Lord Reading of Erleigh, thus symbolizing his debt of gratitude to a constituency that had returned him four times to Parliament within six and a half years.

Why did Isaacs choose to enter the House of Commons in 1904? He had risen, with almost miraculous speed, to the very heights of the legal profession. His work was extraordinarily lucrative, briefs showered on to his table at chambers, he had become well-known to a wide public, and could expect further success and, indeed, advancement. His days were packed full, and he had a wife whose poor health demanded much care and consideration.

He had, however, cherished political ambitions for some time, and in the 'Khaki' election of 1900 had stood as Liberal candidate in North Kensington. This was not a seat that the Liberals had expected to gain, particularly in an election fought when the war in South Africa had apparently been won and the Unionist government could hope to benefit electorally from this. The Liberal organization in North Kensington was rudimentary and, despite the active support of one of the chocolate manufacturing Fry's, Isaacs had lost decisively, although encouraging a handsome swing from the Tory candidate in the process.

Isaacs's impressive progress at the Bar had, in fact, served to obscure his political activities. He had remained a staunch member of the 'Hampstead Parliament' and in 1894 had been chosen as the Liberal 'Prime Minister'. His candidature at North Kensington had come about six years later as a result of an enquiry from Liberal headquarters, and was certainly in the hallowed tradition of trying out promising recruits in hopeless seats.

Rufus Isaacs was no blood-red Radical, and had 'little sympathy with the narrower aspects of the Nonconformist outlook which constituted so powerful an element in contemporary liberalism'.[1] Liberalism, none the less, was the natural party for him to support. Within his own father's lifetime Jews had been obliged to struggle to obtain full civil rights. Moreover, the Liberal party apparently stood for the noble principles of liberty, toleration and progress whereas the Tories, although somewhat disguised within the Unionist coalition, seemed to offer little in the way of enlightened policies. For a man who approved of social reform, yet wanted to stop well short of revolution, the Liberal party was the obvious home.

The Liberal movement in the early 1900s was also a 'broad church', encompassing distinctly contrary views. The Boer War had illuminated these differences to an embarrassing degree. On the left of the party were the 'pro-Boers', led by the up-and-coming David Lloyd George, John Burns and John Morley; the centre was dominated by the party leader Sir Henry Campbell-Bannerman, who had nevertheless antagonized supporters of the British conquest of the Transvaal and the Orange Free State by asking, 'When is a war not a war? When it is carried on by methods of barbarism in South Africa.' On the right of the party were the Liberal Imperialists (or 'Limps'), including such powerful personalities as Asquith, Sir Edward Grey and Haldane. The Liberal Imperialists, though regretting the necessity for the War and deploring the more ruthless tactics deemed necessary by Kitchener and his supporters, wanted an ultimate British victory and looked forward to the establishment of a renewed, purified and unified South Africa under the Union Jack.

Rufus Isaacs belonged, without question, to the Liberal Imperialist wing of his party. His son, indeed, considered 'the description of "Liberal Imperialist" fitted him to perfection and remained the aptest epitome of his political career long after it had fallen into disuse'. Isaacs must also have felt comfortable within a group led by such illustrious members of the Bar as Asquith and Haldane.

After losing at North Kensington in 1900, Isaacs kept in reasonably close contact with organized Liberalism. He travelled, for example, to a great Liberal Imperialist rally at Chesterfield where he addressed an overflow meeting at some length until the chief speaker, the ex-Prime Minister Lord Rosebery, eventually came up behind him, saying in his ear, 'Thanks very much, Mr Isaacs. I think I'll speak now!' In 1902 he went to speak at a miners' rally in the Rhondda Valley where he was promised a warm reception 'in Welsh form' from the 30,000 participants.[2] In August of the same year, the leader of Reading's Wesleyans wrote asking for a contribution to help pay off a debt of £30; Isaacs sent back a pound.[3]

His contribution to the Reading Wesleyans suggests that Isaacs was already nursing that constituency in 1902 hoping to be adopted as Liberal candidate. The sitting MP, George Palmer, head of the prosperous biscuit firm Huntley and Palmer, and a former mayor of Reading, was uncertain, because of increasing deafness, whether to stand at the next general election. Early in 1904 Palmer finally decided not to stand again and the Reading Liberal Committee, with the approval no doubt of the party chiefs at Liberal headquarters, invited Isaacs to become prospective Liberal candidate.

Isaacs accepted the invitation, perhaps encouraged to do so by the likelihood that the next general election was a couple of years off, thus allowing him time both to work at his constituency and to pay proper attention to his legal career. In the event, he was obliged to fight for his seat within a few months, for in July 1904 Palmer announced that, because of his failing health, he was retiring immediately.

Reading had swung between the two great parties in each of the preceding four elections. On that crude analysis it could be expected to return Keyser, the Conservative candidate, in the imminent by-election. Keyser, moreover, was a local man, owning extensive property and backed by most of the area's leading industrialists including Suttons, the seed merchants, and Simmonds, the brewers. Despite Palmer's backing, Isaacs was an outsider and, although it was impossible to calculate its significance, a Jew.

On the other hand, the brilliant KC's national reputation would hardly damage his chances, and, more important, there was clearly a countrywide movement against the Unionist government. In part this disenchantment reflected the natural swing of the pendulum against a party that had been in power since 1895, and had produced next to nothing in the shape of social reform while supervising a fundamentally humiliating war in South Africa. But more damaging still was the great rift in the Unionist coalition caused by Joseph Chamberlain's passionate and divisive tariff reform campaign.

Chamberlain had resigned from Balfour's Cabinet in 1903 in order to mastermind a national campaign to convert the electorate from free trade to tariff reform. Basically tariff reform meant the introduction of protective tariffs to aid the flagging sectors of British industry, while at the same time allowing Britain and her self-governing colonies to give each other preferential fiscal treatment within the tariff system. In order to give Canadian wheat preferential treatment, however, American and Russian wheat, for example, would have to cross a higher tariff barrier before it could be imported into the United Kingdom. The critics of tariff reform thus argued that bread prices, and indeed food prices in general, would rise sharply. Joseph Chamberlain met this criticism head on when he said in the House of Commons in May 1903: 'If you are to give a preference to the colonies ... you must put a tax on food. I make hon. gentlemen opposite a present of that.'[4]

Chamberlain's tariff reform campaign was a godsend to the Liberal party: Lib-Labs, Liberal Imperialists and Gladstonian centrists could all combine in the defence of free trade, and bury their differences on other issues. When Asquith first heard the news of Chamberlain's opening salvoes in the tariff campaign he exclaimed, 'wonderful news ... it is only a question of time when we shall sweep the country'.[5]

Not only were the Liberals suddenly united, the Unionists were split into three broad factions. Chamberlain led a vocal and convinced group of tariff reformers; Tory and Liberal Unionist free traders formed the Free Food League; and Balfour, the Prime Minister, tried to hold the middle ground by issuing pronouncements of an increasingly obscure nature.[6] The electorate were thus presented with the unedifying spectacle of the Unionists divided into warring factions, with the Chamberlainites, in effect, promising the country higher food prices.

All of this made Isaacs's task of holding Reading for the Liberals much easier. His opponent Keyser offered a wary Balfourian prevarication on the tariff issue, stating that 'the question of Fiscal Reform has long had my careful attention, and I am of the opinion that the state of Trade in the Empire necessitates a most careful inquiry into the whole matter, and that some measures should be adopted to preserve to this country the industries and manufactures that are now so seriously handicapped by unfair competition'.

In the opening speech of his campaign in Reading town hall Isaacs

55

fastened on to his rival's bland analysis with the sure grasp of the successful advocate:

I can't help thinking that he must have been reading Mr Balfour's speech at Sheffield and out of the maze of it he must have penned this paragraph: 'The question of Fiscal Reform has long had my careful attention.' Mark that! Mr Keyser is not starting upon his initial study of Fiscal Reform, but it has long had his attention.

'I am of the opinion that the state of Trade in the Empire necessitates a most careful inquiry into the whole matter.' One would have imagined that he might have arrived at that conclusion without long and careful consideration.[7]

He then outlined the platform on which he stood. He was staunchly for free trade, for the taxation of land values, and for reforms in the areas of military organization, licensing, education and the legal standing of trade unions. On the issue of education (a highly contentious one in the light of the current controversy over the 1902 Education Act) he declared himself 'in favour of a great and comprehensive system of education, free and controlled by the people, so that the utmost advantages to be derived from study should be brought within the reach of the poorest in the community'. As one of those most closely involved in the Taff Vale case, he made it clear that he was wholeheartedly 'in favour of amending the laws affecting trade unions so as to afford adequate protection to the association of working men'.

Keyser had no such programme of reform to offer. Nor could he match Isaacs's clear and sophisticated speaking skills, and 'usually contented himself at meetings with a short and stereotyped speech'. Indeed, 'His chief electioneering asset was a magnificent coach-and-four decorated with the Conservative dark blue, on the box seat of which he would parade the town, accompanied by a galaxy of resplendent supporters.'[8]

For his part, Isaacs campaigned, with his wife, from the Liberal headquarters at the Lodge Hotel, a modest temperance house conveniently near to Huntley and Palmer's biscuit factory. This base was not chosen simply out of consideration for Nonconformist views on drink, but because Reading's larger hotels were strongholds of Toryism and the brewing interest. The Lodge Hotel, and much of Reading, was emblazoned with banners and posters in bright Liberal red with the slogan of 'Rufus for Reading'.

Isaacs only encountered one clear example of anti-semitic hostility. During his speech to a public meeting in the town hall, a heckler kept shouting 'Down with the Jews!' At last Isaacs turned on the man and, pointing at him, declared, 'When I came to Reading, I said – as I say now – that I am a Jew and proud of it.' He proceeded to speak of the sufferings of the Jewish race and to remind the audience of the British reputation for justice and fair play. The heckler was silenced, and even Tories in the audience applauded.

The brief campaign, fought over the August Bank Holiday, saw some of the Liberal party's brightest, and youngest, stars speaking for Isaacs: Lloyd George, flaying the government's education bill; Winston Churchill, who had recently crossed the floor of the House of Commons over the tariff issue; Herbert Samuel, and another brilliant young Jewish Liberal, Edwin Montagu, fresh from the Presidency of the Cambridge Union; and John Freeman-Thomas, later Lord Willingdon and Governor of Bombay.

The poll was declared on 4 August 1904 and the returning officer announced that Rufus Daniel Isaacs (Liberal) had received 4,730 votes and Charles E. Keyser (Conservative) 4,540, thus making Isaacs the victor by 230 votes. The first the large crowd waiting outside Reading town hall knew of this was when a placard was produced saying simply: 'Rufus D. Isaacs, KC, MP.'

Noisily acclaimed by his supporters outside the hall, Isaacs next moved a vote of thanks to the returning officer inside the hall, saying candidly: 'I come of course as a stranger. I only wooed you as a politician. I never attempted to do anything else than appeal to you as a politician.' With only nine votes less than Palmer in 1900, the wooing had obviously been very persuasive. Later, from his hotel balcony, he contented himself by telling his supporters, 'Bravo, Reading. This is your victory, not mine.'

Four days after his victory, Isaacs took his seat in a House of Commons about to rise for the summer recess, sponsored by Herbert Gladstone, son of the great William Ewart Gladstone, and by Alfred Rose who held a seat near Reading. Cheers rose from the opposition benches.

At forty-three, Rufus Isaacs was a member of the House of Commons. Press reactions to his campaign and his victory were mostly complimentary. The day before the poll the *Morning Post*, though endorsing the Unionist candidate, spoke of 'the undeniably favourable impression which Mr Rufus Isaacs KC, ... has made on his party'.[9] The *Daily Chronicle* had previously commended 'the inspiring start' to his campaign.[10] On polling day the *Daily News* declared, 'Mr Isaacs has shown by his speeches that he will represent true labour.'[11] After his triumph at the polls the *Pelican* commented that 'Mr Isaacs' whole bearing is that of a man marked out for success',[12] and the *Morning Post* pointed out, rather tartly, that he 'had all the advantages of platform power, for no man is more richly gifted in the art of making the worse appear the better cause'.[13]

But why had the remarkably successful barrister chosen to become a Member of Parliament? Unlike a Joseph Chamberlain, a Lloyd George or a Winston Churchill, he was not a man who wanted passionately to change things, to grab destiny by the scruff of the neck and tame it to his will. He did not clearly represent any powerful national constituency such as organized labour, the City or privilege. There is no impression of a man with fire in his belly, dead set on becoming Prime Minister and leaving an indelible mark upon history.

Asquith's wife, the formidable Margot Tennant, wrote that Isaacs was one of the four most ambitious men that she had ever known. Sir Derek Walker-Smith thought that it was 'fairly clear that Rufus Isaacs never pursued a single goal of attainment, to which he directed all effort and subordinated all activity'.[14] Isaacs's son perhaps comes closer to the truth when he wrote: 'His rise was not the progressive fulfilment of a conscious plan. I do not believe that, with the possible exception of the Attorney-Generalship, he deliberately set out to attain any one of the great offices which he held. Indeed, their very diversity almost excludes design.'[15]

It was quite true that both the Solicitor-Generalship and the Attorney-Generalship were traditionally only open to MPs of the party in power. By climbing on to the Liberal bandwagon just as it was about to roll towards the landslide election victory of 1906, Isaacs was at least making his advancement towards these important law offices possible. In the event, he was appointed to first the Solicitor-Generalship and then the Attorney-Generalship within six years of entering the House of Commons.

There is, however, another way of looking at Isaacs's career in politics and in the law. Perhaps, beneath the calm, reasonable and sophisticated public personality of the mature Rufus Isaacs there still lurked the adventurous, rash and dilettante spirit of the rake of Belsize Park. Arguably Isaacs chopped and changed as much in his illustrious career as he did as an immature young man. A brilliant success as a barrister, he took the Solicitor-Generalship in 1910, thus cutting himself off from his immensely lucrative practice; having been in politics for less than ten years he became Lord Chief Justice, thus apparently abandoning hope of further political advancement; as Lord Chief Justice he found it impossible to resist the temptation of neglecting the duties of this great office and serving as a wartime ambassador; restored to full attendance upon his legal office he soon abandoned it to grasp in 1921 the nettle of the Indian Viceroyalty; at an age when retirement must have seemed most attractive he became briefly Foreign Secretary at a moment of national crisis.

There is a further way of considering Isaacs's apparent lack of political passion and of consistency of purpose, although it is a difficult path to tread. In February 1908 the *Saturday News* wrote bluntly of 'the difference between the English mind and the Jewish mind in relation to British politics. The Jewish mind is essentially outside our politics, despite the sorceries of Disraeli. The Jew is a citizen of the world. He has no patriotism, for he has all patriotisms.'[16] Sir Derek Walker-Smith took a similar line in *Lord Reading and His Cases*, published before Reading's death, saying:

The Jew inevitably surveys national problems in greater detachment, for he sees them against a different background. ... It is perhaps due as much as anything to the fact that he did not altogether share the emotional outlook of his countrymen that Lord Reading has been a ruler rather than a leader. ... Lord Reading is an Occidental, and a lawyer; a man of affairs, romantic in his achievements rather than in his ideas ... a ruler rather than a leader, a diplomat rather than a politician.[17]

There are perils in such interpretations; in the hands of perverted theorists, ideas like these can lead to the extermination camp and the 'final solution'. They put 'race' above 'nationality' and 'religion' higher than 'citizenship'. Given Rufus Isaacs's lack of religious faith and his corresponding lack of enthusiasm for militant Zionism, the criticisms above seem misplaced – reflecting a doctrinaire analysis of a people, and owing little to the characteristics of the individual.

Still, Isaacs was certainly not a committed House of Commons man. He made his maiden speech nearly a year after his by-election victory. It was admittedly an appropriate occasion on which to intervene in the procedures of the House. Partly as a sop to working-class prejudices and partly because a real problem existed, the Unionist government put an Aliens bill before the Commons in 1905. The bill was aimed at restricting alien, mostly Jewish, immigration which had aroused hostility in London's East End and in some northern cities like Leeds.

Isaacs's intervention did not consist of a fiery attack on the principle of restricting immigrants who were mostly fleeing from persecution in Russia and Eastern Europe. Rather it was devoted to a criticism of the procedural inefficiency that had led the government to move a guillotine resolution to cut short the debate.

As reported in Hansard, in the third person, he said:

Hitherto he had been reserving himself for this Bill, upon which he would like to say a few words in view of the current situation.... he would have thought, even without becoming a member and certainly without becoming Prime Minister that it was possible to remedy the situation with the greatest ease. Those who were responsible for the conduct of the business of the House ought to foresee the amount of time that would be required for the measures they intended to introduce and to take precautions to ensure sufficient time for their full discussion. ...

As a new Member he could not help saying that, judging from his short experience of the way in which Parliamentary affairs were conducted, the House of Commons, as a means of passing legislation, was a very ineffective body indeed.[18]

He went on to criticize a proposed government amendment to the bill which excepted from its restrictions those aliens who came to Britain to avoid prosecution or 'punishment on religious grounds'. How, Isaacs argued, did the last phrase properly cover those, like the Russian Jew or the Armenian Christian, who were fleeing their country because of religious persecution?

The *Western Mail* reported on 6 July that 'Mr Rufus Isaacs made a pleasing impression by his maiden speech. Its easy fluency and polished style placed it high above the other men on that side.' The *Manchester Umpire* of 9 July said, somewhat surprisingly, 'It was probably the largest audience that ever assembled in the House for the purpose of listening to a maiden speech. ... It was not a very long speech but it was sufficient to convince the House that a very powerful recruit has joined the ranks of Parliamentary debaters.'

Isaacs's maiden speech did not electrify the House. It had been an astute and polished intervention, but in the style of the experienced barrister rather than of the promising politician.

Balfour, the Prime Minister, none the less paid a graceful tribute to 'the first speech of an honourable and learned gentleman who has a deservedly high reputation in other spheres of activity and whose intervention in our debates I am sure all of us welcome'. From the opposition front benches, Lloyd George was more forthright, declaring that 'He was interested in the admirable speech of the honoured and learned member for Reading. What struck [Isaacs] most of all was that this was a futile place to come and work, and that was what struck every business man.'

Certainly Isaacs did not become a House of Commons man. He rarely frequented the smoking room, and used the library chiefly to work on the next day's briefs. When he did speak in the chamber he did so with authority, but in a rather prosaic fashion. However:

He had no pretensions either to the classic deliberation of Mr Asquith or to the dynamic exuberance of Mr Lloyd George. He was never a maker of phrases and his effects owed little or nothing to choice of words. But he never made the lawyer's mistake of talking above the heads of his hearers. His speeches were simple and direct both in form and content, and they succeeded by the impression of spontaneity and sincerity which they conveyed.[19]

With no aspiration, and perhaps no talent, for imposing his personality upon the House of Commons, Isaacs nevertheless made a number of contributions to its debates from the back benches between 1904 and his appointment as Solicitor-General in March 1910. Hardly had he adjusted to his responsibilities, however, than he was required to fight for his seat again at the general election of January 1906. The tide was by then running so strongly against the Unionists that it would have been difficult to lose Reading for the Liberal party, and Isaacs was returned with a majority of 697, the largest of his parliamentary career.

His task was also lightened by having a young and inexperienced candidate against him. Moreover, he had demonstrated his determination to serve his constituency well by purchasing Fox Hill, a late-Victorian house on what were then the outskirts of Reading. Fox Hill provided him and his wife with a base, on the edge of the countryside, for weekend and holiday stays in Reading, when he played some gentle golf and tennis and went for spins through the Berkshire lanes in a primrose yellow Renault.

During the 1906 election campaign Isaacs fought chiefly upon the free trade issue, and repeated his 1904 by-election calls for reforms in the legal position of trade unions and in the administration of the army. On the issue of Irish Home Rule

he said as little as possible. He was prepared to accept it as a historic, even if inconvenient, plank in the Liberal platform, but he never pretended to any ardent enthusiasm for it, fearing always that in time of crisis the existence of a separate Government in Ireland might constitute a source of danger to Great Britain, and disliking also the possibilities of religious oppression of the Protestant minority.[20]

Yet another controversy, the 'Chinese Slavery' outcry over the government's use of indentured Chinese labour in the Transvaal's gold mines, left him relatively unmoved; he felt that the facts behind the agitation had been substantially misrepresented, and contented himself with a passing reference or two to the matter.

Once safely returned to the Commons, he was shortly to speak during the second reading of the 1906 Trade Disputes bill, supporting the statutory reaffirmation of the privileged legal status of trade unions, although wishing, like Asquith, that their complete immunity had some restrictions upon it. In July 1906 he praised the government's plans to restore self-governing institutions, though within the Empire, to the Transvaal and to the Orange Free State. His next intervention came in February 1907 when, during the debate on the address, he spoke of the problems connected with the Chamberlainite programme of tariff reform and imperial preference.

In June 1907 he made a more substantial contribution to the debate on the resolution of the Prime Minister, Sir Henry Campbell-Bannerman, 'that in order to give effect to the will of the people as expressed by their elected representatives, it is necessary that the power of the other House to alter or reject bills passed by this House should be so restricted by law as to secure that within the limits of a single Parliament the final decision of the Commons shall prevail'. This was the first warning shot in what was destined to be a protracted and momentous battle between the Liberal government, with its overwhelming House of Commons majority, and the unreformed House of Lords with its permanent and in-built Tory majority. Essentially, the Upper House chose to throw out Liberal bills of which their lordships, with no electoral mandate whatsoever, disapproved; the new Education bill and the Plural Voting bill had been savaged in this way. The way was now open for a confrontation that was to lead to the 'People's budget' of 1909 and a constitutional crisis of sometimes disturbing intensity.

Rufus Isaacs's part in the debate on Campbell-Bannerman's resolution was a careful exposition of the problem, 'no outstanding oratorical contribution but ... much as if he had been addressing a jury, preferring logic to rhetoric and argument to invective'. His audience, however, could not doubt that he felt strongly that the House of Lords' destructive tactics should be limited. Interestingly he also rejected the fashionable notion of a referendum to decide the issue, arguing that the electorate could not be expected to exclude all other considerations while concentrating on this one issue.

When Asquith succeeded Campbell-Bannerman to the premiership in April 1908, Isaacs took a clear step nearer to the centres of power. As a Liberal Imperialist he was closely associated with Asquith, and both men knew and respected each other's achievements at the Bar. Asquith and Isaacs became good friends, although their relationship was for a time disrupted after Asquith was overthrown by Lloyd George in 1916.

With Asquith at 10 Downing Street, however, Isaacs could hope for preferment in his political career. Oddly, in view of the bitter antagonism that was to develop between them, Isaacs drew closer at this time to both Asquith and Lloyd George. His relationship with Lloyd George will be scrutinized at some depth in later chapters, but for the moment it will suffice to remark on the complementary qualities that promoted a friendship where, at least superficially, Isaacs had balance, judgement and restraint, and Lloyd George had vision, fire and enthusiasm. Among other leading Liberals, Isaacs became particularly friendly with the urbane and kindly Alec Murray, Master of Elibank, and later the party's chief whip until his retirement from politics in 1912. Isaacs also developed close friendships with other back-bench Liberal MPs, especially with the novelist A.E.W. Mason, Charles Henry and Alfred Mond, later Lord Melchett, whose daughter Eva was to marry Gerald Isaacs in 1914.

During 1908 Isaacs contented himself with a speech on the second reading of the highly controversial Licensing bill, and a further intervention at the committee stage. In 1909 he spoke in support of the government's warship construction programme during the celebrated 'naval scare' prompted by Imperial Germany's threatening naval building programme.

A few months later, in July 1909, he spoke again when Lloyd George's contentious 'People's budget' was passing through the committee stage and the highly charged issue of the taxation of land values was being discussed. The 1909 budget had been framed to raise extra revenue to pay for the cost of proposed social reforms and for the increases in the naval programme. Never loath to attack the 'ruling classes', Lloyd George proposed measures designed to soak, and incidentally provoke, the rich. These included higher death duties, super-tax and taxation of land values, including a duty on unearned increment and on the capital value of underdeveloped land. Although the denunciations by Tories of 'confiscatory socialism' were somewhat exaggerated, the 1909 budget clearly marked a turning-point in the relationship between the old order and the forces of progressive democracy.

Isaacs's view of the taxation of land values controversy was that, since the ownership of land was essentially a monopoly, it ought to be used in the best interests of the whole community. He put his finger on the real reasons for the agitation against the budget proposal by saying: 'The real objection to the land tax is the fear of valuation.... The chief arguments against [it] are the impossibility and difficulty of valuation and the cost.'[21]

The 'People's budget' was thrown out by the House of Lords in an act of self-destructive bravado in November 1909. Asquith had little choice but to ask for a dissolution of Parliament and to appeal to the country on the issue of the Lords' right to reject a budget put forward by the elected representatives of the people. Polling was fixed for January 1910, and Isaacs had to appeal for the third time in five and a half years to the electorate of Reading.

How well had he served his constituents during that period? He had certainly not neglected his local duties, as, for example, when he managed to persuade John Burns, President of the Local Government Board, to put up money for town improvements. Burns wrote on 21 December 1908:

Dear Rufus,

The Reading folks have already received £420. I am sending them today another £266, the entire labour cost of a road across a recreation ground; the Town Council will pay for materials which will cost £450 in loan which I will sanction.

Yours sincerely,

John Burns.[22]

Isaacs thanked Burns for 'his enterprise' and wished him the 'Merriest of Christmases'. Although the two men were never close political associates, it is typical of Isaacs's thoughtfulness that, when Burns's son died in 1922, he found time, amid his viceregal duties, to write a letter of kindly consolation.[23]

The Reading press, in the form of the pro-Liberal *Reading Standard*, expressed its warm approval of their MP, remarking amid the 1906 election that 'Never have the Liberals of Reading had so brilliant and popular a candidate as Mr Isaacs.'[24] The *Standard* a year later gave a sympathetic account of Isaacs's hectic life:

On every weekday morning he rises between four and five o'clock (winter and summer), and before breakfast discharges all the preliminary preparation for his day's work. He is in his chambers from about 9.30 a.m. until 6 or 7 p.m., except when the House of Commons is sitting, so that – allowing for but a brief night's rest – his spare time at home must indeed be limited, even when the Parliament is in recess. When the House is sitting, it is doubtful if even he himself could say how he manages to do the duties that devolve on him.[25]

Although Isaacs was blessed with a strong constitution and had the knack, like Winston Churchill, of being able to snatch a few moments of reinvigorating sleep in the unlikeliest of conditions, his life was indeed almost unbearably full. He admitted himself how tired he so often was during these years, juggling the demands of the Bar, the House of

Commons and his family. It was perhaps partly his inability to devote his energies chiefly to his parliamentary career that led the *Saturday News* to describe him in February 1908 as a political lightweight: 'Mr Isaacs is not an avid figure in the House. His personality is too piquant, his outlook too bright and human. But he is not a great Parliamentary figure. The impression he creates is one of a light skirmisher on the fringe of the battle.'[26]

The pressing demands of his legal practice go some way to explain Rufus Isaacs's apparently lightweight political presence. Between the general election of 1906 and his appointment as Solicitor-General in 1910 he enjoyed an exceptionally lucrative period, which also happened to be his last in private legal practice. His annual earnings averaged a phenomenal £30,000, and his clerk usually refused any brief marked below 500 guineas. Together with Sir Edward Carson, Isaacs was one of the two leading counsels in the country.

Rufus Isaacs's legal cases during this time were varied and often fascinating. They included his successful defence in December 1905 of Sir Edward Russell, editor of the Liberal *Liverpool Daily Post and Mercury*, against criminal libel proceedings taken against him by eight Conservative members of the Licensing Committee of the Liverpool justices. Isaacs also received the then record fee of £12,000 for his triumphant defence in 1908 in the case of Wyler and the Ibo and Nyasa Corporation Limited v. Lewis and Others.

In the previous year he had been retained in a hopeless cause defending Lord Northcliffe, proprietor of the *Daily Mail*, in a libel against him brought by William Lever of the soap manufacturing concern based at Port Sunlight, Liverpool. Carson was retained for Lever. Isaacs soon decided that Northcliffe's case was a hopeless one and proceeded to offer Carson in court, in an audible whisper, sums in settlement beginning at £10,000 and ending finally at the huge amount of £50,000 – the largest sum hitherto awarded to a successful litigant in the English courts. Despite his client losing the case, Isaacs did well out of it on two counts: he won the liking and respect of Lord Northcliffe – which was to be a valuable asset during the ensuing Marconi scandal; he also formed a closer friendship with his great rival Carson.

In 1909 Isaacs had the opportunity of cementing another friendship. This arose when Lloyd George brought an action for gross libel on his private reputation against the owners of the *People* newspaper. As with so many of the rumours circulating about the Chancellor of the Exchequer's private life, the libel, though not mentioning him by name, concerned his alleged adultery with a married woman and his imminent appearance as alleged co-respondent in the ensuing divorce case. Lloyd George's extramarital adventures were, in fact, very real, but on this occasion, with Rufus Isaacs leading F.E. Smith and Raymond Asquith, the premier's son, on the plaintiff's behalf the *People* were obliged to make an unreserved apology and to pay £1,000 in damages – which were promptly handed over to charity.

In January 1910, concentrating his energies once more on politics, Isaacs appealed again to the electors of Reading, aided by huge posters reading 'What's the matter with Rufus? He's all right!' His election address put the constitutional issue plainly:

By the unconstitutional and revolutionary action of the House of Lords this Budget, passed by an overwhelming majority of the representatives of the people in the House of Commons, has been rejected by the Peers. Thus the House of Lords has, for the first time in the history of our constitution, which is based upon usage, practice and custom, asserted a right to force a dissolution of Parliament by refusing to assent to the necessary supplies, and has revived a claim to control the finances of the country which we all thought had been disposed of in favour of the House of Commons, once and for all, long ago. In my view, careful and deliberate provision should be made to prevent any possible recurrence by the House of Lords with the Budget or the finances of the country. Never again should the Budget be liable to rejection by the Peers.

In my view, the taxation imposed on the people through their representatives in the House of Commons should be preserved to the people's protectors, their duly elected Members of Parliament.

I would also support a definite limitation of the power of the Peers to mutilate and reject measures passed by the House of Commons and am in favour of steps being taken to ensure that the will of the people must and shall prevail.

Lloyd George came down to speak for his friend at an election meeting on 4 January 1910. Reminding his audience that he had spoken at Isaacs's first election meeting in 1904, the Chancellor of the Exchequer said:

I am proud that I had that privilege to help to return one of the ablest, most brilliant and distinguished men in the House of Commons. [Cheers.] His constituency is a credit to him, and, if you will allow me to say so, he is a credit to his constituency. [Cheers and cries of 'He's all right'.] Oh, yes, I am quite certain that he is all right.

Why are we here, when we could be enjoying ourselves in other ways at Christmas time? The reason is that the rich landlords who are represented specially in one branch of the legislature decline to bear their fair share of the burden of taxation. ... [The] Budget raises money not only for Dreadnoughts but for social reform!' [Loud cheers.][27]

The electors of Reading returned Rufus Isaacs, though with a majority cut to 207 out of a poll of some 10,000. The swing against the Liberals at Reading was very similar to a nationwide return to the Unionists of voters alarmed at the radicalism of Lloyd George, Winston Churchill and others, and can therefore not be seen as a personal failure for Isaacs. In the new House of Commons the Liberals had 275 seats against the Unionists' 273; the Liberals were, however, sustained in power by the votes of the Irish Nationalists and the Labour party, and could, in normal circumstances, look for a working majority over the Unionists of some 112 votes. Although the Liberals could now proceed to curb the power of the Lords, they would have to pay a price for Irish support. The price was quite a plain one, though disquieting to some, like Isaacs, on the Liberal right – the introduction of a bill for Irish Home Rule.

For a while Isaacs was able to bask in the pleasure of his success in the general election, his mood doubtless heightened by a warm letter from his recent client, the Tory press magnate, Lord Northcliffe, who confessed that he had waited by the telephone for the Reading result 'with more party disloyalty than I care to confess and I congratulate you heartily on a splendid win. ... Today I motored through your constituency and was immensely struck by the brilliance of your poster artist. "He's all right." I never saw such a splendid show.'

Within two months he was to receive further congratulations, for in March 1910 the Solicitor-General, Sir Samuel Evans, was made President of the Probate, Admiralty and Divorce division of the High Court, and Isaacs was invited to succeed him.

6 Solicitor-General, 1910

Mr Rufus Isaacs, who is counted among our most brilliant and successful advocates, follows Sir Samuel Evans as Solicitor-General. No-one has better earned the rank of Law Officer of the Crown.
Daily Mail, 7 March 1910

Rufus Isaacs accepted the Solicitor-Generalship with the alacrity of a man who had hoped for an advancement that could only have resulted from his entering Parliament. Although he could not have anticipated it, he was destined never to return to private practice, and for the next sixteen years held official positions of considerable importance culminating in the Viceroyalty of India.

Reactions to his appointment were generous, both within and without his profession. The *Law Journal* claimed that:

> ... among the profession no more popular appointment has ever been made. The great powers which this brilliant advocate and acute judge of men and affairs has applied to the vindication of private rights will now be employed in the service of the State; and there can be no doubt that his cool judgement and shrewd intelligence will be an advantage to the country in general, as well as to his party, at this period of serious constitutional crisis.[1]

The *Lancashire Post* reiterated his usefulness to the government 'in the critical times that lie ahead', and paid tribute to his 'dynamic quality' and 'great abilities'.[2] The *Manchester Evening Chronicle* said 'of the Solicitor-Generalship, his new post, a barrister said: "There is too much work for one man and Mr Isaacs is the only one I know equal to the task." '[3] The *Evening Standard* called him a 'master of lucid statement', pointing out that 'hitherto his enormous practice has prevented him from doing full justice in the Commons to his remarkable powers of logic and perspicacity'.[4] The *Reading Standard* loyally, and charitably, made the same point, while the Tory *Daily Mail* reflected Northcliffe's mellow view of Isaacs with an assessment of the sort normally reserved for Conservative Law Officers: 'Mr Rufus Isaacs, who is counted among our most brilliant and successful advocates, follows Sir Samuel Evans as Solicitor-General. No-one has better earned the rank of Law Officer of the Crown.'[5]

While warmly applauding Isaacs's promotion, the *Daily Mirror* drew attention to the undoubted financial sacrifice the new post entailed: 'In accepting the office of Solicitor-General at the comparatively early age of forty-nine, Mr Isaacs will not benefit pecuniarily. The income of the office is £6000, with fees that amount to about £4000 per annum. While at the Bar Mr Isaacs' income has been estimated at about £20,000 a year.'[6]

As it happened, Isaacs's average income from private practice had been running at a little under £30,000 a year, and in the seven months that he held the post of Solicitor-General his fees from Crown work amounted to a modest £2,200. The adjustments made necessary by these changed circumstances were neatly illustrated shortly after his taking up the office when a Treasury messenger arrived at his chambers, now at 2 Garden Court, and handed in a fat brief, marked ten guineas for Isaacs and two for his clerk. The clerk condescendingly pointed out that his master did not take ten-guinea briefs, whereupon the messenger, who knew his job, replied, 'He'll take that one, and he'll take dozens more like it before he's finished.'

There were, of course, compensations of a non-financial kind. To begin with, the Solicitor-Generalship traditionally carried a knighthood with it. Isaacs did not receive the honour straightaway because of the disruption caused to the monarchical programme by the sudden death of Edward VII on 7 May 1910. Eventually Isaacs was the first man dubbed knight by the new King George V, who said afterwards, while shaking hands, 'How much pleasure it would have given my father to do this.' Also, although he was obliged, under a statute dating from Queen Anne's reign, to offer himself for re-election on accepting a ministerial post, the Reading Tories (perhaps licking their wounds, and in any case anticipating another general election in the near future) allowed him an uncontested walk-over.

Then there were the compliments of men whose good opinion Isaacs valued more than material rewards. Lord Alverstone, the Lord Chief Justice, wrote: 'My very best congratulations. You have won your great position by your rare abilities and honourable conduct. All your thousand friends will be delighted to see you SG, and none more than your faithful friend the LCJ.' Sir Edward Clarke, one of the most illustrious members of the Bar, said: 'I congratulate you with all my heart. You have nobly earned the honour, and any others which in due course may follow from it. I know your future will be worthy of yourself and of our profession and I hope it may be full of success and happiness. Always your faithful friend.'

So, in the spring of 1910, Sir Rufus Isaacs had scaled yet more heights: he had achieved ministerial rank (though not within the Cabinet), he had been knighted, he was soon to move to Curzon Street from Park Lane, he had a modest country seat, he was a popular member of Parliament and an illustrious King's Counsel. Fortune seemed to smile upon him with a consistency denied to other men. Could this really be Rufus Isaacs, rebellious fruiterer's apprentice, ex-ship's boy and 'hammered' stockjobber? It was a miraculous transformation like that in the world of nature when the caterpillar turns into the gorgeous butterfly.

It was Isaacs's misfortune that he at once inherited a most difficult case from his predecessor as Solicitor-General. It was a subject of much legal and national controversy, and his handling of it was to prove one of the rare occasions when his professional conduct was sharply criticized.

The case of George Archer-Shee was of such dramatic content that Terence Rattigan was later to write a successful play, *The Winslow Boy*, based upon its salient points. The bare bones of the case were that a thirteen-year-old naval cadet, George Archer-Shee, had been expelled from the Royal Naval College at Osborne, on the Isle of Wight, for allegedly stealing a five-shilling postal order from a fellow cadet and for forging his comrade's signature on the back before cashing it at a post office. The authorities at Osborne had got Archer-Shee to write the name of the other cadet, Terence Back, upon a blank piece of paper, and had apparently been justified in their suspicions when a handwriting expert had declared that the signature on the back of the postal order was in the same hand as the specimen produced by the suspect.

No more would have been heard of this trifling incident if Archer-Shee had not adamantly insisted upon his innocence. His family believed him and eventually consulted the great Edward Carson. After an intensive three-hour interview with Archer-Shee, Carson declared himself convinced that the boy was telling the truth.

As a result of pressure from Archer-Shee's family, the Admiralty conducted two enquiries into the affair. These proved unsatisfactory in that none of the witnesses against Archer-Shee was subjected to cross-examination, and the Admiralty predictably refused to reinstate the boy or to alter the original decision.

Carson proceeded to advise the boy's father to sue the Crown on his son's behalf for breach of contract, claiming that the authorities had broken their agreement to provide him with a full course of naval training.

On 12 July 1910 the case came before the High Court, with Sir Edward Carson leading for the plaintiff and Sir Rufus Isaacs, as Solicitor-General, leading for the Crown. Isaacs persisted in the Crown contention that the action brought by Archer-Shee was not maintainable in law; if the judge upheld this contention, the plaintiff would not be able to put the facts of the case before the court.

It is clear that Isaacs was personally unhappy about this crude defence of the Crown's legal position, but felt himself morally bound to uphold the decision of the outgoing Solicitor-General. Carson expressed heartfelt fury at the stratagem, arguing that the legal point as to whether the action was maintainable should have been settled before the case came to court. At one point he said heatedly, 'The Crown is shirking the issue of fact. It is a public scandal. The Crown can, I suppose, be high-handed out of Court, but in open Court it is not to be tolerated.' After a while, he asserted that 'This is a case of the grossest oppression without remedy that I have known since I have been at the Bar.' When, after some terse exchanges between Carson, Isaacs and the judge, the latter upheld the Crown view, Carson picked up his papers and walked angrily from the court.

Carson appealed, and the Court of Appeal unanimously ruled against Isaacs's stand, ordering that the case should be tried before a judge and jury before the legal points in dispute should be argued at all. In July 1910 the case came on before Mr Justice Phillimore and a jury.

George Archer-Shee acquitted himself well during nearly two days of cross-examination, and on the fourth day Sir Rufus Isaacs announced that the Admiralty was prepared to surrender its position and to accept the complete innocence of the dismissed cadet.

Although Archer-Shee's name was thus triumphantly cleared, he was not taken back by the naval college at Osborne. The Admiralty, moreover, had to be forced, by questions in the House of Commons, to offer any compensation to the boy's family, eventually paying out £7,120 in costs and compensation.

Rufus Isaacs's first case as a Law Officer provided him with the rare experience of suffering hard-hitting criticism in the press and Parliament. As he admitted afterwards, he would have much preferred to order a proper trial for the case, but his sense of duty and loyalty to his predecessor led him into too rigid a position.

In the Commons he made his first speech as a minister at the end of March 1910, presenting an authoritative assessment of the fiscal and constitutional relationship between the two Houses of Parliament. On 5 April he took part in an informal, behind-the-scenes meeting, attended by the future King George v, to try to resolve the deadlock; there was a 'luncheon in Thurloe Square, Alick Murray's house, between Murray and Rufus Isaacs and the Prince of Wales with Sir A. Bigge [Private Secretary to the Prince of Wales]. The Prince of Wales being very anxious for an accommodation between the two Houses.'[7] Clearly Isaacs's ministerial position, and his friendly association with powerful figures like Murray, Lloyd George and, to a lesser extent, Asquith, was bringing him closer to the centres of power in Liberal Britain. Although no revolutionary, his advice was plainly in support of the government's intention to assert their mastery over the House of Lords by informal, or if necessary by statutory, means.

Occupancy of the front bench, some noticed, 'gave him increased assurance'. Certainly he was in great demand throughout the country as a distinguished and weighty public speaker, though his son noticed that

the responsibilities of office seriously hampered him on a platform. The spontaneity and zest which made him effective as a private member were replaced by close adherence to carefully prepared notes. ... Whereas he had formerly been eloquent in his own style, he was now at times almost hesitating; whereas he had been vigorous he was now almost laboured. Even his voice lost something of its characteristic and compelling ring and became measured and grave.[8]

Isaacs adopted this graver style quite consciously, shying away from a spontaneity that might let slip a statement embarrassing to his ministerial colleagues during such tense times.

In the middle of 1910 Sir Rufus and Lady Isaacs moved to 32 Curzon Street, a far larger house than the one in Park Lane. They came to love this early Georgian building, with its high, finely proportioned rooms. Since Alice found it difficult to get to the first floor without a lift, they converted the ground floor to serve her needs: 'The two front rooms, one small and one large, became her boudoir and the drawing room respectively. The two similar back rooms were converted into her bathroom and bedroom, in mauve and grey, while the farthest room of all was his dressing room and study combined, the end being partitioned off to provide him with his own bathroom.'⁹

These quarters were a far cry from the relatively cramped conditions of Park Lane. Gerald Isaacs, for instance, had the run of the first floor, except when some of the rooms were needed for entertaining guests. This freedom was in marked contrast to his living quarters at Park Lane where he only had a bedroom on the third floor next to a small study used by his father. Gerald had been an Oxford undergraduate during the last years the family spent at Park Lane and he recalls:

there were times during vacations when, on mounting to my room at an early hour of the morning on my return from a party, I encountered on the staircase my father on his way to start work. He always behaved perfectly on such occasions, and after the exchange of a few impersonal remarks we withdrew to our respective sanctums. By common consent no reference was made at breakfast to our earlier meeting and his 'Good morning' carried no hint of recollection or reproach.¹⁰

Breakfast, indeed, seems to have been Rufus Isaacs's best meal of the day in that he invariably appeared lively and ate heartily. Certainly sleep restored him like a sorcerer's elixir, and he remarked of his capacity to doze off in unlikely places that 'many people consider that to be my best qualification for the Bench!' Holidays, too, continued to be a further recuperative necessity:

When the courts rose, he would appear to be almost at his last gasp. His face, never highly coloured, would be the ivory white of old parchment; his eyes would be sunken and encircled with black rings; his shoulders would stoop; even his voice would be hoarse and toneless. In forty-eight hours he would have shed twenty years. Sunburned, bright-eyed, upright, gay and active, he was almost unrecognizably transformed, and by the end of a week he would be cheerfully complaining that his son was so much older than himself that he had no one with whom to get into mischief.

For this startling rejuvenation he had to thank his almost unlimited capacity, so rare among hard-working men, for suddenly and for a prolonged period doing absolutely nothing at all. Both mind and body were so perfectly under control that he could switch the engine off and drift idly for days on end as soon as the opportunity offered.

He required no form of amusement to distract his mind from its recent responsibilities and labours. The change from hectic activity to placid passivity was effortless and immediate and continued until he felt his mental and physical batteries to be sufficiently recharged. He never made the mistake of plunging into violent physical exercise as soon as he was free from the enforced confinement of his working life. If the weather allowed, he would sit for hours in the hottest sun, hatless and content, until he was surprised and slightly aggrieved to find that the skin of his face had become scorched and painful in the process. If the weather was bad, he would sit indoors paying casual attention to a novel. In either case the bulk of the day would be dedicated to making up arrears of sleep. This result might have been best achieved by staying for a day or two in bed, but he detested the experience so heartily on the rare occasions when he was compelled to endure it that he would never submit to it voluntarily; he would always come down to breakfast, however late, rather than have it in his own room.[11]

In the summer of 1910 the Isaacs went for the first time to take the cure at the newly fashionable spa of Marienbad, then in the Austro-Hungarian Empire. Among other British visitors to Marienbad were the judges Lord Dunedin and Lord Justice Vaughan Williams, Charles Gill from the Bar, T. P. O'Connor, an Irish Nationalist MP, and Colonel Mark Lockwood, from the House of Commons, and three amusing stage celebrities, Squire Bancroft, Herbert Beerbohm Tree and Charles Hawtrey – famous as a mimic.

Such vivacious company suited Sir Rufus and Lady Isaacs very well, even though the latter missed the morning meetings of the group, preferring to rise later in the day. She was, however, at ease after that, and able to accompany her husband out to dinner. Once when they were dining on grouse at the table of Sir John Barker, head of the great London department store, a frivolous lady called out to her host, 'Oh, Sir John! How too lovely! I am sure they must be your own birds. Do tell me – where is your moor?' To which Sir John replied blandly, 'High Street, Kensington.' The Isaacs were to return each year to Marienbad until the outbreak of the First World War.

Shortly after Isaacs's return to his official duties in London he was faced with another change in his position. In October 1910 the Attorney-General, Sir William Robson, was nominated to a judicial vacancy in the Court of Appeal. This meant that Isaacs would be automatically offered the Attorney-Generalship. Thus after seven months as Solicitor-General, Sir Rufus Isaacs became the senior Law Officer of the Crown and the official leader of the English Bar. He was still under fifty years of age, and had only been a barrister for half of that time. His promotion, moreover, opened up the prospect of even higher office, for it was a tradition that the Attorney-General could expect to move into any vacant senior judicial position, including that of Lord Chief Justice.

7 Attorney-General, 1910-13

Asquith proposed to put Rufus Isaacs into the Cabinet. The King spoke to me about it, as he wanted to know what precedents there are. None, so far as I know ... But precedents are really quite unimportant nowadays. Rufus Isaacs is a very clever, sensible, and charming fellow.
Lord Esher, 1912

Sir Rufus Isaacs had hardly settled into his new post before the country was pitched into the second general election of 1910. The inter-party constitutional conference of the summer and autumn had failed to reach an agreement on the crisis over the powers of the House of Lords, and on 28 November Asquith asked King George v for a dissolution of Parliament.

The election campaign of December 1910 was unusually bitter. Liberal reformers campaigned on the platform of 'The Peers versus the People', while the Conservatives and Unionists caricatured their opponents' desire to restrict the right of the House of Lords to delay legislation passed in the House of Commons as a revolutionary assault on constitutional liberties. Although the Lords had finally passed the 1909 'People's Budget' on 28 April 1910, the battle had by then shifted to the Parliament bill which, based on the scheme outlined by Campbell-Bannerman in 1907, proposed that the Upper House should lose any power to veto finance bills and should be allowed to delay other pieces of legislation for only two years. It was not generally known that Asquith had extracted a commitment from the King that, if the Liberals won the election and the Lords still refused to pass the Parliament bill, he would be prepared to create enough new Liberal peers to swamp the Tory majority in the House of Lords.

The election of December 1910 produced an almost exact replica of the January result. Although fifty-six seats changed hands, the final tally was: Liberals 272 seats, Unionists 272, Labour 42, Irish Nationalists 84. The electorate had recorded the same verdict as eleven months earlier: they supported the Liberal government against the Lords, giving it a practical working majority of 126. With 42 per cent of males, mostly from the working and lower middle classes, unable to vote under the franchise, the feeling in the country was almost certainly even more strongly in favour of Lords' reform than the balance of parliamentary seats indicated.

Rufus Isaacs's campaign in Reading was the third occasion inside a year that he had presented himself to the electors, a task which few others had ever faced. He once more had stalwart support from party chiefs, and on 29 November the Prime Minister himself addressed a crowd of eight thousand packed into the corporation tram sheds. Isaacs concentrated his campaign on the two issues of constitutional reform and tariff reform versus free trade. His son, Gerald, helped by some of his friends from Oxford, worked hard for him, even warming up audiences with speeches before his arrival. It was clearly going to be a tight-run thing, with the Unionists putting up a strong candidate, Captain Leslie Wilson, destined to serve as Governor of Bombay during Lord Reading's Viceroyalty.

On polling day the Liberal headquarters was for a time gripped with panic as rumour insisted that the Unionists were heading for a win. In the event Rufus Isaacs was returned with a majority of ninety-nine votes, less than half of his majority in January 1910.

Reappointed as Attorney-General, Isaacs could now settle down to a post which gave him a unique opportunity to observe, and participate in, the working of nearly every ministry without having to carry the burden of ministerial responsibility. His advice on various legal matters would be sought by government departments, and he would sometimes be required on the front bench in the Commons to explain the finer points of a difficult clause. When, moreover, the Crown was involved in important legal cases, the Attorney-General was expected to lead on the Crown's behalf.

An early example of Isaacs's legal expertise being needed was in the preparation of Lloyd George's Insurance bill, a proposed measure of social welfare reform that was to provide for health and unemployment insurance for most categories of workers. After the general election of December 1910, Lloyd George invited Rufus Isaacs, together with the brilliantly promising, but soon eclipsed, Charles Masterman, then Under-Secretary at the Home Office, to join him on a working vacation at Cap Martin in the south of France. Two senior civil servants came too, as did Mrs Lucy Masterman.

Lucy Masterman recorded her impressions of both Lloyd George and Rufus Isaacs during these weeks in France. She was touched, and sometimes embarrassed, by both men's generosity:

We all had breakfast, and indeed every other meal together, and it must be said that George was setting the scale of expenditure very high. He was extraordinarily generous towards Charlie and me, on one pretext or another, and he did his best to pay for nearly every meal we had. When he was not trying to, Rufus was. When we moved to Nice and Charlie and I made efforts to get cheaper rooms, he engaged a suite and tried to insist on our paying only what we had paid at Cap Martin, where we had to put up practically in the servants' room. Of course we would not consent to it, and Rufus who has been a poor man himself was quick to notice, and very ready to help if we looked at all dubious at any of the expenditure.[1]

She also gave a vivid impression of the mutual regard, and the differences, between the Welsh solicitor and the Jewish barrister:

[Lloyd] George used to listen interminably to Rufus Isaacs' description of his cases and appreciated them enormously. But the difference between the two men was extremely marked. Whenever George began to tell us of his experiences among his Welsh preachers, Rufus simply could not understand why he was so interested in them. To him these things seemed simply ridiculous. On the other hand, one could see that Isaacs had an extremely high standard in his profession, a high standard of honour and of permissible things to do. . . .

It was very curious to watch George and Isaacs discussing the Insurance Bill. George was inclined to judge everything by his own experiences in Wales. Rufus very naturally knew but little about the subject.[2]

Isaacs struck her, too, by his verve and vitality. As the party motored through the French countryside:

It was during these drives, I think, that Rufus Isaacs gave his most amazing exhibitions of vitality. We usually started early in the morning. It was very cold at the time. Rufus was either talking or singing the whole time. Other people fell asleep in turn, but never he. Among other things he sang me the Hebrew version of the 'Song of Miriam', which he learned at school. George stared at him open mouthed. 'You are an astonishing fellow. I never knew anybody like you,' was his comment.[3]

Although, apart from Lloyd George and the Master of Elibank, he did not develop any really close friendships with his colleagues, Isaacs had a warm, and reciprocated, regard for Asquith, admiring his 'classic rotundity of mind and serene geniality of temperament' and also 'Mrs Asquith's coruscating swiftness of brain and tongue'. Both Asquith and Isaacs enjoyed playing bridge, often with considerable originality and enterprise. Isaacs was on very cordial terms with Masterman, Churchill and Reginald McKenna, but was unable to draw close either to Sir Edward Grey, the Foreign Secretary, or to Lord Haldane.

Sir Rufus was, none the less, a sociable being, or, at least, much sought after socially:

As a talker he was at his best when in a reminiscent mood, especially when his thoughts reverted to his days at sea or the more reprehensible escapades of his youth. He would then tell his story with so mischievous a light in his eye, so much animation and gusto, and so evident an enjoyment both in the tale and in the telling of it that he would keep his hearers enthralled. He enjoyed wit in others, even if he rarely achieved it himself. But humour he possessed in a high degree and, perhaps even more than a sense of humour, a vivid sense of fun. Gossip about people bored him intensely and he rarely embarked upon a discussion of abstract ideas, preferring to keep the talk to the affairs of the day. But intimacy had never come easily to him. His gaiety, vitality and charm, his power of appearing absorbedly interested in the conversation of wholly uninteresting people, were neither artificial nor superficial, but beneath them lay a core of reserve which grew more impenetrable with the passing of years. There was in his composition a strange blend of sentimentality and stoicism.[4]

There remained, however, an impenetrable reserve, a disinclination to reveal his feelings, though he enjoyed the private catharsis of weeping during a film or stage show, 'secure in the knowledge that as soon as the lights went up, his private safety curtain would fall again over his self-indulgence and shield it again from the eyes of the world'. Otherwise:

He guarded jealously his own rigid self-control, and his embarrassed loathing of openly displayed emotions in others was his instinctive reaction against any possible assault upon his own. He hated rows and scenes, for the spectacle of human beings casting aside the decencies of normal intercourse made him acutely uncomfortable, and for the same reason he looked with icy disapproval at eccentricities of dress or behaviour. Moreover, he had a dislike almost amounting to prudishness of questionable jokes and stories, and any attempt to repeat one to him encountered so discouraging a reception that it would have taken a bold man and a still bolder woman to make the experiment twice. All these traits, seemingly so much at variance with his early life, were no doubt defensive in origin, outworks thrown up in the course of years as additional protection for that inner reserve which the stresses of his own life and the circumstances of his wife's prolonged ill-health had combined to impose upon him.[5]

The Insurance bill, which finally became law in December 1911, occupied a good deal of Rufus Isaacs's time, although naturally it was Lloyd George who bore by far the greater burden in piloting it through the House of Commons. It was a lengthy and hazardous course that Lloyd George had to steer, fighting off attacks from both the Labour party and the Tories. Isaacs's main contribution to placing the bill on the statute books was through negotiations outside the Commons:

His years at the Bar had given him wide experience of conducting delicate negotiations for the settlement of cases as well as of handling many types of people in different moods. Much of his time was consequently spent in receiving, either alone or in company with Mr Lloyd George, indignant deputations which came to voice their grievances against the new proposals, listening to their objections, placating their wrath and ushering them out, if not converted, at least reassured. In this way many of the more formidable obstacles which would otherwise have blocked the progress of the bill ... were removed from its path.[6]

Isaacs's performance in the Commons was not always so skilful or effective. On 19 July 1911 the Labour party bitterly attacked Clause 11 of the bill, which was meant to avoid duplication of benefit in workmen's compensation cases, and proposed its rejection: 'Labour party broke loose on Clause 11 and went on till 5 a.m.! Rufus and McKenna did not manage very well; shortly before breaking up the Chancellor took the House in hand again.'[7]

Isaacs was in more commanding form when he introduced the government's Trade Unions bill which became law in 1913. This bill reversed the effects of the controversial 1909 Osborne judgment which had ruled that compulsory political levies upon members of trade unions for the purpose of paying salaries to their representatives in Parliament were illegal. The trade unions and the Labour party had agitated for legislation to overturn the Osborne judgment and, although many middle-class Liberals had qualms over the political levy, the need to placate working-class Liberals and the Labour MPs in the Commons after the 'dead-heat' elections of 1910 proved irresistible.

As early as 1909 Rufus Isaacs had expressed his sympathy with trade union indignation over the Osborne judgment, and it was appropriate that he should play a leading part in piloting the bill that allowed unions to reintroduce the political levy through the Commons. Ironically, the Trade Unions Act of 1913 enabled the Labour party to restore its finances, thus making them a much more threatening rival to the Liberals than in the period from 1909 to 1913.

Isaacs was also involved in giving advice on the land reform question. From the time of Cobden and Bright, and via Joseph Chamberlain's 'three acres and a cow' campaign of 1885, the Liberal party had toyed with the idea of land reform. Eventually, having put through his National Insurance Act, Lloyd George took up the cause of land reform with his customary vigour, castigating selfish landlords and demanding a sweeping reform of the system to ensure a living wage for country labourers, a policy of rural slum clearance, an end to 'capricious eviction', and proper protection against the destruction of crops through hunting game, also claiming that 'Labourers had diminished, game had tripled. The landlord was no more necessary to agriculture than a gold chain to a watch.'[8]

Land reform was, of course, a tricky matter, and, until Lloyd George launched his campaign, there seemed comparatively little electoral interest in it. By 1913, however, the campaign had made its impact, and the swing against Liberal candidates in rural by-elections in 1912 and 1913 averaged only 2.4 per cent as compared with 5.1 per cent in non-agricultural constituencies.

Although no supporter of extreme confiscatory policies, Rufus Isaacs gave staunch official backing to Lloyd George's initiative on land reform. In 1909, amid the uproar over the 'People's Budget', he had supported the tax on land values thus:

The answer is that land is a monopoly not created by man, and where it increases in value through no effort, expenditure or enterprise of the owner but because of the growth and the activity and the expenditure of the community it is consistent with natural justice that the State should levy toll.[9]

Four years later he prepared a Cabinet paper which coolly justified the need to employ government to ensure the fairest and best use of land:

The cardinal point of the present proposals is that a commission should have discretionary power to intervene in any case in which it was alleged that an unfairness of contract existed which prevented land being used in the best interests of the community.

The question must be looked at, not only from the point of view of obtaining the maximum amount of produce from the land, but also from the point of view of the maintenance of the general physical and moral well being of the people as a whole.[10]

Although a Land Inquiry Committee published a report in two hefty volumes in 1913 and 1914, and despite Seebohm Rowntree's convincing exposure of rural poverty in his *How the Labourer Lives* (1913), the outbreak of the First World War put an end to any Liberal plans to introduce land reform legislation.

Other, more momentous, affairs had absorbed Isaacs as Attorney-General in the years between 1910 and 1913. He was involved in the attempts to bring about an end to the great coal strike of 1912 by introducing a Coal Mines (Minimum Wages) bill and forcing it through Parliament under great pressure.

Hardly had the national coal strike ended when Asquith introduced the long-awaited Irish Home Rule bill into the House of Commons. In the face of vehement Unionist opposition in Parliament, and with Sir Edward Carson acting as the main spokesman for militant Ulster protestantism, the Home Rule bill devoured the time of all those responsible for its legislative passage. Sir Rufus Isaacs 'found himself for the rest of the year involved in the lengthy debates which centred about [the bill] and obliged to take a prominent part especially upon its legal and constitutional aspects'.

It was not easy work. Isaacs spoke in 'the full dress debate' on the second reading. He was also constantly in attendance during the bitterly controversial committee stage of the bill, and, in one infamous episode, was shouted down by the Unionist opposition, one of whose members, the Ulster MP Ronald McNeill, proceeded to throw a weighty book at Winston Churchill. The Irish Home Rule bill was yet another piece of Liberal initiative that was thwarted (to the relief of some Liberals) by the advent of war in 1914.

So heated, however, had the controversy become before then that there had been a clamour from supporters of Home Rule for the prosecution of Carson on a charge of sedition. Isaacs, as Attorney-General, was the man who had to decide whether there were sufficient grounds for such an action – a step that would have been rendered personally delicate by the warm professional regard he and Carson held for each other. Although 'he would not have hesitated to proceed against his old friend if he thought it his duty to do so', Isaacs considered that a prosecution of Carson would merely have created another martyr to an Irish cause. Despite Carson's provocation, no such action was taken.

The agitation for women's suffrage was another thorn in the government's flesh. It was not simply a matter of party politics: 'Campbell-Bannerman was inclined to be favourable, Asquith to be hostile. Churchill's attitude fluctuated. Balfour was friendly, Bonar Law rather less so. ... Lloyd George concluded that the Liberals must either allow universal suffrage for both sexes or nothing, since enfranchisement of only middle class women would strengthen the Conservative vote.'[11] Not surprisingly, nothing was done for women's suffrage until after the First World War. Isaacs was sympathetic to the suffragists, though less so to the militant suffragettes. In December 1911 Lloyd George, in a speech at a meeting of the Women's Liberal Federation, remarked on how impressed Isaacs had been on meeting a women's delegation, saying 'And yet they say that women are not fitted for the vote.'[12] Indeed the Attorney-General 'had gone so far as to say that he saw no reason why a woman should not be Lord Chancellor if she were the best qualified candidate for the office'.

Suffragette activity, however, included acts of violence against public figures, the pouring of vitriol through letter boxes, and the smashing of hundreds of plate glass windows. In his ministerial position Isaacs was obliged to prosecute Mrs Pankhurst, Mr and Mrs Pethick Lawrence and Mrs Turke, the leaders of the militant Women's Social and Political Union, on a charge of conspiracy to commit damage and injury. The defendants were sentenced to nine months' imprisonment to hisses and cries of 'Shame!' from the public gallery. Isaacs was implicated in the official policy of the forcible feeding of suffragette hunger-strikers and the iniquities of the 'Cat and Mouse Act' which allowed hunger-strikers out of prison and then sanctioned their rearrest once they had sufficiently recovered from the effects of their protest. Isaacs was quite clearly troubled by these developments.

In June 1912 Isaacs was given a seat in the Cabinet. The precedent for such a step went back to 1806, and Asquith's desire to promote his Attorney-General to the inner circle of ministers was undoubtedly a personal compliment, although, as we shall see, there were other pressures. In his journal on 12 June Reginald Brett, Lord Esher, wrote of his conversation upon the subject with George v:

> Asquith proposed to put Rufus Isaacs into the Cabinet. The King spoke to me about it, as he wanted to know what precedents there are. None, so far as I know, except Lord Ellenborough in 1806 and that was not a success! But precedents are really quite unimportant nowadays. Rufus Isaacs is a very clever, sensible, and charming fellow.[13]

According to his son, Isaacs later came to believe that it was in principle a mistake for the Attorney-General to be a member of the Cabinet. He came to this conclusion because of the difficulties facing the Attorney-General when asked to give advice on questions of law as they affect government policy; if the Attorney-General was also a Cabinet member, Isaacs believed that he would view the various legal problems with a less than impartial eye, having probably been deeply involved from the outset in discussing the matters in question. At any rate, he was now a member of the Cabinet, eight years after entering the House of Commons, and privy also to informal meetings like that described by Charles Hobhouse, Chancellor of the Duchy of Lancaster, on 11 November 1912:

> After our defeat on Monday 11th [in a snap division on a financial amendment to the Home Rule bill] those of the Cabinet who had been in the

division held a meeting in the PM's room. Harcourt, Isaacs, Lloyd George, Wood, myself and Birrell. Churchill came in later. The PM took the matter with more concern than most of us, and it awoke him from his lethargic optimism most completely and satisfactorily. No one thought of resigning, only of the delay in time and confusion. Though no one blamed Illingworth, who actually prevented people from continuing the discussion as he believed he had a majority in the House, we were angry at so unnecessary a defeat on a point which on the previous Friday we had carried by 120. While we were talking Grey came in laughing, threw himself down on the sofa at full length, and said 'Well, is it relief?' and then hardly another word. I went to try and find the Speaker for the PM while Samuel hunted for Ilbert and precedents.[14]

Isaacs's promotion to Cabinet rank was perhaps chiefly a compensation for his failure to be made Lord Chancellor in June 1912. Lord Loreburn had resigned from the Woolsack on 4 June, having suffered a severe heart attack and on the advice of his doctors. Although the Attorney-General had no prescriptive right to the office of Lord Chancellor, it had been almost invariable practice, over three hundred years, to promote the senior Law Officer of the Crown to the position. There is no doubt that Isaacs wanted, and expected, to be offered the Lord Chancellorship early in June 1912. In the event Asquith, with the hearty approval of the King, gave the job to Lord Haldane, Secretary of State for War.

Why was Isaacs passed over in this extraordinary fashion? Was it because he was a Jew? Apparently he believed this likely, and 'even hinted to John Simon [the Solicitor-General] at resignation'.[15] Simon went so far as to write a memorandum to Asquith arguing that there was no reason why a Jew should not become Lord Chancellor: 'As to this there can, I consider, be no doubt. ... what formerly excluded a member of that faith was the requirement of an oath taken "on the faith of a Christian". That requirement vanished in 1867.'[16]

A much more likely explanation of Isaacs's being passed over for the Lord Chancellorship lies in Haldane's desire for the post and in the latter's close personal and political relationship with the Prime Minister. In 1911 Haldane had willingly become a peer, which seemed a step hardly likely to advance his political career; but in his *Asquith*, Roy Jenkins says that Haldane's 'principal ambition was still centred on the Woolsack ... so that he lost little by leaving the Commons'.[17] When Isaacs sought out Asquith for an explanation, according to one authority the Prime Minister told him 'that ever since the formation of the Government there had been an understanding between him and Lord Haldane that, if the latter would agree to accept the War Office in the first place, he should have the Lord Chancellorship whenever a vacancy occurred'.[18]

This account, published in the Second Marquess of Reading's biography of his father, is inaccurate in the sense that it refers to a 'private compact' between Asquith and Haldane over the Lord Chancellorship. There are echoes here of the 'Relugas Compact', an undertaking made three months before the Balfour government fell in December 1905, whereby the leading Liberal Imperialists, Asquith, Grey and Haldane, agreed not to take office in a government under Campbell-Bannerman unless the latter was prepared to go to the House of Lords and leave the leadership of the Commons to Asquith. Under the terms of the 'Relugas Compact', Asquith was to be Chancellor of the Exchequer, as well as Commons Leader, Grey was to be Foreign Secretary and Haldane Lord Chancellor.

As it happened, Campbell-Bannerman routed the Relugas plotters, and Asquith was the first to opt out of the 'Compact', taking the Chancellorship of the Exchequer. Haldane, however, did not get the Lord Chancellorship, and ended up with the poisoned chalice of the War Office. Asquith undoubtedly felt, at some level, that he owed it to Haldane to secure him the Lord Chancellorship at some future date. Nor was Asquith alone in this for, according to John Wilson, the biographer of Campbell-Bannerman, on 7 December 1905 'C.B., who had the patience of a saint, received Haldane in a friendly way and promised him the reversion of the Lord Chancellorship if anything happened to Reid [later Lord Loreburn]'. [19]

Looked at in this way, it was Haldane, not Isaacs, who would have had the greater cause for disappointment if he had been passed over for the Lord Chancellorship in 1912 on Loreburn's retirement. This did not prevent Isaacs from expressing his indignation to the Prime Minister, although whether he did this mainly in defence of the precedent of the reversion of the post to the Attorney-General is unclear. After all, did he really want the duties associated with the Lord Chancellorship? The long hours of sitting on the Woolsack during House of Lords debates, 'without even the power of Mr Speaker to preserve order'? The presiding over the judicial sittings of the Lords or of the Privy Council? It seems unlikely, even given Isaacs's erratic switches between legal and political office.

Was Isaacs's protest a way of getting into the Cabinet? His son writes that Asquith

recognized the force of Sir Rufus's representations and readily accepted his proposal that, as a solatium alike to himself and his office, he should join the

Cabinet in order that the world might be shown that the Prime Minister had not doubted Sir Rufus's fitness for high office and that he acknowledged that the appointment of someone other than the Attorney-General to the Lord Chancellorship was a break with custom and called for some compensation.[20]

According to Lord Simon's memoirs, however, Isaacs did not put the proposal to Asquith. Rather the idea was proposed to the Prime Minister by the Master of Elibank, Alec Murray.[21] But since Murray was very close to Isaacs, this may have come to the same thing.

At any rate, Sir Rufus Isaacs was now a member of the Cabinet, taking his seat at the historic table in Downing Street and, for a time, as the most junior minister there, obliged to be door-keeper of the Cabinet room – there being no secretariat present in pre-war days.

While Isaacs was so busily involved in his political duties, he also represented the Crown in some fascinating legal cases. One of these first surfaced shortly after his becoming Attorney-General.

In November 1910 a journal, *The Liberator*, that was printed in Paris under the editorship of an American, Edward Holden James, published an article claiming that King George v had lawfully married the daughter of a British admiral in Malta in 1890. Such an allegation, if true, would have made the King a bigamist and his offspring illegitimate, since he had married Mary of Teck in 1893, three years after the alleged morganatic marriage.

The Liberator was a journal of strong republican sympathies, and the editor was assisted by Edward Mylius who was a British anti-monarchist. Gossip had for some time toyed with the allegation now printed in *The Liberator*, but few gave it credence.

Now, however, it was in the open, with *The Liberator* denouncing 'the spectacle of the immorality of the Monarchy in all its beastly monstrosity', and 'the sickening and disgusting crime which has been committed by the English Church which has married one man to two women'.[22]

Since *The Liberator* circulated in Britain and overseas, there were soon references to the allegation in other English language newspapers. *Reynolds' Newspaper* repeated it in England, and the *Brisbane Telegraph* in Australia.

Having sought the advice of the Attorney-General and the Solicitor-General (Sir John Simon), the King decided to take the matter to law. On 1 February 1911 Edward Mylius was brought before the Lord Chief Justice and a special jury in the Royal Courts of Justice charged with criminal libel. Mylius was charged as the British correspondent of *The Liberator* who had supplied the information on which the offending article was based, and as the journal's distributor in the United Kingdom.

Although there was never much doubt as to the outcome of the case, since Mylius was unable to produce a shred of evidence to support his allegations, the trial was notable for some moments of drama, as when, before the jury was sworn, the defendant said, 'I wish the King to be present.' When asked why he made this request, Mylius continued: 'I demand his presence on the grounds, first that every accused person has the right to be confronted with his accuser in Court; secondly, that no action for libel is usually taken without the prosecutor being in Court, where the jury can see him; and, thirdly, that there is no proof that the prosecutor is at present alive.'

The Lord Chief Justice overruled Mylius and the trial began. The defendant had, however, touched on a delicate point: although the King had expressed his willingness to go into the witness box, both Rufus Isaacs and John Simon had already advised him that there was 'some doubt' as to whether he could appear 'as a witness in his own Court'. Isaacs repeated the legal justification for the King's non-appearance during the trial.

The Attorney-General made a powerful opening to his speech to the jury:

Gentlemen, I am very anxious that you should understand from the outset that in these proceedings in this prosecution no complaint has been lodged because of the Republican sentiments and views which this gentleman and those associated with him in this leaflet may choose to advocate. A man is free in this country to advocate political opinions, even to raise the question of the proper form of government for this country. He is probably freer in this country than in any country in the world to publish his views and to circulate them; and so long as he keeps within the law, which is framed on very broad and generous lines, no complaint is made against him, however much you and I may differ from every sentiment that is expressed in the paper. But I want you quite clearly to appreciate that this prosecution is not in respect of any observations of that character which may have been made in this leaflet.[23]

Having later justified the decision that the King could not appear as a witness, and pointing out that the onus of proof was on Mylius, Isaacs concluded his speech to the jury thus:

It is not for the Monarchy that the protection of this Court has been sought by means of this case. The Monarchy in this country rests upon foundations more secure than any that could be undermined by the attacks of James or the defendant Mylius. But the protection is sought for the King as a man, for the

King as a husband, for the King as a father. Your protection is sought for the honour of the King.

In submitting this case to you, I do not ask you to deal with it in any other way than you would the most ordinary case as between one citizen and another. The same rules of evidence and the same considerations must apply. You have to determine this case, and you will determine it, upon the evidence that will be laid before you. You will judge it fairly and impartially. You will, I am sure, consider everything that can possibly be said or may be urged either as defence or in any other way by the defendant. But you will also, I know, bear in mind this: that the King is none the less entitled to the verdict of a jury and to the protection of an English Court of Justice in any attack made upon his honour because he happens to be the King of England.[24]

Since Mylius called no witnesses in his defence, and the Crown evidence appeared so irrefutable, the verdict was a foregone conclusion. Mylius was sentenced to twelve months' imprisonment. That evening George v wrote in his diary: 'The whole story is a damnable lie and has been in existence now for over twenty years. I trust that this will settle it once and for all.' As a mark of the King's personal gratitude, both Rufus Isaacs and John Simon were appointed Knights Commander of the Royal Victorian Order. On 5 July 1911, a few weeks later, Isaacs was appointed a Privy Councillor in the Coronation Honours list.

The second case of great interest in which Sir Rufus Isaacs was involved while Attorney-General was the trial of Frederick Seddon and his wife for murder. Surprisingly it was the only murder trial in which Isaacs ever appeared, and his experience convinced him that he never wished to feature in another one. Since, however, the Seddons were accused of poisoning their alleged victim, Isaacs was more or less obliged to lead for the prosecution because of the tradition that either the Attorney-General or the Solicitor-General should represent the Crown in cases involving poison.

The case against the Seddons was that they had poisoned a middle-aged maiden lady, Eliza Barrow, whom they had taken in as a lodger and whose fortune of £3000 Seddon had taken over in exchange for an annuity of £155. Before she died Miss Barrow had made a will leaving her property to a young boy called Ernest Grant, whom she had virtually adopted, and appointing Seddon as her executor.

Although a post-mortem revealed two-thirds of a grain of arsenic in her corpse, there was nothing but circumstantial evidence to show that either of the Seddons had administered the poison. The trial turned on Isaacs's cross-examination of Seddon, who only went into the witness box on his own insistence.

The trial began on 12 March 1912 at the Old Bailey, and it was clear when Isaacs opened the prosecution case that the Crown was going all out for a conviction. Even so, if Seddon had not offered himself as a witness he might have been acquitted, but the Attorney-General's questioning revealed him as a ruthless, conceited and miserly man who could well have committed the crime of which he was accused.

Early in his cross-examination of Seddon, Isaacs suddenly asked: 'Did you like her?' 'Did I like her?' replied Seddon, unsure as to the best answer. 'Yes, that is the question.' 'She was not a woman that you could be in love with,' answered Seddon, having gained time by repeating the question, 'but I deeply sympathized with her.' Isaacs then took him through all the financial transactions, and in this field Seddon felt more confident and able to give as good as he got. Asked whether Miss Barrow was not living well within her income, he replied brusquely: 'I was the superintendent of an insurance company. I was not the housekeeper.'

As the prosecution proceeded, however, Isaacs was able to throw further doubt on Seddon's integrity and goodwill towards the dead woman. Finally he asked: 'Have you ever heard of poisoning by arsenic taken from fly papers?' 'Yes, since I have been arrested.' 'Do you know that two-thirds of a grain of arsenic was found in the stomach and intestines of this lady ... two months after her death?' 'I have heard that.' Can you account for the arsenic having got into her stomach and intestines?' 'It's a Chinese puzzle to me.'

The jury, however, were not puzzled. After an hour's deliberation they found Seddon guilty of murder and acquitted Mrs Seddon. Seddon remained self-assured to the last and, before Mr Justice Bucknill sentenced him to death, made the secret sign that binds one freemason to come to the aid of another. The judge, a devoted mason, was greatly moved by this, but eventually regained his poise and passed sentence. Seddon was hanged at Pentonville prison, still protesting his innocence.

Some observers considered that Rufus Isaacs had conducted the prosecution case with 'more of the vengeance of a destroying angel than the scrupulous moderation of a high officer of the Crown'. But Mr Justice Humphreys, who was one of Isaacs's juniors, later said:

The case for the prosecution rested upon circumstantial evidence. It depended, to quote the opening speech of the Attorney-General, upon proof of three things – interest, opportunity, conduct. In such a case the explanation of the accused, if given in the witness box, is of the first importance, and this trial was distinguished by the most deadly cross-examination of an accused person which I can recall – all the more deadly because it was perfectly fair. The male prisoner was under cross-examination by Sir Rufus Isaacs for the greater part of a day. During that time the Attorney-General never raised his voice, never argued with the witness, never interrupted an answer, and scarely put a leading question. The questions and the manner of putting them were pre-eminently fair. Seddon was taken through the history of the case and invited to give his own explanation of every material matter. The result was to turn what was always a strongish case into a conclusive one.[25]

If Rufus Isaacs did not altogether relish his triumph in the Seddon case, he was soon to be involved in an investigation that was to cause him far greater anguish.

8 The Marconi Scandal, 1912–13

Never from the beginning, when the shares were fourteen shillings or nine pounds, have I had one single transaction with the shares of that company.
Sir Rufus Isaacs, House of Commons, 11 October 1912

We are of [the] opinion that the Attorney-General acted with grave impropriety in making an advantageous purchase of shares in the Marconi Company of America upon advice and information not then fully available to the public. . . .
Minority Report of the Commons Select Committee, 1913

He [Asquith] saved Ll[oyd] G[eorge] over Marconi. Why? – because Ll.G. was young and he loved you. Had it not been for you he would have let Ll.G. go.
Lady Oxford (Margot Asquith) to Lord Reading

The bitter controversy that engulfed Sir Rufus Isaacs in the summer of 1912 over the purchase of shares in the American Marconi Company raged well into 1913. Indeed, for a time it seemed as if not only the Attorney-General but also Lloyd George, the Liberal Chief Whip (the Master of Elibank), Herbert Samuel (the Postmaster-General), and even the Liberal government itself would be swept aside by the flood tide of rumour, libel and, eventually, official investigation.

The Marconi scandal stands as a monument to the temptations, perils and pitfalls of public life. It provided the unedifying spectacle of the British press, public and Parliament indulging in one of their bouts of hysterical and essentially hypocritical self-righteousness. It was certainly not destined to be the last example of this vindictive frenzy. Of course there were real issues at stake, notably the allegation of corrupt financial dealings by senior government ministers, and none of the protagonists emerged from the affair with an enhanced reputation. The scandal was shot through with evidence of politically-inspired malice and ugly racial prejudice on the part of many of those who denounced the ministers, but it also brought out some of the nobler national traditions of tolerance, loyalty and fair-mindedness.

The case against the four ministers was this: Herbert Samuel, the Postmaster-General, was alleged to have awarded, at Rufus Isaacs's behest, an unduly favourable government contract for the construction of wireless stations to the British Marconi Company, whose managing director was Godfrey Isaacs, brother of the Attorney-General; further-more, Samuel, Rufus Isaacs, Lloyd George and the Master of Elibank were accused of speculating in Marconi shares, using Isaacs's fraternal link and inside government information about the contract to buy the shares at a very favourable price.

Rumours concerning the Marconi contract had been circulating during the summer of 1912. The matter was brought to a head early in August by the publication of an apparently libellous article in a journal, *The Eye-Witness*, edited by Cecil Chesterton, the younger brother of the poet, G.K. Chesterton. *The Eye-Witness* had been founded by the poet and Liberal MP Hilaire Belloc, a close friend of G.K. Chesterton; although it published articles of high literary quality from contributors as diverse as H.G. Wells, Arthur Quiller-Couch and Arthur Ransome, its editorial policy included a ferocious and unrelenting anti-semitism. *The Eye-Witness*'s assault on the Cabinet ministers and Godfrey Isaacs was soon enthusiastically supported by the *National Review* edited by L.J. Maxse 'who detested Liberals and Jews with equal vehemence'.[1]

Rumour and speculation ran riot during the parliamentary summer recess of 1912. On 11 October, after Parliament reassembled, and on a motion in the name of the Postmaster-General, a Select Committee of the House of Commons was appointed to investigate the issuing of the government contract to the Marconi Company. On 11 October in the House of Commons both Rufus Isaacs and Lloyd George denied having bought shares 'in *that* company' [author's italics] – that is, in the British Marconi Company. Samuel seemed to have cleared his name at the same time.

The controversy did not, however, end there; in January 1913, spurred on by yet more accusations, Isaacs and Lloyd George (Murray of Elibank having resigned his post and his seat for a commercial career in the summer of 1912) admitted that they had bought shares in the *American* Marconi Company in April 1912. At the same time, in January

1913, the two men offered Asquith their resignation, which the Prime Minister stoutly and loyally refused.

The Select Committee of Inquiry reported finally in June 1913, but in the unsatisfactory form of a majority report, completely clearing the ministers and carried on the committee by a narrow majority of eight votes to six. The final Commons debate on the affair ended with a healthy government majority of seventy-eight, with the whips on. By August 1913 Isaacs's foolish, earlier misdemeanour of lying over his age to gain admission to the Stock Exchange had been dug up, and the Attorney-General had once more offered his resignation to Asquith, who had once more refused it. Nearly three months later Sir Rufus Isaacs's appointment as Lord Chief Justice was announced. The announcement was not without adverse criticism.[2]

These were the bare bones of the Marconi scandal. It is necessary, however, to probe more deeply – to scrutinize the conduct of the accused ministers, and Godfrey Isaacs, and to examine carefully the motives of those who provoked and sustained the controversy.

The role of Herbert Samuel is most easily dealt with. The government contract with the Marconi Company had been agreed in principle on 7 March 1912. Had the contract been awarded because of influence brought to bear by Rufus Isaacs on his brother's behalf? Furthermore, had Samuel profited in any way out of the awarding of the contract?

There is no evidence that Samuel awarded the contract to the British Marconi Company due to representations by Rufus Isaacs on behalf of his brother. Of course Samuel knew of the family connection, but it must be remembered that the pioneering Marconi Company was, in any case, supremely well placed to win the contract. In his Commons statement of 11 October 1912, Isaacs categorically denied that he had, in any shape or form, taken part in negotiations with Samuel, and that

I never knew there was such a contract in contemplation until a few days before [it was agreed], when I was told at a private social function by the managing director, who is my brother, that he did hope to get a contract with the Government and was in negotiation with them for it. That was a few days before I saw the announcement in the papers that there had in fact been a contract accepted.[3]

Although, as we shall see, Rufus Isaacs's Commons statement of 11 October 1912 contained one deliberate evasion of the truth, there is no reason to suppose that he was employing similar tactics on Samuel's behalf. Samuel did not buy, nor did he already own, any shares in any of the Marconi Companies. In the minority report submitted by Lord

Robert Cecil and Leopold Amery, who had sat on the Select Committee as Conservative representatives, the worst that could be said of Samuel's conduct was: first, that he had not corrected a misleading account of the tender put out by the Marconi Company; and, second, that his action in trying to obtain ratification of the agreement by the House of Commons without enquiry, after he knew of the share transactions of the Attorney-General and the Chancellor of the Exchequer, was regrettable.[4]

Next, there was the Master of Elibank, Alec Murray. At first sight the circumstantial evidence against him was strong: in the summer of 1912 Murray resigned from his post as Liberal Chief Whip and after a few months went off to Bogota in South America on a business trip. Before going he had, according to his brother, given him 3,000 shares in the American Marconi Company which he claimed he had purchased on behalf of the Liberal party fund. Captain Arthur Murray went on to tell the Select Committee that his brother had apparently told none of his colleagues (apart from Isaacs and Lloyd George?) about these shares because he proposed to keep them until the Marconi business was 'cleared up'.[5]

Murray's purchase of the shares might, indeed, have remained a secret but for the awkward fact that the broker, Charles Fenner, through whom they had been bought, defaulted and absconded, and the press pounced upon the fact. Moreover, Murray himself went to Bogota at the time when the various dealings in the American Marconi Company were made public. On 7 April 1913 the chairman of the Select Committee cabled Murray in Bogota asking him when he could attend to give evidence. Murray replied:

shall be glad to testify on my return. May I explain that I am over one month's journey from London and in the midst of highly important negotiations with Colombian Government for my firm. . . . In ordinary circumstances I calculate to return July [1913]. I trust delay will not be gravely inconvenient. Please inform Committee that I have never held any interest whatever in English Marconi Company.

When told that July would be too late, Murray declined to alter his plans.

It is clear that Murray had acted less than openly over his American Marconi shares, and one can only agree with the Select Committee's minority report that his failure to appear before them was 'very regrettable'. It is also clear that Isaacs and Lloyd George were anxious that Murray's involvement should not leak out; therefore the contention that none of Murray's colleagues *knew* of the share transaction was only true if the Attorney-General and the Chancellor of the Exchequer were left out of the picture – a very dubious device.

All the same, Murray was not corrupt in the sense of having profited unfairly from inside information available to him as a government minister – indeed there was no profit, rather a final loss, from the shares purchased. Although his refusal to return from Bogota to give evidence was unfortunate, and open to misrepresentation, it was defensible in view of his very real business responsibilities in South America and the length of time that would have been taken up in travelling back to London by land and boat. The view that Murray had been 'indulging in a half guilty flutter' perhaps best sums up his involvement.[6]

In April 1912 Lloyd George had bought a thousand shares in the American Marconi Company from Rufus Isaacs, who had himself bought ten thousand shares from his brother Harry, who had in turn purchased them from Godfrey Isaacs, the managing director of the British Marconi Company. Although wise in many of the world's ways, Lloyd George was a comparative novice when it came to the intricacies of financial speculation. He was in receipt of a salary from his post as Chancellor of the Exchequer, but he was by no means wealthy in the sense that his friend Rufus Isaacs was wealthy. No doubt he hoped to make a handsome profit from the shares he had bought: indeed, he later purchased further shares.

He did not, however, end up with money in his pocket. At the end of 1913 Isaacs sent him a final account of their losses at Lloyd George's request:

> You have asked me so often to let you know the amount you owe me and I have so often said I would work it out....
>
> I paid 8129. 15. 0.
> I received 5997. 11. 6.
> ————————
> £2132. 3. 6.

of which you and [Murray] each owe one tenth namely £213. 4. 0. The account is simple enough and the balance represents the amount I lost on the whole transaction.

> Don't bother about the amount. I would not have told you but that you seemed annoyed I hadn't yet ascertained it when last you mentioned it.[7]

During a weekend before the Chancellor gave evidence to the Select Committee at the end of March 1913, Rufus Isaacs found it necessary, with the help of Charles Masterman, to coach his friend in some of the technical terms of the stock market. Lucy Masterman has left an account in her biography of her husband; it shows the Chancellor in a less than commanding position:

There was a really very comic, though somewhat alarming, scene between Rufus and George on the following Sunday. George had to give evidence on the Monday – the following day – and Rufus discovered that George was still in a perfect fog as to what his transaction really had been, and began talking about 'buying a bear'. I have never seen Rufus so nearly lose his temper, and George got extremely sulky, while Rufus patiently reminded him what he had paid, what he still owed, when he had paid it, who to, and what for. It was on that occasion also that Charlie and Rufus tried to impress upon him with all the force in their power to avoid technical terms and to stick as closely as possible to the plainest and most ordinary language. As is well known, George made a great success of his evidence.[8]

Lucy Masterman also recorded Isaacs's attempt to think through the problem of how a minister ought to conduct his financial affairs:

'I have thought out four points,' he said. 'First, that no Minister should hold a directorship in any company contracting with the Government. That is a platitude. But,' he added, 'that is a much stricter standard than had ever been set for any Minister before. Then, no Minister should hold shares in any company having contractual relations with the Government. That is obvious, but it is difficult. Then no Minister should take shares in any company under circumstances which might cause his private interest and his public duty to be opposed. That is absolutely impossible. I have been thinking it out,' he continued. 'And you could not put your money on deposit even. The Bank rate is directly affected by Cabinet policy.'

How far was Lloyd George's involvement in the scandal the fault of Rufus Isaacs? In a way it was entirely due to his friendship with the Attorney-General that he was in the position to purchase the initial batch of shares at a favourable price. When, early in April 1912, Rufus Isaacs bought ten thousand shares in the American Company from his brother Harry (who had purchased fifty-six thousand from Godfrey Isaacs on 9 April) he promptly visited Lloyd George at 11 Downing Street, where the Master of Elibank was also staying, in order to share his good fortune with him. Both Lloyd George and Murray bought one thousand shares each at £2 a share – the price Rufus Isaacs had paid. The Attorney-General even went on to tell his friends that, since the shares were not yet issued, they had no need to pay him for a while.

None of the three men seem to have thought twice about the propriety of their action; when, later on, some of their shares were sold, they used their own names. It is true that Murray subsequently disguised his purchase of further shares, but that was not the prevailing mood in

April 1912. All three were important members of the government, deeply involved in public affairs, and perhaps too busy, too buoyed up by their current success, to have misgivings over their transaction.

It was in their later deportment that they can be most strongly criticized, and of the three it is perhaps Rufus Isaacs who acted with the least good sense while being ironically the best equipped to cope with the situation.

Rufus Isaacs's conduct is open to criticism on several counts; in essence it displayed a lack of openness that was potentially very damaging to himself and to his friends. The first example of his lack of complete openness arose when *The Eye-Witness* published its libellous attack upon himself and Herbert Samuel on 8 August 1912.

Samuel's initial response to this 'gross and unrestrained libel', as he explained in a letter to Isaacs, was 'at once to have an application made for a writ, and I am not at all sure that that is not the right course. There can be no possible doubt as to the result of the action.'

The Postmaster-General did, however, see certain problems:

The circumstances that deter me from at once coming to the conclusion that proceedings ought to be taken are obvious ones: first, that this contemptible rag has a very small circulation, its pages are always full of personal abuse, its articles cannot influence any opinion which is worth having, and an action would give an immense publicity to the libel; secondly, it would not be a good thing for the Jewish community for the first two Jews who have ever entered a British Cabinet to be enmeshed in an affair of this kind; and thirdly, one does not wish to soil one's hands with the thing.

As there will in all probability be a Select Committee of the House of Commons in the autumn to inquire into the wisdom of the contract, the Report of that Committee will supply a sufficient answer.

On the other hand, it is a grave thing when Ministers are directly accused of corrupt action by a newspaper, no matter how obscure and scurrilous, for them to do nothing.

With your unrivalled experience of the law you are better able than I to judge what is best to do, and I will very gladly join you in proceedings if you think it advisable, or do nothing if you consider that the best course.

If you are of opinion that a writ should be issued and will wire to me to that effect, I will go to town and see a solicitor and start the proceedings on behalf of both of us if you wish. But in that event I should be glad if you would nominate the solicitor, as my own solicitor is my brother, and I think in a case like this it would be better to have someone else.

If you are in doubt as to the proper course, you might think it well to consult the Prime Minister, and in that case I should be glad if you would send on this letter to him.[9]

Although Rufus Isaacs's reply four days later to Samuel, by telegram from Marienbad, said 'Agree with you but have sent your letter and have written to the chief', he wrote on 14 August 1912 that 'a little reflection convinced me that it was better to treat the rag with contempt', rather than take legal action.[10] This cautious view was reinforced by Asquith who wrote to his Attorney-General on 15 August: 'My Dear Rufus, I return the enclosed. I have read carefully this scurrilous rubbish, and I am clearly of the opinion that you should take no notice of it.... I suspect *The Eye-Witness* has a very meagre circulation. I notice only one page of advertisements, and that occupied entirely by Belloc's publishers. A prosecution would secure notoriety and might bring in subscribers.'[11] On 31 August Isaacs cabled Samuel from Paris: 'Definitely decided take no step he [Godfrey Isaacs] agrees our views.'[12]

Isaacs, therefore, held others back from a prompt legal action. Why was he so cautious? His brother Godfrey, a renowned litigant, had at first no such inhibitions, and on 27 August asked Samuel to appear, with Rufus Isaacs, as witnesses in the action Godfrey was preparing to take against *The Eye-Witness*.[13] By 9 September, however, Godfrey, on his brother's advice, had been persuaded to drop proceedings.[14] There was, of course, the argument that some sort of public enquiry would eventually deal more effectively with *The Eye-Witness*'s accusations. The Prime Minister's advice not to proceed was, moreover, probably decisive. All of the ministers under suspicion would need his backing every inch of the way, and it would have been singularly tactless to ignore the first piece of advice he offered them. The decision not to proceed, however, had the effect of giving the rumours over the Marconi contract nearly two more months of headway.

Although Rufus Isaacs had admitted in his letter to the Prime Minister in August 1912 that he had bought shares in the American Marconi Company, and later told the Select Committee that 'I certainly told him [Asquith] ... as I knew that he already knew', his statement to the House of Commons on 11 October 1912, when Parliament reassembled, was very different.

After discussing accusations that he had used his influence to obtain a contract for the British Marconi Company with the government, he went on:

Never from the beginning, when the shares were fourteen shillings or nine pounds, have I had one single transaction with the shares of that company. I am not only speaking for myself, but I am also speaking on behalf, I know, of both my right hon. friend the Postmaster-General and the Chancellor of the

Exchequer, who in some way or other, in some of the articles have been brought into this matter.[15]

These sentences contain the most blatant example of Rufus Isaacs's lack of candour, when he denied having bought or sold shares in '*that* company'. Within the context of his statement '*that* company' could only mean the British Marconi Company. In this sense the statement was quite accurate, but in effect it concealed the share transactions with the American Company. Nor did Isaacs mention Alec Murray in the same breath as Lloyd George and Samuel. Lloyd George followed the same line. When the purchase of the American Marconi shares was admitted in January 1913, the revelation could only damage Isaacs's and Lloyd George's public reputations.

The failure to be candid before their fellow MPs was essentially the personal responsibility of both Lloyd George and Isaacs, but it is difficult not to believe that the latter, with his brilliant legal background and his astute grasp of financial matters, ought to have ensured that both men made a clean breast of it. Here, once more, we have a resounding echo of the brash and erratic younger Rufus Isaacs.

Was it the same rashness, or innocence, that had allowed him to send, in March 1912, a telegram on the occasion of a public dinner held in New York in honour of Guglielmo Marconi himself? The telegram read: 'Please congratulate Marconi and my brother on the successful development of a marvellous enterprise. I wish them all success in New York, and I hope by the time they come back the coal strike will be finished.'[16] Was there, critics wanted to know, some devilish code in the telegram – especially in its second sentence? Was it an attempt to boost the reputation of the Marconi companies and thus to increase the value of Rufus Isaacs's holdings in the American Company?

The Attorney-General's explanation to the House of Commons on 11 October 1912 was straightforward enough:

What happened was this. I was asked whether in conjunction with a number of other public men I would send a telegram, because there was a banquet to be given by the *New York Times* to Mr Marconi and others.... They had made arrangements to have a Marconi apparatus fitted up on the table ... and as a matter of interest to guests they wanted to see how long it would take to get the messages through to the dinner table.[17]

The affair of the telegram helps to illustrate the ambiguities of Rufus Isaacs's involvement in the Marconi scandal. There is, on the one hand, the light-hearted, 'bullish' purchase of the original shares and the sending of the congratulatory telegram to New York. On the other hand, there is the subsequent failure to seek immediate legal redress against *The Eye-Witness*, and the cynical, or frightened, cover-up in the Commons debate of 11 October 1912.

How far was Asquith responsible for the decision to cover up the purchase of American Marconi shares? We have seen his advice to Isaacs and Samuel not to proceed against *The Eye-Witness*. There is, moreover, no doubt that he knew of the purchase of shares in the American Marconi Company *before* the Commons debate of 11 October, yet allowed his ministers to tell, at best, half-truths to their fellow MPs. However, he was later to claim during an interview with King George v in January 1913 that he had only *just* been told of Isaacs's and Lloyd George's 'lamentable' dealings in the American shares.[18]

There seems abundant evidence that Asquith knew of the transactions well before then. In July 1912 he was told, in one way or another, by at least three of the men at the centre of the controversy. The Master of Elibank told the Prime Minister that 'Rufus Isaacs, Lloyd George and myself have bought a few shares in an American Company' – though he did not say 'Marconi'. Herbert Samuel's *Memoirs* also state that in July 1912 he had told Asquith about the American purchases, and the Prime Minister had commented that 'our colleagues could not have done a more foolish thing'.[19] Moreover, in his evidence before the Select Committee on 27 March 1913, Rufus Isaacs made plain that before Samuel saw Asquith in July he had been told of the involvement of the three ministers in the American transactions. He also told the Committee that when he wrote asking Asquith's advice over *The Eye-Witness* article in August 1912: 'I told him about the American shares. I do not mean that I went into figures, but I certainly told him that I had bought, *as I knew that he already knew* [author's italics], American Marconi shares, of which Mr Lloyd George and the Master of Elibank had part.'[20] Finally, it is clear from the diary of Lord Stamfordham (George v's Private Secretary) that the King had been told of the details of the share dealings in August 1912 while Asquith was staying with him at Balmoral.[21]

Asquith backed up his erring ministers with unwavering loyalty throughout. In doing so he undoubtedly connived at the misleading statements made in the Commons on 11 October 1912. Was he merely anxious to preserve his ministerial team amid the turmoil of these last years of the Edwardian age? After all, he had just lost the Master of Elibank, and his Chancellor and Attorney-General were highly prized assets. On the other hand, he could have been forgiven for wishing, at some level, for the overthrow of Lloyd George, treading so hard on his heels. As it was, he was able in private to take some pleasure in his Chancellor's discomfiture, remarking one day to Charles Masterman, as they sat on the front bench while Lloyd George spoke, 'I think the idol's wings are a bit clipped.'[22]

Another explanation of Asquith's conduct is that he was broadly tolerant of Cabinet ministers' private dealings, and disinclined to take a high moral line in such matters. 'Lloyd George and Isaacs', Roy Jenkins has commented, 'were both lucky in the Prime Minister under whom they made their errors of judgement.'[23] That he even felt some sympathy for their temptation is shown in Charles Hobhouse's diary entry for the Cabinet meeting of 22 June 1913 which discussed the Marconi affair: 'Asquith curiously said that while at the Exchequer [1905-8] it had never occurred to him that he was not free to buy Govt. or any other stocks, although he had never had even a single transaction as a matter of fact.'[24]

Writing to Rufus Isaacs nearly two decades after the Marconi scandal, Asquith's widow Margot, Lady Oxford, explained her husband's attitude in typically flamboyant fashion. Even allowing for Lady Oxford's taste for hyperbole, and her distaste for Lloyd George as the coarse adventurer who had ruined her husband, her letters are extremely interesting.

Lady Oxford made clear her late husband's affection for Isaacs: 'Henry once said to me "Rufus is one of the finest natures I have ever known."'[25] She then made reference, in two letters, to the Marconi controversy: 'I've not forgotten what Curzon said to H[enry] when he asked Curzon to stand by him in the Marconi case, "I'll do nothing for the dirty little cheat [Lloyd George] but for Rufus I'll do anything."'[26] Then, on the motives behind Asquith's unfaltering support of his two ministers: 'He saved Ll.G. over Marconi. Why? – because Ll.G. was young and he loved you. Had it not been for you he would have let Ll.G. go.'[27]

Asquith also gave very practical help to Isaacs and Lloyd George. On 16 June 1913 he sent letters to both men with a draft of what they might say in the final Commons debate. His letter to Lloyd George simply said: 'I enclose a rough draft of what I think (after consultation with Grey) you might say without any loss of self-respect or the respect of others. I shall be at the House after dinner, and could talk with you and Rufus I. about it then.'[28] To Isaacs the Prime Minister said, with a slightly different emphasis: 'I drew this up at LL-G's request ... as a rough draft of the sort of thing you and he might say.'[29] Asquith's draft was consistent with his attitude throughout the crisis: that there had been no possible conflict between the ministers' purchase of shares and their official duties regarding the Marconi contract; that they none the less regretted what had happened; that it would have been better to disclose the facts to the Commons during the debate on 11 October 1912; and that they repudiated any suggestion that their reticence was due to a lack of candour or a desire for concealment. The two ministers obediently followed these guidelines in the ensuing debate.

How did other members of the government view the scandal? McKenna, the Home Secretary, and Walter Runciman, President of the Board of Agriculture, were both staunch supporters of Lloyd George, McKenna believing that, since the Chancellor 'was the greatest platform asset the Liberal party possessed, we could not allow him to say anything that would damage *that* reputation by quotation of words torn from their context, which could be twisted into an admission of guilt. ... His value as a demagogue was retrievable, and it was the business of the party to pull that out of the mire.'[30]

Charles Hobhouse, the Chancellor of the Duchy of Lancaster, however, disagreed

entirely with this reasoning. It may be true as Lord Northcliffe says that Marconis don't sell an extra copy of the *Daily Mail*, but first I am certain that the bulk of the Liberal Nonconformists are shocked at his levity and his speculating at all, and will not easily be won back to allegiance. Secondly the Tory newspapers will not allow this to be forgotten. It is unnecessary to penalize a man for ever for a single mistake, but if Ll.G. had the courage to now resign, I believe he would come back in less than a year universally admitted to be purged of 'error', of which alone he is charged.[31]

John Burns, the Liberal and Labour MP and President of the Local Government Board, was all for a frank confession in the final Commons debate on the Marconi affair at the end of June 1913: 'Burns said [in Cabinet] that it was much better to admit an error of judgement in the original purchase, regret any apparent reticence, ask the House to believe it was a single mistake never to be repeated. This view would be generally and generously accepted – and the whole question would fall to the ground.'[32]

Winston Churchill, First Lord of the Admiralty and a strong supporter of Lloyd George's radical initiatives, intervened with Lord Northcliffe, the proprietor of *The Times*, the *Daily Mirror* and the *Daily Mail*, begging him to hold his fire over the Marconi scandal. Northcliffe, who as we have seen had considerable respect and affection for Isaacs, promised that as far as possible his journals would treat Marconi on non-party lines. When, however, it was revealed in the spring of 1913 that Lloyd George had, after the initial transaction of April 1912, bought a further batch of shares in the American Company, Northcliffe wrote angrily to Churchill: 'Your Marconi friends stage-manage their affairs most damnably. For a couple of clever people, I cannot understand such muddling.'[33] His newspapers were subsequently less sympathetic.

Northcliffe went on to give a shrewd and, in some respects, surprising analysis of the scandal's effect on the public:

Moreover the system of making mysteries of pieces of evidence in the inquiry, and doling them out like a serial story had a bad effect on the public, though, as a matter of fact, the whole Marconi business looms much larger in Downing Street than among the mass of the people. The total number of letters received by my newspapers has been exactly three, one of which was printed – the other two were foolish.[34]

Although for a time public interest in the scandal had been intense, and for months after the final debate Liberal public meetings were interrupted with shouts of 'Mar-con-i! Mar-con-i!' and for good measure 'Bog-o-tah!', after a while the nation's appetite for sensation was gorged; in any case, the complexities of the inquiry were baffling to all but a few. Nor did political activity centre solely upon the Marconi affair: there was the Irish Home Rule bill, suffragette militancy, increasing trade union belligerency and a host of other diversions.

Why, then, was the Marconi affair so long sustained? The Conservative and Unionist opposition were undoubtedly tempted by the chance to embarrass, and perhaps fatally injure, a government that had worsted them in the constitutional crisis and was now pressing ahead with Irish Home Rule. Yet in some ways the Conservatives did not create the impression of a party hell-bent on destroying their opponents. Winston Churchill was later to say that, if the scandal had been properly handled, the opposition might have brought down the government, but 'some of them were too stupid and, frankly, some of them were too nice'.[35] Balfour, even Lord Robert Cecil, were perhaps too nice; Bonar Law, whom Charles Hobhouse dismissed as 'a repulsive party hack', and the Tory backwoodsmen, were perhaps too stupid. Two of the most formidable Conservatives, moreover, F.E. Smith and Edward Carson, were effectively muzzled by their agreement to represent Rufus Isaacs and Herbert Samuel in their legal action against alleged libel in the French newspaper *Le Matin*; here friendships forged at the Bar were of great benefit to Isaacs. Also, in the last resort, Tory MPs were not without their own experience of stocks and shares, and some must have had qualms over casting the first stone at the erring ministers.

If the opposition made a somewhat predictable, and not even excessive, fuss, the same thing cannot be said of other groups. The press's ranks had recently been swollen by the new mass circulation popular daily and Sunday papers, hungry for gossip and, on the whole, writing for people who did not find reading easy. The serious journals, of course, had an eager readership far more deeply concerned with the minutiae of political infighting. Frances Donaldson explains how difficult it must have been for Isaacs and Lloyd George to have made a clean breast of it in October 1912, 'after all those months of rumour and slander, while the Opposition sat silently listening, and the avid heartless journalists waited in the gallery above'.[36]

There was also the anti-semitic lobby, prone to see Jews, not Reds, under every bed. Before fascist persecution and the holocaust of the Second World War brought the sufferings of Jews so dramatically to the attention of a global audience, anti-semitic feeling was by no means confined to the ignorant and to the politically extreme. In socialist and radical Liberal circles in Britain it was often suggested that the machinations of international Jewish finance had led to the South African War of 1899-1902.[37] Moreover, as Imperial Germany presented an ever greater challenge to British naval supremacy as she sought for her place in the sun, it was tempting in some quarters to see German Jews as agents of German expansion. Leo Maxse's *National Review* was obsessed with this notion, and portrayed German Jews in the United Kingdom busily and surreptitiously working for the submission of Britain to Germany; denouncing, for example, 'Hebrew journalists at the beck and call of German diplomats'.[38]

The *National Review*, edited by a disillusioned Tory, was surpassed in vituperation by *The Eye-Witness*, under the control of disillusioned Liberals. Belloc and the Chestertons emerged from the Marconi affair with a huge and dirty stain upon their reputations. Cecil Chesterton, the journal's editor, was particularly repugnant. Leonard Woolf said of him: 'I never liked Cecil Chesterton, partly because his physical appearance was so unprepossessing, and partly because ... he had a streak of that kind of fanatical intolerance which seems to be fertilized, not by profound convictions, but by personal animosities.'[39] To *The Eye-Witness*, and to those of similar convictions, the Marconi affair provided a wonderful opportunity to denounce two Isaacs and one Samuel enmeshed in 'a corrupt conspiracy'.

Their joy was unconfined when in November 1912 a fresh example of alleged Jewish chicanery supplemented the Marconi scandal: this was the Indian silver affair, which centred on Sir Stuart Montagu Samuel, the Liberal MP for Whitechapel, who was Herbert Samuel's brother and a partner in the firm of Samuel Montagu, bankers and bullion dealers. Samuel Montagu had purchased large amounts of silver for the government of India on behalf of Edwin Montagu, Under-Secretary of State for India, Samuel's first cousin, whose father Lord Swaythling was the senior partner in the firm. Once more it could be claimed that Jewish business and Jewish MPs were involved in some sort of plot to profit from government spending. Although Edwin Montagu was eventually cleared of any impropriety, Sir Stuart Samuel was not so fortunate and, accused of involvement in the silver dealings, was obliged, under the 1782 Contractors' Act reinforced by a ruling of the Judicial Committee of the Privy Council, to vacate his parliamentary seat. Samuel subsequently fought and won a by-election in Whitechapel.

If the Indian silver affair and the Marconi scandal were exploited by anti-semites, there was yet another factor to consider in the latter case. One of the early critics of Rufus Isaacs and Herbert Samuel was Major Martin Archer-Shee MP, who began the press campaign with a letter to *The Times* and went on to write an article for Maxse's *National Review*. Archer-Shee was the half-brother of the Osborne cadet dismissed for allegedly stealing a postal order in the famous case of 1910. Rufus Isaacs, it will be remembered, was the Crown Law Officer who at first adopted a very inflexible attitude to the case. Indeed, during the trial, Major Archer-Shee had been cross-examined as a witness by Isaacs. There was clearly no love lost between the Archer-Shees and Isaacs, and one is irresistibly drawn to the conclusion that the Marconi affair provided a chance to even the scores.

In the end, how did the Marconi affair affect the lives of those at the centre of the storm? Godfrey Isaacs, smeared by *The Eye-Witness* for his 'Ghastly Record', but with nothing of substance proved against him during the Select Committee's inquiries, continued to be one of the driving forces behind the Marconi Company until his retirement in 1924. At his death a year later he left £195,490 gross (£139,428 net), and received the following compliment in *The Times*' obituary: 'It is hardly too much to say that the Company owes as great a debt to Mr Isaacs on the business side as it does to Mr Marconi on the scientific side. He will be long remembered as a man of remarkable gifts and boundless enthusiasm for the new science with which he had linked his commercial fortunes.'[40]

Godfrey Isaacs was a man of attractive personal qualities, some vision and a certain recklessness. He was never long out of the news. Indeed, shortly after the clamour of the Marconi scandal of 1912-13 died away, he was involved in a 'Second Marconi affair'. The first government contract with Marconi had been ratified in the Commons in August 1913 and provided for the building of six long-distance wireless stations for the Imperial Wireless Chain, but contained a provision for the cancellation of the second three wireless stations in certain circumstances. In February 1914 Charles Hobhouse, now Postmaster-General, went to Berlin to examine the Telefunken Company's long-distance wireless installations. As a result, work on the Marconi project was held up during the summer of 1914 and stopped entirely after the outbreak of war on 4 August. On 30 December the Post Office cancelled the contract with Marconi, and early in 1915 Isaacs took Hobhouse to law for redress for certain remarks allegedly made to him by the Postmaster-General. The jury found for Hobhouse.[41] One result of the two Marconi affairs and of Godfrey Isaacs's taste for litigation was that the government entered the First World War with its chain of Empire-wide wireless stations unbuilt.

Herbert Samuel, cleared of any impropriety in the first Marconi controversy, went on to high office, including the Home Secretaryship in 1916 and between 1931 and 1932, the post of British High Commissioner in Palestine from 1920 to 1925, and the leadership of the Liberal party in the House of Commons from 1931 to 1933, and in the Lords from 1944 to 1955. Created a Viscount in 1937, he died in 1963, a year before Harold Wilson became Labour Prime Minister for the first time. His career was clearly not damaged by his involvement in the Marconi affair.

Of the chief journalistic assailants of the Isaacs brothers, Samuel and Lloyd George, Cecil Chesterton and G.K. Chesterton continued to harry British Jews and to denounce alleged Jewish influence over national affairs, though the latter showed some misgivings over Hitler's brutal treatment of German Jewry. Cecil Chesterton was killed in the First World War. A second cousin of the Chestertons, A.K. Chesterton, joined Mosley's British Union of Fascists in 1933, and in 1937 wrote a biography of his hero in which he claimed, 'every vitiating and demoralizing factor in our national life was Jew-ridden where it was not Jew-controlled'.[42] Hilaire Belloc was to swing hopelessly between undisguised anti-semitic prejudice and a belief that the Nazi persecution of Jews in Germany was 'abominable'.[43]

The two ministers in the eye of the storm went on to far greater

things: Lloyd George to 10 Downing Street and an international standing enjoyed by few British statesmen in the twentieth century; Sir Rufus
Isaacs to the very pinnacle of the legal profession and to high office in
the service of his country.

Both men were, for a time, marked – even subdued – by their
experiences during the Marconi affair. Asquith, as we have seen, believed that Lloyd George's wings had been 'clipped', and some observers
thought that the Welshman did not recover his full zest for political
activity until the excitement and challenge of the First World War.

Rufus Isaacs carried the scars from his public mauling for a good
many years: there were constant reminders of his humiliation in the
immediate aftermath of the scandal, as Lord Winterton recalled in his
Orders of the Day:

One of the ugliest incidents in this era of mutual party hatred in the
Commons occurred just after the Marconi case. . . . Sir Rufus Isaacs . . . rose to
answer a question; he was assailed with cries from the Conservative back
benches of 'sticky fingers'. Usually calm, collected and complete master of
himself, he was so taken aback by this affront that he turned a deadly white
and, for a moment or so, was unable to read out his answer. Mr Lloyd George
glared at our benches with a look of furious anger on his face which I never saw
on it before or since; Mr Churchill, the most generous of friends, ever ready to
come to the help of a colleague, shouted out something at the top of his voice
which, perhaps fortunately, could not be heard amid the tumult, whilst a
colleague next to him put a restraining hand upon his shoulder; Mr Asquith
sat calm and impassive with his eyes fixed upon the ceiling. The Speaker
managed to restore order just before both sides were apparently going to start
a fist-fight.[44]

Isaacs's son, in his biography of his father, recalls coming across the
Attorney-General in his chambers at Garden Court at the height of the
controversy, and finding him

sitting at his desk, his head resting on his hands, gazing silently before him.
For some minutes he neither moved nor spoke and then, turning towards me,
he said:

'I had hoped to hand on to you so much, and now it looks as if I shall have
nothing to hand on to you that you will want.' From a man of so high a faith
and courage, so little given to demonstrativeness, so steeped in reticence, that
one sentence was the most poignant evidence of all that he was going through.
After he became Lord Chief Justice, I never heard him refer to the Marconi
episode again. It was as if he had determined to blot out of his memory so
harrowing and so embittering an ordeal.[45]

The relationship between Isaacs and Lloyd George was tested and
proved by their mutual ordeal. During the war and as a peacetime

Prime Minister, Lloyd George was to prefer his friend to great offices and assignments of the utmost national importance. Isaacs was to send Lloyd George gifts (a new copy of *The Call of the Wild* in October 1913), to advise him on financial matters in 1919,[46] and to be personally concerned when Viceroy at not having heard from him in July 1922.[47] Innuendoes from the Marconi affair were still liable to be used occasionally against them, as when the editor of the *Financial News* wrote to Lloyd George in January 1918 saying 'the rumour is persistently and mischievously spread that Lord Reading has a "hold" over you, and that he can make you dance to any tune he pleases'.[48]

In the last resort, Rufus Isaacs's involvement in the Marconi scandal throws doubt on his judgement, not on his capacity to be loyal to friends, family and colleagues. Perhaps the worst that can be said of him is that 'Proud and sensitive, he was constitutionally unable to believe that he had put himself in the wrong; and his mind rejected reasoning that, if applied to another, he would have found self-evident.'[49] At the same time, he can perhaps be accused of moral cowardice in not taking *The Eye-Witness* to court, but waiting until the more specific libel in *Le Matin* (a libel, some said, that had been stage-managed by himself and his supporters) to exonerate Samuel and himself at law and to make the whole truth public.

By 1913, therefore, Isaacs's reputation, despite the findings of the Select Committee, despite his victory in the *Le Matin* libel case, had been clouded. Asquith's decision to stand by him and Lloyd George, though explicable in narrow party terms, had saved them both.

Almost immediately the Prime Minister had to give further proof of his confidence in Isaacs, for in October 1913 Lord Alverstone resigned as Lord Chief Justice, an office that customarily reverted to the Attorney-General.

9 Lord Chief Justice, 1913-19

R[ufus] I [saacs] did not feel comfortable about it at first and had thought of not accepting. ... One wonders whether, perhaps, the Marconi episode 'forced' him to accept. Had there been no Marconi affair is it inconceivable that he would have refused?

Edgar Davis, one-time clerk to Rufus Isaacs

It is difficult to realize at once what a great honour has been conferred upon me.

Sir Rufus Isaacs to Lord Riddell, 1913

Lord Alverstone's resignation as Lord Chief Justice in October 1913 provided a decidedly uncomfortable epilogue to the protracted Marconi affair. From Asquith's and Sir Rufus Isaacs's point of view, Alverstone's decision could hardly have come at a worse time, although at least the final Commons debate and division on Marconi had taken place two months earlier, and in theory Isaacs's reputation had been cleared.

In fact, with the wounds inflicted during the controversy largely unhealed, and with many among the Conservative and Unionist opposition still indignant at the alleged 'whitewashing' by the Select Committee, Alverstone's resignation pushed the whole squalid business back into the headlines. Alverstone, however, was a dying man by the late summer of 1913, and his desire to lay down his high office and to make the most of whatever days remained to him was perfectly understandable.

On the last day of the parliamentary session before the summer recess, Andrew Bonar Law, leader of the Opposition since Balfour's resignation in 1911, asked Asquith whether press reports that the Lord Chief Justice had resigned were true, and, if they were true, who was to replace him. The Prime Minister replied that 'as far as I am aware the Lord Chief Justice has not resigned. The last communication I had from him, I am glad to say, led me to entertain the hope that he would in course of time be able to resume his active duties.'

Rufus Isaacs returned from his summer vacation in Marienbad with the Lord Chief Justice still in office. When he resumed work in October he seemed, according to his son, 'largely restored to his old vigour, though at times, as his thoughts turned back to the past year, there would fall over his face a shadow that could not be misunderstood'.[1] His wife, too, seemed better after the long ordeal of the Marconi controversy which had 'left them both exhausted in body and mind. They had fought so hard to put a brave face upon things that, when it was no longer necessary to keep up appearances, they found that they had half-forgotten how to be natural.'[2]

As it happened Lord Alverstone had written Asquith a letter of resignation before the Isaacs's returned from Marienbad. The Attorney-General's right to succeed to the post was firmly established by precedent. In his *Asquith*, Roy Jenkins says the Prime Minister 'did not hesitate about appointing Isaacs'.[3] This is not how it seems to the present author.

Although the demands of consistency and logic made Isaacs's appointment inevitable (for how could Asquith's earlier resolute defence of his Attorney-General now be cast aside?) it is clear that the Prime Minister gave an unusual amount of consideration to the matter. The problem was naturally raised with George V, who found it 'most embarrassing'. As Lord Stamfordham, the King's Private Secretary, wrote: 'if the PM does not recommend him, it will be tantamount to condemning his action', and 'if Mr Asquith *does* recommend him, he will be equally condemned by the other side'.[4] Apparently both men agreed that if Isaacs was not appointed Lord Chief Justice he could not remain in the Cabinet – an unusual conclusion, and perhaps an attempt by Asquith to obtain the King's blessing for the Attorney-General's promotion.

Isaacs was plainly aware of the hesitation that prevailed: he was stricken with a sharp attack of gout, which was perhaps an outward and physical sign of the internal anguish to which he was prey. The press's attitude could not have helped his peace of mind. Both the *Morning Post* and the *Daily Express* were loud in their protests against the possible appointment, the *Express* asking:

Can it be pretended for a moment that the contemplated appointment is either prudent or feasible? To attempt it is, for Mr Asquith, to flout public opinion with a brazen effrontery almost beyond belief. To accept it would be, for Sir Rufus Isaacs, to run the gravest risk both of imperilling an office of which he must hold the honour very dear and of covering himself with an odium which he would wisely dread.[5]

Asquith and Isaacs discussed the appointment at 10 Downing Street before the official letter of 16 October 1913 offering the post was written. Asquith confirmed his intention of making the offer, but it must not be supposed that Isaacs seized the opportunity without hesitation. To accept the promotion would unleash more controversy, would mean resigning his seat in the Commons (which he was to do with a heavy heart), and would signify yet another abrupt change of direction in a career which continued to swing between the law and politics.

There is indeed evidence that Rufus Isaacs was reluctant to accept the post. According to notes made by Edgar Davis, Isaacs's clerk for some years and a distant relation:

R.I. did not feel comfortable about it [the offer] at first and had thought of not accepting. It was suggested that if he did refuse it would be said by those who were attacking him that he did not accept because of the Marconi affair, then why remain Attorney-General?

One wonders whether, perhaps, the Marconi episode 'forced' him to accept. Had there been no Marconi affair is it inconceivable that he would have refused? The observations respecting the Lord Chancellor's Office apply here, I believe with greater force. On the Bench he was immediately cut off from the active life which interested him so much and which he liked. There may have been one or two other reasons why he might have liked to have refused.[6]

Asquith's letter of 16 October 1913 offering Isaacs the post said simply: 'Lord Alverstone having now formally resigned his office, I have the pleasure of proposing to you, with the King's approval, that you should become Lord Chief Justice of England, Yours very sincerely, H.H. Asquith.'[7] Isaacs accepted the post: indeed, he had very little option but to accept – apart from quitting public life.

He immediately motored to Lord Alverstone's house at Cranleigh in Surrey. There he

found the former Lord Chief Justice obviously close to death; even the great domed forehead seemed to have shrunk, and he seemed feeble and frail. At the end of what was obviously a highly charged meeting, Alverstone took Isaacs's hand and said: I want you to know that, if there was an error of judgement on your part in the Marconi affair – and I am not for a moment saying there was – I was disgusted at the disgraceful way in which the whole business was used for party purposes, and you had my deepest sympathy all along.[8]

According to Gerald Isaacs, who had waited outside in the car during the interview, his father emerged 'deeply touched. ... he was for some moments quite unable to speak'.[9]

On 22 October Sir Rufus Isaacs was sworn into his office in the Law Courts in a ceremony attended by Haldane, the Lord Chancellor, most of the judges and a good many members of the Bar. After the swearing-in, Lord Haldane, having made a short speech introducing Isaacs, went on to pay tribute to Lord Alverstone. At this point a barrister, thinking the eulogy was for the new Lord Chief Justice, shouted, 'Speak for yourself, Lord Haldane!'

Although the interrupter was sent packing, the incident symbolized the controversy that surrounded the appointment. The *Morning Post* and the *Daily Express* were no more friendly than they had been before Lord Alverstone's retirement, and the Tory press were in general cool. The most vicious verbal attack on Isaacs, however, came from Rudyard Kipling. Poet of Empire, supreme storyteller and a telling critic of decadent sloth, Kipling's passionate patriotism contained an ugly prejudice against 'lesser breeds without the law'. Disliking radicals and Jews, Kipling had found in the Marconi scandal ample confirmation of his dislikes. Isaacs's appointment prompted him to write a poem of vitriolic hatred, in which he likened the new Lord Chief Justice to Gehazi, the servant of Elisha in the Old Testament. Although not published until 1919, when Isaacs chose not to prosecute Kipling for libel, the verses were circulated widely in private during 1915:

> WHENCE comest thou, Gehazi,
>   So reverend to behold,
> In scarlet and in ermines
>   And chain of England's gold?
> 'From following after Naaman
>   To tell him all is well,
> Whereby my zeal hath made me
>   A Judge in Israel.'
>
> Well done, well done, Gehazi!
>   Stretch forth thy ready hand.
> Thou barely 'scaped from judgment,
>   Take oath to judge the land
> Unswayed by gift of money
>   Or privy bribe, more base,
> Of knowledge which is profit
>   In any market-place.

Search out and probe, Gehazi,
  As thou of all canst try,
The truthful, well-weighed answer
  That tells the blacker lie –
The loud, uneasy virtue,
  The anger feigned at will,
To overbear a witness
  And make the Court keep still.

Take order now, Gehazi,
  That no man talk aside
In secret with his judges
  The while his case is tried.
Lest he should show them – reason
  To keep a matter hid,
And subtly lead the questions
  Away from what he did.

Thou mirror of uprightness,
  What ails thee at thy vows?
What means the risen whiteness
  Of the skin between thy brows?
The boils that shine and burrow,
  The sores that slough and bleed –
The leprosy of Naaman
  On thee and all thy seed?
Stand up, stand up, Gehazi,
  Draw close thy robe and go,
Gehazi, Judge in Israel,
  A leper white as snow![10]

On the other hand, Isaacs could bask in a huge number of compliments. George v sent him 'a very kind and charming message', and Edward Carson's letter of congratulation led him to reply: 'My Dear Ned, you behaved towards me [during the Marconi affair] with all that nobility which is characteristic of you. There I must leave it – it almost overwhelms me.' Sir Edward Clarke, veteran of so many great legal battles, wrote, having appeared before him in court for the first time in February 1914:

It is a very great pleasure to me to appear this morning before the fifth Lord Chief Justice before whom I have practised.
    Cockburn.
    Coleridge.
    Russell.

Alverstone.
Reading.
It is a fine series.
Always yours,
EDWARD CLARKE.[11]

The Times, in a leading article, put the views of many others with a characteristic, balanced gravity:

For our part, we trust and believe that his career on the Bench, when it comes to be reckoned up, will be no less distinguished than his astonishing career at the Bar. Meanwhile it can only be regarded as a great misfortune that an absorbing controversy should have brought hesitation and discord into what would otherwise have been a unanimous chorus of approval.[12]

The post of Lord Chief Justice traditionally carried with it a barony, and the New Year's Honours list for 1914 announced Sir Rufus Isaacs's translation to Baron Reading of Erleigh in the County of Berkshire. Isaacs had earlier bought some land at a small village named Earley (sometimes spelled Erleigh) near to his modest country house at Fox Hill. On his elevation to the peerage it had seemed appropriate both to pay a compliment to his loyal constituency of Reading and to acknowledge his status as a Berkshire landowner. The title Lord Reading of Erleigh did exactly that.

Lord Reading was probably the least active and attentive Lord Chief Justice in England's history. Not, it must be made clear, through sloth or the wilful neglect of his duties, but because the outbreak of the First World War in August 1914 brought in its train a host of demands for his particular skills. A few months after his promotion to the Bench, Reading told Lloyd George that, although he liked his new work, he felt 'the loss of the old constant companionship and never-ceasing turmoil in which all are involved who work intimately with you. Only those who have lived in it can appreciate the loss of it.'

He need not have worried; the extraordinary demands of war were to pluck him from his high judicial office and embroil him, in the most intense fashion, in international politics, diplomacy and finance until 1919. His wartime activities will be examined at length in subsequent chapters. His judicial functions, however, were still significant and often challenging.

Lord Reading's work as Lord Chief Justice began while ten more months of peace remained. The pattern of judicial routine in London and on the legal circuits, broken up by country weekends at Fox Hill, golf, companionship and the annual summer cure at Marienbad with his wife, must have seemed at first very seductive – almost a rest after the traumatic events of 1912 and 1913. His salary was £8,000, a considerable sum in 1914; in any case, he had money invested from his lucrative years at the Bar. After fifteen years he would be entitled to retire on a generous pension.

His family life was enhanced in 1914 by the engagement of his son Gerald to Eva, eldest daughter of Sir Alfred and Lady Mond; since Sir Alfred had made a fortune out of chemical engineering (Imperial Chemical Industries was his later creation) and controlled the *English Review* and the Reuter's new agency, Eva was hardly a poor catch. Eva Mond, eventually to become Lady Erleigh and the Second Marchioness of Reading, had a lively mind and a great interest in child development. She published two books in the 1920s. The first was *In the Beginning: a first history for little children*, published in 1926 and dedicated to her son Michael, the future Third Marquess of Reading. The book is a basic history of ancient times ending with the fall of Rome and the upsurge of Christianity. The bibliography includes Kipling's *Puck of Pook's Hill* and 'The Knife and the Naked Chalk' from his *Rewards and Fairies* – a token of forgiveness for the author of 'Gehazi'? Her second book, dedicated to her daughters Joan and Elizabeth Ann, was *Little One's Log*, published in 1927 with drawings by Ernest H. Shepard, the illustrator of the *Winnie the Pooh* books; this book provides space for the parents to fill in details of their child's development – weight, progress at eighteen months, religious record, reading skills and so forth.[13]

Lord Reading's first circuit in the summer of 1914 was the Midlands circuit, thus enabling him to spend some nights at Fox Hill before travelling to Oxford for the day's hearings. His experiences were sometimes harrowing. He found the trying of criminal cases distasteful and of those involving 'sexual crimes utterly repellent'.[14] Lord Riddell, proprietor of the *News of the World* and a crony of Lloyd George's and Reading's, recalled how the new Lord Chief Justice spent a day with him and the Chancellor of the Exchequer on returning from his first circuit. Reading recounted the trial of a girl who had been abandoned by a man, and who was then charged with concealing the birth of her illegitimate child. In the dock she had sobbed with grief and shame:

The Chief said, 'Having read the depositions, I endeavoured to catch her eye as she sat there sobbing her heart out, but could not attract her attention. I wanted to convey to her that she had at least one friend in Court.' Ultimately, owing to the evidence, he was able to tell the jury that the prisoner must be acquitted.

The Chief told the story well and was visibly affected. When he had finished, I said, 'You earned a lot of good marks in the Recording Angel's diary this week, Chief.' He had made my eyes glisten, and as I looked at him I saw his were glistening too. He is very kind-hearted.[15]

This side of Lord Reading's character has been discussed earlier in the book: how the habitual repression of the expression of his deeper feelings often found release in weeping in the darkened auditorium of the cinema or at the theatre. Assizes, however, were venues for dramas drawn from real life, and he clearly sometimes found them equally moving. Given also his puritanical and fastidious dislike of hearing the details of sexual activity, his presence on the Bench must sometimes have been a purgatory for this gentle and sensitive man.

Although the outbreak of war diverted Lord Reading to certain non-judicial duties, it also provided him with some extraordinary trials arising out of the hostilities. Two of these trials became important cases in the law of treason.

The first, Rex v. Ahlers, which came before Reading on appeal in 1915, illustrated with horrifying clarity the dilemmas facing ordinary, civilized men when their respective countries go to war with each other. Ahlers was the German consul in Sunderland; on 5 August 1914, the day after Britain declared war on Germany, he gave two German citizens of military age money and information to enable them to return to Germany. He was arrested and charged at Durham assizes that he 'with force of arms, unlawfully, maliciously and traitorously, was adhering to, aiding and comforting the German Emperor against our Lord the King'. Ahlers pleaded not guilty, claiming that he had merely been doing his duty as a consul. In the summing up, however, the judge directed the jury that, if they believed that Ahlers had indeed assisted the King's enemies when he knew that war had been declared, they must return a verdict of guilty. This the jury did, and Ahlers was sentenced to death.

Ahlers's appeal was heard by a full bench of the Court of Criminal Appeal. Reading reflected the unanimous opinion of the appeal judges when he described the trial judge's direction to the jury as unduly prejudicial to the accused. What the jury should have been told to consider was whether Ahlers had acted with deliberate intent to assist the King's enemies or whether he was simply carrying out his consular duties. Reading further argued that, in the original trial, insufficient consideration had been given to the contemporary practice of allowing enemy subjects a reasonable time in which to return home – indeed, an order of the Home Secretary, published on 6 August, had allowed enemy aliens until 11 August to make their departure. The Court of Appeal accordingly quashed Ahlers's conviction and he was set free.

If Ahlers had been in the end treated with understanding and humanity, no such benevolence was extended to Lord Reading's second treason case. This was the celebrated trial of Sir Roger Casement in 1916, which provided a lethal compound of treason, Irish rebellion and, more discreetly, allegations of the accused's homosexual excesses.[16]

Casement, a fervent Irish nationalist, had quit the British consular service early in the war and had subsequently gone to Germany trying, with meagre success, to recruit prisoners-of-war of Irish extraction to form an Irish Brigade to liberate Ireland from British rule. On the eve of the Dublin Easter Rising of 1916, Casement had been landed, on the west coast of Ireland, from a German submarine, but had been captured and imprisoned in the Tower of London.

The trial, which began on 26 June 1916, was a sensational episode in a war which was not going smoothly for Britain, and was an uncomfortable epilogue to the Easter rebellion which had, in some eyes, made nonsense of the British claim to fighting for the liberties of small nations, notably Belgium.

The charge of treason centred on Casement's recruiting activities in Germany. The prosecution case rested on a particular interpretation of a medieval Statute of Treason under which Casement was accused of being 'adherent to the King's enemies in his realm giving them aid or comfort in the realm or elsewhere'. Casement's defence counsel argued that the charge of high treason could not stand since the accused could not be shown to have adhered to the King's enemies *inside* his realm, but only in Germany.

Lord Reading's summing up to the jury rejected the defence's interpretation of the Statute. His direction to them was plainly to convict:

> You have to determine whether the prisoner was contriving and intending to assist the enemy. If what he did was calculated to aid and assist the enemy, and he knew it was so calculated, then, although he had another or ulterior purpose in view, he was contriving and intending to assist the enemy. It is necessary that you should pay particular attention to this direction, which is a direction of law to you. The questions of fact upon it, of course, you will determine for yourselves, but it is necessary that you should understand that ... if he knew or believed that the Irish Brigade was to be sent to Ireland during the War with a view to securing the national freedom of Ireland, that is, to engage in a civil war which would necessarily weaken and embarrass this country, then he was contriving to assist the enemy.[17]

Casement was sentenced to death and, despite an appeal, and three discussions in Cabinet, was hanged at Pentonville prison.

While patriots applauded Casement's conviction, Lord Reading was also involved in certain civil law cases where his judgments provoked sharp criticism in jingo circles. The anti-German hysteria so blatantly displayed in Britain during the First World War was based on feelings of national insecurity that had been fed on pre-war portrayals of a besieged United Kingdom, threatened by Germany's military ambitions from without and within riddled with German and Jewish agents and immigrants. Anti-German sentiment even caused the resignation in 1914 of the stoutly patriotic Louis of Battenberg as First Sea Lord, and in 1917 prompted the sailor-King George v to change his family name to 'Windsor' from the Teutonic-sounding 'Saxe-Coburg-Gotha'.

Humbler men than the King and Prince Louis of Battenberg were involved in similar difficulties. Not long after the outbreak of war, two naturalized British subjects of German-Jewish origin, Sir Ernest Cassel and Sir Edgar Speyer, both successful men of business and Privy Councillors, were attacked for their German backgrounds. Cassel had been an intimate adviser to Edward vii, while Speyer was well connected with the Liberal party. The Jewish origins of both men seem to have been of less importance to their enemies than their German birth. Speyer, indeed, felt the criticism so keenly that in May 1915 he asked Asquith to accept his resignation from the Privy Council and to revoke his baronetcy. Although the Prime Minister was, in any case, not empowered to accept such resignations, he resolutely refused to countenance any such step.

Despite rumours over Speyer's continuing business connections with Germany, the matter might have ended there but for the intervention of a Scottish baronet, Sir George Makgill. Makgill brought an action against Cassel and Speyer in November 1915 calling on them both to show by what authority they claimed to be Privy Councillors since they were not natural-born British subjects.

Reading presided over the court that judged Makgill's action to have failed, and the two men, as far as the law was concerned, were entitled to remain Privy Councillors. Although Cassel was content with the decision of the court, Speyer expressed his resentment by resigning from his offices and going to New York, where he became identified with pro-German elements there supported by his brother James Speyer; in 1921 Edgar Speyer had his certificate of naturalization revoked and was struck off the roll of Privy Councillors.[18]

The Lord Chief Justice's part in upholding the rights of Cassel and

Speyer brought him some abuse, as did his judgment, supported by the entire Court of Appeal, in the case of Porter v. Freudenberg, given in January 1915. Porter had begun an action to recover from Freudenberg, a German citizen, rent due under a lease of property carried on before the outbreak of war caused Freudenberg to return to Berlin. At issue was the question as to whether Freudenberg could be sued, and, if so, whether he had the right to appear in court to defend himself, and also to appeal, if that proved necessary.

Reading delivered the judgment that 'To deny him that right would be to deny him justice and would be quite contrary to the principles guiding the King's Courts in the administration of justice.' Since, however, there was a war in progress, an enemy alien's right to sue was necessarily suspended during the hostilities.

The First World War was, however, to demand far more of Lord Reading than legal rulings. Wartime financing posed complex problems for the government, and at the Treasury David Lloyd George called upon his friend to help him deal with them. The war had broken out during the two months' legal vacation and was not very old before Reading was installed in his own room at the Treasury in Whitehall.

10 Wartime Duties, 1914–18

His knowledge of finance, his mastery of figures, his dexterity and calm and sure judgement helped at many turns.
Lloyd George on Reading's role in the early months of the war

Reading is working indefatigably, amidst great difficulties. He was able to obtain fifty million dollars [to buy] Canadian wheat, which really was an inroad on the basic principle that every cent of money advanced to the Allies should be spent in the United States.
Lord Northcliffe to Loyd George, New York, 30 September 1917

Reading's influence with Lloyd George is greater perhaps than any man in England . . . .
Colonel House, November 1917

The First World War arguably began on 28 June 1914 with the assassination at Sarajevo of the Austrian Archduke Ferdinand, while the Lord Chief Justice was progressing round the Oxford circuit. Thereafter the great powers of Europe, too rigidly bound by their alliances, strategic needs, national prejudices and mobilization arrangements, stumbled, often protesting, into a conflict which was effectively underway in the first days of August.

Throughout July, however, Great Britain seemed somewhat detached from the frenetic diplomatic and military activity on the continent: the London money market showed no signs of panic until the last week of the month, and the government expended most of its energies on agonizing over where, in a partitioned Ireland, Counties Tyrone and Fermanagh should go. In the strictest sense, Britain and her Empire were not obliged to enter the war against Germany and the Austro-Hungarian Empire; the *ententes* with France and Russia were not binding military alliances, rather expressions of intent and practical goodwill; Britain's only formal alliance was with Japan – who did not see her security threatened by Austria's belated assault on Serbia in retaliation for the killing at Sarajevo.

Lord Reading, however, was one of those who, during July, 'watched the situation with a double dread; the first, that war was inevitably coming and that Great Britain could not escape from being involved, the second, that at the moment of the country's greatest trial he might be debarred by his judicial office from making any direct contribution to the national effort'.[1] He need not have worried. On 3 August, Bank Holiday Monday, Lord Riddell telephoned Reading at Fox Hill, telling him that the European situation was desperately serious and that France and Germany might be at war at any moment. Riddell added that the Cabinet was divided as to whether Britain should intervene or not (in fact, John Morley and John Burns resigned from the Cabinet, and Sir John Simon, the Attorney-General, and the Earl of Beauchamp, First Commissioner of Works, threatened to do so).[2] Lord Riddell ended the conversation by asking Reading to come to London as soon as possible to advise Lloyd George on the unprecedented currency and financial problems that now faced him.[3]

On arriving at Lord Riddell's house for dinner, Reading found the Chancellor and Charles Masterman waiting for him with the news that German troops had invaded Belgium. The assault on Belgium both gave Britain the strong moral pretext she needed for entering the war, and also faced her with the unacceptable prospect of a great European power in control of the Low Countries. War was now inevitable. 'When I came here today I did not appreciate the position,' Reading said to Lord Riddell, 'I seem to have come into another world.'

Despite his natural apprehension at the end of peace, Reading was a strong supporter of the government's ultimatum to Germany. Indeed 'he had no love of the Germans', and had 'long been alarmed by the trend of Germany's policy'. Furthermore, according to his son, 'Their arrogance as a nation outraged his tolerance and their grossness as individuals offended his fastidiousness.' His son recalled one startling example of that fastidiousness:

Sitting opposite him one day in 1911 in a Munich restaurant I was suddenly aware that his gaze was fixed in disgust on something behind me. I asked what he was looking at and he replied: 'There is a repulsive German over there eating French beans, and he is making a sort of symbolic rite of it, as if with each mouthful he was chewing up a bit of France. They are a frightening people.'[4]

It was, therefore, with some enthusiasm that Lord Reading put his skills at Lloyd George's service during the early weeks of the war. Later, in his *War Memoirs*, Lloyd George was to speak of his friend's 'invaluable aid', adding, 'His knowledge of finance, his mastery of figures, his dexterity and calm and sure judgement helped at many turns.'[5] An odd tribute, perhaps, to a Lord Chief Justice on vacation, but indicative once more of Reading's wide-ranging, almost hybrid, professional talents.

Lloyd George certainly needed expert help at the Treasury:

> The Chancellor had to learn in the midst of a raging world financial crisis. It was the London money market which moved commodities round the world through the medium of bills of exchange. The Chancellor had never seen a bill of exchange and knew little or nothing of the delicate and complicated mechanism by which international trade is regulated.[6]

There was undoubtedly a crisis in international financial circles at the outbreak of war, though the panic on the London money market was kept within the bounds of national decency and restraint. But there was a massive failure of remittances from abroad, exchanges collapsing in Lloyd George's words as if 'a shell had broken an aqueduct', and Britain, owed some £400,000,000 by the Argentine, consequently unable to buy against this enormous credit even one shipload of frozen meat. The government stepped in, proclaimed a halt, or moratorium, and took over responsibility for bills on neutral or enemy countries. Other emergency measures to restore some degree of stability included the issuing by the Treasury of £1 and 10 shilling banknotes to prevent a dangerous run on gold (and the extension of the August Bank holiday for three extra days to enable the notes to be printed), the temporary closing of the Stock Exchange, the suspension of the Bank Charter Act, and a reduction in the bank rate to 5 per cent from the panic-inflated 10 per cent. The government 'also took over the insurance of war risks on shipping – an arrangement which showed a profit at the end of the war'.[7]

Lloyd George needed Reading to bring the banks into line with government policy – for example to discourage them from restricting further advances to customers or from refusing to accept new customers. Reading used his influence with Sir Felix Schuster, governor of the Union Bank, to this effect. Reading was also instrumental in formulating other measures to get the discount market working again, and so to revive flagging foreign trade: for instance the government guaranteed the Bank of England against any losses incurred by discounting approved bills accepted before the moratorium on bills of exchange; the government also agreed to put up half of the sums involved in provincial traders supplying goods to continental customers on credit, provided that the traders' own local banks put up a further quarter of the amount. In such ways did the government try to ensure that the slogan of 'business as usual' had some meaning, and by the start of October 1914 it looked as if they had largely succeeded.

Lord Reading's work for the Treasury did not end with the reopening of the Law Sittings in October; when the courts rose he would then go on, almost every day, to his office in Whitehall and assist the Chancellor. Just as he had coached Lloyd George before giving evidence before the Select Committee on the Marconi affair, Reading helped his friend with the statements he was obliged to make before the House of Commons.

The advice was essentially the same: not to get entangled in technical details, and to be wary of giving any openings for criticism to those in the Commons who had a better grasp of the technicalities than he did. Also, 'You will probably find the House wants to hear very little of the details – it wants a broad statement. As it cannot criticize effectively, it will be bored by detail, and you are not enamoured of it!!' Reading was also convinced that Lloyd George should not refer to banks facing ruin: 'There is nothing so sensitive as the public with money in the bank at these times. Perhaps I exaggerate the importance of the reference but I do not think so and you may be criticized as Chancellor for the suggestion.'

Reading was largely responsible for, and took a leading part in the drafting of, the Courts (Emergency Powers) Act, which was aimed at relieving the difficulties of debtors, particularly by deferring the execution of judgment, whose financial plight could be shown to be directly or indirectly due to the war. So successful was the Act that its provisions were re-enacted when the Second World War broke out in 1939. Reading was also insistent that the moratorium on bills of exchange should be lifted as soon as possible; this was done on 4 November 1914, and trade with neutral countries more or less returned to its normal commercial routine.

Early in 1915 Lloyd George sent Lord Reading a handsome cigarette holder with his thanks for the invaluable assistance he had given. Reading's reply was warm, and contained an interesting reference to his part in embroiling Lloyd George in the Marconi controversy:

I am unfeignedly glad you think my assistance has been of value to you. Whatever its quality it was and always will be most willingly given whenever it is required. I have always felt proud that I was able to help at such a critical period. Then the work fascinated me, and added to it all the close companionship of former days delighted me.

Shall I tell you my innermost thoughts? It was joy that I who so unintentionally had caused you trouble should be able to help in however small a capacity to put you on your highest pinnacle where you now are and must remain till a taller one is made for you.[8]

Not long afterwards, Lloyd George took Reading and Sir John Simon on a trip to France to review the munitions situation and to see if ways could be found of speeding up production – thus ending the Allies' embarrassing shortages in this essential material of war.

The party crossed the Channel from Newhaven to Dieppe in a small and elderly destroyer, *The Flirt*, zigzagging in rough seas to avoid a prowling German U-boat. From Dieppe they were driven to Paris in a convoy of motor cars, passing Senlis in ruins, and seeing some British troops, led by a subaltern wheeling a bicycle, near Beauvais. They entered Paris in the evening with the city apparently deserted and with the business of government being carried on from the security of Bordeaux.

In Paris, where the Hotel Mirabeau was especially opened up to receive them, they met various generals and officials, and discovered that the French faced serious problems over the production of munitions – mainly because so many skilled men had been called up at the outbreak of war. One solution was to buy munitions from the United States, and Reading promised to look into this possibility with the Ordnance Department in London.

The trip included a visit to the General Headquarters of the French Northern Army and a tour of the front line. The shells whistling overhead 'made them shudder', and they perceived that the war was settling down, as Lloyd George said, into 'a siege operation on a colossal scale'. Before returning to Britain the party paid an unscheduled call at the Headquarters of the British Expeditionary Force at St Omer; Sir John French was not there, having gone north to observe some fighting that was to develop into the costly first Battle of Ypres.

Reading's contribution to the war effort during the first six months of the fighting was rewarded by his being created a Knight Grand Commander of the Bath in the King's Birthday Honours list of June 1915. Reading replied, by way of thanks, 'All are, I am sure, willing to help, but it is given to few to have the opportunity.'

In May 1915 the last Liberal government broke up and was replaced by a wartime coalition, though one in which Liberal ministers held the more influential posts – Asquith remained Prime Minister, for example, and Grey stayed at the Foreign Office; Reginald Mckenna became Chancellor of the Exchequer, Sir John Simon took the Home Office and

Lloyd George threw his dynamic qualities into his work as the newly created Minister of Munitions. Lord Reading was not offered a post, nor, indeed, was there any need for him to hanker after a return to the Cabinet; his continuing close friendship with Lloyd George and his friendship with Asquith, together with his undoubted expertise in formulating financial policy, kept him in regular touch with the government as it struggled to adjust to the demands of a wartime economy. McKenna was anxious to retain Reading's services when he took over as Chancellor of the Exchequer, and the Lord Chief Justice continued working part time in his room in Whitehall.

The problems of financing the war, which was demonstrably *not* over by Christmas, were immense. By January 1915 the war was costing the nation a staggering £3,500,000 a day, and Britain's £90,000,000 credit balance with the United States had nearly all been used up. Contracts for war material worth tens of millions of pounds had been placed in the United States and the British government had both to pay for these orders and to raise huge credit advances from American banks. Britain's supply of gold was not inexhaustible nor, moreover, was she helped by the steady decline in the value of the pound against the dollar which made it more difficult to meet American creditors.

So desperate had the situation become by the summer of 1915 that J.P. Morgan and Company, the New York bankers acting as financial agents for the British government, telegraphed that contracts for £52,000,000 of war supplies could not be signed unless $65,000,000 (about £13,000,000) was paid as a deposit. Morgan's, in fact, had no more British money to pay. The Governor of the Bank of England, when asked by McKenna to cope with the demand, replied irritably, 'Oh don't talk like that! What is to be done?' The Chancellor, recognizing the Bank of England's inadequacy with a crisp 'Leave it to me!', then proceeded to twist the arm of the Prudential Assurance Company to let him have their $40,000,000 lodged in American securities.[9] The contracts were duly signed.

Asquith, supported by Reading and Edwin Montagu, the capable Financial Secretary to the Treasury, expressed his 'disquietude' at this extraordinary transaction. It was clear that the British government could not permanently finance its war effort by limping from one great national company to another asking whether it could borrow from their American holdings to pay for essential war materials. These were the economics of the piggy bank, not of a great nation fighting for survival and honour.

In August 1915 the situation deteriorated further when Morgan's informed the British and French governments that the maximum loan they could negotiate in the United States, against the security of government notes, was £20,000,000, whereas the Allies needed a sum more like £200,000,000! The State Department, with President Wilson's backing, had also made plain its dislike of any loans which might be judged 'inconsistent with the true spirit of neutrality'.

The British and French governments promptly decided to send a joint Financial Mission to New York to negotiate for the £200,000,000 loan. Since a British official was to lead the mission, Lloyd George, with McKenna's approval, proposed Lord Reading's name. Reading consulted his fellow-judges who agreed that he should accept the post, leaving Mr Justice Darling, the senior puisne King's Bench judge, to act as Lord Chief Justice in his absence.

Reading chose a high-powered and experienced team of bankers and Treasury civil servants to accompany him. The French were represented by Octave Hombert from the Quai d'Orsay and the well-known banker Ernest Mallet. Less than two years from his appointment as Lord Chief Justice, Reading had left the job to another and sailed, on 1 September 1915, aboard the SS *Lapland* for New York as his country's senior representative.

The Anglo-French mission landed at New York on 10 September and were met by J. P. Morgan and his partner Henry P. Davidson. Reading had met J. P. Morgan before in Britain in the houses of the great banker's American cousins Mrs Lewis Harcourt (wife of the Liberal MP 'Lulu' Harcourt) and Mrs Walter Burns; unfortunately, this was of little use when it came to persuading other American bankers to meet the Allies' needs.

Reading's first two telegrams to McKenna, sent on 12 September, clearly illustrated his basic problems. The first telegram said:

Great activity since arrival. We have met most leading bankers. Situation is very difficult and will require much time and effort.

Press have talked of big loan in collateral of American securities. Have emphatically informed Morgan that suggestion impossible. We want £200 million sterling.[10]

The second telegram read:

Have told Morgan we want £200 million sterling. We meet tomorrow to begin business. Will inform you of progress which must be slow and laborious. American public unaccustomed to such loans even for small accounts. Negotiations very delicate.[11]

For the next two weeks the mission bargained hard to get what they wanted. They were obstructed by the activities of anti-loan groups drawn from the German and Irish-American sections of the population, by isolationist influences and by the ignorance and prejudice of several leading American politicians who opposed the transaction. The British and French governments, moreover, were not prepared to offer collateral security in, for example, the form of British- or French-owned American stocks, proposing instead that their word of honour was sufficient.

Eventually the terms of a loan were announced on 28 September; they fell a good way short of the Allies' target. Morgan's made the deal possible by forming a syndicate to underwrite a loan of approximately £100,000,000 sterling against the issue of five-year 5 per cent bonds, which could be converted at the holder's option, after four years, into $4\frac{1}{2}$ per cent bonds redeemable between 1930 and 1940.

Reading was reluctant to sanction this arrangement, but McKenna settled for the smaller sum (which he acknowledged 'will not be enough to see us right through') rather than risk the mission's complete failure. As it happened the loan was repaid in full at the end of five years, and was presented by the British government as 'a brilliant success'. The Americans had every reason to be pleased with the result, especially since the loan had to be spent in the United States.

The mission sailed for home on 16 October 1915 having formally signed the loan agreement two days earlier. Reading's part in the negotiations had clearly been a most successful one, and he had made a point of meeting as many influential Americans as possible, including President Wilson, Colonel House, the Chief Justice Oliver Wendell Holmes and Joseph H. Choate, former American Ambassador to the United Kingdom. Sir Cecil Spring Rice, the British Ambassador, spoke warmly of Reading's work, telling Sir Edward Grey at the Foreign Office that 'It was to a very large extent due to the personal qualities of Lord Reading that the operation of floating the loan was brought to a successful conclusion. He made an impression on all who met him such as is rare in the case of visiting Englishmen.' Choate, toasting Reading at the Pilgrims' dinner in New York, said, 'He has dealt splendidly with the American people,' to which the leader of the mission replied, 'We came as strangers and you have received us as relatives. You have clasped us to your hearts and made us realize more than ever what the great bond of humanity is.'

Reading's newly established contact with Colonel House was to prove to be of the utmost significance. House was President Wilson's closest confidant, sharing the President's liberalism, dislike of war, and his desire to give discreet encouragement to the Allies. A conversation with Colonel House would usually be relayed to Wilson within a matter of hours. It had been a conversation with House that had led Reading to cable Asquith on 2 October:

Have had important conversation with influential person, which strongly confirms opinions I had formed and expressed for myself and all Mission in telegrams of yesterday.

The attitude of at least four-fifths of the American people is most friendly, but they are very sensitive especially to criticism from England as to American greed and mercenary motives. I am convinced that there is genuine desire to help the Allies and that many welcome loan as an opportunity of helping.[12]

When Reading left the United States on 16 October 1915, House noted in his diary: 'Reading and I agreed to keep in touch with one another and he is to write in an unofficial way as often as necessary to have me fully informed.'[13]

Reading and House were henceforth to maintain a close contact during the war, and, indeed, to remain good friends until the former's death in 1935. It is clear that House's influence with President Wilson was crucial in enabling Reading to be appointed Ambassador to the United States early in 1918. In the interim both men acted as go-betweens for their respective governments, a role they both seem to have relished and to have carried out with purpose and enjoyment. In short, Reading became Britain's Colonel House, and House became the United States' Lord Reading.

In particular, Reading was able to be the link between Lloyd George and Colonel House, and thus with the President. This was to be a connection of tremendous importance after Lloyd George's accession to the premiership in December 1916, but before then there are examples of Reading working assiduously at promoting his friend's contact with the American administration.

For example, when House arrived in Britain in January 1916 on the first leg of an American peace mission that was later to take him on to Berlin, Reading arranged a private meeting between Lloyd George and the American in a private dining room at the Savoy Hotel, believing, according to House, that neither 'George nor I would be willing to open our minds fully to one another unless we were alone'.

The American peace initiative of 1916 consisted chiefly of the proposition (or threat) that 'it was the President's purpose to intervene and stop this destructive war, provided the weight of the United States thrown on the side that accepted our proposal could do it'. If the Central Powers proved unresponsive to the peace mission, Wilson was prepared to consider joining 'the Allies and force the issue'. Asquith and Grey were happy to support the American initiative, particularly since the Foreign Secretary's support for the establishment of a League of Nations after the war had been enthusiastically endorsed by the President.

In the event, the peace initiative was wrecked by the German conviction that they were winning the war anyway, and by the difficulties in getting the Allied powers to call a halt in what many of their people considered to be a just war.

Reading's personal contribution to the discussions between House and various British ministers seems to have been relatively insubstantial, and was once encapsulated by House in the sentence: 'The Lord Chief Justice sat by and said nothing, leaving George and me to thresh it out alone.'

None the less, Reading's diplomatic activities did help to bring about some accord between leading members of the coalition government about the desirability of attempting to set up a peace conference at the Hague, which President Wilson would also attend. The discussions arranged by Reading and House only included Asquith, Grey, Balfour and Lloyd George. Of these, Grey was initially the most enthusiastic supporter of a peace conference and Lloyd George the least eager – though the Minister of Munitions did recognize that the war could be brought to an end by a vigorous intervention and a virtual dictation of terms by President Wilson. For his part, House was deeply impressed by Lloyd George and noted, 'I wish Lloyd George was Prime Minister, with Sir Edward Grey as Foreign Minister, for I believe we could then do something. The Cabinet are all too conservative, and boldness is needed at this time. George has this quality, I believe.'[14]

One of the difficulties in getting agreement between the Prime Minister, Grey, Balfour and Lloyd George lay in the mistrust that was already evident between them. As House recorded in his diary for 11 February 1916:

It is evident that Lloyd George is somewhat distrustful of the Prime Minister, Grey and Balfour, and they are equally so of him. Neither group wants the other to have the advantage, and both are afraid to go as far in the direction as I am pushing as their inclination would lead them for fear capital might be made of it by the others.

Both Reading and George assured me that a peace proposal would be the most unpopular move that could be thought of in England. George said England was aroused for the first time. John Bull was grown fat and lazy, and he was working off his flesh and getting as lean and fit as an athlete, and had no fear of the result. George believes the War has done the nation good –

greater good than harm; that it had aroused the best in the people and that they will come out of it rejuvenated, with better impulses and purposes.[15]

By 17 February, however, much progress had been made, and Reading's efforts to this end are clearly acknowledged by House:

The Lord Chief Justice called this morning. He came to say that in his opinion the conference at his home the other evening was a great success. Like Sir Edward Grey, he thought it remarkable that Lloyd George, Balfour and Asquith should talk so freely before one another. He considered a great work had been accomplished by getting them all committed to the general proposition in the presence of each other. There was no way now by which one could attack the other to his disadvantage. This is because Reading knows, as I know and they know, that peace discussion at this time would be about as popular in England as the coronation of the Kaiser in Westminster Abbey.

I told Reading that both Grey and Balfour had complimented Lloyd George upon the breadth of vision and courage displayed. They both said they had not believed it was in him. This, however, I did not add. Reading thought the Prime Minister had committed himself much more strongly than he thought he would. He thought Asquith had in the back of his mind the feeling that the President was being represented by proxy, while whatever he, Asquith, said was at first hand. He could not repudiate, while the President might conceivably do so.

Reading considered it inadvisable to tell the other members of the Cabinet at present. In this I agree with him. He said it would leak, and would probably lead to a certain cabal getting together to defeat the object we had in mind. I was going directly to see Grey and told Reading I would call this to his attention.[16]

A few days afterwards, House received a visit from Reading who had seen Asquith alone and who now seemed much more in favour of the proposal to set up a peace conference. A little later Sir Edward Grey was able to initial the Anglo-American agreement on the peace plan. The memorandum began:

Colonel House told me [Grey] that President Wilson was ready, on hearing from France and England that the moment was opportune, to propose that a Conference should be summoned to put an end to the war. Should the Allies accept this proposal, and should Germany refuse it, the United States would *probably* [author's italics] enter the war against Germany.[17]

President Wilson's 'probably' was never put to the test: the projected triumphant Allied advance on the Western front ground to a bloody halt at the Somme in July, and the German government consequently felt no need to negotiate a peace; President Wilson, moreover, had to seek re-election in November 1916 and could hardly plunge his nation into war while campaigning on a non-interventionist platform. The House–Grey memorandum thus sank, like so many soldiers' corpses had done, into the mud of the battlefield.

Although Sir William Robertson, Chief of the Imperial General Staff, and Sir Douglas Haig, Commander-in-Chief in France, insisted that the Allies' military prospects for 1917 were excellent, this is not how it appeared to many in Britain as 1916 drew to its close. The military incompetence shown by the army's commanders was compounded by the lack of firm political leadership at the very top. Asquith, for all his fine qualities, still hoped that the war would be won through a combination of the Liberal virtues of *laissez-faire* and the professional skills of the military chiefs. Who was to set this to rights – the man to 'win the war'?

Although there was no concerted move to overthrow Asquith until November 1916, the Prime Minister's doom had in effect been sealed several months earlier. On 5 June, Field Marshal Lord Kitchener of Khartoum, Secretary of State for War, had been drowned when HMS *Hampshire* had struck a mine two hours after leaving Scapa Flow on a secret mission to Russia. The strong man, though an ineffective minister, was dead. A month later another strong man, David Lloyd George, succeeded to his office.

Lloyd George became Secretary of State for War on 4 July 1916 despite Asquith's misgivings – perhaps the Prime Minister already sensed his eventual downfall. On 7 December Lloyd George kissed hands as Prime Minister. What part did Lord Reading play in the overthrow of the man who had loyally advanced his career, and in the triumph of his closest political associate?

Reading was not a man who relished the rougher side of political conflict; his chosen weapon was the pen not the cudgel; his favourite arena the drawing room not the rowdy public meeting; his tactics were those of persuasion and reason not of brute force. This sensitivity and fastidiousness sometimes led to inappropriate indecisiveness. In the struggle between Asquith and Lloyd George, however, he was forced to choose, and he chose Lloyd George.

He was none the less a discreet champion of his friend, and it is clear that he strove to retain Asquith as a member of the new government. Edwin Montagu, an intimate of Asquith, thought that he and Reading had tried, and failed, during the crisis to bring the two men closer together. Reading's son wrote that 'it was a real sorrow for him to find himself gradually forced into line with the advocates of change. But the evidence pointed in his view inexorably in one direction, and he could not allow private affection to conflict with public interest.'[18] Although Reading's role in Asquith's overthrow temporarily estranged him from his old colleague, Margot Asquith, not by nature the most forgiving of women, was later able to express forgiveness:

> I felt in choosing Ll.G. . . . you had chosen a lower type of man, a man of less fine nature, fine intellect and education and even of character . . . but I forgave you because you have one unique quality added to a perfect nature, you have gratitude, and you have compassion and you have simplicity under all the tact and diplomacy.[19]

It is clear that Reading's backing of Lloyd George was neither immediate nor complete. The crisis over the direction of the war finally surfaced on 1 December 1916 when Lloyd George, encouraged by Sir Edward Carson, Lord Northcliffe (who loathed Asquith) and Bonar Law, the Unionist leader, formally proposed a war council of three with himself in the chair. Asquith refused to take a back seat, and insisted that he must preside over such a council.

Bonar Law then called on Asquith and almost certainly gave him a garbled version of his earlier meeting with the three leading Unionists – Lord Robert Cecil, Austen Chamberlain and Lord Curzon, the 'three Cs'.[20] The Prime Minister assumed that Law and the 'three Cs' would resign from the coalition government if he did not accept the war council and he accordingly wrote to Lloyd George agreeing to the proposed council. At the urging of Edwin Montagu, the Prime Minister issued a press release that the government was to be reconstructed. It seemed that he had accepted becoming a figurehead.

Reading's part in the crisis up to this point had been to act as the 'peacemaker on Lloyd George's side', while Montagu acted in a similar role for Asquith. On 2 December, the day after Lloyd George formally proposed the war council, Montagu had breakfasted with Reading, and both men then went to the War Office to persuade Lloyd George not to resign from the government if he did not become chairman of the war council and if he did not also secure Balfour's removal as First Lord of the Admiralty. Lloyd George, however, had not been interested in compromise, and Montagu at once wrote gloomily to Asquith:

> The situation is probably irretrievably serious. I have just come from L.G., with whom I have spent an hour of hard fighting, but it seems to be of no avail and I fear he has committed himself. I have done everything in my power and you know that Rufus has also done his best. Rufus has been with him throughout and I left him there. He [Lloyd George] says that he submitted proposals to you which are not acceptable to you, and that you have submitted proposals

to him which are not acceptable to him. We then tried to arrange a compromise, but so far none is possible.[21]

At Reading's request, Lloyd George had agreed to hold back from resignation for twenty-four hours. Reading had then walked to Downing Street where he proposed, with Montagu's assent, a workable compromise to Eric Drummond, one of Asquith's private secretaries. It was a compromise that would have left Asquith as Prime Minister and nominal president of the war council but have given Lloyd George the council's chairmanship and hence the overall control of running the war.

Sir Maurice Hankey, Secretary of the War Cabinet, also talked to Reading and recorded the common dilemma in his diary:

> We both agreed that the whole crisis is intolerable. There is really very little between them [Lloyd George and Asquith]. Everyone agrees that the methods of the War Committee call for reform. Everyone agrees that the Prime Minister possesses the best judgment. The only thing is that Lloyd George and Bonar Law insist that the former and not the Prime Minister must be the man to run the War. ... The obvious compromise is for the Prime Minister to retain the Presidency of the War Committee with Lloyd George as Chairman, and to give Lloyd George a fairly free run for his money.

News of this compromise had brought Asquith hurrying back to London from Wolmer Castle on Sunday 3 December. There he was confronted by Law and the 'three Cs', and also met Lloyd George. From these meetings there had emerged the press statement of Monday 4 December dealing with the government's reconstruction.

Unfortunately, Northcliffe's *Times* also carried a leading article critical of Asquith, and written by the editor Dawson on Sir Edward Carson's prompting. This seemed to rub salt into the wound of Asquith's demotion. At the same time, those Liberal ministers who had known nothing of the Lloyd George proposal and the compromise 'came to Asquith in high indignation. They demanded a fight. The "three Cs" also indicated that they were on Asquith's side. Curzon declared that no Unionist except Law would join a Lloyd George government.'[22]

Asquith took heart from these tokens of support – insubstantial as many were later to prove – and decided to fight Lloyd George. He told his rival that he could not go on with their agreement unless Lloyd George corrected the impression of his 'relegation' to 'the position of an irresponsible spectator of the War'.

Lloyd George refused to accommodate the man who had so recently stood by him during the Marconi scandal – he resigned. Doubtless he put his country before his honour, or at least hoped that if he saved his country his reputation would be saved with it.

Instead of pausing for recuperation, Asquith promptly decided to destroy his enemies with one blow; he, too, resigned on 5 December and, in effect, challenged anyone else to form a government.

Forty-eight hours of political jostling ensued. Law, the leader of the Unionists, would only form a government if Asquith joined; Asquith refused – indeed he declared his unwillingness to serve under any viable Prime Minister, including Balfour who had been premier barely a decade earlier. Law acknowledged defeat.

George v then sent for Lloyd George on 6 December. By the evening of 7 December, Lloyd George was able to tell the King that he had formed an administration: the Labour party had backed him, so had Law and the back-bench Unionists, and Addison and the back-bench Liberals. The other Unionist leaders were quickly won over by the promise of high office and an undertaking to keep Churchill (Lloyd George's erstwhile ally) and Northcliffe out of office. Curzon, who had declared a few hours before that he would 'rather die than serve under Lloyd George', became Lord President of the Council. The 'last of the Romans' had been overthrown, superseded by the 'first of the Goths'.

Montagu's immediate reaction was distress that he and Reading had failed in their efforts to bring Asquith and Lloyd George closer together. But, while Reading would have preferred to see Asquith associated with the government in some capacity, Lloyd George's accession to supreme power could only benefit him. Anxious to escape from the uninspiring demands of his high judicial office, he could expect preferment and consideration from the new Prime Minister – above all, some exciting assignments as Britain struggled to win the war.

One of Reading's first assignments on Lloyd George's behalf was to try in May 1917 to wheedle Asquith back into the government as Lord Chancellor. To achieve this end, Reading got himself invited to a Whitsun country-house party with the Asquiths. When Reading had left empty-handed, Asquith wrote down a record of their discussions. The document reveals Reading's tactics as Lloyd George's emissary, and also shows that the early failure to reconcile the two great Liberal leaders was fundamentally the fault of Asquith:

Secret

The Wharf,
Sutton Courtney
Whit Monday,
May 28, 1917

We came down here for Whitsuntide on Friday, and among our guests was the Lord Chief Justice, who arrived that evening and left this afternoon. I soon found out that he had come on a political mission – whether self-imposed, or inspired by others, or (as is more probable) a little of both, I cannot say. He twice sought me out for private confabulation on the subject.

The first time (on Saturday morning) he began by referring to McKenna's acceptance of a Bank Directorship from which he inferred that Holden the Chairman had marked McKenna out, with his own assent, as his successor. He (the Lord Chief Justice) and others had drawn the conclusion that this meant McKenna's abandonment, for the time being at any rate, of politics for business: and 'this' he remarked 'would remove a great obstacle in the way of possible reconstruction of the Government'.

I replied that he and his friends were living in a fool's paradise: that I was sure from what McKenna had said to me that he had no such intention: that he had accepted the directorship, partly for pecuniary reasons, partly to fill his time, and partly to familiarize himself with the routine of City business. I added that in my opinion McKenna (and also Runciman), whom I know to be almost equally obnoxious in some quarters, was an indispensable member of any really capable Administration.

My friend was a little discouraged by this unpromising opening, but proceeded to throw out other feelers. Bonar Law, e.g., was anxious to get away from the Exchequer, Balfour would soon find the Foreign Office too much for him; the War Cabinet could well drop one or two of its present members, &c. &c. I said that if he wanted my opinion, without going into individual cases, I regarded the whole thing as a hopeless and unworkable experiment. A ridiculous and insupportable weight was cast upon two or three not overcompetent men, while the administrators of most of the great departments were deprived of all responsibility, and even of any real knowledge of what was going on. Self-respecting statesmen could not be expected to take part in such a crazy adventure.

This (Monday) morning the Lord Chief Justice returned to the charge, with something more like a frontal attack. He said that he, and many others, regarded my active participation in the Government as essential, and he hinted that this was the view of the Prime Minister. I gathered that I could have almost any post I chose except that of the head of the Government.

I answered that I must use preferably plain language, since he had raised the subject. I was quite ready to go on giving the Government full support so long as they carried on the War in the proper spirit, and use my influence within my party, and in the country, in the same sense. But he and others had better understand clearly, and at once, that under no conditions would I serve in a Government of which Lloyd George was the head. I had learned by long and close association to mistrust him profoundly. I knew him to be incapable of loyalty and lasting gratitude. I had always acknowledged, and did still, to the full his many brilliant and useful faculties, but he needed to have someone over him. In my judgment he had incurable defects, both of intellect and character, which totally unfitted him to be at the head.

The Lord Chief Justice with rather a wry face acquiesced. To some further vaguely tentative overtures, I replied that I could not associate myself with what he called 'the counsel' of any Government unless I had supreme and ultimate authority.[23]

In August 1917 Reading, plainly anxious to undertake more war work, wrote to Lloyd George from the Prospect Hotel, Harrogate, where he and his wife had been taking the waters. He began: 'My Dear Lloyd George, I have been imbibing sulphur water but you must have been living near the warmth of hell lately,' and went on to remark that this was the first long vacation in which he had no war work to do: 'I should be very glad to do anything that would be of service and would have liked to have been a member of the Committee to deal with the constitution of the House of Lords. Whilst I was Attorney-General, I had much to do with this matter and collected some information about Second Chambers. Can it be managed?'[24]

Within a week of this almost pathetic appeal to Lloyd George, Reading was asked to go to the United States as High Commissioner to deal chiefly with the complexities of Anglo-American finance and also to survey the effectiveness of the British government's representation there.

At first sight, Reading's appointment as High Commissioner looks like an incredibly quick and warm response to his letter of 18 August to the Prime Minister. In fact, pressure to appoint Reading in such a capacity had been put on Lloyd George for some seven weeks before he agreed to it. This seems an unusual way to treat a man who, quite apart from his earlier close association with Lloyd George, had played an active part in getting him into 10 Downing Street. The Prime Minister was not alone in his initial misgivings; Bonar Law, Chancellor of the Exchequer, wanted a Conservative to undertake the task, and the Treasury officials argued the case for a civil servant.

Lloyd George's own hesitation, according to Northcliffe's brother Lord Rothermere, was due to 'fears of a revival of the Marconi allegations'. Since Reading was to be in charge of delicate financial negotiations, there was some sort of basis for this anxiety. On the other hand,

Reading's loan mission of 1915 had awoken none of these grisly spectres. Nor had Lloyd George refused the premiership for fear of echoes of his own involvement in the Marconi affair. The Prime Minister seems to have paid the most serious attention to Bonar Law's objections; once these were overcome he appointed Reading. At least Lloyd George's initial hesitation was awkward to square with the whispers that he was 'run by Reading'.

Lord Northcliffe, the head of the special war mission to the United States, campaigned for Reading; so did Colonel House, who recorded in his diary of 16 July 1917 that: 'Northcliffe spoke of Lloyd George's intimacy with the Lord Chief Justice, saying that Reading was "the Colonel House of their Government". We decided that the Lord Chief Justice would be a good man to come over and negotiate ... upon financial questions.'[25] Colonel Sir William Wiseman, the thirty-two-year-old head of British Intelligence in the United States, and a close friend of House, was also convinced that Reading was the man for the job. Wiseman, in fact, had returned to Britain early in August 1916 in part at least to persuade the War Cabinet to send Reading back with him.

Lord and Lady Reading landed at New York during the second week of September, and then moved on to Washington and more permanent accommodation supplied by the British Embassy. As part of his team, Reading took, on Sir Maurice Hankey's advice, Ernest Swinton, Assistant Secretary to both the War Cabinet and the Committee of Imperial Defence, as well as an outstanding young economist John Maynard Keynes, head of the Treasury department dealing with external financing.

The United States had entered the war in April after the depredations of Germany's unrestricted submarine warfare, and the revelation, through 'the Zimmerman telegram', that Germany had offered Mexico an offensive alliance against Washington with the unlikely prospect of recapturing pieces of Mexican territory long since annexed by the Americans.

Reading's main tasks in the United States were to integrate the American war effort as closely as possible with that of the Allies, and to get a firm commitment from the Americans to provide regular credit for the duration of the war. The British government also wanted to be able to spend some of their American credit on goods produced elsewhere – Canadian wheat, for example.

As if these tasks were not difficult enough, Reading also had to face some obstruction from Sir Cecil Spring Rice, the British Ambassador to the United States. Spring Rice, emotional, impulsive and sometimes incoherent in discussion, saw Reading – quite correctly as it turned out – ultimately as a rival for his post. On 22 September 1917, within a few days of arriving in America, Reading was discussing the Spring Rice problem with Colonel House:

Strangely enough the larger part of his time was taken up by a discussion of his troubles with Sir Cecil Spring Rice and proposed remedies. ... Reading feels he is in a precarious position with Spring Rice working against him at every turn, and in a perfectly unbalanced way. We agreed it was best for him to ask his Government to recall Spring Rice, giving the reason Lord Reading's presence here and the consequent possibility of a vacation for the Ambassador, and also the desire of the Government to confer upon him certain honours because of the United States' entrance into the War on the side of the Allies. ... Reading is to write a despatch to his Government on the question of recalling Spring Rice, and is to submit it to me for approval. We agreed that he, Reading, is to remain here as long as it was possible for him to do so consistent with his position as Lord Chief Justice.[26]

Nor was Reading's relationship with the more flamboyant Northcliffe free of stress. Northcliffe was generally an enthusiastic supporter of Reading's work in the United States, for example telling Lloyd George on 30 September that the achievement of getting the Americans to allow Britain to use loaned money to spend on Canadian wheat was 'one that could not be brought about by anyone not possessed of Reading's ability, charm and tact in handling these difficult people'. On the other hand, he did not want his own work as head of the British mission to America eclipsed by that of a newcomer, whose precise status had been kept vague by the British government, and aspired to overall control of British representation in the United States. There is even evidence that he used his position as a press magnate to minimize Reading's role in America. Arthur Murray, Assistant Military Attaché to the British Embassy in Washington, and the brother of Murray of Elibank, gave the details in a confidential report to the Foreign Office of 23 October 1917:

Two things have happened which have brought this to my notice, and Rufus is conscious of it, and has talked to me about it. *You* of course will understand that he talks freely to me as an old friend, and has not and would not speak to anyone else here about it. Nor, I think, would he like it 'passed around', and I pass it on to you only in order that you may be fully seized of the *personal* situation.

As to the actual methods: Rufus's recent visit to Canada where as you know he was the 'guest of honour', and pulled off a 'big thing', was announced in

The Times (London) and the Press over here in which Northcliffe has a 'pull'
as 'a visit to Canada of Lord Northcliffe accompanied by Treasury Officials
and Lord Reading!' Secondly: Rufus addressed a most successful meeting in
New York last week for the Liberty Loan. There was no report of it in the *New
York Times*. In nosing about quietly to discover the reason for this I found that
Northcliffe had kept out (by the means at his hand) any report of the meeting,
because, as he said to my informant, he thought that too much publicity would
harm the work that Rufus is doing!

It is difficult to convey by letter a personal situation such as this without
perhaps creating the impression that there is at the same time a sense of
antagonism between the two. This is not so, though *privately* Rufus is a bit
sore.[27]

Sir Arthur Willert, *The Times*' Washington correspondent, dined
with the Readings a few days after their arrival in the capital and left
an interesting account of the High Commissioner as both host and
negotiator, recalling Reading

with his dark aquiline face, which would have made up well as that of an
elderly Hamlet, graceful body, strong shoulders, delicate sensitive hands toying
with a chicken wing, sipping gingerly from a glass of good claret, gently
drawing them out, elegant in evening dress – a tail-coat, though the dinner
was small and the evening warm.

Advanced middle age had left his energy unimpaired. As a negotiator and
advocate he was Northcliffe's superior. Northcliffe's methods were pyrotech-
nical, and the fuses did not always go off; he relied upon the inspiration of the
moment and his own forcefulness, rather than upon preparation. Reading was
always perfectly prepared. He had the great lawyer's power of mastering a case
quickly, unravelling its complications and marshalling in the right order the
arguments most likely to impress the other side. Sometimes I was called in to
assist in this preparation where politics were concerned, and in my mind's eye
there is still the picture of Reading pacing softly about the room or standing in
front of the mantelpiece, deciding how to start some conversation, how his
interlocutor would be likely to meet his presentation of the case, what his own
answer would be, and so on.

I used also to think that the fact that he was a Jew and Chief Justice of
England helped considerably. It 'spotlighted' his ability, and British open-
mindedness. It impressed Americans that a Jew should plead the British cause
with such sincerity and feeling.[28]

On the other hand, there was, according to Northcliffe's official
biographers, 'a strong prejudice against him, and also against his
German-Jewish wife, which did not exist in England'.[29] Wiseman,
however, gave a more accurate appraisal when he wrote to Sir Eric
Drummond, Foreign Secretary Balfour's Principal Private Secretary in
London, shortly after Reading's arrival:

138

There are serious financial problems unsolved, but Reading is approaching them in the right spirit and is a very acceptable person to all the Administration. House as usual is very helpful, and I believe we are now tackling the situation properly. While I cannot say that there is any popular enthusiasm for the War, there is a very solid determination to carry on with all the resources of the country until the German military power is crushed. The position of the President remains very strong. Feeling towards the British is improving.[30]

Although Reading was successful in obtaining the necessary credits for Britain and thus ensuring that the war could, for the time being, be paid for, serious problems remained.

Chief among these was the need to co-ordinate the supply demands of the Allies in Europe with those of the United States. As the United States' armed forces were built up, pressure upon American armaments and supply industries threatened to disrupt production of war material needed by Britain and France. With the collapse of Russia as a reliable fighting ally in the Autumn of 1917, Lloyd George urged the necessity for 'some kind of Allied Joint Council, with permanent military and probably naval and economic staff attached to work out plans for the Allies, for submission to the several Governments concerned'.

One of Reading's primary tasks, therefore, was to persuade the American government to participate in such a consultative scheme. Although President Wilson was initially reluctant to send American representatives to Europe to sit in council with the Allies, he eventually agreed to send Colonel House for a short visit to Britain accompanied by the appropriate representatives of the American army, navy and various supply boards. This concession was not solely Reading's doing, but Arthur Murray gave him most of the credit, writing on 23 October 1917:

In my humble opinion, Rufus in pulling off the 'War Council' has achieved one of the biggest things of the War. The vital importance of the immediate allocation of shipping to various urgent needs over a long period ahead impresses itself upon one more and more every day. A section of public opinion here is out to send as large a number of American troops across as quickly as possible without regard to other (and Allied particularly) demands for shipping.

Early in November 1917 Colonel House sailed for Britain, to be followed a few days later by Reading, Northcliffe and Wiseman. Although the ensuing discussions in London were generally useful, Lloyd George proved reluctant to commit himself at once and wholeheartedly to the proposed Inter-Allied Conference, and all of Reading's diplomatic skills were brought to bear on the situation. House noted gratefully that 'Reading's influence with Lloyd George is greater perhaps than any other man's in England, and it is on this that I am playing.'

Amid these negotiations, Reading received two honours: firstly, it was announced at the end of November 1917 that he would continue to assist the British War Cabinet in financial matters, and that he would consequently attend the meeting of the newly created Supreme War Council in Paris; secondly, at Lloyd George's insistence, King George v created him Earl of Reading, with the title of Viscount Erleigh for his son.

On 7 January 1918, Reading received the appointment that both he and his closest supporters wanted – he was made Ambassador Extraordinary and High Commissioner on Special Mission to the United States. Sir Cecil Spring Rice was, at the same time, recalled for consultation. As early as August 1917 Lord Rothermere had concluded that there was going to be a change of ambassador in Washington, and asked his brother Northcliffe, 'Why do you not suggest Reading for the job? He is dying to get away from the Bench.' Less than five months later Reading had once more got away from the duties of Lord Chief Justice.

11 Ambassador to the United States, 1918–19

He is one of the ablest Englishmen living – everybody concedes that. But, with that, agreement about him here ends.
Walter Page Hines to President Wilson, January 1918

Add ... his appointment to Washington, a position for which, in public opinion, (in spite of the applause of an obvious claque) he is the most unsuitable man who could have been chosen, and you will understand why you ... are suffering inestimable damage by this prominent public association with an individual who is more distrusted even than Lord Haldane.
Ellis T. Powell to Lloyd George, January 1918

Reading's appointment as Ambassador did not gladden every heart. Spring Rice was deeply upset both by his dismissal and by the necessarily blunt telegram bearing the news from the Foreign Secretary, Balfour. Although he had not enjoyed a happy relationship with President Wilson, Colonel House or anyone in the Democratic hierarchy (had, indeed, coined witticisms like 'If the President is the Shepherd of his people, then McAdoo* is his crook!') he was an over-sensitive and sick man who, according to Wiseman, 'felt his dismissal very keenly'. Having composed the sonnet 'I vow to thee, my country' in a farewell letter to the former Secretary of State, William Jennings Bryan, Spring Rice made a tearful departure from Washington and went on to Ottawa planning to travel home from there with his wife. He was never to reach Britain, however, dying of a sudden heart attack while staying as the guest of the Canadian Governor-General, the Duke of Devonshire, at

* William G. McAdoo was Secretary of the US Treasury.

Ottawa. Spring Rice had for some time ceased to be a useful ambassador, and in October 1917 Arthur Murray and Maynard Keynes had sent a telegram to Bonar Law's Private Secretary, John C.C. Davidson, saying, 'We have come to the conclusion separately that Spring Rice cannot be regarded as mentally responsible. It should be realized on your side that he is in a serious nervous condition and incapable of properly conducting business.'[1] None the less, many of the Embassy staff were sorry to see Spring Rice bundled so unceremoniously out of Washington.

The appointment prompted Ellis T. Powell, editor of the *Financial News*, to write Lloyd George a long letter in which anti-semitic innuendo and patriotic paranoia jostled with the downright insulting insistence that the Prime Minister was dancing to any tune that Reading chose. Powell was no Northcliffe in terms of influence and prestige, but the letter is worth considering in some detail as typical of a section of British opinion, although oddly the *Financial News* had been founded by Harry Marks in 1884 and had often been accused of being under Jewish 'influence'.[2]

After denouncing the perilous influence of 'naturalized Germans' upon the government, Powell went on to claim that the 'second influence that is doing you incalculable injury is your prominent public association with Lord Reading. Rightly or wrongly, that individual is the most profoundly distrusted individual in the country.' Powell added that often, after he had addressed public meetings on the war effort, his audience would say: 'If Lloyd George is such a patriotic man as you say, why does he allow himself to be "run" by a man like Lord Reading?'[3]

Powell went on to allege that 'the Marconi gang' had been able to secure War Office contracts 'as long as L.G. was there', that Mrs Godfrey Isaacs had been speculating in Marconi shares in the name of Lea Perelli, and that 'the public now knows that Lord Reading and his associates concealed from the Marconi Committee a vast army of ghastly facts vital to the formation of its judgement'.

Claiming that Lord Reading had declined to make him an admission of his guilt, Powell complained that twice Reading and 'his financial group' had prompted Lloyd George's government

to threaten me with a prosecution unless I remained silent – or risk a trial before a judicial creature of Lord Reading himself. The public infers, therefore, that Lord Reading is afraid lest the truth should come out, and that he exerts sufficient control over your Government to make them his instruments in a policy directed to hushing up the facts. The public infers, moreover, that these facts have some bearing upon German influence in our midst.

In fact ... the rumour is persistently and mischievously spread that Lord

Reading has a 'hold' upon you, and that he can make you dance to any tune he pleases. ... [he] is able to obtain an earldom for arranging one of the most disastrous financial deals that it is possible to imagine, and which, as the public has not been slow to discern, would be singularly profitable to that group of his co-religionists who dominate the Silver Market. Add the continual appearance of Lord Reading's name in combination with yours as if you were his secretary or his servant, and the reiterated (and of course carefully arranged) publication of his portrait showing you in his company, and finally his appointment to Washington, a position for which, in public opinion, (in spite of the applause of an obvious claque) he is the most unsuitable man who could possibly have been chosen, and you will understand why you ... are suffering inestimable damage by this prominent public association with an individual who is more distrusted even than Lord Haldane.

P.S.   If I can ever serve you by an inspired indiscretion Sir George Riddell or Sir H[arry] Dalziel will tell you I am to be trusted.[4]

This unedifying letter was accompanied by an even more distasteful pamphlet, published in America, and entitled 'The Wireless Ghost'. Consisting of a vicious attack upon Godfrey Isaacs – 'That hideous face with a horrible grin is finding his way into one of the largest financial counting rooms in the world' – it also attempted to smear 'the Lord Chief Justice of England' for alleged undercover Marconi dealings.[5]

In the United States, apart from scurrilous pamphleteers like the author of 'The Wireless Ghost', Reading's appointment was generally welcomed. Walter Page Hines, the American Ambassador in London, wrote an interesting and warm assessment of his new British counterpart to President Wilson on 16 January 1918:

You know Lord Reading and have taken the measure of him, but the following facts and gossip may interest you. He is one of the ablest Englishmen living – everybody concedes that. But, with that, agreement about him here ends. The very general Conservative view of him is that he cannot be trusted. See and compare the view taken of Disraeli, the other Hebrew Earl, by his political enemies. He is not so spectacular as old Dizzy was, but he is far sounder. I doubt if Dizzy was honest and I think that Reading is. ...

He is the son of a London merchant and he married a daughter of a merchant named Cohen. The Isaacs and the Cohen are now swallowed up in the Earl and Countess, and 'Reading' gives no hint of Jewry.

Lord Reading does not give up the Lord Chief Justiceship. He remarked to me the other day that his Ambassadorship would be temporary. Lady Reading told Mrs Page that they expected to be gone only three months. But I take it that he will not return till the end of the War. ...

I think there is no doubt that to do a concrete job Lord Reading will succeed, during war time, better than any man who was considered for the post. ...

Of course the immediate problems to be met in the relations of the two Governments will continue to be financial – till we have to slacken our pace. The British, God knows, need money, but God knows also that they are not slow in making their wants known. I doubt if anybody, but the Germans, will ever wage war on less than twice what it ought to cost. But, if it could be more extravagantly conducted than they (the British) conduct it, I can't imagine how it could be done.[6]

In Britain, *The Times* welcomed Reading's appointment, recalling the 'proud period when English judges were, as he is, versed in state-craft', and praising the government's evident desire 'to make use of indisputable financial and diplomatic ability'. From Kent, Sir Henry Lucy wrote to Reading that he had read 'with some amusement the adulation lavished upon Lloyd George and yourself by the [Tory] Press, who a few years back were united in an unscrupulous conspiracy to drive you both out of public life'.[7]

Lord Beaverbrook in his *Men and Power, 1917–18* was later to assess Reading's suitability to his wartime functions:

Lord Reading ... was an important influence in war-time finance. He had financial understanding, a legal training, a career in government and experience in Cabinet. He was well equipped to give good counsel and good guidance. Holding a non-political post, he had immense advantage in relation with ministers irrespective of Party allegiance.

Reading's outstanding quality was his tact. This gift enabled him to be on intimate terms with Lloyd George, McKenna and Bonar Law, three successive Chancellors of the Exchequer, all of varying natures and diverging temperaments, yet all willing and anxious to avail themselves of Reading's fundamental qualities. Reading kept in with all three, just as he managed to keep on terms with Asquith and Lloyd George throughout the strife between these two Liberal leaders.[8]

Beaverbrook also pointed out how 'dignified and dull' Reading's speeches always were: 'It is acknowledged that at the Bar he was magnificent, yet in private conversation his vocabulary was limited. He never resorted to picturesque phrases. ... He was just and a most likeable fellow. Indeed he was a lovable man with an abundance of personal charm.'[9]

Tact, diplomacy and charm were to be useful qualities in wartime Washington, and it is clear that Reading exercised them to the full and generally to good effect. These gifts, however, were linked to a caution which helped to make Reading a superb negotiator but a poor innovator of policy. Equipped with a clear brief, few could surpass him in getting the desired result, but he lacked the fire and inspirational egotism of the dynamic policy-maker – hence his mutually supportive relationship with Lloyd George.

Beaverbrook described Reading as 'cautious, so cautious that he never gave an opinion until he was forced to do so', and several times in his papers Colonel House produces a phrase like '[Lloyd] George and I did practically all the talking, Reading as usual being the listener'. And in December 1918 Maynard Keynes wrote a tart description of Reading's indecisiveness over whether Britain should continue to enforce the blockade against a defeated Germany:

I hardly know why we, the English, decided to promote its continuance. I attribute it in part to the irresolution of Lord Reading, who was in charge of the business on our side; for he was intriguing at that time day and night to be one of the party for Paris and was terrified of identifying himself too decidedly with anything controversial. I recall him picking at the nail of his left thumb for minutes together in his room in the War Cabinet offices in Whitehall Gardens in an agony of doubt which way the cat was jumping; his top hat perfect; his whole face and person so chiselled and polished, reflecting pinpoints of light from so many angles that one longed to wear him as a tie pin; tie pin on tie pin, till one hardly knew which was Earl and which was jewel; poor Earl![10]

How did Lord Reading square his lengthy absence from his judicial duties with his conscience? There is no doubt that he was eager to escape from the Bench for reasons of personal satisfaction and ambition; the special circumstances of war smoothed his path and helped clear his conscience at the same time. His appointment to the Washington Embassy prompted the Lord Chancellor, Lord Finlay, to write a letter to the Prime Minister expressing his anxiety over Reading's absence in the United States.[11] Reading himself expressed some disquiet at the implications of his appointment in a letter to Balfour on 29 January 1918, stressing that he must return to his office of Lord Chief Justice 'in a few months', and emphasizing that he 'must be careful not to overstrain the position or cause any public discussion or agitation about it'. Reading argued that he could only be in America for six months since otherwise he 'would be committing a wrong to the high office of Lord Chief Justice and one for which I could not possibly hold myself responsible'.[12] Lloyd George also received a copy of this letter.

While there is no need to doubt that, at one level, Reading meant what he said, almost exactly a year later he was again writing to Balfour and Lloyd George from London asking to be finally relieved of his ambassadorial responsibilities. He told the Prime Minister: 'After four and a half years' activities on war problems I have come to the conclusion that I should return to my judicial duties.'[13] He promised Balfour that, if he wished it, he would return to Washington to take formal and public leave, but before sailing would come to Paris (where Balfour was one of the leading British peace delegates) to get the latest views on 'the Anglo-American situation'.[14]

Reading's appointment as 'His Majesty's High Commissioner, Ambassador Extraordinary and Plenipotentiary on Special Mission to the United States' was on favourable financial terms. He continued to draw his salary as Lord Chief Justice, was granted an initial outfit allowance of £2,000, and was repaid for 'the cost of establishing and maintaining the Embassy'. Reading asked for Sir Eric Drummond from the Foreign Office to be sent with him to Washington. Balfour refused this request, hoping that his refusal did not seem 'ungrateful' and remarking, perhaps with a touch of Balfourian irony, 'I know well with what reluctance you have accepted the Mission, and how much you have sacrificed to duty and patriotism.'[15]

Once installed in Washington, how effective was Reading's ambassadorship? The answer must be divided, like the broad sweep of Reading's duties, into two parts.

First, how well did he handle the basic matters of supply and finance? Balfour's valedictory letter of 24 May 1919 warmly congratulated him on solving 'problems ... quite outside ordinary diplomatic routine. They involved the most complicated questions of finance, shipping, food supply, troop transportations and armaments. ... you provided the most important personal link between the two great Associated Powers.'[16] These were precisely the areas where Reading's tact and lack of overt aggressiveness, allied to his mastery of detail and finance, could really be expected to count.

In anticipating Reading's arrival in Washington, William Wiseman had written to Balfour on 25 January 1918:

America's contribution to the War during ten months has undoubtedly fallen far short of this country's expectations and is a shock to America's self-satisfaction. ...

I believe Reading's firm insistence on our essential needs and helpful suggestions and sympathy for their difficulties will achieve far more than the hostile criticisms of the Administration's methods which are too noticeable amongst certain British officials here.

President Wilson may be led but certainly not driven.[17]

Wiseman also wrote to Eric Drummond the same day that 'I am hoping a lot from Reading. He has a wonderful chance. If he is well backed up with a constant stream of information, and his recommendations are promptly acted upon, he can assume a great position in Washington and do very much to guide the Administration. . . . We are all getting ready to make Reading a big success over here.'[18]

Even before Reading had called at the White House to present his credentials, President Wilson made an important speech before Congress in which he outlined the four principles upon which a lasting peace could be based: the essential justice of each part of the settlement; no bartering of peoples and provinces; every territorial settlement to be for the benefit of the people concerned; the attempt to satisfy national aspirations, without stirring up old or new discord. These four principles were somewhat bland generalizations compared with the more specific, celebrated 'Fourteen Points' on which peace could be based, which had been enunciated by Wilson on 8 January 1917.

Lord Reading was warmly appreciative of Wilson's speech, telling Colonel House, 'I would have given a year of my life to have made the last half of the President's speech.' House then 'returned to the White House, where the President was waiting to hear if I had any news of Reading. He was delighted when I told him what Reading . . . had to say.'

Settled in his old quarters at Number 2315 Massachusetts Avenue, Reading presented his ambassadorial credentials to the President on 13 February 1918. Shortly afterwards he told Wiseman: 'I am rather staggered by the amount of work to be tackled, but it will get easier when I have got the personnel properly to work.'

Reading's effectiveness in dealing with matters of supply prompted Wiseman to write an enthusiastic letter to Drummond at the Foreign Office on 14 March 1918, a month after the Ambassador had got down to work:

Reading has done splendid work here. He found a good deal of confusion when he arrived owing to the Northcliffe regime at the War Mission and the entire lack of cooperation between the Embassy and the Mission. It is important you should remember that Reading, on his arrival, was faced with a number of awkward and unpleasant personal questions which you heard nothing about, but which had to be settled before he could get the machine to run smoothly. I do not suppose they are by any means settled yet, but the organization has certainly improved. . . .

Immediately he arrived Reading was faced with the urgent problem of Food. The Americans, as you know, had fallen far short of their promised deliveries for January and February. This time it was not a question of ships, as there was enough tonnage available. The difficulty was that the Administration could not transport the food to the seaports. This was partly due to a general breakdown of the railroad organization, and partly due to the exceptionally bad weather which tied up a lot of the railroads for days at a time. The Government in control of the railroads took various measures to remedy this, and have succeeded to a large extent; but the truth is that the railways running from the Middle West farming districts and the great industrial centres to the eastern seaboard are not capable of handling the produce of the country. . . .

Reading is excellent in dealing with the Food Controller, Railways, Treasury and shipping people. He masters each complicated subject himself, and is very patient and tactful in dealing with the Ministers at Washington. He has established also a dominant position among the Allied Ambassadors, who seem willing to let him take the lead in joint negotiations. This, of course, is all very excellent. It is not easy work for a British Ambassador, as you can well imagine. At every turn he is met by the obvious but unpleasant truth that we are very largely in the hands of the American Administration – that they are in a position almost to dictate the war policy of the Allies. This would make any lesser man irritable and disheartened, but Reading knows them well enough to realize that the President at any rate is in no mind to misuse his great power, or take advantage of difficulties in which the Allies may find themselves. But, of course, it does make negotiations very hard.

Politically they are so unfamiliar with European, in fact with international, affairs that the Foreign Ambassador must be very patient indeed. The Administration also seemed inclined to be slow to face unpleasant truths; particularly they still cling to the hope that they may still 'talk' the Germans into a just peace. But this attitude must not be mistaken for any weakening in their determination to win. After they have done their talking, you will find they will go on fighting whatever the sacrifices may be.[19]

The second main area of Reading's ambassadorial activities was concerned with the overall diplomatic conduct of the war. This was far more complex, yielded less tangible results than matters of supply, and it is clear that Reading found his work here less fulfilling. The delicacy needed in urging the United States to commit itself to war more fully, both morally and materially, was considerable.

The great German counter-offensive beginning on 21 March 1918 on the Western front, however, did much of Lord Reading's advocacy for him. With its ranks swollen by the divisions switched from the Eastern front after the peace treaty signed with the Bolshevik government at Brest-Litovsk on 3 March 1918, the German army threatened to drive a wedge between the British and French forces. By 23 March the British Fifth Army was in full retreat to the Somme and the German advance seemed irresistible.

Hitherto the United States had been slow to commit its troops to the battlefield. Instead of the agreed seventeen divisions to be in France by March, only four were actually in Europe, and those four not yet in the front line. Reinforcements were desperately needed on the Western front to stop the German advance and to counterbalance the forces recently released from the Eastern front. Reading was helped to stress the urgency of the position by the response of American public opinion to the great German offensive. His summary of this sea change was promptly cabled to the Foreign Office:

Effect of the great battle on American public opinion is wholly advantageous to the Allied cause. Nothing has occurred since America entered the War which has stirred more fully the national feeling or united the people so thoroughly against Germany. Display of German military power is a shock to America and the people at large realize for the first time that the Allies in general and England in particular have been standing between her and German militarism. It has produced feeling of admiration and sympathy for the British, quite contrary to the usual attitude. People of America are for the War and anxious to know how they can most effectively help. They have realized as it were in a flash their own military shortcomings and time they have lost since they entered the War. This has already produced outburst in the Press and Congress which naturally enough takes form of attack on the Administration. ...

To the Administration the battle has been no less of a shock. They had hoped and believed that the effect of the President's speeches had been to strengthen Liberal party in Germany and sap morale of the Army and influence of the military party. Today they are very conscious of their delusion and realize that there is no hope that speeches and propaganda will turn the German people against their military party or detach Austria from Germany. At last they face the fact that, if Germany is to be beaten, she must be beaten by force.[20]

To capitalize upon this changing mood, Reading made use of his invitation to address the Lotus Club in New York on 27 March by asking Lloyd George to send a telegram of exhortation that could be read out to the audience.

Lloyd George responded promptly and Reading was able to read out the following telegram which, though unashamedly melodramatic in parts, expressed the dire circumstances of the Allied position on the Western front:

We are at the crisis of the War. Attacked by an immense superiority of German troops our Army has been forced to retire. The retirement has been carried out methodically before the pressure of a steady succession of fresh German reserves which are suffering enormous losses. The situation is being faced with splendid courage and resolution. The dogged pluck of our troops has for the moment checked the ceaseless onrush of the enemy and the French have now joined in the struggle.

But this battle, the greatest and most momentous in the history of the world, is only just beginning. Throughout it French and British are buoyed up with the knowledge that the great Republic of the West will neglect no effort which can hasten its troops and its ships to Europe. In war, time is vital. It is impossible to exaggerate the importance of getting American reinforcements across the Atlantic in the shortest possible space of time.[21]

To ram home the urgency of the situation, the Prime Minister dispatched a second telegram for President Wilson calling for American troops to be poured into the broken Allied lines. Reading received this cable on 28 March and as soon as it was deciphered drove to the White House to see the President.

Reading's interview with Wilson ended satisfactorily with the President for once showing his inner feelings when bidding farewell: 'Mr Ambassador,' he said, putting his hand on Reading's shoulder in an untypical show of warmth, 'you need say no more. I'll do my damnedest!'

However, unknown to Reading at the time, only Colonel House's intervention had prevented an unpleasant 'diplomatic incident'. According to House, Wilson had been 'much annoyed at Lloyd George's [first] cable to Reading and at Reading's lack of judgement in reading it'. The President felt that 'it was most discourteous to give out publicly a message from his Government directly to the people of another country without addressing it to the head of that Government. He said it was sufficient cause to send an ambassador home.' House smoothed the President's ruffled feelings, telling him, 'it was all meant in good part, and that Reading himself had no diplomatic experience. I thought we ought not to be too critical since he was our sincere friend and doing the best he knew.'[22]

Despite President Wilson's personal assurances of active support, it was still necessary to badger the Americans into quickly sending as many troops as possible across the Atlantic. On 29 March Lloyd George cabled once more and asked Reading to see Wilson again and ask for the embarkation of 120,000 infantry a month for the next four months. Wilson detected 'a note of alarm which was almost panic in the telegram' [of 29 March], and remarked to Reading: 'I hope your Generals are not as rattled as your politicians.' Reading's feelings were also depressed at this critical moment of the war, and House observed, on 30 March, that 'He is very nervous and anxious, and Wiseman and I have to be constantly around to cheer him up.'

Joseph and Sarah Isaacs,
Rufus's parents, on their
Golden Wedding day, 25 July 1905

Below: Rufus aged eleven and a half
standing by the side of
his brother Godfrey

Below right: Rufus Isaacs, aged
twenty-six, the rake of Belsize Park,
soon to be transformed into
the brilliant barrister

Above left: Rufus Isaacs, QC

Above: Liberal lawyers: Isaacs (right) Attorney-General, with John Simon, the Solicitor General, at a levée at St James's Palace in 1911

Sir Rufus and Lady Isaacs walking to St Paul's to attend a thanksgiving service in February 1912 for George V's safe return from India after his durbar

Above: Asquith, Prime Minister 1908–16.
He resolutely supported Isaacs during
the Marconi scandal

Above right: Godfrey Isaacs, Rufus's
younger brother, photographed in
October 1912 at the height of
the Marconi controversy

Max Beerbohm's ironic view of the
Marconi scandal showing Isaacs
besieged by members of the Liberal
Cabinet. The caption reads: 'Some
Ministers of the Crown, who
(monstrous though it seem) have
severally some spare pounds to invest,
implore Sir Rufus Isaacs to tell them
if he knows of any stocks which they
could buy without fear of ultimate
profit.' From left: Winston Churchill,
Colonel Seely, Asquith, Sir Edward
Grey, Isaacs, Reginald McKennon,
Augustine Birrell, John Burns, Lewis
Harcourt.

Lloyd George, flanked by his two 'Guardians', Isaacs and Charles Masterman (left) on the government front ben A Max Beerbohm cartoo

Lloyd George at Cannes in February 1913 with Sir Rufus and Lady Isaacs

A grim-faced Lord Reading, the
newly appointed Lord Chief Justice,
leads the procession to the Lord
Chancellor's breakfast in 1913

Wartime associates: Colonel
House (left) and President Woodrow
Wilson photographed in 1918

Lord and Lady Reading in Viceregal poses

The Viceroy and Vicereine are welcomed at Victoria Station at the start
of a period of leave in April 1925 by the Secretary of State for India,
Lord Birkenhead (centre, with walking stick) and assorted officials and relations

Old friends: Margot Asquith bids Reading
farewell before his return to India
in July 1925

The Viceroy about to shoot a tiger in the line
of duty. Reading's marksmanship
left much to be desired

The human touch: the Viceroy doffs his sun hat to respectful subjects
at Calcutta before beginning the first part of his journey home
in February 1926

Reading as Foreign Secretary in the first National government in 1931.
BACK ROW (from left): Sir Philip Cunliffe-Lister, J.H. Thomas, Reading,
Neville Chamberlain, Sir Samuel Hoare. FRONT ROW: Philip Snowden,
Stanley Baldwin, Ramsay MacDonald, Sir Herbert Samuel, Lord Sankey

Below left: Reading with his second wife, formerly Stella Charnaud, after their wedding in 1931;
below right: Reading, the newly installed Lord Warden and Admiral of the Cinque Ports, inspects
the Silver Oar, his symbol of office, at Dover in June 1934

Reading could hardly have been cheered up by a telegram from Lloyd George received on 2 April 1918:

Urgent. Secret.
London. April 2, 1918. It is very difficult for you at this distance, without being in close touch with the realities of the position, to realize how success or disaster in this battle will be decided by the exertions which America puts forth in the next few weeks or even days. I believe that the German chances now depend mainly upon whether or not America can get her troops effectively into the line in time. The difference of even a week in the date of arrival may be absolutely vital. In this contest an advance of a week in the arrival of troops may win a battle, and the delay of a week may lose it. And remember that no troops can be put into the battle line for at least a month after they land. They must be put through the final training by men acquainted with the conditions at first hand and this, I understand, is alone possible in France. . . .[23]

In fact, as Reading was able to inform the Prime Minister, the American government was committed to calling up fresh drafts at the rate of 150,000 a month. Although this was enormously encouraging, a further obstacle to the plan's smooth implementation soon presented itself.

Essentially the new problem centred on who was to command the American troops pouring into the Western front. General Pershing, commander of the American forces, had no intention of letting his divisions be absorbed into the British and French armies in Europe. Partly as a counter, he now insisted that he could only agree to 60,000 infantry per month being shipped to France in British vessels.

With a second massive German offensive beginning on 9 April and the Allied armies near to disintegration, this muddle had to be sorted out as soon as possible. Wilson was inclined to overrule Pershing, though in a somewhat ambiguous manner. In London the British War Cabinet, with French backing, named General Foch as 'commander-in-chief of the Allied armies' on 14 April.

After frantic negotiations between Reading, Wilson and House in Washington, the American War Department issued a memorandum on 19 April which confirmed the promise to transport 120,000 troops (infantry and machine-gunners) per month to France, but which declined to place them under General Foch's overall command, instead leaving them 'under the direction and at the discretion of General Pershing' to 'be assigned for training and use with British, French or American divisions, as the exigencies of the situation from time to time require'.

Reading cabled the War Cabinet to accept this agreement as the best that could be done. He believed that Wilson meant to stick to his original undertaking, and was merely making concessions to Pershing's pride. Pershing, however, proceeded to upset the already shaky understanding between the United States' War Department and the Allies by concluding a separate agreement with Lord Milner, newly appointed Secretary of State for War, while on a visit to London at the end of April 1918.

The Milner-Pershing agreement, though confirming that six American divisions would be shipped during May, also stipulated that afterwards artillery and other divisional units should be sent over so that 'American divisions and corps, when trained and organized, shall be utilized under the American commander-in-chief in an American group'.

Reading was keenly disappointed by this development, and felt his impotence to alter the arrangements effectively. In this he was at least at one with Lloyd George and, to a lesser extent, with President Wilson. In the event, Pershing's obstructive tactics inflicted little damage on the Allied cause: the German April offensive was contained, General Foch's position could accommodate American military independence, and American troops did arrive in large numbers in Europe – 950,000 between 1 April and 31 July 1918, and in August and September at a monthly average of over 280,000. By early autumn it was clear that Germany's spring offensive had failed and that victory was now the Allies' for the taking, no matter that Foch, far from precisely controlling the armies nominally under him, was merely 'a conductor who beat time well'.

The Ambassador's difficulties over the American reinforcements for the Western front were not lightened by an extraordinary diplomatic incident in the middle of May 1918. Sir Robert Borden, the Canadian Prime Minister, received, in the weekly information sent by the Ministry of Information in London on the progress of the war, the following statement, apparently from the War Cabinet, that the Allies 'are so confident that, having been given the choice of a small immediate American army for defence or waiting until they are reinforced by a complete, powerful, self-supporting American army, they have chosen the latter'.

This was clearly nonsense, and ran counter to all that Reading had been struggling to achieve. To clear up the confusion, and without waiting for advice from London, he immediately issued a strong denial, and told the Foreign Office: 'It is obvious a glaring blunder has been committed and I trust recurrence will be prevented by strong measures.'

It turned out that the error had originated with the compiler of the telegram at the Foreign Office. Reading rushed to Ottawa to investigate and to set matters straight. Although some American newspapers tried to exploit the mistake, the President and the bulk of the American people were firmly committed to aiding the Allies as quickly as possible, and the incident was merely deeply embarrassing for a few days.

Apart from his main task of helping to co-ordinate the United States' war effort with that of the Allied powers, Lord Reading had to cope with several other pressing problems of policy.

One of these concerned Allied policy towards Bolshevik Russia. The Russian Revolution of 1917 had effectively ended Russia's participation in the war, and in March 1918 the Bolshevik government had signed a separate peace treaty with Germany at Brest-Litovsk. The dramatic effect of this settlement upon the balance of power on the Western front has been described earlier in the chapter.

Apart from tilting the balance against Germany by rushing American troops to France, there was another, complementary, strategy. This involved the reopening of a second front in the far east of Russia, thus drawing German divisions away from the Western front and at the same time encouraging the Russians to resist German colonization of the Ukraine and other food-producing areas. There was a further motive lurking behind these relatively honourable ones. If an Allied force could establish itself in eastern Russia, it might be possible to give assistance to elements fighting the Red Army and even 'to strangle Bolshevism in its cradle' as Winston Churchill and certain other Western politicians wanted to do.

Unfortunately the Allied powers were not in agreement over what to do. The British government, for instance, worked its way round to an interventionist policy. In February 1918 the Foreign Secretary, Balfour, had put the current British point of view in a telegram to William Wiseman:

The internal affairs of Russia are no concern of ours. We only consider them in so far as they affect the war. If at this moment large parts of the country accept the particular type of Socialism favoured by the Bolsheviks, this is the affair of Russia, not of Britain, and it appears to us quite irrelevant to the problem of diplomatic recognition. Full and complete recognition of the Bolshevik Government is at present impossible, and a complete rupture is very undesirable.[24]

By April 1918, however, with the armies on the Western front reeling back before the German offensive, the Foreign Office attitude had changed. On 19 April Reading received a Foreign Office cypher, sent at the request of the War Cabinet, that argued cogently for intervention:

> if we are to win the war we must treat Europe and Asia as a single front, for the purpose not of command, but of strategy. . . .
>
> We must therefore create an effective Allied front in the East. . . . If we could bring about a national revival in Russia such as freed Russia from the despotism of Napoleon, very great results might ensue. . . .
>
> [Trotsky now shows signs] that he recognizes that cooperation with the Allies in a war to free Russia from German domination is the only hope either of Russia or the Revolution, or possibly for the maintenance of his own power.[25]

But where could this second front be opened? Japan, Britain's loyal ally since 1902, solved the problem in April 1918 by landing a small force of marines at Vladivostok with the avowed intent of protecting Japanese nationals in that part of the world, though with the more serious purpose of arousing Cossack and other anti-Bolshevik, and anti-German, elements.

Of the other major Allied powers, Britain's response was also to send a small force of troops to Vladivostok to ensure that the Japanese presence there was transformed into an Allied presence. France, more closely pressed than its Allies by the great spring German offensive, strongly supported the intervention. Only the United States hung back on the grounds that American policy did not include interference in the domestic affairs of foreign states. There was, moreover, growing anti-Japanese sentiment in the United States – particularly on the Pacific coast, which not only had a considerable number of Japanese immigrants, but which had most to fear from Japan's potential for aggressive expansion.

Despite Reading's arguments, the most that Wilson would do was to accept the principle of Anglo-Japanese intervention at Vladivostok. However, Reading was instructed further to ask the President whether his government would co-operate with Britain in giving practical assistance to the Bolshevik government in the event of renewed German aggression, and whether the Americans would send some sort of force to the Far East. This initiative was blunted by Wilson's refusal at this stage to be drawn into an interventionist policy, and Reading reported back to Balfour on 5 May 1918 that, 'There is a steady influence on the President which makes him decline to commit himself. It is partly that the reports he receives make him very apprehensive of the effect upon the Russian people and partly because he thinks the military advantage will not be worth the risk.'[26]

On 22 May Wilson again told Reading that he thought the moment for intervention 'inopportune, in other words that he did not think the circumstances sufficiently warranted the proposed action'. In fact Paul Reinsch, the United States Minister in China, had just told the President in a dispatch that the chaos in Siberia opened the way for an Allied initiative – the sending of a relief commission to reconstruct Siberia economically and place the region in the Allied camp.

Wilson was favourably inclined towards this scheme and on 29 May told William Wiseman of his doubts over the feasibility of creating a Russian front but that he did favour sending 'a Civil Commission of British, French and Americans to Russia to help organize the railroads and food supplies, and, since currency is worthless, to organize a system of barter. . . .' He was still firmly opposed to relying mainly upon the Japanese.

On 21 June 1918 Reading had managed to convince Colonel House that 'something must be done immediately about Russia, otherwise it will become the prey of Germany. It has now become a question of days rather than months.' House proceeded to urge the President to send out the proposed relief mission.

The delicacy of diplomatic relations with Russia was plainly illustrated a few days later. Alexander Kerensky, who had been ousted as the leader of the Provisional Russian government when the Bolsheviks seized power in October 1917, wanted to come to the United States to argue the case for intervention – and, incidentally, for his own return to power. Reading was anxious lest Kerensky should upset his diplomatic campaign to commit the United States to intervention. He sent a secret telegram to Balfour on 24 June, saying:

It would be most unfortunate if M. Kerensky came here at present. There is a distinct movement here in favour of some steps being taken as regards intervention in Russia. President is now considering matter and will probably in a short time consult you as to his proposals before making an announcement in public. If he made it soon after M. Kerensky's arrival, it would be most unfortunate.

Colonel House whom I have seen and to whom I have mentioned your telegram feels very strongly upon advisability of Kerensky's arrival at present. I trust M. Kerensky's arrival may be postponed. . . .[27]

Although Kerensky was prevented from coming to plead his cause in America, the President still prevaricated over intervention, despite a strongly worded appeal from Foch on 27 June.

Early in July, however, events in the Far East helped to move Wilson more towards supporting intervention. On 3 July Reading called on the President and presented a document from the British, French and Italian Prime Ministers, and approved by the Supreme War Council, that claimed that 'a complete change had come over the situation in Russia and Siberia, which makes Allied intervention in these countries an imperative necessity'.

The 'complete change' was the result of the military success of the Czech Legion which had captured Vladivostok from its Bolshevik government at the end of June 1918. The Czech Legion was a force, led by Thomas Masaryk and composed of some 300,000 Czechs who had deserted to Russia from the armies of the Austrian Empire, and which had been formed into a unit dedicated to the overthrow of the Central Powers in exchange for Allied backing for the eventual establishment of a Czech national state. After the Treaty of Brest-Litovsk, however, the Czechs had fought their way eastwards, believing that the Bolshevik authorities meant to intern them and thus prevent them from giving active military support to the Allies.

After the Czech Legion had captured Vladivostok, and set up a government sympathetic to the Allied cause, Britain sent a battalion of troops there from Hong Kong to support them. These events put extra pressure on President Wilson to take action, and on 8 July he told House: 'I have been sweating blood what is right and feasible to do in Russia. It goes to pieces like quicksilver under my touch, but I hope I see and can report some progress presently along the double lines of economic assistance and aid to the Czechoslovaks.'

Lord Reading promptly cabled Lloyd George on 12 July with his assessment of the situation:

The overthrow of the Czar and establishment of a republic was welcomed with the utmost enthusiasm in America. The sympathy and hope for the new republic was, I believe, far stronger and more genuine here than in Europe. Ever since the question of intervention was first discussed, Americans have feared that the interventionist movement would be controlled by friends of the old Imperial régime, and, however disguised, intervention would eventually prove to be a reactionary weapon and an anti-republican influence. Further, the President is apprehensive lest any intervention should be converted into an anti-Soviet movement and an interference with the right of Russians to choose their own form of government. . . .

We should take care to reassure opinion here in order to carry the President with us in any further movement that may become necessary. At present his intention is to help the Czechoslovaks, but nevertheless as I read his mind, it is still opposed to intervention and somewhat apprehensive lest the step he is now willing to take should lead him into a much more extended policy. It is for this reason that I think it is important to give a liberal turn to our assistance to Russia. . . .[28]

The 'liberal turn' which Reading suggested was that the Prime Minister should send to Siberia, in addition to military officers, 'a labour or socialist delegation headed by some prominent labour leader'. Arthur Murray, now back in London, told Wiseman on 16 July that 'The idea seems to me to be a very good one . . . but a very delicate one to handle and carry out.' Nothing, however, came of this good idea.

Reading had also shown a similar sensitivity to Bolshevik (and American) feelings when he had vetoed Lloyd George's suggestion that General Knox, who was sent by the British government to Siberia to sound out the situation, should make the journey via Washington and discuss the problem with the President. Reading cabled the Foreign Office on 14 July that this would be a mistake since Knox 'is much too identified with past regimes and there is too much suspicion given that Allies (confidential, chiefly the French but also ourselves) are striving for a reactionary political regime and especially are anti-Sovyet [sic] in their policy. Nothing makes President more apprehensive than notion that intervention may develop by Allies taking sides in political contest.'[29]

Reading's restraint in dealing with the American administration's misgivings over the interventionist strategy was recognized by William Wiseman when he cabled to Drummond at the Foreign Office that 'Lord Reading realizes that undue pressure on President, and particularly too many interviews with him, may have the opposite effect to that desired, but he is taking every opportunity of pressing firmly but tactfully the policy of HM Government'.[30]

On 17 July Reading's patience was rewarded with the news that President Wilson had agreed to the dispatch of a small number of American troops to Vladivostok, and also to Murmansk, 'to guard the military stores at Kola, and to make it safe for Russian forces to come together in organized bodies in the north. But [the United States] can go no further. It is not in a position . . . to take part in organized intervention in adequate force from either Vladivostok or Murmansk and Archangel. . . .'

Before he sailed for Britain at the end of July for a period of consultation and reflection, Reading tried to reassure Wilson that America would not be dragged into a policy of interference in Russia's domestic affairs. But he left the President convinced that he had only decided to back intervention to placate Allied demands for action.

As it happened, by the spring of 1919 there were only some 7,500

American troops in Siberia against 28,000 Japanese, 12,000 Poles, 4,000 each of Canadians, Serbians and Romanians, 2,000 Italians, 1,600 British and 750 French. The military achievements of these interventionist forces did nothing to alter the balance of political power within Russia and very little to undermine Germany's war effort during the last few months of the First World War, although further eastwards German expansion was blocked. The American presence was of more symbolic than practical use, and grudging at that. Even in September 1918, Colville Barclay, at the Washington Embassy, sent a cyphered telegram to Reading in Britain warning him 'that there is a strong feeling in highest quarters here that French and British Government [sic] are trying to force the hand of the Administration, not merely in Siberian matter but in general, it being even thought that the British Military Mission was sent for the purpose of "rushing them"'.[31]

Reading replied on 19 September:

Very Secret and Personal.
Let me know if you detect any signs of improved relations between US Administration and ourselves. I am neglecting no opportunity here to promote a better situation, and have reason to think our friends there are doing their utmost to help.[32]

By January 1920, with power more or less securely in Bolshevik hands, the last Allied forces were withdrawn from Archangel, and the way was clear for the eventual rise of Soviet Russia to the status of super power – a position to be uneasily shared with the United States.

While in Washington, Reading had to deal with several other matters of major concern. One of these was the problem of Irish home rule. Given the strength of the Irish-American community's feeling, and its political power within Wilson's Democratic party, there was bound to be renewed pressure on Britain, once the United States had entered the war, to move towards an equitable solution of the 'Irish problem'.

Reading, as the judge who had condemned Sir Roger Casement to death, was not, at first sight, the ideal ambassador to placate Irish-American hostility towards British policy in Ireland. Nor did the apparent determination of the British government to put the home rule problem into cold storage for the duration of the war make the Ambassador's task any easier.

As it happened, Reading was soon urging London to make a positive step over the home rule issue, and at the same time to keep him fully informed of any developments. Early in April 1918 he complained to Drummond at the Foreign Office that, 'I am asked [about developments] in high quarters and, as I know nothing and I think they obtain information elsewhere, it produces the impression that I do not wish to tell them.'[33] Drummond cabled back his agreement the next day.

Drummond's assurances were not, however, acted upon in full. On 16 May 1918 Balfour cabled Reading warning him that the government was about to arrest some prominent Sinn Fein leaders under the Defence of the Realm Act for allegedly conspiring to raise rebellion in Ireland with German backing. Reading replied on 4 June, complaining that he had been kept in the dark over the contents of documents allegedly implicating the Sinn Fein leaders, and asking, with justifiable impatience, how he was going to back up the government's conspiracy theory in America without knowing all the facts.[34]

This example of slipshod government communication with the Embassy in Washington was all the more infuriating in view of Reading's conviction that the War Cabinet should make an immediate grant of home rule to Ireland. On 15 April 1918 he had cabled Arthur Murray to put these views before the Cabinet:

To carry opinion here, and particularly Irish opinion of moderate tendencies, it would be necessary for the British Government to declare its intention not only to stake its existence on the passing of a Home Rule measure but also its intention to put the Act into operation at once. The fundamental trouble is that unfortunately the Irish and their friends have lost confidence in the passing of an Act. What they require is to see an Act put into operation by a Government that will not shrink from it if serious opposition is raised. If the Government is pledged to Home Rule and strives without delay to pass it, the President will, I think, find satisfactory answers to any representations made.[35]

Lloyd George, ever anxious to reach compromise behind the scenes, had in fact been involved in secret negotiations with Irish nationalists, through the Irish Convention, since the winter of 1917. Reading's cable of 15 April 1918 was thus warmly received by the bulk of the Cabinet who then decided to offer the Irish a deal: accept conscription (which had only been applied to the mainland since 1916), and home rule would shortly follow.

Reading had misgivings over this sequence, quite apart from the problems of Ulster Protestant resistance to anything like coercion. He returned, on 5 May, to his advocacy of prompt action, telling Lloyd George: 'If only you can get a good Home Rule Bill into operation, the effect here will be very marked and will remove almost the chief cause of anti-British feeling.' He also told Murray that 'The intelligent American understands that of course Ulster cannot be sacrificed, but he fails to understand why it cannot be safeguarded. Generally my impression is that America would welcome a fair and generous treatment of Ulster, provided it forms part of the Government of Ireland.' Reading believed that a generous Irish settlement would satisfy everyone except 'the extremists who would never be satisfied'.

Apart from advocating immediate home rule, Reading had, early in his ambassadorship, made informal contacts with certain leaders of Irish-American opinion. Shane Leslie, son of a Unionist baronet, a convert to both Irish nationalism and Roman Catholicism, and now an American citizen, was invited to dine at the Embassy. Leslie was instrumental in arranging a meeting between Reading and Cardinal Gibbons, the influential Archbishop of Baltimore. Reading met Gibbons first at Baltimore, where a bottle of Rhine wine on the luncheon table prompted the Cardinal to remark genially: 'Here is a protest against two tendencies of our age, prohibition and the idea that we should not take advantage of anything good the enemy may produce!'

The two men later met in February on 'neutral' territory, the rectory of St Aloysius church in Washington, where Shane Leslie announced them epigrammatically saying to Gibbons, 'Your Eminence, I introduce the Old Testament to the New!' According to Leslie, the two men ('their profiles made a splendid picture') got on so well that 'Given full powers they could have settled the troubles of Dublin and Jerusalem.'

It transpired, rather alarmingly, from these meetings that the Pope wished to sit at any future peace conference! More realistically, Reading saw in his friendship with Cardinal Gibbons a means of furthering President Wilson's policy of detaching Catholic Austria from her alliance with Germany. On 14 May 1918 Reading told Eric Drummond at the Foreign Office that he would try to get 'one of the United States' cardinals to write to the Pope urging him to make effective the President's policy of detaching Austria. Could the cardinal be assured that such a letter would be sent on its way "unread"?'[36] A few days later, however, Reading recognized that the President was unwilling to negotiate directly with the Vatican and that he could thus not press the matter hard.

The Lloyd George plan for Irish conscription plus home rule had, meanwhile, come to nothing. The arrest of the Sinn Fein leaders in May 1918 signalled the end of such aspirations. There was to be no immediate grant of home rule, and on 17 May Walter Long, Tory Colonial Secretary in the wartime coalition government, told Reading that the 1914 Home Rule Act 'has been vetoed by all parties in many of its most important provisions', and that the government must therefore draw up what amounted to a new scheme, and for this to be done properly extra time was needed. The government was, however, according to Long, quite sincere in its desire to introduce home rule. Could Reading please explain all of this to President Wilson?[37]

So, despite a brief flowering of hope, promoted skilfully by Reading, that home rule could be speedily introduced, the settlement of Irish nationalist aspirations had to wait until the untidy compromise of 1921-2.

If the British government continued to struggle in the bogs of Irish nationalism, Reading was able to offer far greater satisfaction to American Jews. The Balfour Declaration of 1917 had offered Palestine to world Jewry as a national homeland. General Allenby's conquest of Palestine, and the symbolically significant occupation of Jerusalem at the end of 1917, brought the fulfilment of this dream much nearer – despite the inconvenient fact that the proposed Jewish national home was already inhabited by an Arab population.

Reading's arrival in the United States in January 1918 was enthusiastically received by American Jews, of whom one of the most influential was Mr Justice Brandeis, later a Supreme Court judge.

The new Ambassador was deluged with invitations to speak at Zionist and Jewish functions and meetings, and to contribute articles to Jewish journals. Although he declined all but a very few of these requests, it did seem necessary to make some sort of public statement to satisfy American Jewry anxious to see flesh put on to the bare bones of the Balfour Declaration.

Accordingly a press release appeared on 27 March 1918 in Reading's name. The statement was warmly appreciative of the American Jewish and Zionist contribution to the war effort. It also paid tribute to the Jewish recruits about to serve overseas: 'It would be magnificent if some of them could strike a blow for the freedom of the world in the land of our ancestors.' Reading waxed enthusiastic over the investment of Jewish money and settlers in Palestine, saying, 'My good wishes are with the Zionists in the United States in the great work that is before them in giving effect to the Declaration of the British Government, and I shall esteem anything that I may be called upon to do in connection with that work as not the least important or the least satisfactory part of my duties as British Ambassador in Washington.'

Ironically, Reading was himself lukewarm to the cause of Zionism. Indeed he did not even bother to draft the statement of 27 March, leaving it to Arthur Willert, saying 'You see, I have no great personal sympathy with Zionism. Why should I have? Here I am, Ambassador, Lord Chief Justice, Peer, and I started from nothing. I owe it all to

England. I am English. How can I help it if I don't feel strongly about a national home for the Jews?'[38]

Of course someone with Reading's spectacular public success and considerable private wealth was not an obvious recruit for the labour of citrus farming in parched deserts, but there is more to it than that. His robust rejection of orthodox religion when a boy, aided and abetted by his mother's lack of faith, had made him unenthusiastic for religious zealotry. Nor did a passion for Zionist activity square with Reading's dapper English image, shining top hat and all.

In this respect Reading was destined throughout his life to be a disappointment to those who expected him actively to promote Jewish and Zionist causes. When approached for his support in Zionist causes his response was almost invariably rational, even guarded, as if, like his other emotions, any residual feelings of Jewishness must be kept from public view. A brief survey of his career clearly confirms this view.

He responded generously enough to requests for financial support: from the Serbian Chief Rabbi in 1915, for example, who appealed to 'your own well-known sympathy with the unfortunate ones of our race in general',[39] and in October 1918, from Israel Cohen of the National Jewish Fund, who asked for money on the grounds of the 'sympathy that you recently expressed with Zionist aspirations when your Lordship was in the United States . . .'.[40] In September 1914 Field Marshal Lord Roberts of Kandahar made an appeal of a different nature, asking Reading to help recruit Jews into the British army by speaking at a meeting. In May 1917 Alfred Milner suggested to Lloyd George that Reading should lead a group of British Jews to revolutionary Russia to help counteract the pro-German propaganda being spread by Jews sympathetic to the Central Powers within Russian Jewry.[41] Reading took no part in the proposal.

Although in 1921 and 1923 Herbert Samuel, High Commissioner to Palestine from 1920 to 1925, wrote Reading letters explaining the progress of Zionist settlement there,[42] it is difficult to imagine Reading enthusing over the news, and impossible to see him accepting Samuel's post. As early as March 1916 Reading had written Edwin Montagu a lengthy and by no means orthodox appraisal of the Jewish question, giving almost grudging support to the idea of Palestine as the Jewish homeland:

The moment one considers the Jewish question one realizes that its aspects differ so materially according to the country of which Jews are subjects that it is impossible to regard them as a nation. In England, for example, a Jew is an

Englishman with the religious beliefs of a Jew, but I doubt whether it is so with a Russian Jew.

But even so – those with whom I have discussed the subject and speak with authority tell me that the Russian Jew clings to Russia, if he can only manage to struggle on there.

I am emphatically of the opinion that to put them in a position of privileged ascendancy over other races with the status of a nation under an International Protectorate would be injurious to them. Wherever they reside they would be regarded as aliens.

One hates to think that anything one may say or do would help to prevent realization of an ideal which attracts so many who are less fortunate than we who live in this country.

Instead I think it [the idea of Palestine] would appeal to the [majority] as it does to you and also to me – equal political rights with religious liberty in all countries and with facilities for administration in Palestine, with special rights in those parts where the Jews are in the majority, would seem to be the right policy.[43]

There is a detachment about this letter which is significant and in keeping with Reading's views on Jewishness. For example, Reading mostly refers to Jews as 'they', not 'we', and it is as if he was analysing a problem of which he did not fundamentally consider himself a part.

Later, the rise to power of Hitler and the Nazis had the effect of making Reading rather more actively sympathetic to the plight of fellow Jews in Germany and more resolute in his defence of the national homeland in Palestine. In October 1930 he spoke in the House of Lords chiding the government for appearing to retreat from its commitment to the principle of a national homeland. At the same time he prefaced his remarks with a denial of active Zionist sympathies:

Let me state first that I have never been a member of the Zionist Association; I have never been a member of the Jewish Agency, or taken any active part in the work of Palestine. My interest in the main is as a citizen of this country and, I will add, as a member of the Jewish community.[44]

Four years afterwards, with Hitler in his second year of power, Reading wrote to Wauchcope, the Governor of Palestine, saying that he was 'deeply concerned in Palestine and the National Home and am anxious to find opportunities of settling German Jewish Refugees of the more advanced and cultured type there'.[45] All the same, he prefaced his remarks by saying, 'As you know I am not a Zionist', and eight months later, in November 1934, once more wrote to Wauchcope, putting the case for closer co-operation with the Arabs:

I have always maintained that there will be no true security for Judaism in Palestine until there is more employment by Jews of Arabs, more mixing of the two peoples and consequent understanding and goodwill.[46]

It was, indeed, quite consistent with his feelings on the subject of race and religion that, when he remarried in August 1931, a year and a half after his first wife's death, the second Lady Reading should have been a gentile, Miss Stella Charnaud. They were married in a Registry Office.

In his *Rufus Isaacs*, published a year after Lord Reading's death, Stanley Jackson gave a good summary of his subject's attitude to Jewishness, especially to those Jews lucky enough to live under British liberalism:

His race proved no obstacle to success. He did not regard his Jewishness as a kind of poor relation. Unlike so many Jews, Rufus Isaacs did not shun his compatriots and eagerly seek out Gentiles. He had no Ghetto complex and was equally at home with Jews and Gentiles. He was proud of his race and never afraid to justify that pride. But he blended his Jewish intensity with the diplomatic moderation of a man of the world. On Rufus Isaacs' lips racial pride was never a challenge of defiance. Years later, he was to remind the Jewish community that there was 'no bar, by reason of religion or race, to the position which a man might attain to in this country'.[47]

Whatever his private views, Lord Reading's Jewish origins were a positive advantage during his Washington ambassadorship. By May 1918, however, he was not measuring his satisfaction by the plaudits of American Jewry. On 30 May he cabled Lloyd George and Balfour asking to be allowed to come home after July, or at least by October, when the courts resumed, to discuss whether he had to continue as ambassador.

Balfour replied on 5 June saying:

I cannot express to you how much Prime Minister and I appreciate the work you are doing in US. From every quarter, whether Democratic or Republican, testimony arrives of great value of your services in your present position. We feel that it is of highest national interest that you should prolong your period of appointment beyond that originally stipulated though we fully understand greatness of sacrifice we ask you to make.

We cannot think in the circumstances the judiciary would insist on your early return to your high office, as, however great their deprivation may be, it is after all domestic, while duties you are now executing are essential to effective prosecution of the War and cannot be performed by another.

We therefore sincerely trust that you will consent to continue your Ambassadorship. . . .[48]

Why did Reading wish to leave the Washington Embassy, perhaps permanently, in the summer of 1918? As we have seen, the judicial bench held no seductive glamour for him; rather he viewed his duties as Lord Chief Justice as a chore. His wife's health at this time seemed good enough. His work as ambassador had been almost universally acclaimed. There was demonstrably enough variety and prestige attached to his post. Was there, perhaps, yet another echo of the restless, ambitious side of Rufus Isaacs's personality: having conquered Washington, and with America's increasing military presence about to tip the balance on the Western front, did he long for a more stimulating, more central role in any future peacemaking? Certainly he was shortly to become closely involved in the peacemaking process.

Of course, his Embassy in Washington had not been without its frustrations. Early in June 1918 he sent an uncharacteristically sharp telegram to Lloyd George and Balfour complaining that he had just learnt from the American newspapers that honours had been awarded to members of the British War Mission in the United States

without any reference or communication with me. ... To my amazement I find matter of recognition of services of men under me has been taken out of my hands without first consulting me or even informing me of proposals. ... I need not tell you that my authority and influence are not likely to be enhanced by course taken in London.[49]

The tone adopted by Reading in this telegram is not that of a man basking in his contemporaries' warm appreciation. A major cause of his disenchantment with Washington undoubtedly lay in what he considered to be his failure to establish a really close diplomatic relationship with President Wilson. William Wiseman gave this problem an airing in an astute letter written to Eric Drummond on 19 July shortly before Reading sailed for Britain:

You may find it difficult to persuade Reading to return here permanently. He is disappointed that the President has not taken him more into his confidence. While this is perfectly true – and I think a great mistake from the President's own point of view – I am sure that the President likes him and that he can get more out of the Administration than anyone I can think of. In all respects he has been an unqualified success – the French and Italian representatives just follow after him. He has raised our influence and prestige right throughout the country. Among all the people of both political parties he is a great favorite [sic], and has made friends and no enemies wherever he goes. ...[50]

In a letter to Arthur Murray, Wiseman expanded on his theme:

Reading feels that he came out here not as an ordinary Ambassador, or High Commissioner, but because he thought, owing to his close connection with the Cabinet at home and his friendship on this side with members of the Administration, that he would be able to gain the President's confidence to such an extent that he would be able to discuss with him and consult with him on important questions affecting the War. He has now come to the conclusion that it is quite impossible to break down the barrier between the President and the foreign representatives and that he is unable to do more than any ordinary Ambassador could accomplish. In this I think he is quite wrong, and I have told him so.

In the first place, the President does trust him and values his opinion very highly, but it is simply not the President's nature to be communicative or to discuss affairs of state with anyone. In this respect Reading achieves far more than anyone else I can think of whom the Government could send out. Furthermore, Reading does not realize that the many problems (almost daily problems) which arise regarding finance, shipping, food, supplies, etc., which he negotiates and settles with comparative ease, would present real difficulties to anyone else, and furthermore would probably lead to friction. He has a particular gift for putting his case in a way that will appeal to the American officials and a very nice sense of how far he can go without causing trouble.

He is worried, too, about the question of the Chief Justiceship. He feels more and more that if he stays out here any longer he must resign his position, and, of course, that would be a terrible wrench for him, and in my humble opinion a sacrifice he ought not to be called upon to make. His present plan is to go home and put this position to the Prime Minister, and agree to come back for a short time, say a month or six weeks, in order to clear up here and hand over to somebody else; but I am afraid that his mind is very much against coming back here permanently.

I have discussed the whole situation frankly with House, and more cautiously with the State Department. The opinion is unanimous that it would be a disaster to the Allied Cause if Reading did not remain here until the War is over. I must say, however, that I think it is a pity for him to stay here too long without going home. He soon begins to feel out of touch (much more out of touch than he really is) and becomes restless and very anxious to have a full discussion of problems with the Cabinet at home.[51]

Some further indication of Reading's prestige in Washington is also contained in Wiseman's letter to Drummond of 19 July. It provides a counterbalance to the generally bland, almost inhibited, image of Reading the Ambassador:

At the Embassy, the staff like him and admire him, but are a bit afraid of him. . . .

Barclay [Embassy Counsellor] is eminently safe and reliable, but quite terrified of Reading. . . .

There has really been remarkably little friction between the many missions here; I think that this is partly due to the fact that they are all a little afraid of Reading. ...

Reading insists on my staying here while he is away, which annoys me a great deal as I was just about ready to go back and see you all.[52]

At any rate, Reading got his way and sailed with his wife in the *Mauretania*, arriving in Britain early in August. From Washington Arthur Willert, *The Times'* correspondent, cabled his editor, Dawson, asking him to ensure a good press reception for the returning Ambassador:

His prompt realization of the danger and his masterly handling of the American officials involved had as much to do with the saving of the food crisis as Hoover's organization. To him more than anybody else belongs the credit for the American troop movements. I am convinced that but for his diplomacy and the success of his personal contact with the President, the Russian issue, the delicacy of which cannot be exaggerated, would have never been pushed to a successful conclusion. He has made himself a commanding position in Washington and in a few months has effectively rescued the Embassy from the slough into which it had fallen. He has been untiring in his work and has never hesitated to spend himself in the making of speeches which have helped us greatly with public opinion. It is essential that he should return here shortly.[53]

Although Willert himself wrote in *The Times* that 'Washington expect Lord Reading back soon', Washington was to be disappointed.

12 Peacemaking, 1918–19

Reading ... was intriguing at that time day and night to be one of the party for Paris and was terrified of identifying himself ... with anything controversial. I recall him picking at the nail of his left thumb for minutes together in his room at the War Cabinet offices ... in an agony of doubt which way the cat was jumping....

Maynard Keynes, on Reading in the winter of 1918

Your tact, energy and counsel have been of inestimable value to the Allied cause, and I have the best of reasons for knowing that you have won the same measure of confidence on the other side of the Atlantic that you enjoy in the British Isles.

Lloyd George to Reading, 1919

When he left the United States at the end of July 1918, Lord Reading compounded one absence, and arguably one dereliction of duty, with another. Already an absentee Lord Chief Justice, he now became an absentee ambassador. Reading did not sail again for New York until 21 February 1919, and then only to engage in a lengthy winding-up of his ambassadorship. He and Lady Reading finally returned to Britain on 9 May 1919.

It is clear that Reading returned to Britain in August with the real purpose of deciding whether he should continue as Ambassador to the United States. It would have been better for his reputation in the short term if he had then resigned his diplomatic post and returned to his judicial duties. Instead he allowed himself to be persuaded by his old friend Lloyd George to play a significant part in the peacemaking process after the armistice of November 1918 – although it should be said that he generally relished his new assignments; indeed, as we have seen, Maynard Keynes described him as 'intriguing day and night to be one of the party for Paris'.

Reading's son has left an account of his father's predicament during these months:

Those of his staff who had returned with him from the United States begged him to spare himself as he was obviously over-tired, but he replied that he could not refuse help to anyone. ... He was unhappy at being absent from his post in Washington but unable to free himself from fresh daily preoccupations in London. ... There is no doubt it was a mistake on his part to allow himself to be persuaded to undertake this task. ...[1]

This over-sympathetic picture portrays a man tossed helplessly this way and that by the demands of duty and patriotism, and gives no indication of the high ambition that so often fired Lord Reading's varied and exciting career.

Others were less sympathetic. There were soon complaints in the United States at the protracted leave of the chief Allied Ambassador, and, as his son admits, American 'public opinion was ... both puzzled and affronted by his continued absence'.[2] On 14 February 1919 *The Times* presented the criticisms fairly and squarely in a leading article:

Lord Reading left Washington as long ago as last July, for a flying visit home, and he has been detained until this week by a series of unexpected duties in London and Paris. Doubtless these duties have been of great importance to the affairs of the Allies. But his failure to return to the United States has not prevented serious heart-searchings among our friends across the Atlantic. There is abundant evidence of dissatisfaction there that during the last six critical months the Embassy in Washington should have been left without a head. The evidence has accumulated by every American mail until it is obvious that, however much modern means of swift intercourse may have impaired the independence and hence the prestige of Ambassadors, Americans are convinced that their local conditions require, as one of the key-stones of really satisfactory Anglo-American relations, a first-class British representative in Washington.[3]

Reading's return to Britain was made aboard the *Mauretania*, which was crowded with United States troops whom he described as

fine stalwart expressions of American manhood. Their conduct was remarkably good and earned the greatest praise of the British generals and officers on board. One could not see those American soldiers without realizing that they were earnest, thoughtful men, intent upon acquitting themselves well for the sake of their country and inspired by the great ideals so well expressed by the President.[4]

This extract comes from a statement Reading wrote for *The Times* under the heading 'America's Prompt Aid' and which provided an assessment of his ambassadorship up to that point. The article was a conventional paeon of praise to the United States' contribution in men, money and materials to the war effort. It skated over the very real difficulties that Reading had encountered, not least with President Wilson, and was liberally laced with phrases like:

> The events in America ... are proving a wonderful inspiration to us and our Allies. ... If I speak in terms of enthusiastic admiration, it is because none other would convey my thoughts. ... In no direction, however, is the spirit of wholehearted cooperation more striking than in the magnificent contribution which America has made and is continuing to make to the man-power of the Allies.[5]

Once on British soil, Reading was cordially received and even fêted. On 21 August a luncheon was given in his honour at the American Luncheon Club in London, and at the end of the month he spoke at a reception given to Samuel Gompers, the pro-British and powerful President of the American Federation of Labour. Shortly after his arrival, Reading was summoned to Windsor to report to George v. There he found the King's views on a number of issues, including the need to provide prompt help for the Czech Legion in Russia, very close to the mainstream of public opinion; this was hardly surprising since George v laid no claims to originality of intellect, presenting instead a comfortable 'plain man's' image.

Reading, who once told a colleague how much he hated needlessly inactive holidays, was soon back at work. A room was made available in the War Cabinet offices in Whitehall Gardens, and he was thus available for dealing with American affairs and undertaking any tasks that the Prime Minister or the government might give him.

On 20 August 1918 Arthur Murray sent Wiseman an account of Reading back in harness:

> Reading is still very busy, in my opinion much too busy as he is getting no rest at all. He attends all the meetings of the War Cabinet. This in itself is, of course, a good thing because it helps to take him out of and puts him on a higher plane than the ordinary run of Ambassadors. He spends the rest of his time seeing various members of the Cabinet individually and many other people, British and American, on important affairs. In addition, he has had unloaded on to him (unfairly in my opinion) an inquiry into the whole problem of shipping and tonnage. This is not his legitimate work and it should not have been put upon him. ... In the meantime he is looking and feeling somewhat tired, and I am pressing him hard to take his week-ends off and to go out of town. ...[6]

Reading's tasks were hardly likely to induce inertia: he still carried out his ambassadorial duties, at the end of a cable, and he acted as legal adviser and emissary to the government.

On 3 September he left for a week in France to confer with French ministers and to visit Allied commanders at the front. In Paris there was a diplomatic flurry when the British Ambassador, Lord Derby, protested at Reading's brief from Lloyd George to negotiate with the French for an independent British air offensive. Derby had already been discussing this matter with Clemenceau, the French Prime Minister, and resented Reading's intrusion as well as what he perceived as his 'special relationship' with Lloyd George. On 9 September Reading told Lloyd George from Paris that Lord Derby was 'very disturbed at my coming here', mainly because of the message he had brought from the British Prime Minister for Clemenceau, but also because of the independent air offensive issue.[7]

Although Lloyd George promptly smoothed Lord Derby's ruffled feathers, the latter was to some extent justified in his resentment of Reading's visit. Before Reading left for France, Lloyd George had given him particular instructions as to how to negotiate with the French. Basically, the Prime Minister wanted Reading

to bring pressure to bear upon the French and the Americans to take over part of our line and thus enable us to give a rest to our troops. Clemenceau and Foch mean to compel us to keep up our numbers on the British front by refusing to take over the line. This policy would be fatal to the British Empire as we have no reserve of men here to keep up the number of divisions we now maintain in the field, and if we tried to keep that number up until the summer of 1919 we should be left with no army at all for the rest of the war.[8]

The lever that Lloyd George proposed to use against the French and the Americans was the threat of giving no further assistance in shipping American troops to France. Knowing how desperately the French wanted American reinforcements to relieve their troops at the front, Lloyd George instructed Reading not to give the French minister, Tardieu, 'any promises' over shipping facilities; after all, because of the diversion of British shipping to the transport of American troops, Britain was 'losing' 250,000 tons of essential cargo every month. The French were to think that the shipping problem could only be solved after an agreement over who should man what sections of the front line.[9]

Quite apart from illustrating that the British government was not anticipating an early end to the war, and was considering troop numbers for the summer of 1919, Lloyd George's brief to Reading shows how determined he was to show no quarter to his Allies. Of course Clemenceau was a formidable colleague, whom Lloyd George described at their first meeting as 'a short, broad-shouldered and full chested man, with an aggressive and rather truculent countenance, illuminated by a pair of brilliant and fierce eyes set deeply under overhanging eyebrows. The size and hardness of his great head struck me. It seemed enormous, but there was no dome of benevolence, reverence or kindliness.'[10] Not lacking in aggressive qualities himself, Lloyd George reinforced Reading's mission by telling him tersely on 9 September that he feared that Clemenceau still believed that Britain could maintain a full number of divisions at the front, but that 'You must get that entirely out of his mind.'[11]

Arthur Murray left a clear account of Reading's negotiations with Clemenceau and Tardieu:

Reading saw everyone of importance whom it was necessary for him to see. Clemenceau he saw twice, in order to discuss with him the question of British manpower for next year's campaign. The French have for some time past hinted that our manpower was not being made available up to its maximum limit. Memoranda on the question were therefore prepared and submitted for the consideration of the French Government. The situation was rapidly, it seems to me, developing into one in which France would dictate to us how our manpower should be used. Reading was commissioned by the Prime Minister to discuss the whole matter with Clemenceau.

Previous to seeing Clemenceau, he talked with Tardieu, who is more and more becoming one of Clemenceau's right-hand men and a growing power in official Government circles in Paris. Tardieu suggested to Reading that the latter and himself should be appointed by their respective Governments to go into the whole question of British manpower and decide what should be done. Reading headed this off by saying that if this course were adopted, a very difficult situation might develop. He thought it much better, therefore, that the two Governments should agree that Great Britain, realizing the seriousness of the situation, would do all that she possibly could to put the maximum number of men into the field by April 1st next year. Tardieu expressed himself in agreement with this view.

Subsequently Reading had a conversation with Clemenceau and took the same line as in his talk with Tardieu. Clemenceau agreed that on the whole the course suggested by Reading would be the best course to adopt, although he said that he might still have to make an official request in the matter. Unquestionably Reading succeeded in thus ending satisfactorily a very unsatisfactory situation, and credit is due to him for the manner in which he handled it. At the same time I would observe that the situation ought never to have been allowed to develop in the way that it did. Seeing that we have been and are keeping France's head above water in so many different ways, it is difficult to see why the proposition that we should in any way allow her to dictate to us on the manpower question should have been countenanced for a single moment.

I did not myself see Clemenceau, but Reading told me that he found him in good fettle and in high spirits. Derby told me that Clemenceau took him out a couple of weeks ago at half-past five in the morning to visit the battle front. They spent the whole day driving about, coming back to Paris at eight o'clock in the evening. 'By that time,' said Derby, 'I was dog tired, but the old man stepped out of the car as fresh as a daisy, and after having something to eat proceeded to work until close on midnight.'[12]

Reading also had a meeting with Marshal Foch, and discussed the best way of organizing the Allies' military resources. Foch put more faith in the power of infantry divisions than in new-fangled weapons of war such as tanks and aircraft. Reading left a record of this encounter:

He thought we were in great danger of over-production of tanks and aeroplanes which required large personnel which could otherwise be made available for infantry. Tanks were auxiliaries which required infantry to make effective advance. Aeroplanes intended for independent offensive could be better employed certainly when required to assist military attack. He begged the Prime Minister to take these matters into consideration and to keep up the number of divisions.

I said I had delivered detailed particulars to M. Clemenceau which showed that it was quite impossible for us to provide necessary requirements and also keep up numbers of divisions. I said of course more divisions could be kept if not maintained at full strength. He answered, 'by all means reduce strength in winter' provided we had divisions fully completed by April 1st next year.

Advantage must be taken of disorganized condition of German Army. The High Command was straining to save stores and supply, which would otherwise be booty, and was thus fighting comparatively small actions which were costing them dear. He thought they should have retired a long way straight off to enable them to reform. Policy now and to be continued as long as weather lasted must be to give them no rest – here, there and everywhere. No one could say where they would halt as the present retreat was continuing. He said we should keep at it as long as we could and prepare to throw everything in for next year.

He again and again reverted to this which he was obviously most anxious to impress upon me and thus upon the Prime Minister. . . .

I said Germany's hope must rest now more than ever upon disagreements between the Allies which of course would not happen. He agreed and said, 'They must not happen.'

I suggested that good will and confidence in each other were better than exchanges of documents.

His view was that we were preparing for too long ahead instead of the immediate future. . . .

Foch referred also to point made by M. Clemenceau that France and England, having held the fort for four years, should put their full fighting strength into the year of victory and not leave it to America, whose troops although splendid had not the training of those long in the field....[13]

Reading was able to put some of these points to General Pershing, whom he also met. He found Pershing as committed as ever to the principle of American troops fighting as part of an American army: 'All questions of brigading troops with the French or ourselves have completely disappeared. He even dislikes divisions fighting with British and French troops and Foch is somewhat nervous in giving orders lest Pershing should fall out with him.' So anxious were the French on this point, that Clemenceau asked Reading whether President Wilson would back Foch up if Pershing failed to carry out the orders of the Supreme Commander on the Western front. Reading reassured Clemenceau by saying that 'the President . . . would in my judgement insist on Pershing acting in accordance . . .'.[14]

During his visit to the front, Reading let out his feelings on his American ambassadorship to Colonel C.A. Repington, *The Times'* military correspondent, at a lunch at the British Liaison Mission headquarters attached to Foch: '[Reading] had read in some novel the advice of a sage lady to her son, "that when he had made a good impression in a house he should firmly leave". He felt that about himself and America. But he expressed his intention to return.'[15]

The next day Reading visited American troops in the front line at Juvigny. Here in a deep dug-out, as darkness fell, this generally reserved and punctilious man for once allowed his feelings full flood when he spoke spontaneously and warmly to the American troops assembled to hear him. Later printed by the American High Command and handed out to American troops under the title 'In Our Hour of Need', Reading's impromptu speech ended: 'the people of America are watching you. . . . I shall tell them to be of good cheer, that America is here, that the Star Spangled Banner is waving, and that you are taking a noble part in this great struggle, and will continue to do so till the end, till victory is ours. Good luck to you and God bless you all!'

On his way back to the coast, Reading motored along the British front line to visit General Headquarters at Montreuil, where he stopped to take tea with his son Gerald who was serving on the staff of a divisional HQ near Noeux-les-Mines.

He sailed for home in a destroyer HMS *Termagant* together with Lloyd George, Lord Riddell and Edwin Montagu who had all come to France for a brief visit. *Termagant* 'crossed the Channel at full speed, cutting through the waves and sending up columns of sea on either side. Lord Reading was in his element and it was only out of deference to his fellow passengers that he ultimately went below.' [16]

Back in Britain, Reading had various problems to deal with in connection with American policy. The Allied intervention in Russia was still a cause of some vexation, especially as the Czech Legion, in US Secretary of State Lansing's words, were 'moving west when they ought to be going east'. More Allied troops were landed at Vladivostok, which caused the Bolshevik government to react suspiciously and to arrest the British Agent in Russia, Bruce Lockhart. Barclay, as we have seen, had cabled Reading in cypher from Washington on 9 September 1918 telling him that he had heard, through reliable sources, 'that there is a strong feeling in highest quarters here that French and British Government [sic] are trying to force the hand of the Administration, not merely in Siberian matter but in general . . .'.[17] Reading had replied that 'I am neglecting no opportunity to promote a better situation . . .'.

In the event, Wilson seemed content to accept Allied policy on intervention more readily than before, causing Wiseman to write: 'As far as the President's position is concerned, he has lost faith and curiously enough practically lost interest in the Bolsheviks and is, I think, much more inclined to fall in with our programme than he was a few months ago.' The collapse of the Central Powers in November 1918 in any case solved America's problem and the United States proceeded to withdraw its troops, leaving British and French forces to stay on and become entangled in a futile attempt to help the White Russians defeat the Red Army. As for the Czech Legion, it made its way home and played an important part in establishing the new republic of Czechoslovakia.

Wilson's views on the establishment of a League of Nations after the war also occupied Reading's mind. On 18 August 1918 Wiseman had presented Wilson's current thinking in a telegram he sent to Reading and which the latter immediately passed on to Lloyd George. Wiseman portrayed Wilson as caught between American isolationists and League enthusiasts: Wilson 'has ideas on the subject but not worked out in detail. I asked him what his ideas were. He replied: "Two main principles; there must be a League of Nations, and this must be virile, a reality, not a paper League of Nations." '[18]

According to Wiseman, Wilson 'would like nothing better than to discuss the whole matter frankly with the Prime Minister who, he felt, would substantially share his views'. Reading told Lloyd George that Wilson's perception of their agreement on the issue 'is based upon your recent speech in the House of Commons – the "clanking sound" speech. ... The President takes the view that the League should be constituted at the Peace Conference and this seems to approximate closely to your position.'[19]

Before he had left the United States, Reading had, at Colonel House's request, looked over a draft covenant that had been shown to Wilson. House had wanted 'to get Reading's legal mind to bear upon the different points. He expressed himself pleased with the document as a whole. His feeling, however, was that unless Germany changed her form of government and its personnel, it would be useless to include her in the League.' Reading had made his notes of the conversation with House, and saw the fundamental problem to be one of what the power of the League might be:

How to enforce rulings or decrees is the inevitable puzzle which must be solved if the League is to be fully effective. The financial, economic and commercial alliance of the various contracting parties is the only means yet suggested. Whilst this affords on paper a better guarantee to my mind than an international military police, it has within it the possibility of ineffectiveness at the critical moment and consequently there can be no security to nations that they may not be attacked by a combination which has made up its mind at the critical moment not to carry out its treaty obligations. With Germany a party to the Convention and with her past history and avowed policy the only security would be that, when the favourable moment came, Germany would refuse to be bound, and she would probably carry with her certain other States.[20]

President Wilson, according to Wiseman, 'looks to the economic pressures to supply the main force which might be used to support a League of Nations. He feels there must be force but recognizes the practical difficulties.'[21] By the time of Wilson's visit to Britain at the end of December 1918, the President, his party worsted in the mid-term congressional elections by a Republican upsurge, gave Lloyd George and Balfour the impression that the League was 'the only thing he really cared much about'. Wilson had also been insistent that the League should only be constituted at the Peace Conference, and Reading had persuaded the British government to avoid a premature public discussion of the proposal which might otherwise have put a serious strain upon Anglo-American relations. Ironically, once the League was constituted, Wilson was overwhelmed by a stroke and the opposition of his domestic opponents, and the United States did not as a consequence join the League of Nations.

By the start of October 1918 the German armies on the Western front were in full retreat. On 5 October the new German Chancellor, Prince Max of Baden, sent a note to President Wilson, through the Swiss government, urging him to invite the belligerent powers to begin peace negotiations on the basis of the President's proposed 'Fourteen Points'. The Austro-Hungarian government was also anxious to sue for peace.

An untidy episode now took place. The British government was anxious that President Wilson should not make a unilateral, and possibly inappropriate reply, to the German peace note. Reading wondered whether he should ask the President not to reply until he had consulted with the Allies. Eventually, after discussions with Balfour, Reading and Lloyd George agreed to wait and see what happened; an odd decision, as it turned out.

While waiting for the outcome, Reading spent a weekend early in October at Lord Riddell's summer home, Danny Park, with Lloyd George and Philip Kerr (the Prime Minister's Private Secretary, and later Lord Lothian). Although Reading was in two minds whether to return soon to Washington, Lloyd George said after dinner on the first evening, 'It is important that you, Reading, should get back to America to look after our interests there.'

There was some badinage over the different personalities that would be involved in any peace negotiations. Lloyd George said, 'I have been picturing to myself my first interview with President Wilson', to which Reading replied, 'Clemenceau says that after a few hours only feathers would be left to tell the tale. Both would have disappeared!' Lloyd George laughed, and, returning to Wilson's pending reply to the German peace note, wondered whether 'it would not be a good thing for Clemenceau or me to make a speech indicating the position in an inoffensive way'.

Shortly after the Prime Minister had gone to bed, the text of Wilson's reply was telephoned through to Danny Park. After reaffirming that the Germans must accept the Fourteen Points as a basis for peace discussions, the letter went on:

> The President feels bound to say, with regard to the armistice, that he would not feel at liberty to propose a cessation of arms to the Governments with which the Government of the United States is associated against the Central Powers so long as the armies of those powers are upon their soil. The good faith of any discussion would manifestly depend upon the consent of the Central Powers immediately to withdraw their forces everywhere from invaded territory.[22]

Having waited passively for Wilson's reply, Lloyd George and his colleagues now reacted with some dismay to the letter. The Prime

Minister thought, 'the Allies are now in a horrible mess. Wilson has promised them an armistice.' Reading tended to agree, while Riddell believed that 'Wilson may well say "Get out as best you can, and when you are out I will make proposals."' 'He can't mean that,' Kerr insisted. Reading commented that the letter was 'badly drafted'.

The next morning, Sunday 13 October, Lloyd George discussed the problem further with Reading and Riddell while they walked to the top of Wolstonbury Hill, near by. The Prime Minister was still unhappy with Wilson's letter and said, 'The time is coming when we shall have to speak out. We have borne the heat and burden of the day and we are entitled to be consulted. What do the Fourteen Points mean? They are very nebulous.'

Members of the War Cabinet, Maurice Hankey the Cabinet Secretary, and the Service Chiefs had been invited to lunch. After eating, they discussed the problem of Wilson's letter. Eventually, Balfour, Reading, Hankey and Kerr were put in separate rooms with the task of drafting a suitably firm telegram to the President. Balfour was the winner of this exercise, which must have seemed like a deadly serious version of a weekend drawing-room game. The Danny Park telegram had its effect, and President Wilson's next note to the German government was far more explicit and unbending. On 20 October Germany accepted Wilson's conditions for arranging an armistice.

Peacemaking now began in earnest. Although Reading had booked a passage to the United States at the end of October, Lloyd George asked him to cancel his booking and go instead to Paris to join the British ministers there in their deliberations. Despite Reading's subsequent disclaimers, it is clear that he relished the challenge of these new experiences.

It was, in a way, easier to make peace with the Central Powers than to bring universal harmony to Anglo-American diplomatic relations. President Wilson was not an easy man to deal with, and Colonel House in Paris loyally represented his master's views. Earlier in October, before the German agreement to negotiate for peace on Wilson's terms, Reading had been obliged to help smooth out some diplomatic tangles.

For instance on 30 September the President, speaking to the Senate on the subject of women's suffrage, had said, rather tactlessly: '[The American people] have seen their Government accept this interpretation of Democracy – seen old Governments like that of Great Britain, which did not profess to be democratic, promise readily and as of course this justice to women though they had before refused it.'[23] A strong protest had been made on behalf of the British government to Colonel

House, who agreed to write to the President urging him to make some public explanation on the lines that governments which the United States tended to consider less democratic than themselves had in this instance proved more democratic.

A week later, Reading was warned, in a telegram marked 'Very Confidential', that the American State Department had heard, 'from a source they consider reliable', that the British, French and Italian governments were bound by a secret treaty regarding the disposition of Turkish territory and were engaged in negotiating peace terms. There was also another rumour that peace terms had been concluded with Bulgaria. There would be much agitation, Barclay told Reading, if such steps were being taken without consulting the American government.[24]

So the Allies were anxious about President Wilson's peace negotiations with Germany, and the United States was disturbed by rumours of secret treaty-making by the Allies. This was hardly the best prelude to the serious business of concluding a satisfactory peace with the Central Powers. Worse, there was indeed a secret treaty, the Sykes-Picot agreement, the result of negotiations concluded at a preliminary stage early in 1916, for the disposal of Turkish territory. There were subsequent revisions of this agreement – Italy came into the reckoning (as did the idea of a Jewish Homeland) and Russia went out after the Revolution – but the essentials remained fairly static, the establishment of British and French spheres of influence in the Middle East, with Britain getting the lion's share. No wonder the United States, which had hardly entered the war to promote the extension of European imperialism, looked askance at these dealings, although the essential agreement had been reached well before America entered the war.

There were plenty of other potential causes of Anglo-American friction. One of these concerned the second of President Wilson's Fourteen Points which provided for 'Absolute freedom of navigation upon the seas, outside Territorial waters, alike in peace and war, except as the seas may be closed in whole or in part by international action for the enforcement of international covenants.' Britain objected to this point on two counts: first, that it would destroy the continuing blockade of Germany, and second, that it threatened Britain's claim to stop and search neutral vessels when she was at war. The Americans very much disliked this latter activity which was in part the result of Britain's long-established naval supremacy.

As early as January 1918, shortly before leaving for America, Reading had been asked for his legal views on a paper prepared by the Solicitor-General on Britain's view of the 'Freedom of the Seas', and had told Lloyd George that it was 'a good summary of the position'.[25] By the end of the same year, Reading's views had not changed and he was able to advise Lloyd George to state: 'This point we cannot accept under any conditions.... my view is that I should like to see the League of Nations established before I let this power go. If the League of Nations is a reality, I am willing to discuss the matter.'

For the American government, however, House could not be budged, despite Reading's several attempts to persuade him to accept the British position. Even Reading's arguments based on the concept of international law were of no avail; 'I told Reading he was wasting his breath,' House noted after one lengthy discussion. Finally Lloyd George, with his genius for breaking deadlock, proposed that the issue should be left to the Peace Conference proper, where, he told House, 'I don't despair of coming to an agreement'.

Thus on 4 November 1918 the Supreme War Council approved an Allied memorandum to President Wilson accepting his Fourteen Points as a basis for peace negotiations, with the reservation of the contentious Point 2. On 5 November, with her allies Austria-Hungary, Turkey and Bulgaria already suing for peace, Imperial Germany had to accept the inevitability of surrender. On 6 November the German delegates left Berlin and were eventually received by Marshal Foch, for the Allied armies, and Admiral Sir Rosslyn Wemyss, representing the Allied navies, in a railway carriage in the forest of Compiègne. In the early hours of 11 November, the German delegates, with no room for manoeuvre, signed the armistice agreement, which came into force at 11 a.m. that morning. In the meantime, Kaiser Wilhelm II had fled to Holland and a republic was proclaimed as the German Empire collapsed.

During these momentous days, Reading was close at the side of Lloyd George, and sitting as a member of the War Cabinet. On 20 November his legal advice was sought in the War Cabinet on Lord Curzon's proposal that the ex-Kaiser, 'the arch-criminal of the world', should be tried for having brought about the war and suitably punished. Reading, with habitual tact and caution, refused to give an opinion, but instead moved that the Law Officers of the Crown should look into the feasibility of the proposal. Reading was later asked whether he would preside over any tribunal that might be set up to try the Kaiser, but he was 'too conscious of the many legal obstacles and too sceptical of the ultimate practicability of the scheme to commit himself until a more concrete proposition had been laid before him'.[26]

Reading's prevarication was well justified by events. The clamour to 'hang the Kaiser' was partly whipped up to enable Lloyd George, and those coalitionist Unionists and Liberals who supported his premiership, to win the 'coupon' election of November 1918. Demands that Germany should be made to 'pay for the war' also rang from the hustings and found a fierce response from the electorate. At the polls, 339 coalition Unionists and 136 coalition Liberal MPs were returned: the independent Liberals were annihilated, and Labour 'pacifists' like MacDonald, Snowden and Arthur Henderson lost their seats.

Of course the election was not won on the crude threat to hang the Kaiser. Lloyd George was 'the man who had won the war', and consequently reaped the benefit. Moreover, his promise of 'a fit country for heroes to live in', seemed both just, and possible – given his pre-war reputation for social reform. In the event the Kaiser was not hanged, and lived in comfortable retirement in Holland until 1940. On the other hand, the peace negotiations certainly made Germany 'pay for the war' in material terms, thus ensuring that she would find it almost impossible to accept the settlement in the long term.

On Boxing Day 1918 Reading was at Dover officially to greet President Wilson on behalf of the British government. Wilson's state visit to Britain was a prelude to his involvement in the peace negotiations due to open in the New Year at Versailles. Although his arrival was the first time an American President had stepped on British soil, and despite the goodwill of the host nation, Wilson's visit was not a success. Beset by political opposition at home, obsessed with the need to impose his Fourteen Points upon the peace settlement, and of an aloof and academic temper, he turned out to be a trying guest. Lloyd George regretted that 'There was no glow of friendship or of gladness at meeting men who had been partners in a common enterprise and had so narrowly escaped a common danger.' Lloyd George urged Reading somehow to get the President to be more generous to the Allied powers in his public utterances, but Wilson failed, in either of his two major speeches, to offer 'one word of generous allusion to Britain's sacrifices for or achievements on behalf of the common cause'.

Before Wilson's arrival in Britain, Reading had taken yet another step away from a prompt return to Washington. He was invited to be the chief British representative on the Inter-Allied Committee set up in Paris to attend to 'the question of victualling and supplying enemy, Allied and neutral countries in all its aspects, including the use of enemy merchant vessels'.

As we have seen, Reading's son has stated that 'it was a mistake on his part to allow himself to be persuaded to undertake this task'. He was not alone in thinking it a mistake. G.K. Chesterton, who had harried

Reading during the Marconi controversy, took the opportunity to write an offensive open letter, headed 'The Sign of the World's End'. Chesterton objected to Reading's representation of Britain in Paris, and his letter included a number of wounding innuendoes:

Are we to lose the War which we have already won? That and nothing else is involved in losing the full satisfaction of the national claim of Poland. Is there any man who doubts that the Jewish International is unsympathetic with that full national demand? And is there any man who doubts that you will be sympathetic with the Jewish International? ... Are we to set up as the standing representative of England a man who is a standing joke against England? That and nothing else is involved in setting up the chief Marconi Minister as our chief Foreign Minister. ... Daniel son of Isaac, Go in peace; but go.[27]

As chief British representative on the Inter-Allied Committee on victualling and supply, Reading did not impress Maynard Keynes, the principal representative of the British Treasury in Paris. We have seen how Keynes had derided Reading's indecision, before the latter left for Paris, on the blockade question. Reading, however, believed that he was not meant to make policy in such matters. Indeed he sent Lloyd George early in February a balanced assessment of the problem, though leaning towards the preferred British position of maintaining the blockade in order to force Germany's hand during the peace negotiations:

On the one hand, there is pressure to relax or remove the blockade for economic or industrial reasons; on the other, there is military objection to any substantial relaxation of the blockade, based upon the necessity to maintain pressure notably on Germany by means other than the resumption of hostilities to accept the terms of Peace submitted by the Allied Powers.

It will be for the highest authorities to weigh in the balance the advantages of providing food and to some extent employment in Germany and other enemy countries by the blockade restrictions.

... Without attempting to prejudge the matter, it will be found that the British Representatives and probably those of other Governments on the Supreme Council will recommend that it is essential to keep the blockade machinery in existence and in operation so that pressure could always be exercised on Germany if necessary.[28]

Reading found aspects of his work in Paris trying, especially since he had a number of confrontations with Herbert Hoover, his American counterpart. The atmosphere of peacemaking Paris was sometimes uncongenial, and he would have agreed with Keynes's description of the Hotel Majestic where he was staying: 'The feverish, persistent and boring gossip of that hellish place had already developed in full measure the peculiar mixture of smallness, cynicism, self-importance and bored excitement that it was never to lose.'[29]

One of his few sources of pleasure came from his son's brief visit to the Hotel Majestic. On a walk with Gerald in the Bois de Boulogne they met F.E. Smith, now Lord Chancellor and Lord Birkenhead, and the Attorney-General, Sir Gordon Hewart. Birkenhead began to bemoan the fact that he would never again conduct a case in court, and Reading suddenly said, 'Look here F.E., you and I are both too young to be stuck for the rest of our lives as Judges. Let's go back to the Bar.'

So engaging did this fantasy prove that the little party, deep in conversation, 'stepped blindly off the kerb of a side-street just as a large car flashed round the corner. "Good God!" said Lord Birkenhead. "The Lord Chancellor, the Lord Chief Justice and the Attorney-General; what a bag! And how grieved the Bar would have been!"'[30]

Reading had already decided to leave Paris. He had resigned from his official position on 21 January 1919, telling Lloyd George:

After four and a half years' activities in war problems, I have come to the conclusion that I should return to my judicial duties. As you will remember, I came here to help in the formation of the Relief Council and to assist in its first deliberations. The Council is now all on its feet and is working very satisfactorily. I propose therefore to retire from the position of British Representative upon this Council and am returning to London on Friday.

He had already resigned from the War Cabinet on 17 December 1918, and the way was now clear for his return to Washington and the decent winding up of his ambassadorship there. He and Lady Reading were back in London by 9 February, and twelve days later left for the United States.

By the middle of May the Readings were back in Britain. On 17 May Reading visited Paris, where the peace negotiations were drawing to a close and where he spent some time with Balfour and Lloyd George, and bade goodbye to President Wilson and Colonel House.

Reading had certainly not had a dull war. He had undertaken various important missions and had acquitted himself well. He had been created an earl, his wife was to be made a Dame Grand Cross in the Order of the British Empire – the nearest a woman could get to a Knighthood – and his heir Gerald had been moved to tell him, in October 1918, 'although I am not by nature or training the most demonstrative of beings, I am enormously proud of being your son'.[31]

On 21 May Lloyd George sent his old friend the following letter which was widely published in the press:

My Dear Lord Chief Justice,

At the moment when you are about to resume your judicial duties, I wish on behalf of His Majesty's Government to express to you the deep appreciation which we all feel for the manner in which you have discharged the all-important mission which was entrusted to you, and for the conspicuous service which you have rendered to the Empire while acting as His Majesty's Ambassador and Minister Plenipotentiary to the United States.

No mere formal words can give proper recognition for this service. Under strong pressure from the Government, and with great reluctance, you gave up your duties as Lord Chief Justice in order to undertake a mission which has been of singular complexity and extremely arduous. When the time comes for the history of those most critical years of the War to be written, the leading part which you played in co-ordinating the war-effort of the United States and the other Allies, and above all in helping to bring about that dramatic movement of the American Army to Europe in the spring and summer of 1918, which contributed so strikingly to the Allied victory in the later autumn, will be understood in its true perspective.

Your tact, energy and counsel have been of inestimable value to the Allied cause, and I have the best of reasons for knowing that you have won the same measure of confidence on the other side of the Atlantic that you enjoy in the British Isles.

The Government will greatly miss your advice and assistance in the various spheres in which you have rendered service during the War, and I can assure you that you return to your high judicial duties with the gratitude and goodwill of the nation and the Empire.

Believe me, ever sincerely,

D. LLOYD-GEORGE.[32]

Whether Reading would rest content with his 'high judicial duties' was, however, another matter.

13 Unwillingly Back to the Law, 1919–21

For the first time in sixty years the zest had gone out of his life, and he could see nothing ahead of him but stagnation and decay.
Gerald Isaacs describing his father

I will never look at a law report again if I can help it! I never want to see another one!
Reading to Lord Riddell on his appointment as Viceroy, January 1921

Reading spent the second half of 1919 and the whole of 1920 in the Courts, trying special jury actions, presiding over the Court of Criminal Appeal, and serving on a couple of occasions as a member of the tribunal for hearing cases brought before the House of Lords. As his son noted, he 'resumed the duties of Lord Chief Justice with a very heavy heart'.

His reluctant return to the Bench was perfectly comprehensible. He had in reality had little option in the unsavoury aftermath of the Marconi scandal but to accept the post of Lord Chief Justice when it became available. Once installed in this august office, the special demands of the First World War had almost immediately enabled him to escape and to taste the excitement of power and responsibility amid events of earth-shaking magnitude. Although he had not found peace-making in Paris wholly satisfying, it took 'an even sterner effort of renunciation ... in 1919 to compel himself to leave again the swiftly flowing stream of political life for what he had come ... to regard as a depressingly safe and stagnant backwater'.[1]

His son Gerald, who had become his private secretary at this time, was able to observe him closely during this unhappy and frustrating period of his life. Reading grumbled at the physical inactivity forced upon him, 'complaining that it made him feel as if he were only fit to be wheeled up and down Brighton front in a bath-chair'. Day after day in 1919 and 1920 he would come out of Court in a state of exasperation wholly at variance with his usual calm, muttering that 'he really could not be expected to go on trying trumpery "running down" cases for the rest of his life and that his patience was at an end'.[2] In the spring of 1920 he played golf with Lloyd George and Lord Riddell at Walton Heath; both thought he had suddenly aged, and Riddell noted that 'he seems to have lost some of his wonderful spring and vitality'. His son confirmed that, 'For the first time in sixty years the zest had gone out of his life and he could see nothing ahead of him but stagnation and decay. . . .'

Reading's disenchantment with his work sometimes found expression in criticizing the standard of pleading that he had to hear in silence:

He would, however, sometimes come into his room on the rising of the Court, gravely shaking his head, and say to me: 'You know, it was awful to have to listen in silence to — cross-examining a witness this afternoon and fumbling all his points. If only I could have changed places with him for half an hour!' or ' — has got a good case, but he will take all his bad points first and at such length that the jury will be thoroughly bored before he gets to the good ones. I've given him several hints but he won't take them, and it's not my job to do more. All the same it is painful to watch a good case being thrown away.' He was like an old cricketer reduced to umpiring, performing his inactive task all day with alertness and impartiality, but at times passionately longing to seize a bat again and 'have a go' at the bowling, just to show the youngsters how it ought to be played.[3]

He also seriously debated the feasibility of resigning his great office and returning to the Bar, despite the obvious difficulties that lay in such a course.

Time did not lessen his frustration:

Certainly Lord Reading was pining for more active occupation throughout 1920. Even during the blackest and most anxious days of the War he had remained outwardly cheerful and confident whatever his inner doubts may at times have been. Now he became restless, irritable and depressed, finding his unaccustomed leisure to hang heavily upon his hands. As Lord Chief Justice he regarded himself as debarred even from taking part in debate in the House of Lords except on subjects of purely legal concern and he had worked too hard for many years to have had the leisure to acquire outside interests or hobbies with which to fill his spare time. He felt himself caged and helpless, wasting his talents and his energies. He had disposed of Foxhill to Sir Hugo (later Lord Hirst) in 1918 and had not even a country-house to which to go for week-ends, while [the golf courses of] Walton Heath and Swinley Forest had largely lost their savour.[4]

As the Attorney-General Sir Gordon Hewart remarked, Reading 'had learned to enjoy the glitter of diplomacy', and missed its glamour and excitement. Indeed, hardly had he returned from his final leave-taking in Washington than Reading was offering to go back as Ambassador during the long vacation of 1919. Although the post was eventually offered to Viscount Grey, formerly Sir Edward Grey, Reading continued to act as if he had a personal 'special relationship' with the United States, and even went so far as to ask Lloyd George if he could be given copies of all important communications that passed between London and the British Embassy in Washington. That Lloyd George agreed to this unusual request is another indication of the bond that connected the two most illustrious survivors of the Marconi scandal.

Reading assiduously fostered that bond throughout 1919 and 1920, as he ached for more stimulating employment. In June 1919 he congratulated the Prime Minister on the final signature of the Versailles peace treaty, saying, 'It is a splendid achievement of yours. . . .'[5] Two months later he offered Lloyd George his warmest congratulations on the award of the Order of Merit, 'the only distinction I suppose that you would have accepted'.[6] At the end of August 1919 Reading gave his friend some financial advice, remarking:

I am glad to hear of Carnegie's legacy to you and I hope you will have no scruple in accepting it. Why should you? It is intended to relieve you of any pecuniary anxiety during your life – for – careless as you always have been of these personal matters – there must sometimes have been at the back of your mind a passing thought about them.[7]

Lloyd George's finances were probably the subject of a mysterious letter written in November 1919 when Reading says, 'Tomorrow when my brother comes I have not asked any one else as I understood you wanted a private talk.'[8] The Prime Minister even sought his friend's advice over government finance, asking him in October 1919 whether his and Milner's optimism over the financial position for next year was justified.[9] Reading replied that Lloyd George was being over-optimistic.

In other letters, Reading showed mild envy of Lloyd George's active life and evident good health. On 19 November 1919 he wrote, 'My Dear P.M., You looked very well last night. I watched you and *thought*.'[10] In July 1920 he sent his friend his heartiest congratulations on the occasion of his birthday and on the award of the Grand Cross of the Legion of Honour: 'You carry your years well – responsibility seems only to increase your vitality and resourceful energy.'[11]

Reading made one positive intervention in Anglo-American

diplomacy in the autumn of 1919. The Prince of Wales, the future King Edward VIII, was due to visit Canada as the first step in an Empire tour. While in Canada, the Prince cabled home for permission to extend his tour to the United States. Reading was asked for his opinion by George V and replied that he was strongly in favour of the Prince visiting the United States, and that he believed that he would be warmly received there. As well as visiting a desperately ill President Wilson in the White House, the Prince was welcomed, on the whole, with spontaneous enthusiasm. Reading was delighted that his advice had resulted in such success, and passed on his feelings to Lord Stamfordham, the King's Private Secretary, on 25 November 1919:

> It shows, as I always insist, that at heart the Americans are with us in spite of their extreme sensitiveness lest Britain should be patronizing them. At this present moment nothing could have been happier than this visit. The reception shows our people another side of American opinion and serves to calm the exacerbation of those who might be disposed to say bitter things and thus not help but mar future prospects.
>
> The Prince has proved a better Ambassador than all of us rolled into one. He has caught the American spirit, so difficult to understand quickly, and has done more in America to make their people comprehend the strength of the democratic support to our monarchy than all [the] books and articles and propaganda.
>
> I trust I may be permitted to tell Their Majesties how much I rejoice at this success.[12]

When the Prince of Wales returned home, Reading was gratified to be among those welcoming him on behalf of the government. A few months later he was equally pleased to go back to Reading to receive the freedom of the borough.

All of this, however, was peripheral activity, far away from the real centres of power and influence. Reading did come near to landing a post that would have satisfied his craving for a more challenging variety of public service early in 1920. For a moment it seemed as if he might succeed Lord Derby as British Ambassador to France, but Curzon, who had succeeded Balfour as Foreign Secretary, insisted that this plum post should go to a senior civil servant and Lord Hardinge, Permanent Under-Secretary of State at the Foreign Office, was duly appointed.

The 1920 Michaelmas law term opened with Reading apparently doomed to stay on as Lord Chief Justice for the foreseeable future. Yet on 6 January 1921 it was officially announced that Reading had been appointed Viceroy of India, and on 2 April, having resigned as Lord Chief Justice, he and Lady Reading landed at Bombay.

How did Reading come to be offered a post which, for all its demands and difficulties, bestowed upon the incumbent a power second to none in the whole of Asia or throughout the British Empire?

The main reason for Reading's appointment lay in his close friendship with Lloyd George, within whose considerable powers of patronage lay the Governor-Generalship of British India. As we shall see, the Prime Minister was prepared to enter into convoluted, and in some respects unprecedented, negotiations to smooth Reading's path to the Viceroyalty.

There were, of course, other factors. One vital point was that Austen Chamberlain, who was first offered the post, finally refused it. From early in 1920 Edwin Montagu, Secretary of State for India, had been considering a replacement for Lord Chelmsford, who was due to retire as Viceroy in April 1921. Montagu had even toyed with the idea of taking the post himself for a limited period of three years, and then handing over to one of George v's sons, but the Prime Minister had rejected the proposal. On 7 December Montagu told Lloyd George of the state of play: 'Austen would not accept. After him Reading is probably the best, then Winston, then Lytton and then Willingdon or Willingdon and then Lytton.'

So, in the often difficult game of 'find the Viceroy', Austen Chamberlain's refusal opened the way for Reading. Did Reading really want the post? It was not the easiest time in which to exercise viceregal power: the demands of Indian nationalists for self-rule, inspired by Gandhi's philosophy of *satyagraha* (or truth-force), were pressing hard upon the Raj. The inhospitable climate and the traditional risks to health had to be reconciled to Lady Reading's fragile constitution and her perennial illnesses. Moreover, the Viceroyalty carried no pension and by taking it Reading would cut himself off from the long-term financial security of the post of Lord Chief Justice.

Reading's first impulse was to accept the offer: 'The temptation to accept outright was strong. He was still as adventurous as ever at heart, and here was a prospect of adventure on a hitherto unimagined scale. He enjoyed responsibility, and here was responsibility in full measure. He was tied to an uncongenial routine, and here was the certainty of release.'[13] Lloyd George believed that he was 'very anxious' to accept the post.

He did not accept straightaway, however, and asked for time to consult his wife and to consider his personal and financial position.

There seems little doubt that Lady Reading would not have been able even to consider going to India, but for the death of her mother, the widowed Mrs Cohen, in October 1920, just before Lloyd George approached Reading over the Viceroyalty.

Alice Reading's persistent ill-health, despite its very real physical manifestations, none the less owed a good deal to the claustrophobic atmosphere of her upbringing. Even when her father, with his obsessional rituals, died in 1896, her mother continued to display enough symptoms of ill-health and dependence to bind Lady Reading to her in a relationship that was at least partly neurotic in its anxieties.

Lady Reading's son Gerald, though stoutly denying that his mother's 'ill health was exclusively, or even primarily, nervous in character', none the less left a clear description of the inhibiting effect of old Mrs Cohen's demands upon her:

In October, 1920, Mrs Cohen, Lady Reading's mother, died at the age of 81, and her death had indirectly a great influence upon Lord Reading's subsequent career. Her husband had died in 1896 and for the last twenty-four years of her life she had had no permanent home, preferring to live in a series of hotels and to be thus freed from the cares of housekeeping. She had, however, few interests outside her immediate family with which to occupy her time and it accordingly became her habit at an early stage of her widowhood to visit each afternoon at least one of her three daughters in London. This routine almost invariably included a visit to Alice, whom her mother regarded as requiring particular attention on account of her indifferent health. If by some rare mischance her daughter was not at home, Mrs Cohen strongly resented her absence. If other callers were announced, she was apt silently to indicate her view that they were unwelcome. In short, after her husband's death she exhibited in a wider field much the same despotic qualities as he had possessed and she had suppressed during his lifetime within their home. Her daughter was in the position that for reasons of health it was very often impossible for her to go out during the afternoon, so that she was of necessity there to be visited. Moreover, she was most deeply devoted to her mother, whose loneliness and lack of resource filled her with pity, and she was genuinely ready to abandon any other calls upon her time in order to provide the old lady with some measure of daily companionship.

The convention of the regular afternoon visit was thus imperceptibly established, neither mother nor daughter realizing that the effect of it was to impose upon the younger woman a habit of invalidism, escape from which became increasingly impossible as the years passed.[14]

When Lady Reading managed to escape, however, as when she accompanied her husband on his American ambassadorship, her health and her spirits markedly improved. In fact she flourished, like her husband, in the new environment, and doubtless drew strength from being free of her mother's demands upon her time and her patience.

It is surely significant that, after her mother's death, when Lady Reading first heard of the offer of the Viceroyalty to her husband, 'summoning her doctor privately before her husband could interview him and probably receive an unfavourable opinion, she persuaded him at least to say that he saw no reason why, if she exercised reasonable care and took with her an excellent nurse who had already looked after her several times, her health should be worse in India than in England'.[15] She best summed up her attitude when she told her son: 'It will be a marvellous experience, and if it does take a few years off the rest of my life, it will have been well worthwhile.' Certainly she took India in her stride, and on 31 January 1923 the *Bristol Times and Mirror* told its readers that 'Lady Reading, whose desires and interests have great weight with her husband, finds the position of Vicereine quite an attractive and brilliant one'.[16]

Reassured by his wife's optimism, Reading considered whether his own constitution could take the strain. To help himself come to a reasonable decision on this question, he called upon Lord Curzon, who had served as a rash and reforming Viceroy from 1898 to 1905, and who had done so despite bouts of ill-health. He found Curzon ill at his home in Carlton House Terrace and lying in 'a small, almost bare, room ... on the simplest of brass bedsteads'. Curzon swept Reading's doubts aside with a magnificent flourish redolent of viceregal grandeur: 'Climate?' he said. 'The Viceroy has not to concern himself with climate. He goes where he wishes.'

Satisfied that his and his wife's health could stand the strain, and with Emma Squires, Gerald's old nurse, determined to accompany them, the remaining problem was one of money.

Early in December 1920 Lloyd George had acknowledged that there was 'a difficulty about money'. Although Reading's private means were substantial, he lived fairly lavishly and his wife's medical bills were a steady expense. To sacrifice the pensionable post of Lord Chief Justice, and then to return to Britain from India at the age of sixty-six to begin a search for new sources of income, seemed foolhardy.

In order to satisfy his friend's anxieties on this score, Lloyd George went to extraordinary lengths, using all his powers of persuasion and innovative skill, to find a solution. If not all of his tactics make edifying reading, they at least bear witness to the Prime Minister's warm regard for Reading, and to his determination to appoint him Viceroy.

Lloyd George's first move was to confide in Sir Edward Carson and, outlining Reading's financial worries and pointing out that he had not nearly earned his judicial pension, propose this plan: Reading would go to India, leaving an elderly judge as a stopgap Lord Chief Justice, would resume his judicial post on his return, and then go on to earn his pension.

Carson was taken aback. He told the Prime Minister 'that it was a shocking and impossible plan, that it would be an affront to the Bench, and that it would be an affront to [Hewart] the best Attorney there ever had been'.[17] Here was a real stumbling-block. How could Hewart be reconciled to such a plan, when he was entitled to succeed to the post of Lord Chief Justice on Reading's resignation?

Lloyd George then tackled Hewart in mid-December 1920, and genially proposed this solution to the problem. Hewart made a note of the proposal:

The plan which he immediately proceeded to unfold was as follows: that Rufus should go to India, that the office of Lord Chief Justice should then be offered to me, that I should for the moment decline it, and that then it should be offered to and accepted by one of the more elderly judges, who had earned or almost earned his pension, upon the terms that he should give it up at any time when requested by the Prime Minister, which request might be made in a few months' time and certainly would be made before he (Lloyd George) ceased to be head of this Administration or before the next General Election, whichever event should first happen, and that thereupon I should be appointed Lord Chief Justice.

The Prime Minister told me that he had thought over this plan with great care, and wanted to know what I thought of it. I said at once that there seemed to me to be grave objections to it, but that it was too serious a matter to dispose of in a moment, and that I should like to think it over for a few hours. He answered that that was most reasonable, and asked me to see him again on the following afternoon.[18]

The next day Hewart went to see Lloyd George to discuss the matter further. Having thought the proposal over, the Attorney-General had grave doubts on two counts. First, would it be possible to find the elderly and compliant judge to stand in for Reading, and then to go quietly when required? Second, if Hewart stood aside as the Prime Minister asked, would not the public, unaware of the private agreement, assume that the Attorney-General had not been considered suitable to succeed to the post of Lord Chief Justice? Lloyd George made no secret of his feelings, saying ruefully, 'The Government simply cannot do without you. I am very sorry. I thought my little plan would have worked. But now I have your decision – a very reasonable decision, no doubt – there is an end of the matter. Our friend Rufus must stay where he is.'[19]

The whole affair had now reached a most extraordinary stage. Lloyd

George's original idea that Reading should return to the post of Lord Chief Justice on his return from India seemed to have been scrapped. Did that mean that Reading had reconciled himself to his apparently precarious financial position if he could no longer count upon a judicial pension? In the event Reading died an extremely wealthy man, leaving £290,487. 11s. 9d. in his will – so the financial anxieties he expressed to Lloyd George when first approached over the Viceroyalty were clearly insubstantial.

If Reading was in the process of reconciling himself to taking the Viceroyalty without the prospect of returning to the office of Lord Chief Justice, why did Lloyd George take such a strong line with Hewart? Did the government really need Hewart's services as Attorney-General so much? His mark upon history is not a profound one. Why did Lloyd George make Hewart's compliance with his plan the essential prelude to Reading's appointment as Viceroy?

Reading himself later told Hewart that Lloyd George and Bonar Law, the Conservative leader, would not agree to his becoming Viceroy if the Attorney-General would not agree to stand aside, saying, 'We have been over all the ground again, and they are as adamant as ever. They will not part with you at the present time, and I am not going to India. I have just left them, and they are in the act of arranging another appointment as Viceroy.' Hewart sought out Bonar Law, whom he trusted a great deal more than Lloyd George, to find out the truth and Law backed up Lloyd George, saying, 'There are thousands of men who can be Viceroy of India, but we only have one Attorney.'

Tremendous pressure was put on Hewart during the course of a fortnight running into the new year of 1921. The newspapers, from *The Times* to the *Daily Mail*, wrote as if Reading's appointment was imminent. Hewart learned from a lobby correspondent that 'you prefer a political career and that you are not to be appointed to the Chief Justiceship', and Lloyd George told his harried Attorney-General that he might never succeed at all to that great office.

Hewart was not the only man under pressure. Reading's feelings swung between elation and depression as the Viceroyalty seemed to be within his grasp one minute and to be eluding him the next. Hewart described him on 4 January 1921 as having 'that look of pallor and that earnest demeanour which I had so often noticed upon him on occasions of great importance'; the next morning Reading struck Hewart as a different being, like a man who had just seen a ghost; a little later the same day, on a further visit to 32 Curzon Street, Hewart found him peevish, complaining, 'The delay is not consistent with my position.

Everybody is expecting a definite announcement in the newspapers one way or the other today, or at the latest tomorrow.'[20]

At last Hewart gave way to the pressure, perhaps swayed finally by the belief that he might never become Lord Chief Justice if he continued to thwart Lloyd George, and, incidentally, Bonar Law, a potential Prime Minister. He went to Reading and made his offer:

> Rufus was, as before, alone. I told him that I was prepared, if need be, to give way provided that the Prime Minister would assent to two further conditions. One was that when Rufus resigned the post of Lord Chief Justice and the vacancy actually occurred, the post should be definitely offered to me, and that I should be given a real opportunity of declining it, and that the offer and the refusal if made should be officially announced.
>
> The other condition was that the plan now proposed should not in any degree prejudice my claim to the Lord Chancellorship if and when it became vacant.
>
> Rufus thought that there would be no difficulty about either condition.[21]

Lloyd George was delighted with Hewart's capitulation, and heaped fulsome praise upon him. Although the Attorney-General had some second thoughts, wondering whether perhaps the Prime Minister and Reading had both been bluffing, Lloyd George pulled two draft telegrams out of his pocket which did indeed offer the Viceroyalty to someone other than Reading – almost certainly Lord Lytton, then Parliamentary Under-Secretary for India.

Hewart's act of self-sacrifice had a satisfactory ending. A seventy-seven-year-old judge, A.T. Lawrence, later Lord Trevethin, was appointed Lord Chief Justice in Reading's place, allegedly furnishing Lloyd George with an undated letter of resignation to be used when the Prime Minister wanted him to go. Lord Trevethin lasted less than a year in the post, only learning of his 'resignation' in the morning newspapers as he travelled by train to court! Hewart succeeded him according to plan, although the letter of resignation required by Lloyd George from Trevethin possibly eased a potentially awkward situation since the stand-in Lord Chief Justice went on to ninety-three years of age, outliving Reading, and only dying in 1936 as a result of falling into the river Wye while salmon fishing!

Reading's appointment could now go ahead. He was overjoyed by the announcement, causing Lord Riddell to remark shrewdly: 'For some time past he has been on the gloomy side. Now he is like a schoolboy let out on holiday.' On 17 January 1921 Reading wrote delightedly to Lloyd George: 'Don't you think the Press has been very good on your appointment of me?'[22] Press comment had indeed been very friendly except for the *Morning Post* which objected to Reading being a Jew.

Oddly, Reading's Jewishness seemed a positive advantage to many observers. Several Indian newspapers believed that his Jewish background would enable Reading better to understand the oriental mind – though what the City of London had in common with Calcutta, Belsize Park with the Punjab, or the new Viceroy's lapsed religion with the passionate faith of India's Hindus and Muslims, was not made clear. Curzon, the most illustrious ex-Viceroy living, on the other hand was 'quite prepared ... to overlook [Reading's] race, because of the enormous importance of securing a *first rate* man ...'.[23]

Writing to the Prime Minister before Reading's appointment was finalized, Curzon insisted, 'We want a man with a statesman's knowledge of political life: not merely a courteous figurehead. Strength and character are what tell in India, for the Viceroy has great responsibilities, and, where it is tempting to be weak, he must have the courage to be strong.'[24] Reading was due to leave on the first stage of his journey to India on 16 March 1921; how well he would measure up to Curzon's recipe for viceregal success was uncertain.

14 Viceroy of India, 1921–6

We must strive to the utmost of our human capacities to ensure the success of the Reforms, strive genuinely and honestly to prevent a breakdown. . . .
Lord Reading, 1924

It is pathetic to observe the rapid decline in the power of Gandhi and the frantic attempts he is now making to cling to his position as leader at the expense of practically every principle he has hitherto advocated.
Lord Reading, 1925

Reading is a very weak Viceroy. He never reads a file or studies a subject but has people in who state a case to him orally, just as though he were a lawyer in chambers and then decides.
The Maharajah of Alwar

Reading prepared himself earnestly for the great post that he was about to take up. During more than two months after the announcement of his appointment on 6 January 1921 he set about acquiring as much information about India as he could: he read a good many books, most of them chosen on Curzon's advice; he picked the brains of civil servants and old India hands in the room set aside for him at the India Office; he read through piles of dispatches and official papers, and spent much time closeted with the Secretary of State for India, Edwin Montagu.

At a more private level, he hastened to acquire skills that had not been important to his career before, but which he now considered to be essential to his viceregal status. Since he was out of practice on horseback, and because there were occasions when the Viceroy would need to ride, he took morning riding lessons in Rotten Row. Happily his old equestrian accomplishments were revived and the prestige of the Raj was spared the embarrassment of the King-Emperor's representative being pitched from the saddle before the eyes of thousands of subjects.

He went clay pigeon shooting in order to be able to acquit himself well in the great shoots that viceroys were expected to join when they visited the princely states. He and Lady Reading also took a refresher course in ballroom dancing, reasoning that it would be an intolerable burden to remain seated at receptions in India where lines of people would be brought up for a five-minute introductory chat and that 'their life would be easier if they occasionally took to the floor, when at least conversation would not be expected'.[1]

Edwin Montagu was delighted at the zeal with which Reading set about learning the job, remarking, 'I am delighted with Rufus. We spend much of the day together. No one can say who is going to make a good Viceroy, but one can confidently predict that Rufus ought to make a good one.'[2] Reading's son was relieved at the effect of all this upon his father's spirits: 'he became rejuvenated almost overnight. The weariness and the sense of frustration vanished and, as he set about preparing himself for his greatest adventure, he shed twenty years.'[3]

On 15 March 1921 Reading and his wife were received in audience by King George v. Reading kissed hands on his appointment and was invested with the insignia of the Knight Grand Cross of the Order of the Star of India and of the Order of the Indian Empire, while the Order of the Crown of India was at the same time conferred upon Lady Reading. George v took a particular interest in the Indian Empire which he had visited in 1911 to be crowned King-Emperor at a magnificent durbar in Delhi, and Reading corresponded with him regularly during his Viceroyalty.

The next day Reading was given a farewell dinner in the Middle Temple Hall by leading members of the Bench and Bar, and at which F.E. Smith, now Lord Birkenhead and Lord Chancellor, presided. Birkenhead, who was to be Secretary of State for India during Reading's last year and a half of office, made a warm and eloquent speech in which he praised the Viceroy-designate for three qualities: a courtesy 'so exquisite that, while it was shown to everyone, it was perhaps most scrupulously shown to him who was most humble'; inexhaustible patience; and a vehement and passionate desire to do justice.

Next morning the Readings, accompanied by Emma Squires, left 32 Curzon Street on the first stage of their journey, their luggage no doubt containing the exact number of grey and black top hats recommended by Lord Curzon, as well as an extensive array of clothes for Lady Reading. With them as the train steamed towards Dover was Colonel Cranford-Stewart, the Military Secretary, two Aides-de-Camp, Lady Reading's private secretary and nurse, and Emma Squires, acting as her maid. Once in India this staff was to be increased by ten: the Viceroy's Private Secretary, his Assistant Private Secretary, his Comptroller, a surgeon and six more ADCs – of whom two were Indian.

The party, which included Gerald Isaacs and Edwin Montagu, spent the night at the Lord Warden Hotel in Dover, from where Reading cleared his conscience by writing to Lloyd George urging him to appoint Hewart Lord Chief Justice. The next day they sailed for Calais, and then took the train to Marseilles. There they embarked for Port Said on a P. & O. liner, with one of its decks drastically altered for their convenience and bearing a cow to supply Lady Reading with fresh milk.

Passing south to pick up the liner *Kaiser-i-Hind* that was to bear them through the Red Sea to Bombay, they spent a night at the British Residency in Cairo. Field Marshal Lord Allenby, conqueror of Palestine, was their host and among the guests was Winston Churchill, now Colonial Secretary and in Cairo for a conference on the Near and Middle East. The renewed fighting between Greece and Turkey was discussed at dinner, and Churchill freely denounced Lloyd George's pro-Greek policy, declaiming, 'We shall everywhere be represented as the chief enemy of Islam.' Appropriately, Britain's relations with Islam was a subject to which Reading had already given a good deal of thought, and which was to be one of the major preoccupations of his Viceroyalty.

On 2 April 1921 Lord and Lady Reading disembarked at Bombay and, to the sound of 'God Save the King', walked up the steps from the water to the great grey archway, the 'Gateway of India', built to commemorate the visit of the King-Emperor ten years before. After some appropriate speeches in a red and gold pavilion, the Readings were driven to the convocation hall of Bombay University for the swearing-in ceremony. They were then taken to government house where they were coolly, though civilly, received by the outgoing Viceroy Lord Chelmsford and his wife – both showing their disappointment that Chelmsford had only been offered a viscountcy at the end of his five-year term rather than an earldom. Reading, of course, came to India bearing his earldom with him, which may have accounted for his cold welcome from the Chelmsfords, and in particular from Lady Chelmsford.

After two days of receptions and speeches, during which time he met the leading people in Bombay, Reading and his wife left for Delhi 845 miles away gratified by 'the large cheering crowds which lined the streets despite the lateness of the hour'. Some idea of the pomp that attended Reading's new post was given by the magnificence of the viceregal train, and by the fact that the railway line to Delhi was guarded at twenty-yard intervals by soldiers holding flickering torches – a lavish deployment of manpower.

At the central station in Delhi, the Viceroy's bodyguard awaited them, resplendent in their red and blue uniforms. The bodyguard escorted the Readings past the Red Fort, the Kashmir Gate, various cantonments and official buildings to Viceregal Lodge, a long, low, white 'temporary' construction which Reading believed he would 'prefer ... infinitely to the far more impossible and palatial abode which will some day be occupied by the Viceroy'. He was now installed at the capital of British India.

What were the chief problems that Reading faced as Viceroy? The centuries-old tasks of keeping the peace between India's diverse peoples and religions, of ensuring justice, and, if possible, of promoting some material improvement in the daily lives of over 350,000,000 subjects, were daunting enough. Not that the Viceroy held sway over the whole subcontinent; approximately one-third of India was composed of princely states, from the enormous territory of Hyderabad to petty provinces of a few acres ruled by hereditary chieftains, which, though closely associated with the British Raj, were not directly under the control of the government of India. When Lord Curzon had become Viceroy in 1898, the equitable ruling of British India, aided by prudent but limited reform, and the fostering of good relations with the princely states, had been the main preoccupation of the Governor-General, or Viceroy. Indian demands for a greater share in government were scattered and insubstantial, and the modest Indian Congress movement was, in Curzon's view expressed in 1900, 'tottering to its fall'.

When Reading landed in Bombay the scene had changed beyond recognition. Far from expecting to rule India for the next one hundred years, as Curzon had imagined, Britain had already made substantial constitutional concessions to the rapidly growing Indian nationalist movement. The Morley-Minto reforms of 1908–9 had taken a bold step in associating Indians in a genuine way with the government of their own country. The conspicuous loyalty of the Indian Empire during the First World War, allied to the continuing development of nationalist feeling, had led to the Montagu-Chelmsford reforms whose cornerstone was the 1919 Government of India Act.

The 1919 Act had been pushed through Parliament by the determination of the reforming Secretary of State Edwin Montagu, who in 1917 had issued the historic declaration that bears his name and upon which the Act of 1919 had been based:

The policy of His Majesty's Government, with which the Government of India are in complete accord, is that of the increasing association of Indians in every branch of the administration and the gradual development of self-governing institutions with a view to the progressive realization of responsible government in India as an integral part of the British Empire.[4]

The Government of India Act of 1919 embodied the reforms recommended by the Montagu-Chelmsford report. The Viceroy's Executive Council was now to be composed of four Europeans and three Indians. It retained wide powers of supervision over the provinces, although surrendering much control over local finance. The central legislature was divided into two houses – a Council of State and an Assembly. In both houses elected members were in a majority, but the franchise was high and reflected, perhaps too nicely, communal differences. In any case, the Viceroy could if need arose legislate with the support of only one house or, subject to approval from London, by himself.

In the provinces and Burma, one-chamber legislatures were established with considerable elected majorities. Furthermore, a system of dyarchy was introduced whereby certain executive posts were handed over to Indian ministers – education, public health, local government and economic development. These ministers had to be members of the provincial legislatures and responsible to them. But significantly the administration of law and order, the press, finance, land revenue, famine relief and irrigation were kept in British hands. Only the lesser keys of the citadel had been surrendered.

Still, the path to responsible government within the Empire seemed clearly marked out. But 1919 brought tragic disillusionment to Indian nationalists. In April 1919 General Dyer ordered troops at Amritsar, in the Punjab, to fire on a large crowd, killing some four hundred and wounding more than a thousand. British restraint seemed to have been replaced by hotheadedness. Worse, the Hunter Committee of Inquiry appeared to many Indians to whitewash Dyer and his colleagues. Early in the year the passing of the controversial Rowlatt Acts, which authorized the government of India to retain the summary powers it had acquired during the Great War to check sedition, provoked an all-India campaign of protest led by Gandhi.

These events suggested that an uglier mood lurked behind the sweet reasonableness of the Montagu-Chelmsford reforms. The character of the Raj apparently had something in common with that of Dr Jekyll. Nor did the unfriendly temper of much of the European community reassure those Indians who hoped to proceed to independence to the strains of the national anthem. Among those alienated by 1919 was the loyalist Gandhi, whose previous desire to co-operate was transformed into non-cooperation and rebellion. Convinced of the value of the British constitutional methods, Gandhi sought to obstruct them in India. Warm in his respect for British qualities, he also wished to goad the British conscience. Motilal Nehru, father of Jawarhalal, also became disillusioned with the Raj. Congress, too, swung away from moderation and pursued a harder line.

Reading thus arrived in India at a crucial point in the history of the Raj and of Indian nationalism. The way in which he handled the various pressures and crises that were bound to arise would be seen as the proof of the British government's real intentions. His son later wrote that 'His primary duty would be to guide the first steps of this vast and heterogeneous population along the path towards ultimate self-government which had been marked out by the Government of India Act of 1919.'[5] Certainly Reading went out to India determined to see justice done, and to give decentralization and dyarchy a fair chance. His innate liberalism, his sympathy with Montagu's policy and his own perception of India's political imperatives made him a just and reforming Viceroy.

The viceregal style that Reading and his wife adopted could only work to their advantage among Indian opinion. Being a Jew set Reading a little aside from the establishment of the Raj, and had made it possible for the Parsee President of the Bombay Municipal Corporation, Sir David Sassoon, to welcome him to India in the name of one great oriental civilization to another. In reply Reading could say, unlike any previous Viceroy:

> I note especially your sympathetic reference to the ancient race to which I belong, and I observe with pleasure that you state that your pride in welcoming me is enhanced by this circumstance. It is my only connection with the East until the present moment and this leads me to wonder whether perhaps, by some fortunate almost indefinably subtle sub-consciousness, it may quicken and facilitate my understanding of the aims and aspirations, the trials and tribulations, the joys and sorrows of the Indian people, and assist me to catch the almost inarticulate cries and inaudible whispers of those multitudes who sometimes suffer most and yet find it most difficult, if not impossible, to express their needs. .... I know that the task that awaits me is as you say 'arduous indeed' – I was aware of it when I gave up my place of serene dignity to accept a place of perhaps greater dignity but certainly of less serenity. But I shall set out, cheered and encouraged by your welcome, with hopefulness in my heart, and mainly because all my experience of human beings and human affairs has convinced me that justice and sympathy never fail to evoke responsive chords in the hearts of men, of whatever race, creed or class.[6]

The official pomp and ceremony that surrounded the Viceroy could not, of course, be cast aside, yet Reading and his wife were able to keep a creditable sense of proportion. When Gerald Isaacs and his wife visited them in Simla, he recalled:

It was a strange experience ... to find myself on our first night in Simla walking in to dinner with my mother on my arm, my father escorting my wife in front of us, while the Viceregal band played 'God Save the King' and some fifty Indian servants in scarlet-and-gold tunics and white and gold pugris [light turbans] raised their white-gloved hands to their foreheads in obeisance. My mind inevitably leaped back to Broadhurst Gardens and I said to my mother: 'You have travelled a long way', and she, following my thoughts answered: 'Yes, but those first years were good too. All this would have meant so much less without them.' Perhaps that attitude of mind was the main secret of their personal success in India. They never lost either their sense of humour or their sense of proportion or forgot the long uphill road that lay behind them.[7]

Lady Reading, despite her capacity for ill-health, flourished at first under India's scorching sun, refusing to return to Britain herself for a holiday as so many of her predecessors had done. She proved to be an indefatigable shopper, busy furnishing various viceregal abodes, and deeply distressed at India's poverty. Soon after their arrival she was quick to visit 'the native hospital ... that was quite the most interesting thing I have done. I felt my work in India ought to be directed in that channel. ...'[8] Appalled by undernourished babies, she took a keen interest in infant nutrition, having, in the words of one Indian journalist, 'a great love for milk-sucking babies', and proceeded to draw attention to the age-old problem by organizing an 'All India Baby Week'. Through her initiative a hospital, bearing her name, was built for women and children at Simla. She threw herself into the committee work that flowed from her position as head of India's most important charities.

She wished 'it were possible for a Viceroy to go down amongst the people and talk to them and nail the lies to the counter',[9] and stressed that 'we give no ball, dinner or party without inviting Indians and this is much appreciated'.[10] In May 1921 she thought Gandhi 'a man of eloquence who interested me by his sincerity',[11] but a little later expressed a prudent housewife's shock at the policy of burning foreign cloth: 'Personally I think he has made a big mistake, it is to say the least of it depressing to see good cloth burnt. ...'[12] She also showed some lack of sympathy for Indian religious scruples as when, in the winter of 1921, 'I told my head man the other day I would light the fire myself if he didn't put a match to it, since then he has condescended but with fear and trembling in case he would lose caste'.[13]

In her social contact with the British establishment in India, Lady Reading was generally a great success. Soon after becoming Vicereine, the following conversation was 'overheard at a garden party: "Oh, my dear – after Lady Chelmsford!" "Isn't she charming!" "Oh, but adorable!" The second lady was one up.'[14] The Maharajah of Bikaner was, however, less impressed, recalling later 'how nice it had been that Lady Reading had enjoyed India so much. She had positively radiated happiness, but it was perhaps a pity that she had eaten cheese on her knife.'[15]

Lady Reading's happiness was cut short six months before her husband's term of office came to an end. She discovered a malignant tumour which, although needing prompt surgery, she did not mention to the Viceroy until after the departure of their visitors King Albert and Queen Elizabeth of the Belgians from Simla at the end of September 1925. She was then taken to Calcutta and the tumour was removed. She recovered slowly, but absolutely refused to consider going home before the due date in April 1926. Although it was not clear at the time, her operation had not eradicated the cancer, and she had less than four years to live.

Her refusal to leave her husband plainly indicates the very deep bond between them and their mutual dependence upon the other for companionship and support. They were zestful and informal hosts, only dreading 'the ceremony after dinners at which no entertainment was provided other than having a series of people brought up to them for a short conversation before giving way to the next comer'.[16] Their preferred way of entertaining guests 'were dinners of varying sizes for people young and old, followed either by dancing or cinema or bridge'.

Lord Reading bore the enormous quantity of work that descended upon him with fortitude and patience. The capacity for grinding toil that had made him his name at the Bar stood him in good stead in Delhi, Simla, Calcutta and elsewhere. His son Gerald, who visited his parents in 1922 and 1924 for two holidays of six weeks, could not remember, apart from his father's morning ride, 'a single occasion other than at the weekend during either visit on which my father ever left the house, even to go into the garden, except on public business of one kind or another'.[17]

The Viceroy began his daily routine by rising early, as he had always done, and riding for an hour between seven and eight o'clock; 'nothing but impenetrable mist or tropical rain could induce him to forgo his only exercise of the day'. Although Simla offered him few changes of route, he avoided monotony by paying close attention to everything that came his way, new effects of light, the unfamiliar types of men and women that he passed, and the wild flowers: 'I rejoice each morning in all the different varieties. Just at present the [hill-side] is full of blossom, my favourites being the wild geraniums, orchids, dahlias and anemones. I am becoming a great nature-student in my dotage.'

He preferred to take breakfast alone on the verandah outside his study at Simla, the summer capital, and afterwards met and received reports from senior government officials. At least once a week he chaired a meeting of the Viceroy's Executive Council. He took lunch with his wife and however many guests happened to be present.

The afternoons were devoted to more meetings with officials, and the reading of documents and dispatches. Sometimes he received a visitor of particular importance. He insisted on taking half an hour to have tea with Lady Reading in her sitting room. The evenings were crammed full with official dinners, more informal dinners, balls, levees, investitures and the like.

To be a fully committed Viceroy it was vital to have a constitution of steel. Reading, despite his enormous workload, was almost invariably polite and thoughtful, picking his way deftly through his files, and sitting back detached and judicial while his officials put their cases to him. According to his son he was 'often worried but never flurried and he never allowed himself to be rushed into a decision after insufficient thought or upon incomplete facts'. His second Secretary of State, Lord Peel, thought of him that 'The judicial habit of looking all round a problem is perhaps prone to retard executive action, but is none the less emphatic in the character it gives to resolution, when once taken.'[18]

As in the past, Reading could relax with swiftness and conviction, 'putting up the shutters at closing time' he called it, and 'he was always astonishing his staff and guests by appearing at dinner in the gayest of humours after long hours of unbroken and anxious toil'. He did his best to accommodate the passion for hunting that possessed so many of India's princely rulers and, indeed, senior servants of the Raj. He duly slaughtered grouse, duck and geese (though later refusing to tell George v, who was a crack shot, how many cartridges he had expended in achieving his tally); he even bagged a tiger in Gwalior, but afterwards confessed, 'In truth I am not so keen upon actually killing the animal as being in the jungle which I love. . . .'[19]

The Readings were widely popular in India, despite some early anti-semitic mutterings from elements in the British establishment there.

They maintained a lively interest in their exotic environment, while not failing to notice and condemn the squalor and human misery that also confronted them. Although Lady Reading asked her family at home, 'Do you think I can ever come back after being spoilt like this?', the magnificence of their viceregal progress never went to either of their heads and they were able to take pleasure in the ridiculous side of so much of the official pomp which surrounded them.

Reading's preparation for his viceregal responsibilities had convinced him of the need to make reasonable concessions to various sections of Indian opinion. Before leaving Britain he told Lloyd George (who was pursuing a pro-Greek anti-Turkish policy) that he had been carrying out research at the India Office into 'the causes of agitation' in India and had concluded that Muslim objections to the Treaty of Sèvres were 'one of the main causes of the unrest'. He wanted to impress upon the Prime Minister 'how important it is, in my judgement, to make some concessions to Mahommedan opinion if you think they can be safely made'.[20]

Was Reading proposing to drive a wedge between the Muslim League and Congress during 1921, the year when both parties were closely involved in a programme of non-cooperation against the Raj? Can we discern an apparently reasonable man's attempt to 'divide and rule'? The character of Muslim unrest, and the delicate relationship between the two great Indian religious communities, is too complex to allow so crude an analysis.

The First World War had both encouraged Hindu–Muslim accord and provided a stick with which Muslim activists could belabour the Raj. The accord had been given structure by the Lucknow Pact of 1916 in which Congress and the Muslim League agreed to give Muslims separate electorates in all provincial legislatures and to allow them special weighting in Hindu majority provinces. This meant that even in the United Provinces, where Muslims accounted for only 14.3 per cent of the population, 30 per cent of the seats allotted to Indians in the legislature would be filled by separately elected Muslims. In the Central Legislature the Muslims would have one-third of the elected seats although they were only 24 per cent of the population of British India. The Montagu-Chelmsford reforms, through the Act of 1919, thus put Muslims in a strong position in the provinces and encouraged most League leaders to believe that they should co-operate with the constitutional plans of the Raj.

On the other hand, the First World War had given rise to the Khilafat movement. The defeat of Turkey by the Allies, and the dismemberment of the Turkish Empire, had aroused Muslim anxieties over the future status of the Khalifa (the Turkish Sultan), the spiritual head of Islam and warden of various sanctuaries, including Jazirat-ul-Arab, the geographical centre of the Islamic faith. The Treaty of Sèvres in 1920, making peace with Turkey, had angered India's Muslims, and the Khilafat movement had become a painful thorn in the side of the Raj.

Although Congress, the Muslim League and the Khilafat movement had combined to support the *satyagraha*, or non-cooperation campaign, inspired by Gandhi in the aftermath of the Rowlatt Acts and the Amritsar massacre, strains were apparent within the alliance by the time Reading had settled in as Viceroy. In particular the Ali brothers, Mahommed and Shaukat, leaders of the Khilafat agitation, were trying to foment mutiny in the army, calling for complete independence, and prepared to welcome an invasion of India by the warrior Muslims of Afghanistan. The Ali brothers were also impatient with Gandhi for preaching the virtues of non-violent pressure for change upon the Raj. As early as the end of April 1921 Reading informed the Secretary of State for India that he was considering prosecuting the Ali brothers for their agitation.

In the event, he decided instead to try to detach Gandhi from his alliance with the Ali brothers. The Viceroy and the newly emerged leader of Indian nationalism met on 14 May 1921, through the good offices of Pandit Madan Mohan Malaviya. It was to be the first of six interviews.

Reading left a graphic account of these meetings in letters written to his son and Montagu:

There is nothing striking about his appearance. He came to visit me in a white dhoti and cap, woven on a spinning-wheel, with bare feet and legs, and my first impression on seeing him ushered into my room was that there was nothing to arrest attention in his appearance and that I should have passed him by in the street without a second look at him. When he talks the impression is different. He is direct and expresses himself well in excellent English with a fine appreciation of the words he uses. There is no hesitation about him and there is a ring of sincerity in all that he utters, save when discussing some political questions.

His religious views are, I believe, genuinely held and he is convinced to a point almost bordering on fanaticism that non-violence and love will give India its independence and enable it to withstand the British Government. His religious and moral views are admirable and indeed are on a remarkably high altitude, but I must confess that I find it difficult to understand his practice of them in politics. To put it quite briefly, he is like the rest of us; when engaged in a political movement he wishes to gather all under his umbrella and to reform them and bring them to his views. He has consequently to accept many with whom he is not in accord, and has to do his best to keep the combination together. This is particularly true of the Hindu–Moslem combination which I think rests upon insecure foundations. . . .

In the course of six interviews – the first of four hours and a half, the second of three hours, the third of an hour and a half, the fourth of an hour and a half, the fifth of an hour and a half and the sixth of three-quarters of an hour – I have had many opportunities of judging him. A critical point came towards the end of the second interview, when I, for the first time, adopted a firm and rather severe attitude. He seemed surprised and I think his attitude changed from that moment.

Our conversations were of the frankest; he was supremely courteous with manners of distinction. A slight incident at our first interview reveals a pleasant Oriental courtesy. I wanted tea and I pressed him to have some. He would take nothing. He then asked for hot water, which was immediately brought whilst I waited for tea. I was concerned lest his hot water should get cold, and when my tea was brought said he was letting his hot water get cold. He replied: 'I could not think of tasting it until you had had your tea.'

He held in every way to his word in the various discussions we had. He explained in public that he had applied for interviews and gave quite an accurate account of the events leading to his letter to my Private Secretary. Altogether you will judge that I liked him and that I believe there are possibilities in the future. Upon leaving he seemed quite affected and earnestly assured me he would come whenever I wanted him.[21]

Reading discussed four main topics with Gandhi: the Punjab disturbances and the Amritsar massacre of 1919; the Treaty of Sèvres; the meaning of Swaraj; and Gandhi's attitude to the possibility of an Afghan invasion. On Amritsar Gandhi 'displayed considerable animus against all those British officers who had come into prominence during the quelling of the dangerous rising in the Punjab, and in particular he inveighed against Sir Michael O'Dwyer [the Governor of the Punjab] and General Dyer, demanding the cancellation of their pensions'. He then spoke in a much more perfunctory manner about the Treaty of Sèvres, clearly aware that he was not an accredited spokesman for Muslim opinion. As to the possible Afghan invasion, Reading asked him how he would deal with it:

He answered that he would go to meet the invaders and conquer them by love. I suggested that whilst he and his disciples were embracing them they would strangle him, to which he replied that even if he knew that would happen he would still take the same course and that the effect upon both Indians and Afghans would be to make his views prevail in the end.[22]

It is worth noting that Gandhi's solution to the possibility of an Afghan invasion was repeated in the face of a much more ominous threat in 1942, when he advocated that the British should immediately quit India which, thus purified, would be able to overcome the Japanese forces poised on her frontiers with love and 'truth-force'.

Reading also cross-examined Gandhi as to precisely what he meant by the word 'Swaraj', which was in fact translated as 'self-rule'. Gandhi began by being evasive, and the Viceroy later recounted this part of their interview in mild exasperation:

Discussion then led to the meaning attributed to Swaraj and frankly I am as much at a loss now to explain it as when he came into the room, although I have tried hard to get a definite meaning from him. All I could gather was that, when the Indians had regained their self-respect and had pursued a policy of non-cooperation with the Government and had refrained from violence, they would have gained Swaraj. I asked the question point blank: 'What is it in the actions of the Government that makes you pursue the policy of non-cooperation with the Government?'

The answer, repeated more than once during our interviews, was that he was filled with distrust of the Government and that all their actions, even though apparently good, made him suspect their motives. I pressed him to be more precise, and eventually he stated that he had some time ago arrived at the conclusion that every action of the Government which appeared good, and indeed was good, was actuated by the sinister motive of trying to fasten British dominion on India. This was his answer to all the arguments about the new reformed Councils, and in my judgment is the root cause of his present attitude to the Government.[23]

Eventually Reading returned to the problem of the Ali brothers, and extracted from Gandhi a commitment to obtain from them a promise to stop their incitements to violence and to apologize publicly for their earlier provocation. In return, Reading undertook to ensure that the charges of sedition against the brothers were not proceeded with. Although Gandhi subsequently tried to insert in his draft letter to the brothers some passages supporting non-cooperation, Reading would have none of it, and finally fixed a time-limit for an accommodation to be worked out. Gandhi deluged the Ali brothers with telegrams and at last obtained their agreement to Reading's demands.

Montagu was full of praise, telling Reading, 'We are all delighted with your skilful treatment of Gandhi. You gained a great victory.' Reading had certainly acted with determination and finesse, and seemed to have succeeded in his objective of undermining the influence of the Ali brothers, particularly Mahommed whom he saw as the

real factor in the situation: he is the ostensible link between Mahommedan and Hindu. If trouble comes between him and Gandhi, it means the collapse of the bridge over the gulf between Hindu and Mahommedan. If Mohammed Ali does as Gandhi desires – and that no doubt will be to make the declaration – Mahommed Ali will be lowered in the public esteem; his position as a leader will be seriously impaired and the most disturbing factor of peace at the moment will be quietened.

Reading was over-optimistic: the Ali brothers were soon busily explaining away their apology, and Gandhi promptly resumed his offensive against the Raj. None the less, Reading's move to isolate and humiliate the Alis, while generally showing broad sympathy with Muslim opinion, was effective in drawing Muslims closer to the Raj.

Towards the end of 1921 the differences between the Muslim League and the Hindu-dominated Congress party were accentuated. In August the fierce rebellion of the Moplahs, the Muslim peasantry of the Malabar coast, against their Hindu landlords reinforced communal antagonisms. On the other hand, Gandhi's calling-off non-cooperation a little later left his Muslim supporters feeling aggrieved.

The Khilafat movement waned from the middle of 1921. Mahommed Ali, and to a lesser extent his brother, tried to reassert his influence, causing Reading to remark in July 1921 that 'It seems clear ... that Mahommed Ali is trying hard to recover his position and is indulging in fairly wild talk.' He added, however, 'Our reports indicate that he has become very high-handed and is upsetting some of his own followers in consequence.'[24] Two months later the brothers were arrested for incitement during the Moplah rebellion and Reading told Montagu, 'I believe generally throughout the community, excepting of course the extremists, there is a feeling of relief that the Ali brothers have been incarcerated and are to be prosecuted.'[25]

Reading pressed home his counter-attack against the Khilafat extremists on 28 February 1922 when he sent Montagu a dispatch formally asking the British government, on the eve of the Paris Conference, to try to reconcile Greek and Turkish differences, to revise the Treaty of Sèvres. Reading requested the following three revisions which 'we ourselves regard as essential: first, evacuation of Constantinople; second, the Sultan's suzerainty over the holy places; third, restoration of Ottoman Thrace, including the sacred Moslem city of Adrianople, and the unreserved restoration of Smyrna'.

Throughout 1922 and 1923 events conspired to weaken the Khilafat cause further. In 1922 the Turkish revolutionary leader Kemal Ataturk overthrew the Sultan of Turkey, thus denying the Khalifa any further pretence to temporal power and undermining his claim to spiritual power as well. Ataturk's military success against the Greeks, while causing the Chanak crisis in the autumn of 1922, also reasserted Muslim authority in territory dear to the hearts of Indian Khilafat supporters. Peace between Turkey and Greece was finally concluded on 24 July 1923 at Lausanne, with Stanley Baldwin's Conservative government confirming much of Turkey's military success. In 1924 Ataturk completed the discomfiture of the die-hard Khilafatists by abolishing the Khilafat.

Meanwhile prominent Muslim politicians in India were beginning to question the value of long-term League-Congress co-operation. As early as December 1921 Hasrat Mohani, the Khilafatist president of the Muslim League, advocated a federation of free Indian states where Kashmir, the Punjab, Sind, Bengal and Assam would be ruled by their Muslim majorities and where Hindu majority states like Madras, Bombay and the United Provinces 'will not be allowed to overstep the limits of moderation against the Mussulmans'.[26] In the 1923 council elections Muslims accounted for only 3.6 per cent of Congress delegates, and many of their co-religionists preferred to stand on the Swarajist ticket. In Bengal, between 1923 and 1926, Fazlul Huq urged the province's Muslims not to enter into alliance with C.R. Das but 'to stand on their own feet, in co-operation with the government and against the Hindus'.[27] In December 1924 the Muslim League met as a separate body from Congress for the first time since 1920. The League now demanded an all-India federation but with full provincial autonomy and separate electoral rolls for Muslims and Hindus.

Hindu–Muslim co-operation thus suffered a serious set-back during Reading's Viceroyalty. The man who was eventually to play a major part in establishing the state of Pakistan in 1947, Mahommed Ali Jinnah, led the predominantly Muslim Independent party within the Muslim League when Reading arrived in India. In November 1921 Jinnah called upon Reading, who recounted the meeting to Montagu:

Jinnah came to me yesterday and had long interview. I found him distinctly able, rather extremist, not a non-cooperationist, but somewhere between moderate and extremist. I think he stands politically where Malaviya [the moderate Hindu leader] does, i.e. he holds strong views about acceleration of Swaraj, redress of Punjab wrongs, in favour of Khilafat agitation, but has not joined Gandhi, whose policy he regards as destructive and not constructive. ... Punjab grievances were capable, he thought, of settlement on basis of expressions of regret, and perhaps more emphasized statement that humiliation orders must be made impossible for future, and that some officers inculpated should be dismissed. On Swaraj he realized the difficulty of making any definite statement at moment, but thought it would not be difficult to agree upon some formula. ...

I definitely declined to commit myself in any shape or form, save in expressions of sympathy with Moslem Indian opinion which I had already publicly made. On Punjab grievances I reiterated the various steps we had taken, and added that I could not countenance even discussion of dismissal of subordinate officers who had merely obeyed superior orders. ... I pointed out the injury that would be done to India and to obtaining of Swaraj if any insult or affront was offered to the Prince of Wales. ... He agreed, but thought that it was very difficult for the general public to take this view. ... I was impressed by his evident desire to use the present moment for settlement, which is on the eve of the All India Congress Committee Meeting on the 4th.

He left me on the understanding that if better conditions prevail with regard to Greece and Turkey, and I find that I can give greater hope, I should let him know and he would come again at any minute I called him. I am left under the impression that there is a real desire to arrive at a settlement, particularly as he told me he had seen both Gandhi and Malaviya before he left [Bombay] for Delhi. I have no solid ground for this impression, and therefore give it with caution. I was not particularly desirous of encouraging him in his role of broker, as he termed it, for I see little if any prospect of agreement between Gandhi and myself. Moreover, anxious as I am to banish illegal and substitute constitutional agitation, I am not at present prepared to make substantial sacrifices to arrive at it.

Jinnah's personality, as distinguished from intellect, did not favourably impress me. I thought I discerned strong anti-British feeling, although masked at the moment, and some want of scruple. He has acute sensibility and subtlety of mind, and yet I think he lacks perception of impression he is creating. I prefer Malaviya.[28]

Reading could be pleased as his Viceroyalty came to an end, with the Lucknow Pact and Hindu–Muslim co-operation in a sorry state, that he had encouraged a substantial Muslim movement away from support of Gandhi. In 1923 he had made his early intentions plain when he wrote:

For the first year that I was in India and when the Ali brothers were much to the fore, the menace was more serious from the Mahommedans than the Hindus, for they were fierce and fanatical. It is very striking that in all the troubles we had which culminated in violent disturbances or in imprisonment, the larger proportion was Mahommedan. The Gandhi movement could never have gained its strength but for the Treaty of Sèvres, which made the Mahommedans so frantic that they joined up with the Hindus.[29]

Once back in Britain, however, Reading vehemently rejected the charge that he and the government of India had encouraged religious and communal separatism. Speaking in the House of Lords on 28 July

1926, a few months after ending his Viceroyalty, he asserted that: 'Throughout the five years of my life in India I not only most carefully watched but sought every opportunity of ascertaining whether there was the slightest foundation for this charge, and I never found even the merest breath of evidence to support it.'[30]

Despite Reading's disclaimer, there is no doubt as to the effects of his policy of placating Muslim opinion. Perhaps he saw it partly as a necessary dispensation of justice to a powerful minority; certainly he wanted to undermine the potency of Gandhi's appeal to the masses, an appeal made doubly dangerous for the Raj by the Mahatma's success in encouraging co-operation between Hindus and Muslims. With Gandhi's influence reduced, Reading hoped for a more predictable approach to constitutional reform.

Apart from Hindu–Muslim co-operation there was another major casualty of Reading's policy of placating Islam. As an indirect result of the official request for the British government to renegotiate the Treaty of Sèvres, Edwin Montagu was forced to resign as Secretary of State for India.

When Montagu authorized Reading to publish the dispatch of 28 February 1922, specifying those parts of the treaty to be revised, he did so without consulting either the Prime Minister, Lloyd George, or Lord Curzon, the Foreign Secretary. Although the telegram containing Reading's proposals had been circulated to Cabinet members on 4 March, this was a Saturday and there was thus no chance to discuss the request. Reading put pressure on Montagu in a second telegram, saying that he was planning to arrest Gandhi within the next few days, and that, because of this and reports of Muslim violence in certain provinces, he needed an immediate reply. Montagu thus authorized publication of Reading's first telegram.

On Monday 6 March 1922, at a Cabinet meeting presided over by Austen Chamberlain in Lloyd George's absence, Montagu, while not raising the matter officially, admitted to Curzon that he had authorized publication two days earlier. Curzon, who was about to attend the Conference in Paris on the problem, was staggered; he later wrote Montagu an angry letter, saying:

Had I, when Viceroy, ventured to make a public pronouncement in India about the foreign policy of the Government in Europe I should certainly have been recalled. ... That I should go into a Conference at Paris, while a subordinate branch of the British Government 6,000 miles away dictated to the British Government what line it thinks I ought to pursue in Thrace seems to me quite intolerable.

Curzon's righteous indignation was particularly ironical in view of his own conflict with the Balfour government over exactly the same issue some twenty years earlier. Balfour had then fought a protracted campaign to limit Curzon's high-handed approach to foreign policy, complaining, 'To allow a Viceroy to run his own foreign policy ... irrespective of the foreign policy of the Home Government, would be to copy the blunder which has brought Russia to disaster and humiliation – the blunder, namely, of having one Foreign Minister in the Far East and another at home, not necessarily acting in accord.'[31] Balfour had also remarked wryly that Curzon, if unbridled, 'would raise India to the position of an independent and not always friendly power'.

These earlier conflicts conveniently forgotten, Curzon's anger was communicated to Lloyd George, who called Montagu before him on 9 March and demanded his resignation for an action 'totally incompatible with the collective responsibility of the Cabinet to the Sovereign and Parliament'.

Reading was horrified by the news, and telegraphed his distress to Lloyd George on 13 March; he wondered whether he, too, ought to resign. The Prime Minister promptly let him know he should do no such thing, and that,'There is no imputation against you or your Government. Montagu did not suggest that he relied on you or seek in any way to shelter himself behind you.'

There is no doubt that there were many in the Tory party (including Curzon), and among the British in India, who were glad to see the reforming Montagu go. Montagu told Reading on 10 March 1922 that, 'You are too shrewd to make it necessary to warn you that the general political situation was not without its bearing on the causes of which led to my resignation.'[32] Lloyd George's passionate support of Greece against Turkey must also have encouraged him to dismiss a man who was wholeheartedly backing the renegotiation of the Treaty of Sèvres.

One unpleasant reaction to the resignation, containing a reminder of the anti-semitism so common in British ruling circles, came in a letter written to Curzon by Sir Walter Lawrence on 14 March 1922. In a tone later to be commonplace in Nazi Germany, and hinting at the 'Jewish international conspiracy', Lawrence wrote:

You have been very much in our thoughts lately, as we feel, as do all our friends, very bitter against that malicious and dangerous Jew. My inference is that he deliberately created this situation to get out of office before the [crisis?] came in India. He suggests intrigue – he who has intrigued with his agents in India, British and Indian, to be made Viceroy.

It ought to be emphasized that the problems that are coming to India are due, not so much to our policy, as to the intrigues and methods of this mischievous Jew.[33]

The Jewish Viceroy, however, remained in office, though confiding to his son, 'I am very doubtful whether I ought to let Edwin go into the wilderness without following him, not merely because we are both children of Israel and both anathema to a certain section of people, but because I find it very difficult to understand why he should have been drummed out of the Cabinet post haste.' Reading told Montagu that, though contemplating resignation, he had decided to stay on because 'my departure from office simultaneously with you would have a remarkably bad effect in India – not because of my own personality, but because I had become identified in Indian minds with the Liberal policy you had pursued'. Montagu, for his part, replied, 'May I say how much I hope you will "stick to it", and continue your wise rule.'[34]

Reading was desperately anxious to avoid the public impression that Montagu had been dismissed because of government disapproval of his policies. On 11 March 1922 he telegraphed his own alterations to Montagu's draft message explaining his resignation to the princes and people of India. Reading wanted this statement to be included: 'Another point I must emphasize is that my resignation involves no change in the policy of His Majesty's Government on the subject of Reforms, as announced in the Declaration of August 1917, and as later embodied in the provisions of the Government of India Act [of 1919].'[35] Austen Chamberlain, a former Secretary of State for India himself, who dealt with Reading's proposed amendment, told Reading two days later that he was quite unable to authorize the publication of Montagu's proposed message, but emphasized that 'the resignation of Mr Montagu has nothing whatever to do with the Government's Indian policy'.[36]

The controversy continued fiercely for some days. Reading complained to Lloyd George on 13 March that press reports were suggesting 'some particular cunning' underlying his initial request for a revision to the Treaty of Sèvres, and that he owed it to his self-respect to resign with Montagu. The Viceroy was adamant that the impression that Montagu had been sacrificed to the Cabinet's hard-liners must be avoided. Montagu stirred up more controversy by speaking on 12 March at the Cambridge Liberal Club, enabling *The Times* the next day to head its report of the speech 'Victim of Die-Hard Dislike', and 'Prime Minister as Dictator'.[37] Curzon also waded into the fray, publishing a letter which Austen Chamberlain described to Lloyd George as 'the first public criticism directed at the conduct of Reading and his Government'.[38]

That Edwin Montagu's resignation was partly a response to Tory die-hard pressure within the Lloyd George coalition is indicated by a vote of censure put down in the House of Commons in February 1922. A die-hard Tory MP Sir William Joynson-Hicks had moved the censure motion, accusing Montagu of the 'criminal betrayal of every white man and woman in India all through 1919, 1920, and 1921', and also, rather fancifully, of having 'broken the heart of the [Indian] Civil Service'. Although ninety MPs supported the motion, Montagu had come through the censure debate triumphantly, securing a large majority in his favour.

Shortly afterwards Montagu had written a letter to Reading in which he gave a frank analysis of the political pressures at work in Britain, including the view that Lloyd George 'if anything is endeavouring to right himself with the Conservatives', and considering the effects of the current instability within the coalition government upon Indian policy:

Meanwhile the Conservative Party seems to be getting more and more restive at the existence of the Coalition. The trend of events is by no means closer alliance but rather towards separation, and whatever happens it looks as if Liberalism at the moment is not in a bright position, hopelessly split, more so than ever, between the fires of Ultra-Conservatives on the one hand and Labour on the other.

Lloyd George appears imperturbable, but if anything is endeavouring to right himself with the Conservatives. Chamberlain looks anxious and worried, torn between loyalty to his party and loyalty to the Prime Minister. F.E. is a strangely isolated figure and very unpopular with the Conservatives. Winston jumps from the diehard to the Liberal camp as he works from Egypt or India to Ireland. That is a pithy summary of the position of the more important Members of the Government.

How do these circumstances affect us? Well, they affect us this way, that if we are not to have a reversal of the policy in India, which to my mind would mean the end of the Indian Empire, we must try and avoid, until things get brighter, presenting to the Government or Parliament proposals that they would reject. . . .

Despite the fact that the Indian debate last week had a bad Press, mainly due, I think, to the swinging of the British public against India for the moment, I am informed that it has had a very good parliamentary effect, and after all, I said nothing which could not be found in other language in the Montagu–Chelmsford Report. But the trouble is that nobody will accept the facts merely because Gandhi has not been actually arrested. No statement seems to convince the public that your Government and the Local Governments have been dealing vigorously and effectively with disorder.[39]

Reading felt 'a deep sense of personal loss' at Montagu's removal from office. Quite apart from anything else, he enjoyed nothing like the same degree of intimacy with the new Secretary of State, Lord Peel, a Conservative peer and the great-grandson of Sir Robert Peel, Queen Victoria's second Prime Minister. Although conscientious and steady-going, Peel was a political nonentity, lacking 'not only all knowledge of India but also the occasional flash of visionary insight that had made Mr Montagu so inspiring a colleague'.[40]

Peel was soon putting Lloyd George's anti-Turkish line to Reading, complaining of alleged atrocities against the Greek population in northern Anatolia. Reading countered this by reminding Peel that 'the Moslem does not now suspect the Government of India, indeed I think he believes in it as a friend of the Moslems, but he is firmly convinced, in spite of all that we may say, that the efforts we make are checked by the Government at home'.[41] Peel was soon convinced of the wisdom of Reading's pro-Muslim policy, and their relationship for the next two years was marked by a great deal of harmony.

Reading's first year as Viceroy, working with Montagu, was, however, the most obviously creative of his time in India. Quite apart from their joint initiative to reassure Muslim opinion and head off Khilafat agitation, the two men saw eye to eye on the need to placate the Punjab, still resentful of the Amritsar massacre, of the arbitrary and humiliating treatment meted out to Indians suspected of assaulting a female European missionary, and of the unofficial British support of General Dyer's 'strong measures'.

Reading made an improvised and unannounced visit to the Punjab early in his Viceroyalty. Montagu encouraged Reading's desire to do something positive, with these words:

I do not in the least wish to influence your judgment at this stage about what it is best to do with regard to the Punjab. We have discussed it so often and we are fully aware of the difficulties. I hope, however, you will not take it amiss if I suggest to you that I have no doubt you will be careful, in expressing the repugnance of Englishmen to the humiliation orders, not to let it be inferred that there is not the same horror of the doctrine of preventive murder enunciated by Dyer. If you could see your way to saying that you hope you have taken steps to prevent a recurrence of humiliation orders and that anybody issuing them will in future be at once dismissed from India without pension, I think it will have a good effect.[42]

Once Reading had arrived at Lahore in the Punjab, however, the Governor and Sir William Vincent, Home Member of the Viceroy's Council, strongly advised him not to go on to Amritsar. Reading was unmoved:

I expressed my view that to visit Lahore without going to Amritsar would occasion more comment, and might be taken as implying callousness. My proposal was to pay an informal visit, necessarily hurried by my limitation of time, and in the end both the Governor and Sir William Vincent agreed that it was advisable I should pay the informal visit.

Accordingly the Governor and I and staff went yesterday morning early to Amritsar, where reception was quite friendly and no untoward incident happened. We drove through the streets and visited the Jallianwala Bagh and then saw the Golden Temple, but we had no time to enter it, and indeed I thought perhaps it was inadvisable. Everybody seemed very satisfied with the visit and were very glad we had gone, and so far as one can gather the visit seems to have given satisfaction. I have not yet seen Press comments, but of course am prepared for criticism. . . .[43]

Reading was also prepared to push ahead with a wide range of reforms that flowed from the Montagu–Chelmsford initiative of 1918 and 1919, and agreed with the Secretary of State's assessment of the dilemma of the Raj expressed in September 1920:

As soon as the Indians were told that we agreed with them that they were to become partners with us, it instilled into their minds an increased feeling of existing subordination and a realization of everything by which this subordination was expressed. Similarly, when the Europeans were told that, after driving the Indians for so many years, that régime was to be over and they might find themselves forced to co-operation with the Indians, or even forced to allow Indians to rule India, their race consciousness sprang up afresh.

I am convinced in my own mind that that has been the fatal mistake of our policy in India. We ought to have let Indians run their own show, with all its inefficiency and imperfections. Development would have been much slower, but the inevitable transition would have been less difficult. I am, however, satisfied that the temper of democratic countries such as ours is increasingly against remaining in a country where we are not wanted, and we have either got to make our peace with the Indians, or, as the educated classes grow, we shall find a strenuous desire in this country to get rid of India and all its bother.[44]

Thus Reading supported the genuine Indianization of the Indian Civil Service, and of the army, without which progress towards independence would be merely a farce. Although the process had barely begun in 1921, when Reading arrived in India, there was a good deal of criticism within the Indian Civil Service and at home of what was clearly a trend that could only mean one thing – eventual self-rule for India. Indianization was further writing on the wall for many potential recruits into the ics, and an increasing number of graduates now began to look to the Colonial Service in Africa and elsewhere for their careers.

Reading, while anxious to encourage the Indianization of the Civil Service, was embarrassed by the sudden shortage of suitable recruits coming from Britain. His embarrassment was heightened by a speech made by Lloyd George early in August 1922 when he referred to the services in India as 'the steel frame' of the whole administrative structure, and stated that the recent reforms in India were an 'experiment' and that the government would stand by its responsibilities in the subcontinent and would take whatever steps necessary to uphold them.

Lloyd George's belligerent speech was another example of an attempt to rally the Conservative majority in his peacetime coalition. Reading was shocked by its reactionary tone, telling the Secretary of State, Peel, at the end of August 1922, 'the Prime Minister's speech has upset things tremendously here, and it will take some time before they settle down.' He also resented press criticisms at home, complaining to Peel that 'considerable injustice is being done to us as a government and certainly to me personally, in reference to this question of abandonment or reduction of recruitment in England for the Indian Civil Service'.[45]

In fact Reading wanted to maintain a reasonable level of recruitment into the ics from Britain, since this would maintain efficiency and enable Indian recruits to be properly trained and integrated. On the other hand, Indianization was to go ahead, and in his view should be accelerated when the next great step towards independence should become obvious. British opinion, especially in India, was not reassured, however, and a gloomy picture continued to be painted by the malcontents. The rate of progress was, however, slow: the 1924 Royal Commission on Indianization recommended changes in recruitment to ensure that the ics should be half Indian within fifteen years, and the police force half Indian within twenty-five years. This was hardly setting the services on the slippery path to disintegration or full-blooded Indianization.

The Indianization of the army was even more contentious, firstly because the officering of the Indian army was overwhelmingly British, and secondly because the army ultimately guaranteed law and order and stable government. Reading was in no doubt that political progress went hand in hand with the Indianization of the army as well as of the civil service. On 18 August 1921 he told Montagu:

I have never been able to understand the views of those who comfort themselves by the thought that, supposing ... full Dominion Status was given to Indians, the British Army would still remain in India, controlled by India and not by the War Office at home. Who can possibly expect that such a state of things will happen? ... Consequently, steps must be taken to enable Indians to take the high command and to direct their own Army. ... These considerations apply, though not with such force, to the other Services, and this touches one of the most complex and difficult questions surrounding the future of India. ... The problem is not only in the future: it is in the present.[46]

Reading's positive attitude helped a wind of change blow through the proud structure of the Indian army. Change was certainly needed: in 1917 there had been no fully commissioned Indian officers in the army; by 1918 ten places were reserved for them at Sandhurst. By January 1922 a revolution in thinking had occurred when Reading was able to send the recommendations of a report that proposed that the Indian army, with the exception of the Gurkhas, should be completely Indianized in three distinct stages beginning in 1925. If all went smoothly, the Indian army would be completely controlled by Indians by 1955.

The British government rejected these proposals, preferring a slower time-scale, involving fewer army units for complete Indianization. London proposed four units, but Reading fought for eight and got them; in return, however, he had to give way to Lord Peel's insistence that, even if the experiment with the eight units went well, there could be no question of increasing the number of units to be fully Indianized.

The conflict between Reading and the British government led to wild speculation in the press that the Viceroy was pressing for a complete end to European recruitment into the Indian army – as indeed he was, but in the long term. An authoritative statement in *The Times* of 14 August 1922 helped to still the more irresponsible rumours, but progress towards Indianization was hardly helped by the Commander-in-Chief of the Indian army, Lord Rawlinson, referring in 1924 to the 'supreme difficulty' of Indianizing the army at a rate appropriate to the advance towards self-government. Rawlinson believed, quite simply, that 'it is more than doubtful whether a sufficient number of the right type of Indians will ever come forward to supply the military requirements of the army ...'.[47]

Even after the Skeen (Indian Sandhurst) committee proposed in

1926 an immediate and progressive increase in the number of Indian places at Sandhurst, the projection was an extremely modest one – that the Indian army would be half-Indianized by 1952.

With the Viceroy and the home government in such clear disagreement over essentials like the rate of Indianization in the civil and military services, it was small wonder that many Indian nationalists were suspicious of Britain's real intentions towards their demand for independence. To a large extent, the difficulties were due to changes of government in Britain and to changes at the India Office. Lord Peel, as we have seen, was far less sympathetic to Reading's progressive line than Edwin Montagu had been. Peel continued as Secretary of State when the Lloyd George coalition fell in October 1922, serving first under Bonar Law and then, from May 1923 to January 1924, under Stanley Baldwin. He must have felt more secure in his resistance to some of Reading's proposals as part of a wholly Conservative government.

The advent of the first, minority, Labour government in January 1924 did not, however, open the floodgates of Indian reform. In power on the suffrance of the Liberals, Ramsay MacDonald's administration was in no position to force through radical changes, even if they had seriously wished to do so. Lord Olivier, the distinguished ex-civil servant, and Fabian, who took Lord Peel's place at the India Office, got on remarkably well with Reading, even to the extent of supporting him in his move to revive an old statute empowering India's provincial governments to detain agitators without trial for indefinite periods.

When the Conservatives returned to power in November 1924, Reading was gratified to find his old friend F. E. Smith, now Lord Birkenhead, at the India Office. Despite the warmth of feeling between them, however, the two men had widely divergent views of India's capacity to achieve independence, even within the Empire. Birkenhead, for example, believed 'that a Government founded so completely as ours is upon prestige can stand almost anything except the suspicion of weakness'.

On 4 December 1924 the Secretary of State expressed views to Reading which were openly reactionary:

I think you know that alone in the Cabinet, I distrusted and, to some extent, opposed the Montagu–Chelmsford Report. To me it is frankly inconceivable that India will ever be fit for Dominion self-government. My present view is that we ought rigidly to adhere to the date proposed in the Act for a re-examination of the situation, and that it is not likely, unless matters greatly change in the interval, that such a re-examination will suggest the slightest extension.[48]

He returned to the theme on 22 January 1925:

In ultimate analysis, the strength of the British position is that we are in India for the good of India. The most striking illustration of the truth of the position is of course supplied by the infinite variation of nationality, sect and religion in the sub-continent. The more it is made obvious that these antagonisms are profound, and affect immense and irreconcilable sections of the population, the more conspicuously is the fact illustrated that we, and we alone, can play the part of composers.

I, as you know, never liked, or believed in, the Montagu-Chelmsford reforms. I distrusted dyarchy, though I realized that dyarchy was an indispensable experiment in attempting to begin grafting Western parliamentary institutions upon an Oriental population, wholly uneducated for their receipt. But I realize of course that we must give the reforms a fair chance insisting at the same time that those to whom they were offered shall equally give them a fair chance.[49]

Reading was more than ready to give dyarchy and other reforms a fair chance. Soon after arriving in India he had indicated his willingness to call a Round Table Conference on the constitutional issue and, if necessary, to make appropriate concessions to the nationalists. In this respect he was more progressive than Montagu, who demurred at the prospect of a Round Table Conference. The Round Table Conference did not take place and instead Reading, as we have seen, met Gandhi and other nationalist leaders for face to face discussion – a move derided as a sign of 'weakness' by die-hard observers.

The Viceroy's commitment to making the reforms work is evident from letters written to a good many of his contemporaries. His letter to Lord Chelmsford, his predecessor as Viceroy, and First Lord of the Admiralty in the Labour government of 1924, is a good example of his thinking:

We must strive to the utmost of our human capacities to ensure the success of the Reforms, strive genuinely and honestly to prevent a breakdown, and never allow ourselves to fall back upon the difficulties and obstacles India has put in our way until she has succeeded, by her Extremists (Heaven forbid!), in bringing the Dyarchy and the Constitution generally to a complete standstill.[50]

The obstacles in the path of such progress were not all the creation of Indian 'extremists'. Quite apart from changes of government in Britain, dyarchy was interpreted in completely different ways by India's provincial governors. Thus the progressive Lord Willingdon in Madras welcomed the reforms as a genuine opportunity for Indian politicians to learn the craft of democratic government, and even asked Reading and Peel to grant Madras full responsible self-government, while highly conservative governors like Sir George Lloyd, Bombay, Sir Michael O'Dwyer, Punjab, and Lord Lytton, Bengal, saw things differently. These latter, while accepting dyarchy because it gave them much more provincial autonomy than hitherto, did not work the system of decentralization in the liberal spirit of the Montagu–Chelmsford reforms. Indeed in Bengal, delicately balanced between the two great religious communities, Lytton took the opportunity to break the power of the Hindu nationalists and to establish what amounted to an Anglo-Muslim raj – something that Reading's early initiative to placate Islam unwittingly encouraged.

These divergent interpretations of dyarchy and decentralization were offensive to Indian nationalists. In 1923 leading Indian ministers in the provincial governments of Bombay and the United Provinces resigned, claiming that their departments had been subject to persistent interference by permanent officials of the Raj. When, in 1924, a committee of inquiry investigated the working of the Act of 1919, its Indian members complained that Indian ministers in the provinces 'had not enjoyed real responsibility, and that in several provinces the two halves [Indian and British] of the government had not met in joint session'.[51] Despite his own liberal inclinations, there was no clear-cut way in which Reading could make the more conservative governors change their attitude – an attitude that was much strengthened by Montagu's removal from the India Office and his replacement by Peel and later by Birkenhead.

Not that all Indians wanted dyarchy to work, by any means: the early boycott of the reformed councils by Khilafatists and Congress members, and the obstructive tactics of the many Swarajists who did sit on the councils, all tended to render the experiment in devolution somewhat hollow, almost fraudulent.

Reading acted with dignified restraint in the face of Gandhi's non-cooperation movement. The Mahatma's non-cooperation campaign of 1921–2 he treated with disapproving forbearance. Having successfully set about detaching Muslim support from Gandhi, Reading was disinclined to arrest him fearing that such action would immediately whip up sympathy for the Mahatma. On 9 June 1921 Reading wrote reassuringly to Montagu: 'So long as Gandhi pursues his present policy of less virulence and refrains from preaching active hatred of the Government and all its works, it is plain that no action should be taken by the Government.'[52]

One reason why Reading chose not to arrest Gandhi lay in the delicate situation created by the Prince of Wales's arrival in India on 17

November 1921 for a three-month visit. The day of the Prince's arrival was marked by riots in Bombay, with Gandhi's supporters clashing with rowdier elements bent on violence. The disturbances continued into the next day, leaving fifty-three dead (including several Europeans) and about four hundred injured.

Reading was able to recognize that Gandhi, who had called on his followers to boycott the Prince's reception and to observe *hartal* (or strike), was appalled by this outbreak of violence, and recounted: 'Gandhi has again called forth a spirit which he could not control, as he now admits. I am told that in several quarters in which he appeared to quell trouble, he was powerless. He admits that his emissaries came back having been assaulted, and he is so disappointed that he expresses himself now against civil disobedience for the moment.'

Despite the riots in Bombay, the Prince's tour was never again to occasion such violence, and Gandhi's attempts to persuade his countrymen to boycott the royal progress were largely unsuccessful. Gandhi's prestige thus suffered as Prince Edward was greeted by large crowds wherever he went, culminating in a relatively triumphant visit to Calcutta – often seen as a hotbed of sedition. Reading's decision to let Gandhi have enough rope to hang himself was clearly vindicated by the events. For his part, the Prince of Wales left India convinced that British rule could last for a good deal longer, though conscience stricken by the high cost of his tour, '£25,000 of English money and goodness knows how many lakhs of rupees'.

With the heir to the throne safely departed, Reading moved at last to arrest Gandhi. The more conservative governors, led by Sir George Lloyd of Bombay, had grown impatient at Reading's reluctance to prosecute Gandhi. As we have seen, Reading, though wary of Gandhi's ambiguities, felt that 'His religious views are, I believe, genuinely held and he is convinced to a point almost bordering on fanaticism that non-violence and love will give India its independence and enable it to withstand the British Government.... Altogether you will judge that I liked him and that I believe there are possibilities in the future.'[53] In August 1921, with Gandhi encouraging the boycotting and burning of foreign cloth, Reading had told Montagu, 'He seems to me to be staking everything upon his boycott of foreign cloth, but I cannot think that he can have more than an ephemeral success.'[54] On 24 November Reading mused 'that one of the difficulties of the problem of Gandhi and his movement that is always striking me afresh is that we never quite know how strong the movement is among the ignorant masses'.[55]

By January 1922, however, Reading was weighing the pros and cons of arresting Gandhi. On 5 January he told Montagu that 'If he is arrested another will take his place and carry on in Gandhi's name with the additional stimulus that Gandhi, the saint, is in prison.'[56] Towards the end of the month, the Viceroy had come to the conclusion that he should wait for Gandhi to declare a campaign of civil disobedience against the Raj so that he would have something more concrete for which to arrest him. On 26 January Montagu put pressure on Reading by cabling, 'You are of course aware that public opinion here is becoming even in the circles most favourable to Government and in Cabinet itself more and more perplexed by non-arrest of Gandhi.'[57]

On 11 February Montagu told Reading that 'we have, I think, arrived at a moment when a larger body of Indian opinion will accept Gandhi's arrest than at any time hitherto'.[58] Certainly with Hindu–Muslim co-operation in ruins, and with many Indian moderates alienated by Gandhi's refusal to countenance a conference with the government, the Raj's hand was strengthened. Non-cooperation as conceived by Gandhi seemed to have failed in the face of a government that, on the whole, decorously refrained from violent response, and was led by a Viceroy still firmly committed to the Montagu–Chelmsford reforms. Nor were many leading Indian politicians happy with the non-cooperation movement; writing from the United Provinces as early as April 1921, Sir Grimwood Mears, Chief Justice of the High Court at Allahabad, had told Reading that: 'I believe Motilal [Nehru] is an unhappy man. I think non-cooperation is felt by him to be non-constructive and barren. He wants progress. He wants to be up and doing. He is mentally unsatisfied. He is also disturbed by the conduct of his son Jawaharlal Nehru who is not averse to violence.'[59]

With the Prince of Wales gone and Gandhi's position weak, Reading arrested the Mahatma on 10 March 1922 (ironically the day Edwin Montagu was forced to resign in London). Gandhi was tried on a charge of sedition, and sentenced to six years' imprisonment. Far from provoking a violent national outcry, Gandhi's arrest was received quietly. On 4 May 1922 Reading could tell Lloyd George that 'the internal situation has been quieter than at any period since I have been here'. On 17 October Reading was able to inform Peel at the India Office that the 'Non-co-operation movement ... remains more or less stationary. Hindus took little or no interest in proceedings. ...'[60]

With Gandhi in prison, the Congress leaders C.R. Das, from Bengal, and Motilal Nehru, from the United Provinces, proposed in December 1922 that the party should adopt a policy of 'council entry' – in other words to participate in the provincial and central councils established by the 1919 Act. When Congress rejected their proposal, Das and Nehru formed the Congress-Khilafat-Swaraj party with the support of Vithalbhai Patel and N.C. Kelkar in Bombay. This breakaway pushed Congress into accepting, at a special session in September 1923, the principle that Congressmen could enter the councils, though Congress could not be held responsible for their activities.

In May 1924 Gandhi was released from prison on the grounds of ill-health. Meeting with the Swaraj leaders, whose position had been much strengthened by their party's remarkable successes in the central and provincial elections of 1923, Gandhi still insisted that council entry was inconsistent with non-cooperation but accepted that Swarajists could remain members of Congress. Reading described the negotiations thus: 'After Gandhi's release from prison there were various attempts at compromise which resulted in a more or less patched-up formula given out for the benefit of the public but only faintly concealing the differences that still existed.'[61]

Despite the Swarajist alliance with Jinnah's Independent party in February 1924, and despite Motilal Nehru's 'National Demand' calling for a Round Table Conference to revise the constitution with a view to establishing full responsible government, the nationalist movement was ineffective during 1923-6, the last three years of Reading's Viceroyalty. The official response to the 'National Demand' was to appoint a committee to inquire into the working of the 1919 Act. Nothing much came of the inquiry. Das died in June 1925, and Motilal Nehru finally walked out of the Legislative Assembly on 8 March 1926, completely frustrated by his failure to bring about constitutional progress.

With the Swarajists ineffective, Congress divided, Gandhi passive, and the Muslims disinclined to continue co-operation on a national scale, the Hindu Mahasabha was established in December 1924. Led by Malaviya, it reflected high-caste Hindu anxieties at the political power being wielded by lower-caste Hindus and by the compromises made, principally in Bengal, but also in the Punjab, with Muslim politicians. Communal fears were thus given a new form.

These gaping divisions within Indian nationalism, and particularly within Congress, were certainly not all of Reading's creation, but he could feel well pleased that his liberal and patient responses to agitation had led to a period of tranquillity that was certainly not expected when he began his Viceroyalty. Nothing indicated the containment of militant nationalism more clearly than Gandhi's failure seriously to disrupt the Raj, and on 1 January 1925 Reading was able to write, self-contentedly:

Gandhi is now attached to the tails of Das and Nehru, although they try their utmost to make him and his supporters think that he is one of the heads if not the head. ...

It is pathetic to observe the rapid decline in the power of Gandhi and the frantic attempts he is now making to cling to his position as leader at the expense of practically every principle he has hitherto advocated.[62]

Despite this apparent nadir in Gandhi's fortunes, however, the Raj had not heard the last of him.

Reading also had responsibility for princely India, which accounted for a third of the subcontinent and comprised 362 states of which all but 108 were very small in size. The rulers of these princely states wrongly understood the devolution that flowed from the Montagu–Chelmsford reforms as implying that Britain would eventually liberate their territories from the interference of the Crown in their internal affairs. Moreover, the princes were not encouraged to democratize their own administrations, and still looked to British protection against the threatening flood-tide of nationalist politics in British India.

In 1921 a Chamber of Princes had been established as a consultative assembly of 120 members presided over by the Viceroy and meeting once a year. Despite the concessions made to nationalist demands in British India, however, the Raj still chose to act as the paramount power towards princely India, and the princes protested, to no avail, over examples of British interference.

Late in 1921 some of the princes led by the Maharajah of Bikaner became alarmed by nationalist agitation, and early in 1922 the Chamber of Princes petitioned Reading to confer with a delegation over their anxieties that as British India achieved self-government 'the position of the Princes and States will be an unenviable one and in many respects even worse than that of the loyalists in Ireland'.[63] Reading, with the non-cooperation movement already in disarray, refused the request as indicating panic. A sop was thrown to the princes when Reading, using his viceregal powers, forced a bill through the legislative assembly to prevent the dissemination of printed matter meant to incite disaffection in the princely states.

Reading came to know personally most of the major princes, visiting their territories and being royally entertained. He formed firm friendships with the Maharajah Scindia of Gwalior, the Maharajahs of Bikaner and Patiala, and with the Jam Singh of Nawanagar – previously a hero to the English cricketing public as 'Ranji'. He visited gorgeous palaces, did his best to shoot game, and he and his wife stored up a host of vivid memories:

The old retainers in blue and silver who, carrying silver rods and chanting a weird cry, preceded the Viceroy and Maharajah through the palace of Mysore, showing them where they might safely tread. ... The Maharaj Rana of Dolhpur's legendary pearls, for only one string of which the Czar of Russia was said to have offered a fortune, and the Empress Eugenie's superb diamond necklace around the Maharaja of Patalia's massive throat. ... The Maharajah [of Kashmir] and H. E. ... on two silver thrones ... behind them servants with horsehair whisks in gold to keep flies off. The chiefs handed H.E. the usual gold coin and sprinkled everyone's hand with attar of roses and handed [out] betel nuts wrapped in gold foil.[64]

Some idea of the programme of a viceregal visit to a princely state can be gathered from that printed for Reading's visit to Alwar in March 1922:

PROGRAMME

Saturday the 25th March 1922.

Morning	8.30 a.m.	Arrival of His Excellency the Viceroy (Private Reception).
,,	9.45 a.m.	Breakfast at Lansdowne Palace.
,,	10.45 a.m.	Departure for Seriska.
,,	. .	Shikar [hunting].
Night	. .	Dinner at Seriska.

Sunday the 26th March 1922.

Morning	10.00 a.m.	Breakfast.
,,	. .	Shikar.
Night	. .	Dinner.

Monday the 27th March 1922.

Morning	10.00 a.m.	Breakfast.
,,	. .	Shikar.
Evening		Return to Lansdowne Palace for change [sic].
Night	8.30 p.m.	Banquet at City Palace.
,,	11.00 p.m.	His Excellency's Private departure.[65]

The Alwar programme included elaborate plans of the seating arrangements at banquets, a plan of the accommodation, the arrangements for greeting the Viceroy (including 'Motor Arrangements from Railway Station to Lansdowne Palace', with a 'Racing Rolls', a 'Daimler', a 'New Rolls', a 'State Rolls', a 'Crown Magnet', a 'Touring Rolls', and lorries for the servants and luggage), and a 'List of Officers in Charge of Functions' – for example, 'Patrolling Railway line in Alwar territory: Inspector General of Police assisted by Hakim Mal',

'Arranging crowds: Judicial Minister assisted by Inspector General of Education and the President of the Municipalities', 'Electric light and hot and cold water arrangements at Lansdowne Palace and at Seriska: Mr Bradley', and 'Shikar arrangements: Col. Dhabai Ganeshi Lal'.[66]

Despite the lavish welcome, the Maharajah of Alwar, a sadistic tyrant who once tethered a difficult polo pony to a hillside under a blazing sun and took pleasure in watching it die slowly of thirst, formed a low opinion of the Viceroy, telling Lord Curzon, 'Reading is a very weak Viceroy. He never reads a file or studies a subject but has people in who state a case to him orally, just as though he were a lawyer in chambers and then decides.' Alwar also despised Reading for his poor marksmanship, remarking that 'Lady Reading loves the Viceroyalty, which her health has been good enough to enable her to enjoy, so much so that she was enabled to accompany her husband on a tiger shoot where she had the satisfaction of seeing him miss three tigers running.'[67]

Reading was far more masterful with India's princes than with their tigers. He removed the rulers of Indore and Nabha from their thrones for the ill-treatment of their subjects – a confident assertion of paramountcy that hearkened back to the Governor-General Lord Dalhousie's strong-armed and provocative tactics prior to the great Mutiny of 1857. He settled the Bhopal succession dispute, although the Begum had to go to Britain to look up ancient records in the India Office Library before her request for her third surviving son to succeed rather than her most senior grandson was granted. Finally, Reading acted with great firmness in rejecting the claim of India's greatest prince, the Nizam of Hyderabad, in 1924 for the restoration of the territory of Berar taken under British control by Dalhousie in 1853.

In making his claim for the restoration of Berar, the Nizam asserted his government's 'absolute equality with the British government except in foreign affairs'. Warmly supported by Birkenhead, Reading made a definitive statement of the doctrine of paramountcy:

The Sovereignty of the British Crown is supreme in India, and therefore no Ruler of an Indian State can justifiably claim to negotiate with the British Government on an equal footing. Its supremacy is not based only upon treaties and engagements, but exists independently of them and, quite apart from its prerogative in matters relating to foreign powers and policies, it is the right and duty of the British Government, while scrupulously respecting all treaties and engagements with the Indian States, to preserve peace and good order throughout India. ... The right of the British Government to intervene in the internal affairs of Indian States is [an] instance of the consequences necessarily involved in the supremacy of the British Crown. ... The internal, no less than the external, security which the Ruling Princes enjoy is due ultimately to the protecting power of the British Government. ...[68]

Amid all the problems that confronted Reading in India, he maintained throughout a resolute commitment to the dispensation of justice. He wanted drastic measures taken against the practice of human sacrifice in which Sir Harcourt Butler had reported 'his wild tribes' in the United Provinces indulging.[69] Above all, as he told the Chelmsford Reform Club in Simla, to which Indians were admitted as well as Europeans, in July 1921, 'I say there cannot be and must never be humiliation under the British Rule of any Indian because he is an Indian.'

Almost immediately after this speech, Reading was horrified to learn of a trial which quite clearly reflected racial injustice under the law. A Bengali had been wounded by an Englishman who had made unwelcome advances to the Indian's daughter; the Englishman claimed he had been shooting deer and had accidentally hit the irate father. The case was tried by a British judge, before a jury of nine, eight of whom were Europeans. The Englishman was acquitted by a majority of eight to one – 'a clean racial division'. Reading was also disturbed by the case of a British soldier being charged merely with assault, and fined 50 rupees, by a British magistrate after attempting the rape of an Indian woman.

Reading told Montagu on 7 July 1921 that:

I am seriously perturbed by the results of both these cases, and more particularly by the indignation caused among Indians. I am having the law examined for the purpose of arriving at some solution, but I know that there are grave obstacles in the path of any alteration of the system, and yet I am convinced that we must take steps to put the law on an equal footing. I am only expressing a very hasty view, as I have not yet been able to give full consideration to the subject, but I believe the mischief is in the jury of a majority of Europeans. It is easy to understand the mentality of those who sit on these trials, but sober-minded and justice-loving Englishmen do not like the impression created. My hasty view is that if the trials were by Judges alone there would be no cause for complaint. English Judges would act with justice, but to attempt to abolish juries is a very thorny path to pursue. Equally I fear that to give a corresponding right to Indians of trial by a jury of a majority of Indians presents grave difficulties in the administration of the law. But the problem is there and must be solved. ...

Again complaints come forward of unequal treatment of Indians at railway stations and in the railway trains. You are familiar with the problem – equally it presents troublesome and difficult questions and I am going to devote attention to them.

I am convinced that we shall never persuade the Indian of the justice of our rule until we have overcome racial difficulties of the character above-mentioned. As you and I agreed when we discussed these questions at home the root of most difficulties is the racial problem. However desirous we may be of removing inequalities, I fear that we shall for a long time have before us the social problem even if we manage to solve the legal one. I could go on for a long time discussing this subject, but you are as well aware of it as I and you have known it longer. It is the cause of most of the bitterness.[70]

Despite Reading's determination to ensure racial equality before the law, abuses were to continue for some considerable time after his departure from India.

The new Viceroy, Lord Irwin, and his wife landed at Bombay on 1 April 1926 and were greeted cordially by the Readings. Lady Irwin noted the pallor in Lady Reading's cheeks, and her depressed bearing – her great adventure, and her husband's, was over.

When on 8 April 1926 the Readings left for home, the departing Viceroy could look back on five years of grinding toil and the daily task of confronting problems of great weight and urgency. Yet Reading had acquitted himself as well as any other Viceroy during the final fifty years of the British Raj. He had remained courteous and patient and just in the face of frequent provocation; he had displayed a commendable firmness, tempered with understanding; he had been willing to talk with Indian leaders across the whole political spectrum, and he had tried to put European anxieties into proper perspective.

Reading's Viceroyalty produced both the temporary disintegration of Gandhi's non-cooperation movement, and a lengthy period of peace and stability. Paradoxically he helped to drive a wedge between Hindus and Muslims, and at the same time strove to uphold the principles of the Montagu–Chelmsford reforms. His rule in India was marked by a liberal sympathy and a wise perception. India as a whole had been fortunate in its Viceroy.

15 Elder Statesman, 1926–31

What an immense acquisition of strength to our [Liberal] party as a whole it would be if Reading, with his brilliant ability, wonderful record of achievement, and inexhaustible energy, could be induced to again play an active and influential role in helping to direct the affairs of the party.

Arthur Crosfield to Lord Beauchamp, 1926

I said that if the Government was in favour of Dominion Status for India with temporary reservations, as far as I was concerned there was no good going on with the Conference.

Reading, before the opening of the Round Table Conference on India, 1930

Reading was received in Britain with the honours traditionally bestowed upon a returning viceroy. He and Lady Reading reached Victoria Station on 17 April 1926, having been met at Dover by their son and daughter-in-law. At Victoria, Lord Birkenhead headed the reception party. Lady Reading was garlanded with flowers by Indian admirers, while reporters crowded round the ex-Viceroy asking for a statement. Reading obliged them by simply saying, 'It is the end of five great years for me. If it has been of any use, I am very delighted.'

They had hardly settled into their well-loved house in Curzon Street when Reading was summoned to Windsor Castle. On 20 April he recounted his visit in a letter to his son:

I tried to send you a line last night but could not manage it. Immediately on my arrival HM sent for me and I had about an hour's audience. The King was extraordinarily nice to me and expressed his appreciation of my services to the country, culminating in those to India and the Empire. He informed me that he had just signed the papers announcing that he had raised me to a Marquisate. There was no discussion regarding other possibilities and I heard later that it had been communicated to the PM and would be sent to the Press in the evening.[1]

231

What did Reading mean by 'other possibilities'? He was referring to an earlier speculative conversation with Gerald when the latter had supposed his father would be honoured either by the Garter or by an elevation in the ranks of the peerage, and had expressed the hope that, if he had a choice, he would select the Garter. As it happened, there was no choice to be made. The Garter, the most prestigious of British chivalric orders, could only be awarded to a Christian, and Reading's Jewish origins thus put him into that tiny section of the British population that could never aspire to the honour.

A Marquisate, however, was not to be sniffed at. Reading was the first British citizen since the first Duke of Wellington to rise from commoner to Marquess. There all similarities between the two men ended: Wellington had been born the younger son of a peer, and had won his honours by the sword; Reading was a Jewish fruiterer's son who had climbed the greasy pole through the exercise of his intellect and his wits and by staggeringly hard labour. On 8 June 1926 the First Marquess of Reading received a further honour when he was given the Honorary Freedom of the City of London at a ceremony attended by Lloyd George, Asquith (now ennobled as the Earl of Oxford and Asquith), Birkenhead and Sir John Simon.

Despite these accolades, Reading faced a tremendous problem of readjustment. For five years he had been the ruler of a great subcontinent, living amidst spectacular pomp and ceremony, highly salaried, widely respected, with tens of thousands of subjects jostling to see him whenever he travelled among them, the director and controller of that elaborate administrative machine the British Raj.

Now, despite his Marquisate, he was merely the lessee of a house in Mayfair, without employment, with no prospect of a pension, with his party out of power, his old friend and patron Lloyd George on the opposition benches, and his wife only recently recovered from a major operation for cancer.

One of Reading's immediate reactions to being back again in Britain was to appreciate at least two of the advantages he could now enjoy. The first was that he could again have curry made from tinned curry powder, rather than the exotic and highly spiced dishes that had so often been served up to him in India. The second was that he could once more carry money in his pocket and thus be able to walk into a shop and make a purchase – something which had been deemed inappropriate to his viceregal rank.

How much money he would have, however, was a source of some anxiety. He had saved nothing from his viceregal salary and, according to his son, had not always wisely invested the capital he had built up earlier. He and his wife had also spent freely.

It is evidence of Reading's persistent worries about his financial future that, while in India, he had been reluctantly prepared to sell what remained of the lease of 32 Curzon Street. Several inquiries had been made, but they had eventually fallen through – much to the Readings' relief.

Although Reading no doubt felt genuine anxieties over money, they were misplaced. His illustrious name, his reputation for financial knowledge (though not much in evidence in his apparently 'unsuccessful' investments), and his close links with the world of business, were all saleable commodities, and before long he had been appointed to the boards of a number of companies.

His most useful connection was with Sir Alfred Mond, the father of Eva, Gerald Reading's wife. Alfred Mond was a man of cosmopolitan tastes and with 'a passionate love, at once critical and emotional, for beautiful things', but he 'was not temperamentally a businessman and ... would have been happiest in the life of a student and connoisseur and patron of the arts'.[2] After his daughter's marriage to Reading's son, Mond's and Reading's families became close friends, spending Christmas and Easter together, their grandchildren around them – joyful occasions which have passed into family legend.[3]

Sir Alfred Mond's father had played a major part in creating the companies Brunner, Mond and Company and the Mond Nickel Company. In 1926 Brunner, Mond and Company amalgamated with Nobels and other important groups to establish the giant Imperial Chemical Industries. Mond at once offered Lord Reading a seat on the board of ICI, where he served until his death, becoming chairman in 1930. Reading was duly installed in a 'delightful room' at Imperial Chemical House, Millbank, which became his working headquarters.

Reading was soon deluged with other offers, but contented himself with serving on the boards of the National Provincial Bank and the London and Lancashire Insurance Company; later he became the first chairman of the Palestine Electric Corporation, and for the last two years of his life he was also chairman of Carreras Limited, the tobacco company.

He was also tempted into the newspaper world, becoming in 1926 chairman of United Newspapers, which published the *Daily Chronicle* and other Liberal journals. Reading's somewhat reluctant venture into newspaper publishing was a direct result of his relationship with Lloyd George. In October 1918 Sir Henry Dalziel and others had bought the

Daily Chronicle on Lloyd George's behalf, most of the purchase money of
£1,650,000 coming from Lloyd George's notorious political fund which
the Prime Minister's wealthy admirers had set up for his support, and
often in payment for their peerages and honours.

The *Daily Chronicle* was supposed to promote the Lloyd George brand
of Liberalism, and did so, with varying success. In 1926 Lloyd George
decided to sell out, having sought Lord Beaverbrook's advice. The
ordinary shares of United Newspapers were bought by Sir David Yule
and Sir Thomas Catto, representing the Calcutta Discount Company.[4]
Reading was persuaded by Lloyd George to accept the chairmanship of
the company, but bought no shares.

Reading resigned his chairmanship before long. The newspaper
world was not one in which he felt at home. Moreover, scandal and
speculation surrounded the Lloyd George Fund, thus partly tarnishing
the bright Liberal image of the *Daily Chronicle*. There were more changes
of ownership to come, and in September 1928 William Harrison of the
Inveresk Paper Company Limited bought the controlling interest in the
Daily Chronicle. The newspaper, and its associated journals, was nearly
bought by Beaverbrook in the spring of 1930, and towards the end of
that year the *Daily Chronicle* was sold to the *Daily News*, thus becoming
the *News Chronicle* for the last thirty years of its life.[5]

So, apart from his brief and uneasy chairmanship of United Newspapers, Reading was soundly set up in the world of business within a
few months of returning from India. His financial worries were thus
removed and he could look forward to a prosperous old age.

He reached his sixty-sixth birthday in 1926, and might have been
tempted to stick to his new business responsibilities. However, he was
'active and vigorous both in mind and body, and eager to undertake
any new adventure that might present itself'.[6]

Reading had no intention of renouncing his Liberalism, or of taking
a discreet place on the House of Lords' crossbenches as former Viceroys
had done. There is no doubt he still hoped for political office, but, with
the Liberal party in disarray, his only chance of achieving this lay in
helping his party recover its old purpose and unity.

The Liberals, on Reading's return, were in a sorry plight. In the
election of November 1924 the Liberals, divided between the followers
of Asquith and Lloyd George, had suffered a crushing defeat. Baldwin's
renunciation of fiscal protection some months before the election had
allowed wavering Liberals to vote Conservative with a relatively clear
conscience. The Liberal party had lost over a hundred seats, mainly to
the Conservatives; Asquith, the party leader, had been defeated by a

Labour candidate and went to the House of Lords; the Liberal MPs were reduced to a rump of forty, uneasily marshalled behind Lloyd George; Labour, with 151 seats, was the main opposition party and seemed likely to remain so; the Conservatives had 419 seats out of 615, with 48.3 per cent of the total vote, one of their most commanding majorities for half a century.

How could the Liberals mend their divisions and present themselves to the electorate as a, more or less, united party? There was perhaps one man who could act as peacemaker, a man close to Lloyd George yet reconciled with Asquith, a man whose public service in the war and latterly in India had kept him above party infighting, a man who was known for his discretion and balance, a man who could possibly lead the party and rekindle the fires of a relevant and dignified Liberalism – the Marquess of Reading.

Reading had barely returned to Britain before he was being begged to save the Liberal party. On 30 May 1926 Arthur Crosfield, a senior Liberal and a rich Warrington soap manufacturer, and a close friend of Lloyd George from the early Edwardian era, wrote to Reading on behalf of other concerned Liberals asking him to use his personal influence to try to heal the continuing rift between Lloyd George and Asquith.

It was a request that demanded almost superhuman powers of persuasion and diplomacy. After the loss of his Commons seat in 1924 and his elevation to the peerage, Asquith had been Liberal leader in the Lords, with Lloyd George leading the party remnant in the Commons. This two-headed leadership might have worked if both heads had allowed it to, but it was, in effect, an unsightly aberration. Although in the Lords, Asquith was titular head of the party, while Lloyd George was merely chairman of the small parliamentary party. In addition Lloyd George, through his control of the Lloyd George Fund, had the money with which to force his views on the party. Although the National Liberal Federation had launched the Million Fund Appeal to try to make the party, and Asquith, independent of the Lloyd George Fund, the appeal had flopped and Asquith's hopes of supremacy over, or even parity with, his old foe flopped with it.

Serious differences over policy had surfaced in the autumn of 1925, and were further exacerbated by reaction to the General Strike of early May 1926. While Asquith and Grey in the Lords condemned the strike, and Simon in the Commons declared it illegal, Lloyd George took a different line. In the Commons he condemned the government's handling of the situation more than the strike itself; he went on, in a syndicated article for the American press, to doubt the government's ability to force an end to the strike.[7]

Lloyd George then made these differences more obvious by refusing to attend the next meeting of the Liberal Shadow Cabinet on 10 May on 'policy grounds'. An exchange of plainly antagonistic letters between Asquith and Lloyd George took place, leaving the former feeling that he was unable any longer to communicate directly with the latter. It was this crisis that had prompted Crosfield to write to Reading on 30 May 1926.

In theory Reading was ideally placed to bring about a reconciliation. His friendship with Lloyd George was of long standing and of considerable depth; moreover, both men had benefited from the complementary qualities that each had brought to the relationship. As for Asquith, despite an initial coolness between him and Reading after his downfall in December 1916, he had now repaired his friendship with his former Attorney-General. In February 1918 Reading had reported a conversation with Asquith as being 'in the friendliest spirit'.[8] Nothing had occurred since then to reopen any wounds. Indeed, Reading was to continue on the friendliest terms with Asquith, and Margot Asquith noticed when the disastrous 1918 'coupon' election results were coming in and her husband lost his seat that Reading was 'looking snow white'. A decade later, in 1927, Reading, taking pity on his former chief's relative impoverishment, raised an annual endowment for him of £3,500, of which Lord Beaverbrook agreed to contribute £1,000.[9]

Reading seems not to have made any serious attempt at reconciliation. At any rate the two rivals were not brought together, and Asquith's star faded throughout 1926 as Lloyd George's grew once more bright. By the end of August it was known that Asquith, who had suffered a mild stroke on 12 June, intended to retire from his leadership of the party, and from active political life, in the autumn.

Crosfield, seeking for ways to strengthen a dispirited party, wrote to the leading Liberal peer Lord Beauchamp on 3 September 1926 saying: 'What an immense acquisition of strength to our party as a whole it would be if Reading, with his brilliant ability, wonderful record of achievement, and inexhaustible energy, could be induced to again play an active and influential role in helping to direct the affairs of the Party.'[10] He went on to suggest the setting up of a Committee of Direction for the party, to be chaired by Reading and to exclude some of Lloyd George's most 'violent opponents' such as Runciman.

Beauchamp replied the next day that it was not merely Asquith who was reluctant to come to terms with Lloyd George, but that Lord Grey of Fallodon (Sir Edward Grey) was even more strongly opposed to the Welshman and would be even less willing to meet with him.[11] Crosfield's response was to suggest that perhaps Asquith, Grey and Lloyd George should be excluded from leading the Liberals, and that Reading should be taken on as representing both wings of the party.

Crosfield then wrote directly to Reading on 7 September 1926 saying, 'the best hope of preventing open conflict in the constituencies this autumn, and of bringing about a sensible, practicable working arrangement, lies in your own authoritative personal intervention'.[12]

Reading replied on 12 September, in rather non-committal, but realistic terms, saying that: 'The aim should be to achieve, if not a complete and cordial unity, at least a unity which would satisfy the public and lay the lines for closer and more harmonious working between the various sections of the Parliamentary Liberal Party.'[13]

By the next day Crosfield had established that Lloyd George 'would be willing to agree to Reading's chairmanship of the Party, being confident that he would receive fair and courteous treatment from him'.[14]

On 17 September Crosfield was once more appealing for Reading's active support, telling him: 'As it has been well expressed to me, should any arch be constructed to bridge over personal differences in such a way as to give the whole Liberal party a fresh start in the country, you will be the keystone of that arch.'[15] On the same day, Crosfield was assuring Sir John Simon that 'Reading is due in London on the 22nd [September], and his letter makes it very clear that he will return prepared to do his utmost to serve the best interests of our entire party.'[16]

Although Reading played a constructive part in these attempts to resolve the leadership problems of his party, he did not shape events. Asquith's resignation in October 1926 simply opened the way for Lloyd George's overall control of the Liberals, although Reading approved of this. Lloyd George set about transforming his party's electoral image: with Keynes's help he began to promote new ideas about economic planning; he ditched some old-style Liberals, and encouraged fresh thinking; he was lavish with his infamous Fund, paying out £400,000 to the party between 1927 and 1929.[17] In this way the Liberal party could claim once more to be a viable non-socialist alternative to the Conservatives. The electorate, however, were no longer sufficiently interested and, although the party increased its number of seats in the May 1929 election by nineteen (from forty to fifty-nine), it was Labour who won the election with 288 seats, with the Conservatives twenty-eight seats behind them.

Reading had done his best to help send the Liberals into the 1929 general election in as unified a condition as possible, and a huge campaign poster had portrayed the United Liberals, grouped like a happy family, and comprising Lloyd George, Lord Grey, Herbert Samuel, John Simon, Walter Runciman and Lord Beauchamp.

After the bitter disappointment of the election result, however, the deep rifts within the party once more emerged. In particular Lord Grey, who had earlier described Lloyd George's plans to combat unemployment as 'absolutely right', found cause to distance himself from the party leader. As the most senior of the surviving Asquithian Liberals (Asquith himself had died in 1928), Grey deemed himself their standard-bearer, telling Baldwin in January 1929, 'The iron entered into my soul, when Ll.G.'s Govt. after the war let down and corrupted life at home and destroyed our credit abroad.'[18]

Grey particularly disliked the party's dependence on the Lloyd George Fund, and between August and October 1929 Reading played an intermediary role between the two men. Grey had specifically complained that Lloyd George had paid for his own election expenses out of the private Fund; he even talked of illegal electoral practice.

On 14 August 1929 Lloyd George, made aware of these criticisms by Reading, told his friend: 'I should be only too delighted to meet him and anybody he would care to invite to discuss the question anywhere. I promise to do so quite candidly and put all my cards on the table.' But he asserted: 'The Fund ... is not merely a Lloyd George Fund in its inception, but is especially so in its present form. It is rather a cool proposition to ask me now to hand all over to men who have done nothing but criticize and cast mud at this Fund, when I was sweating hard to increase it.'[19]

He added, somewhat wistfully, 'But I am afraid that the anti-L.G. obsession in some hearts is so deeply rooted as to be incurable.'

Two weeks later Reading, having passed on an edited version of this letter to Grey, told Lloyd George that 'after considerable thought' he had made certain omissions from the letter: 'My reason for cutting out some of the stinging phrases was that I felt sure Grey would want to show the copy to his confidential associates.' After all, Reading added, the object was 'to pave the way for complete unity in the future'.[20]

Grey was not to be placated, however, and on 10 October Reading made an urgent appeal to him to promote party unity:

I am trying hard to find some way of avoiding publicity of differences of opinion between sections of the Liberal Party. I feel sure that you appreciate to the full the serious, I might almost say, grave, consequences of the disunity in the party, so soon after the last election and the subsequent events. . . .

I hope I am wrong but I am very apprehensive that many Liberals will feel tired of the dissensions and will group themselves either with Labour or with the Conservatives.[21]

Grey did not respond to this plea. In January 1930, speaking on behalf of the Liberal Council, he once more condemned the party's dependence on the Lloyd George Fund, and refused to acknowledge him as party leader. The Liberals' dissensions were thus openly displayed to the public.

Some leading Liberals continued to see Reading as the senior statesman to steer the party into calmer waters. Sir Hugh Seely, for example, wrote on 8 October 1930: 'I am persuaded that you are the only man now living who can take the lead and solve the problem.'[22]

The Liberal split was to be further widened by the great economic and political crisis of 1931.

Apart from fitfully attempting to bind up the Liberal party's self-inflicted wounds, Reading was naturally much involved with developments in India. Ex-viceroys had tended to make authoritative, even if inconvenient, pronouncements on the government of the day's policies towards the Indian Empire. Curzon had been a particularly weighty critic of the Liberal initiative under Edwin Montagu, and had the added advantage of being an influential member of the Cabinet almost continuously from 1915 until 1925, the year of his death. Reading was not a member of any government from 1926 to 1931. None the less, he was consulted on several occasions by the government, and made a number of speeches on India in the House of Lords.

A year after Reading's return from India, a Statutory Commission under Sir John Simon was appointed to examine the working of the Montagu–Chelmsford reforms. Reading loyally welcomed Simon's appointment, as one Liberal lawyer to another. Less predictably he also stoutly defended the Commission's all-European composition, drawn in proportion of party strengths from both Houses of Parliament, arguing with legal precision that, since it was a British Parliamentary Commission, appointed under the terms of a British Act of Parliament, it would have been inappropriate to include any Indians as members.

Reading's response to the membership of the Simon Commission demonstrates both his caution and his preference for strict, even ungenerous, legality; it was also somewhat at odds with his generally liberal approach as Viceroy. He went on to demonstrate his firm adherence to, and optimism for, Indian constitutional development by telling the House of Lords on 30 March 1927:

I refuse to regard the Constitution as a failure. I would rather regard it as a monument erected by the generosity of the British Parliament, for the purpose of giving effect to the principles we hold dear and of enabling India in the future, when she is ready for it, and has shown the willingness of spirit we all desire, to govern herself as part of the British Empire. ...

Everything seems to point to the peaceful development of constitutional government.[23]

Reading was woefully wrong in his prediction. Indian nationalist opinion was outraged at the composition of the Simon Commission. There was a concerted move to boycott the Commission, and both Gandhi and the Congress party were able to recover a great deal of the strength they had displayed before Reading's viceregal policy had helped to undermine their appeal.

Before the Simon Commission could report its findings, there was a change of government in Britain. Labour became the biggest party in the Commons in the election of 1929 with 288 seats against the Conservatives' 260, and with the Liberals holding the balance with 59. Ramsay MacDonald sent Wedgwood Benn (later Lord Stansgate, and the father of Tony Benn) to the India Office.

The Labour government wanted to encourage India's rapid advance to Dominion status, and to this end decided to anticipate the findings of the Simon Commission and to call a Round Table Conference to thresh out the next stages for India's progress to self-government within the Empire. All shades of Indian opinion, including the princes, were to be represented at the Conference. In order to promote further its Indian policy, the government also decided to make a positive statement regarding Dominion status through the Viceroy, Lord Irwin, who was personally consulted on the matter while on leave during the summer of 1929.

The government consulted Baldwin for the Conservatives and Reading for the Liberals over its intentions. Both men agreed that a viceregal announcement could be made, as long as the Simon Commission thought it appropriate. Unfortunately, the agreement of members of the Commission was not obtained, although Simon, at lunch at Reading's house, seemed unperturbed, feeling that the intended reference to Dominion status was 'academic'.

The Secretary of State for India, Wedgwood Benn, decided none the less to go ahead with the proposed Irwin declaration. Reading was convinced that a great tactical error was about to be committed and wrote urgently to Wedgwood Benn on 27 October 1929:

The selection of this particular moment immediately after the return of the Viceroy from consultation with you and His Majesty's Government, and when the Simon Commission is engaged in considering its Report, will lead Indians to the conclusion that the declaration imports a change of policy and brings the final stage of constitutional development appreciably nearer in point of time.

I am aware that both you and Lord Irwin maintain that the policy remains unchanged and that the pronouncement is made merely for the purpose of setting at rest doubts which have arisen in the minds of Indian politicians regarding the meaning of 'responsible government' and the ultimate destiny of India within the Empire. I cannot but think that Indian politicians will believe that the making of the declaration now and without waiting for the Report of the Simon Commission is evidence of a new policy....

The effect in this country must, I fear, inevitably lead to a serious political controversy which all parties have desired to exclude in relation to the constitutional position of India. The appointment of the Simon Commission and the selection of its members from the three political Parties with the assent of Parliament led to a general understanding that all questions relating to the constitutional development of India should be postponed until the Commission presented its Report.

For the course you are now proposing to take you have failed to obtain the support of the Liberal Party and, I have reason to believe, of the Conservative Party. So far as I am aware the Simon Commission has not given its assent. Nevertheless it is intended, as I gather, to proceed immediately and to make the declaration which must be regarded as of capital importance, otherwise it seems inconceivable that Government should persist in the face of opposition it has met.

Whatever may be the effect of the Government action in India, there can be no doubt that in this country and in Parliament there will be an end of the general understanding above mentioned.

I would beg of you again to consider whether in these circumstances it would not be more to the advantage of India that no action of the character proposed should be taken until after the Simon Commission has reported and Parliament and the country are in possession of their conclusions and advice.[24]

The government, however, pushed ahead with the declaration, which the Viceroy made on 31 October. In his statement Irwin reaffirmed that it was 'implicit in the Declaration of 1917 [the Montagu Declaration] that the natural issue of India's constitutional progress as there contemplated is the attainment of Dominion status'.

Although Indian nationalists on the whole were well pleased with the

Irwin Declaration, and Congress was soon pressing its claims to a large representation at the Round Table Conference, in Britain the Conservative party and the bulk of the Liberals expressed hostility for the announcement.

Reading promptly proceeded to initiate a debate on the subject in the House of Lords of 5 November 1929, during which he reiterated and extended his objections:

> Is it open to the Government to suggest that there is no misunderstanding with regard to it? I believe that there is a very grave misunderstanding. Unfortunately, I felt sure it was bound to happen and that the words would be extended far beyond their natural meaning.
>
> The consequence is that it will be held as a promise to give at once, or almost at once, Dominion Status. I know that the Government did not mean that. I want them to say it, to state now in plain and explicit terms what undoubtedly is their meaning.
>
> It is my anxiety with regard to that reputation [of fairness] which we have acquired over a period of many years, that makes me put this question.
>
> In conclusion, may I hope that nothing that I have said during my observations could possibly be construed as casting the faintest reflection upon the Viceroy.[25]

Reading opposed the Irwin Declaration partly because he believed (rightly) that it would encourage unrest in India, and partly because the promise of Dominion status had recently been given a new significance. At the Imperial Conference of 1926, the Inter-Imperial Relations Committee chaired by Lord Balfour had produced a liberal definition of Dominion status which, while satisfying most of the Dominions (even the Irish Free State and South Africa), had disturbed traditionalists by its polished ambiguities: for one thing, the Balfour definition seemed to imply that a Dominion could disassociate itself from the Commonwealth.[26] The definition read: 'They [the Dominions] are autonomous Communities within the British Empire, equal in status, in no way subordinate one to another in any aspect of their domestic or external affairs, though united by a common allegiance to the Crown, and freely associated as members of the British Commonwealth of Nations.'[27] Here was an autonomy not formally acknowledged previously.

The Round Table Conference was not due to meet until November 1930. In the interim Gandhi successfully renewed the civil disobedience campaign, there was a good deal of violence (including an attempt to assassinate the Viceroy), and the Simon Commission reported.

Reading spoke out against the renewal of violence, in May 1930, and attacked the civil disobedience campaign:

When I was in India it was threatened and there was some attempt. I am not making any comparison, or attempting to suggest what should have been done at an earlier moment. I am pointing out this, that while at that moment a bridge had been thrown across the chasm which divided Hindu from Muslim ... to that extent the position was more serious ... that bridge, frail as it was, has disappeared.... The situation is in that respect better.

I am not in the slightest degree suggesting blame upon anybody. It is a very difficult problem for the Viceroy.

I desire to say that Civil Disobedience can never be tolerated. It strikes at the very heart of the Government. If it succeeds it is a vital blow, if it manages to survive it has dug the grave of Government in India.[28]

The Simon Commission reported in June 1930. Its basic recommendations were for the scrapping of dyarchy and in favour of the introduction of full responsible government in the provinces; central government, however, was to be reconstructed, with the Viceroy and his council continuing in charge of defence, and the directly elected central assembly to be replaced by a federal assembly composed of members elected indirectly by the provincial legislatures.

Reading, in common with leading Conservatives and Liberals, warmly welcomed the Simon Report, with its strong central executive and reconstituted central assembly. As long as Dominion status was seen as the government's *ultimate* goal for India, Reading was prepared to accept that too, believing that its achievement would now be properly supervised by a strong central government. Simon had kept in close touch with Reading; he had sent him memoranda setting out his early thoughts on his task in July 1929,[29] and 'the first available copy of volume 2' in June 1930.[30] For his part Reading believed that 'the two volumes of the Simon Commission Report are a splendid achievement, and will rank among the most valuable of State Papers'.[31]

It was natural that Reading should have seen eye to eye with Simon: they were both men from modest backgrounds, who had worked their way to the top of their two highly competitive professions – law and politics. They belonged to the same party, and shared many perceptions of the world.

What could Reading now do to support the Simon Commission's view of Indian constitutional development as opposed to the Wedgwood Benn–Irwin view?

The Round Table Conference, of course, provided him with the obvious forum. The Conference opened on 17 November 1930. A week before, Reading, the inevitable leader of the Liberal delegation, after consulting Lord Peel, had sent Wedgwood Benn what amounted to a threat to disrupt the Conference unless the British government was prepared to accommodate the Liberal and Conservative view on Dominion status:

Our view was that a demand would be made from the Indian side to know if we were prepared to agree to Dominion Status with certain reservations. We Liberals took the view that we and the Conservatives should not be put in the position of fighting this demand, with the Government doing nothing. ... I said that if the Government was in favour of Dominion Status for India with temporary reservations, as far as I was concerned there was no good going on with the Conference. We said that presumably the Government would not want to go further than the Government of India's Despatch, but this we have not yet been able to learn from the Government. I said that we must have an answer before [the opening of the Conference on] 17 November.[32]

Privately, Reading had earlier indicated a more flexible attitude, saying, 'I will go as far as I possibly can to support Lord Irwin', and telling the joint meeting of British opposition delegates that he 'did not by any means rule out the Government of India's proposals'.

What had prompted Reading's ultimatum of 10 November to Wedgwood Benn was his anxiety that the Labour government would leave the Liberal and Conservative delegates high and dry to fight the proposal of Dominion status themselves while it stood 'aloft in the position of a judge, remote from the strife in the arena ...'.[33] For his part Benn resented Reading's pressure and assumed that he wanted to take over the running of the Conference.

The Conference was saved from disaster and Reading was able to resume a more liberal approach by two developments: one was that the Indian communal representatives could not agree sufficiently to press home the demand for Dominion status; the other was the declaration, early in the proceedings, by the Maharajah of Bikaner that the princes were in favour of an all-India federation.

Reading was thus let off the hook. All-India federation became the dominant theme of the Conference, not Dominion status and the timetable for its achievement. As Reading became more enthusiastic over the federation proposals, the conclusions of the Simon Commission were quietly shelved. He seized upon the federal proposals as a potential solution to the constitutional problem: within a responsible federal framework, with a responsible federal government at the centre, Britain and India could work towards the complete transfer of authority, subject to certain reserved areas in respect of defence, the army, foreign affairs and relations between the states and the maintenance of safeguards over finance, the services, law and order and the minorities. He was, however, evasive on the issue of separate Muslim electoral representation, to the chagrin of the Muslim delegates at the Conference.

He expressed his views in a speech on 5 January 1931 which marked the turning-point of the Conference, and provided the Prime Minister, Ramsay MacDonald, with a model for his end of Conference speech on 19 January. It is clear that Reading's earlier denial of Dominion status had been largely strategic, designed to find a fitter solution; encouraged by his fellow-Liberal delegates as well as by many Indians, and warmly supported by the *Manchester Guardian*, he was able to take credit for himself and his party in putting India definitely on the path towards Dominion status within a widely acceptable constitutional framework.

This demonstration of political finesse did not go unnoticed. Wedgwood Benn considered, perhaps ruefully, that Reading had made himself the 'hero of the Conference'.[34] Lloyd George sent his old friend a letter packed with lavish praise, and amounting to party political propaganda, on 4 February 1931, saying:

Circumstances prevailed to make the Liberal Party to a very large extent the arbiters of the fate of the Conference. . . . It is the great merit of the Liberal delegates that . . . when the Conference had reached a critical moment . . . they, through their leader, made it known that they and their party accepted the principle of a responsible Federal Government for all India, accompanied by certain safeguards designed primarily in the interests of India herself. . . . This result was achieved by Liberals working assiduously in the light of historic Liberal doctrine, guided throughout by your great knowledge of Indian affairs, by your statesmanship, and by your great personal influence and prestige. . . . [It] will always be reckoned one of British Liberalism's foremost achievements in the realm of constructive statesmanship.[35]

Although all-India federation was to prove a will o' the wisp, disconcerting successive governments in their attempts to make satisfactory progress towards Indian independence, the Round Table Conference of 1930-1 at least enabled Irwin to negotiate a pact with Gandhi whereby non-cooperation was, for the moment, called off. It was also agreed to reconvene the Conference in September 1931.

Among other public preoccupations during this period of his life Reading, as we have seen, gave some consideration to the problem of Jewish immigration to Palestine.[36] While quick to react against antisemitic prejudice, he was careful to disassociate himself from Zionism. After the coming to power of Hitler in 1933, however, he was obliged to reappraise his attitudes.

He was also involved in attempts to settle the General Strike in May 1926. Hardly had he set foot on British soil on his return from India when he was invited by Lord Wimborne, a Liberal peer and an ex-Viceroy of Ireland, to attend a meeting of a group who hoped to bring the government, the Trades Union Council and the mine owners to a prompt and constructive solution of the dispute.

The account of Reading's part in this attempt at mediation can be found in volume four of Osbert Sitwell's autobiography, *Laughter in the Next Room*, first published in 1949. Other members of the group, apart from Lord and Lady Wimborne, Reading and Sitwell, were the coal owners Lord Londonderry (a Tory) and Lord Gainford (a Liberal); J.H. Thomas, a right-wing member of the TUC's General Council and a man much distrusted by the miners whose unresolved conflict with the coal owners had led to the General Strike itself; Philip Snowden; and J.A. Spender, once editor of the Liberal evening paper the *Westminster Gazette*.

Sitwell observed Reading closely at the first meeting of the group, remarking that:

Though he certainly brought with him a feeling of ambitions gratified and of marked worldly success, to me he resembled the phantom of a great man, but a spectre heavy in spite of his phantomhood, and of his light weight physically. One seemed to see him, like an apparition at a séance, through curtains; an affable Caesar, ponderous, though thinly cast in bronze, laurel-wreathed, finely featured, quick witted (that could be deduced from his eyes), but slightly damaged by life and rendered complacent by the progress of the years. He had occupied so many exalted posts that above all men he knew the value of discretion, and in consequence he preferred in his talk to deal in golf values in a proconsular manner or relate some small story about Asquith or Lord Balfour ... rather than discuss high politics.[37]

According to Sitwell, J.H. Thomas and other trades union leaders were pleased that Reading agreed to act as an intermediary since he was 'sympathetic to a degree' with the plight of the miners and their refusal to accept lower wages, and could not be associated with 'ruthless Tory policy'.

Not that Reading was prepared to advocate syndicalism or support socialist revolution. Indeed, 'he thought the only true path out of the present most serious position was for the miners to agree to abide by the recommendations of the Samuel Report', which had ruled out the nationalization of the mines and supported the owners over the need to cut wages, but had balanced this by backing both the miners' refusal to work longer hours and their call for a basic overhaul of the industry's organization. The miners had rejected the report overall, finding several of its recommendations quite unacceptable.

Reading did, however, try to see the premier Baldwin over the crisis, but Sitwell had it from the novelist Arnold Bennett that he 'had been stopped by Churchill and F.E. [Smith]'. On 9 May after a meeting between Thomas, Lord Wimborne and Reading, the three men sent Baldwin a message saying that the TUC General Council might call off the General Strike if the government would resume negotiations to implement the recommendations of the Samuel Report without delay. The Prime Minister rebuffed this overture, replying that he had already conceded as much in his broadcast of Saturday 8 May.

On 11 May Reading's attitude to the crisis had dramatically changed. Gone was his previous mood of patience and faith in careful negotiation. Together with Wimborne, he now pressed Thomas with 'extreme urgency' to get the General Council to call off the strike. What had Reading learnt from his contacts with the establishment? Quite simply, according to Sitwell, that the government 'had resolved to arrest the Trades Union leaders the following day'.

Whether the government actually had such intentions is unclear, although before the start of the General Strike J.H. Thomas and other TUC members had speculated that they might be arrested. Thomas, indeed, went so far as to imagine that some of the Council would be shot: 'Of course, the shooting won't be done direct, it will be done by those damned Fascists and those fellows.'[38] In any case, Reading apparently did not tell Thomas on 11 May why he was now urging him to call off the strike. Nor did most members of the General Council need such a threat to bring them to heel. Their resolve was crumbling throughout 11 and 12 May, and after meeting Baldwin at 10 Downing Street at noon on the 12th the General Strike was called off. The miners, however, held out, and were eventually forced back to work, defeated and humiliated, six months later.

Reading was undoubtedly relieved at the collapse of the General Strike, and his love of law and order must have been upset by the potential for violent confrontation in the dispute. His son Gerald makes no mention in his biography of his father's involvement in the negotiations to end the strike. Nor does he reveal that he himself helped to run a canteen in Hyde Park for strike-breakers. Gerald, according to a contemporary, was made 'C.O. Urns', and proceeded to mix up the tea and the coffee and was not pleased to be told so 'sitting forlornly in front of his two urns, rain dripping steadily off his hat'.[39]

Reading had preoccupations of a deeply personal nature too. He and his wife had found a country house in 1927, occupying Deal Castle near Walmer Sands in Kent. Lord Beauchamp, now Liberal leader in the

Lords, was also Warden of the Cinque Ports, and when Lord Allenby resigned the office of Captain of Deal Castle, offered the sinecure to Reading. The couple thus acquired a country retreat in exchange for duties of the lightest kind.

Lady Reading did not, however, live long to enjoy Deal Castle. The cancer which had first appeared in 1925 had not been eradicated, and she became progressively more ill during 1928 and 1929. She was in considerable pain during 1929 and early 1930, when her husband refused to leave the house for a single night. Reading chose not to let his wife know that her condition was hopeless, although she must have realized it before long. At any rate, she knew shortly before the end, telling him, 'My every prayer is answered. Thank God, I go before you.' She thus remained the perfect platform wife and steady supporter to the last.

Alice Reading died in her Curzon Street house on 30 January 1930 and, in her son's words, 'the perfect partnership of 42 years was dissolved forever'. Lady Reading was buried in the Golders Green cemetery.

Reading was deeply affected. He had undergone enormous strain as he watched his wife slowly die. At the end of the year Lord Melchett (formerly Alfred Mond) also died, and another close family bond was broken.

Gerald Reading recalled that his father was 'bitterly lonely', but often refused invitations to come to his son's home in the evenings, even pretending sometimes that he had friends who were coming to visit him. According to Gerald, 'even work had lost its savour, though he plodded on in search of such distractions as it could provide. Hitherto he had always looked many years younger than his real age; now he seemed suddenly an old man. He had lost his quickness of movement and he walked slowly and with a stoop.'[40]

In a little over a year and a half, however, Reading had remarried. His second wife was Stella Charnaud, who had been for a time his wife's secretary in India, and who had worked for him in a similar capacity on his return to Britain. Gerald Isaacs has written that his mother 'had become deeply attached to her'. Was there any rivalry, even at a subconscious level, between the two women? The present generation of Readings believe not.[41]

The wedding took place early in August 1931. The fact that Reading's new wife was a gentile seems to have been accepted with good grace by his family, though there was some criticism in orthodox Jewish circles. In any case, Gerald's son, the future Third Marquess, had already been baptized into the Anglican faith, and in 1966 became a firm friend of the American evangelical preacher Billy Graham.[42] Reading himself, as we have seen, was hardly a man of faith, which was just as well since his new wife saw no merit in emphasizing their different backgrounds.

Stella Reading was, in any case, a woman of great force and charm. Her husband adored her, and they could be seen holding hands at the dinner table like a courting couple. Stella certainly endeared herself to her newly acquired grandchildren and, later on, to their children. Lady Zuckerman, Gerald Reading's daughter, recalls how Stella later kept her husband's memory alive for her and for others in the family.[43] Stella Reading went on to found the Women's Voluntary Service in June 1938, and by the end of 1939 had helped to boost its membership from 165,000 in September, when war broke out, to 300,000 by the end of the year. She was as energetic and hard-working as Reading had been, travelling an average 1,200 miles and speaking at nearly a hundred meetings a month during this successful recruiting drive. Among her favourite exhortations to her female audiences were: 'The greatest disservice a woman can do, at the moment, is to consider herself useless', and 'It is no good relying on the next person to do the job, she is probably relying on you.'[44] Appropriately she was one of the first women to be made a Life Peeress, in 1958. Her outgoing personality and drive provide an interesting contrast to the more secluded and circumscribed life-style of Reading's first wife.

Remarriage, according to his son, revived Reading: 'the transformation in him was immediate and immense. Much of his old buoyancy returned and he resumed work with fresh vigour and zest.'

This was just as well, for hardly was he back from his honeymoon when he was invited once more to fill a great office of state.

16 Foreign Secretary, 1931

The ideal would be to banish party division and to unite in a National government for say five years to deal with India, the Dole, Tariffs and Empire, but alas I fear this is Utopian....
Reading to Lord Willingdon, May 1931

They [the National government] could never face your defection. You mean far more to the country than a party leader and they know it, that is why they are so anxious to keep you with them.
Lloyd George to Reading, 25 September 1931

I was sorry to leave the FO. I liked both the office and those officials with whom I was in closest contact very much indeed.
Reading to Arthur Murray, 1932

1931 was to be a year of great significance in Reading's life. Although he reached the age of seventy-one in 1931, his private and his public life were to be as active as when he was half that age. Early in the year he succeeded Lord Beauchamp as Liberal leader in the House of Lords; he remarried at the beginning of August; and three weeks later he had been sworn in as Secretary of State for Foreign Affairs in Ramsay MacDonald's first National government.

Reading's appointment as Foreign Secretary was a direct result of the economic and political crisis that had been building up in the wake of the Wall Street crash of 1929 and the development of the Great Slump of the early 1930s.

As revenue from taxes fell and expenditure, especially on unemployment benefit (the dole) increased, the Labour Chancellor of the Exchequer, Philip Snowden, had been unable to balance the budget. He had produced a stopgap budget in April 1931, intending to produce a more realistic, and almost certainly punitive budget in the autumn. Moreover, for the first time, estimates, haphazard at best, of Britain's balance of payments with the rest of the world, were being published: they showed deficits, which many took to be connected in some way with the budget deficit. As it happened, the nation's balance of payments had never shown a credit balance since 1822, but the deficit had always been made up, except in three years since then, by earnings from the 'invisibles' – banking, insurance, shipping and the interest on foreign investments. By 1931, however, these 'invisible' earnings had been badly hit by the Slump.

As unease, not to say panic, grew in orthodox economic and financial circles, the tension was increased by the news early in August that there was a run on the pound and foreigners were making haste to sell sterling. On 11 August MacDonald was recalled to London to be told by leading bankers that the nation was 'on the edge of a precipice'. Some experts were convinced that the pound would lose its value as dramatically as the German mark during its recent collapse. The Governor of the Bank of England, Montagu Norman, even advocated 'that ration books should be printed in case the currency collapsed and the country had to revert to barter'.[1]

What could the government do? The bankers agreed that the budget must be balanced through reducing government expenditure, especially unemployment benefit. The Conservative party, and many Liberals, were not prepared to see direct taxation increased. Many Labour supporters and the TUC refused to countenance a cut in unemployment benefit or indeed in public spending generally. MacDonald was also told by the London bankers that 'The cause of the trouble was not financial but political, and lay in the complete want of confidence in HMG existing among foreigners.'[2]

Between 20 and 23 August the Cabinet struggled to find an acceptable solution to the crisis. They failed. Snowden, a harsh man for harsh times, insisted on a 10 per cent cut in unemployment relief; MacDonald held no firm economic views, though favouring the proposed cuts; nine Cabinet ministers indicated that they would resign rather than support the unemployment cuts.

As the crisis unfolded, Reading hurried back to London to confer with Sir Herbert Samuel, who was acting leader of the Liberal party while Lloyd George recovered from a serious operation to remove a prostate gland. The Liberal leaders had for some months been considering how they could help ease the nation's difficulties. Sir John Simon and Leslie Hore-Belisha had entered into discussions with the Conservatives. Lloyd George, however, favoured a Liberal alliance with Labour; towards the end of July 1931 he had met with the Prime Minister, and had returned believing that 'Generally speaking, Labour would like an alliance. They would be willing to drop certain of their present Ministers. ... Ramsay would be Prime Minister, Lloyd George would be Leader [of the House] at the Foreign Office or the Treasury.'[3]

Reading had been involved in discussions as early as May 1931 and had given Lord Willingdon, the new Viceroy of India, his appraisal of the situation: 'The ideal would be to banish party division and to unite in a National Government for say five years to deal with India, the Dole, Tariffs and Empire, but alas I fear this is Utopian and I see no prospect of it although there is talk amongst some of us of the urgent need of unity.'[4]

On 24 August, with Lloyd George safely out of the way, Reading's utopia became a reality. MacDonald, having gone to Buckingham Palace to hand in his government's resignation, found George v anxious to retain him as Prime Minister, and well disposed to the idea of a National government. Could MacDonald form such a government?

Reading and Samuel had met the day before. Both believed in the necessity of such a government, and Samuel, as acting party leader, duly proposed it when he met the King for consultation. He later made a note of his meeting with the King:

We thought that, in view of the unpalatable character to the masses of the people of many of the economies which were indispensable, it would be to the general interest if a Labour Government were in office during their enactment. If Mr MacDonald, with this or a reconstituted Labour Cabinet, was able to propose economies which were really adequate, that would be the best solution. The proposals hitherto made by the Cabinet were, however, quite insufficient, and I gave some illustrations as to Unemployment.

If that solution proved to be impracticable, then a National Government of members of the three parties would be the best alternative. It would be preferable that Mr MacDonald should be the Premier, unless he found that he could not carry with him a sufficient number of his colleagues.

We deprecated a purely Conservative Government, as we thought it would have great difficulty in securing popular support for the necessary measures. If, however, His Majesty found that no other solution could be reached, we should of course support the Government of the day in the steps immediately necessary to save the financial situation.

I said nothing as to the possibility of a Conservative-Liberal or Labour-Liberal Administration, and the King did not raise the point.[5]

Other Liberals followed this lead, with Lloyd George sending his blessing from his sick bed. The dissident, largely Asquithian Liberals, grouped under Sir John Simon, were less enthusiastic, and were eventually passed over for office.

Baldwin, the Conservative leader, was prepared to join a government led by MacDonald. Perhaps he shied away from the idea of leading a Conservative government supported by the Liberals, which was a real alternative, because he did not want his party to bear sole responsibility for the unpleasant economies that would have to be made. At any rate, he gave MacDonald his support.

MacDonald thus formed the National government in a day. His biggest problem lay with his own party, the bulk of which hastened to disassociate themselves from the venture. Three senior colleagues, however, were willing to serve with him: Snowden, of course, J.H. Thomas, the Dominions' Secretary and the National Union of Railwaymen's leader, and Lord Sankey, the Lord Chancellor.

The offices were shared out in rough proportion to party strengths in the House of Commons: MacDonald remained Prime Minister, Snowden Chancellor of the Exchequer, Thomas stayed as Dominions' Secretary and took on the Colonial Office, and Sankey was still Lord Chancellor; for the Conservatives, Baldwin became Lord President of the Council, Sir Samuel Hoare Secretary of State for India, Neville Chamberlain Minister of Health and Sir Philip Cunliffe Lister President of the Board of Trade; Sir Herbert Samuel went to the Home Office, and Lord Reading to the Foreign Office.

Why was Reading included? A simple explanation is that the Liberals were offered two posts and it was natural for the leaders of both Houses of Parliament to take office. But there were other considerations. One was that Reading and Samuel had seen eye to eye as to how to respond to the crisis and had reaped an immediate reward. Another lay in Reading's considerable prestige; as a successful ex-Ambassador to the United States and as a much acclaimed Viceroy, he had a statesmanlike reputation to take to the Foreign Office. Moreover, he had Lloyd George's blessing. MacDonald, too, had wanted him in, and had 'urgently pressed him' to accept office.[6]

For his part, Reading relished the challenge. His son has claimed that 'he felt bound to play his part particularly since the one office which had always had a powerful attraction for him and one for which his gifts and experience admirably qualified him, was at his disposal'.[7] Perhaps it was this sudden promotion to high office, as much as his recent remarriage, that allowed Reading so noticeably to cast aside his years during the second half of 1931.

Congratulations poured in as soon as his appointment became

known. Among his well-wishers was J.L. Garvin, editor of the *Observer*, who wrote: 'I rejoice to see you in the forefront of the State in these extraordinary circumstances. It is another phase, and not the last, in your equally extraordinary career. Although I strain my memory I cannot recall anyone whatever in the history of England who filled so many different great offices.'[8] Philip Guedalla thought, 'It is a great thing for England that you are now at the Foreign Office. Yours is an appointment which will be welcome all over Europe and particularly in Washington.'[9]

On 28 August Reading presided over a well-attended Liberal party meeting, and assured his audience that Lloyd George was in 'complete accord' with what had happened though he had also expressed the conviction that the crisis should never have arisen in the first place given the nation's real wealth.

Reading had to choose a Parliamentary Under-Secretary of State. This was of particular importance since Reading was in the House of Lords. There was some talk of the Prime Minister's son Malcolm Mac-Donald filling the post, but Austen Chamberlain, with Baldwin's backing, strongly recommended a young man called Anthony Eden whom he believed had the makings of a future Foreign Secretary. Eden and Reading seem to have got on extremely well during their short time together at the Foreign Office, and in 1934 Eden told Reading: 'I shall always remember your many kindnesses to me when it was my privilege to serve under you at the FO, and I am quite sure that I shall never again enjoy a political experience as much as I did those few months.'[10] Although this letter is one more tribute to Reading's courtesy and consideration, Eden may have been reinforced in his fond memories of his work with Reading in the light of his much less satisfactory relationship with Reading's successor at the Foreign Office, Sir John Simon.[11]

One of Reading's first duties was to receive all the foreign ambassadors in London. The meetings were brief, but Reading asked each ambassador what he thought of world affairs at that moment and later recalled, somewhat wryly, that only the Turkish ambassador expressed a cheerful view.

Reading's workload was a heavy one. Apart from his duties as Foreign Secretary, which included making a detailed record for the Cabinet and for the relevant British diplomatic missions overseas of any interviews with foreign representatives, he was asked to lead the government in the House of Lords. This latter responsibility meant that he was responsible for getting all of the government's business through the Upper House. At the Foreign Office Reading was well served by his permanent officials, notably Sir Robert Vansittart, the Permanent Under-Secretary, and his Private Secretary, Sir Walford Selby.

As he sat at his huge desk in the Foreign Secretary's spacious room overlooking St James's Park, Reading must have wondered at a career that had begun so inauspiciously and had now taken him, so late in life, to one of the great offices of state.

Not that Reading had much time for nostalgic musing; in addition to his responsibility for foreign affairs, he was closely involved in formulating policy on the financial crisis and whether Britain was to go off the gold standard, as well as keeping a watchful eye on Liberal party interests.

Reading's impact upon foreign policy was less significant than his influence on matters of domestic concern. Early in October he made a short visit to Paris, accompanied by Sir Frederick Leith-Ross from the Treasury, 'to get into contact with the French Ministers and to lay the basis for future co-operation wherever it was possible'.

The most obvious purpose of Reading's trip to Paris was to express thanks for the French government's tactful support of the British Cabinet's decision, a fortnight earlier, to suspend the gold standard as a result of a massive depletion of Britain's gold reserves. Pierre Laval, the French Prime Minister, and a future collaborator with the Nazis, had put a loan of 3,000,000,000 gold francs at the disposal of the British government, and had arranged for the Paris Bourse to be closed at the same time as the London Stock Exchange while the emergency legislation was being rushed through Parliament.

Reading met, in addition to Laval, Flandin, the French Finance Minister, and Briand, the Foreign Minister. The future stabilization of the pound was discussed, though little could be decided in the way of policy.

The same could be said of Reading's conversations with Laval and Briand over the problem of Germany's reparation repayments. To help the struggling German government, reparations had been suspended on the initiative of President Hoover of the United States. France was eager for the reparations to resume at the end of the Hoover moratorium, and Laval asserted that France could not wipe the slate completely clean, though he hinted that his government might accept a partial writing-off of the reparations if France was given adequate guarantees for her national security. Laval also made it plain that France would refuse to support any scheme for general disarmament unless she had such guarantees.

For his part, Reading was hampered in these exchanges by the caretaker nature of the National government, and told the French that he 'could not therefore take decisions on a long policy or make any promises'. He did, however, emphasize that the British government was 'very anxious to do everything in their power to keep in close agreement with France'. After these bland exchanges, Laval and Reading parted on good terms, and the Foreign Secretary later informed the Cabinet that, in his view, his mission to Paris had been a success.

On 11 October 1931 Reading left for Geneva to attend a meeting of the League of Nations. The willingness of the Cabinet to allow him to go to Geneva was in strong contrast to the attitude expressed at the end of August. Then the Cabinet view had been that 'in principle it would be undesirable that a Government, formed to deal with a particular emergency, should be weakened at the present juncture by the detachment of a member of the Cabinet to attend an international meeting'.[12] By 16 September, however, the Cabinet view was that

a visit from the Foreign Secretary [to the League of Nations' Assembly] would be much appreciated. ... The Foreign Secretary could reaffirm the announced intention of the Government to support the meeting of the Disarmament Conference in February; he could make a friendly reference to Signor Grandi's proposals for a holiday in armaments. ... he could explain the aims and intensive activities of the National Government, and say a strong word about the maintenance of the £ sterling.[13]

More than a month later, with the financial crisis under better control, Reading arrived at Geneva. There, apart from demonstrating by his presence the comparative stability of the National government, he was mainly involved in the Manchuria crisis that had followed Japan's intervention in that country. Reading joined with the Foreign Ministers of France, Italy and Germany in urging the United States, which was not a member of the League of Nations but had been one of the prime movers of the Kellogg Pact, to send a representative to sit in on the proceedings of the League's Council when it tried to resolve the Sino-Japanese conflict over Manchuria.

Nothing much came of this initiative. Although China and Japan were formally reminded of their international obligations under the Kellogg Pact to settle their differences by peaceful means, there was to be no such solution. By the time the League of Nations met again to discuss Manchuria, Reading was no longer Foreign Secretary and could only regret in private the League's total failure to prevent the Japanese conquest of Manchuria.

Reading had next to no impact upon British foreign policy. This was understandable, given his mere ten weeks at the Foreign Office, and his naturally cautious disposition.

His role within the National government, however, was by no means negligible. This is particularly true in regard to the financial crisis.

In this context, the expertise which had made Reading so indispensable to Lloyd George at the outset of the First World War was once more of service to the country. Within a week of joining the National government, Reading had joined the Cabinet's Finance Committee; indeed, he had been invited to become a member as soon as he took Cabinet office but 'had been obliged to refuse membership as there were urgent matters requiring his attendance at the Foreign Office'.[14]

Since the National government owed its birth to the need to stabilize the nation's financial and economic position, the Finance Committee was a body of the utmost importance.

Reading was quick to assert his influence. On 11 September he put to MacDonald a proposal to 'enter into an arrangement with Canada ... for the purchase of wheat, of which they have so large a surplus in hand, to be paid for by exports of manufactured goods'.[15] The same day Reading wrote to the Chancellor, Snowden, making a suggestion based on his wartime experiences in the United States:

May I make a suggestion to you which I have no doubt will have already occurred to you, – I make it only because you are so dreadfully pressed at the moment. Would it not be [as] well to give instructions to the Treasury officials to have ready for us on Monday a statement of the procedure which was adopted in the war for the purpose of obtaining American securities, in case we should require them.[16]

On 14 September Reading made the Cabinet's special Finance Committee look at the possibility of restricting the withdrawal of capital from the London market. He gave the Committee 'some evidence to show that persons in London may be withdrawing capital on a considerable scale'. He quoted the meetings of three boards of directors where

it had been suggested that the business of the Directors was to make profits as long as this was possible and to prevent loss, and that this could best be accomplished by transferring into foreign currencies. To the suggestion that this was not patriotic the reply had been that if this was the case the Government ought to prevent it.[17]

Faced with the traditional selfishness of many City businessmen and financiers who had clamoured for a cut in the dole while busily protecting their own profits, Reading boldly proposed that 'the Government ought to consider what powers they could take, and how far it was possible to exercise them'. Predictably, Sir Ernest Harvey, Deputy Governor of the Bank of England, replied 'that it was impossible to impose restrictions as it would endanger the position of foreign business'.[18]

Three days later Reading tried again to convince the Committee, asking 'if it was certain that no results could be obtained from restrictions. The stage might be reached where it was necessary to go to all lengths and he felt that the matter ought to be fully considered.'[19] Harvey replied briefly that if restrictions were to have 'any effect it would be one of alarm'.

While Reading was arguing for official action to stop the run on sterling, and perusing the Treasury proposals for balancing the budget, events elsewhere were pushing the government into an intervention of far greater symbolism. On 15 September sailors in the Atlantic Fleet at Invergordon refused their duties as a protest against cuts, some of more than 10 per cent, in lower deck pay. The Invergordon 'mutiny' was soon over, ended by the Admiralty's promise to revise the cuts, but this act of defiance in the ranks of the senior service helped to increase the panic felt by foreign holders of sterling. On 19 September, two days after Sir Ernest Harvey had rejected Reading's proposal to restrict the run on the pound, the Bank of England had been forced to part with such huge sums of gold that they told the government that they could no longer sell bullion at the fixed price. The Cabinet had no alternative but to suspend the gold standard.

Legislation to suspend the gold standard was rushed through Parliament on 21 September 1931. The evening before a telegram to the principal British missions abroad had been issued in Reading's name, and reflected his views:

His Majesty's Government have arrived at their decision with the greatest reluctance. But during the last few days the International financial markets have become demoralized and have been liquidating their sterling assets regardless of their intrinsic worth. In the circumstances there was no alternative but to protect the financial position of this country by the only means at our disposal.

His Majesty's Government are securing a balanced budget and the internal position of the country is sound. This position must be maintained. It is one thing to go off the gold standard with an unbalanced budget and uncontrolled inflation; it is quite another to take this measure, not because of internal financial difficulties, but because of excessive withdrawals of borrowed capital. The ultimate resources of this country are enormous, and there is no doubt that the present exchange difficulties will prove only temporary.[20]

258

Many contemporaries viewed the suspension of the gold standard as a cataclysm only a little removed from Judgement Day. The value of the pound did, of course, fall from 4.86 dollars to 3.80 dollars, then to 3.23 dollars, and ended up hovering about the 3.40 dollar mark. Apart from that, very little of note occurred. Paper money seemed as real to most people, especially those of the younger generations, as gold sovereigns. Moreover, the devaluation of the pound was a great help to British exporters, enabling them to compete more effectively with their foreign rivals. A few days before the suspension of the gold standard, as A.J.P. Taylor has remarked, 'a managed currency had seemed as wicked as family planning. Now, like contraception, it became a commonplace. This was the end of an era.'[21]

Reading was one of those responsible for ending the era. As we have seen, he viewed the managing of the currency with equanimity, even approval. His financial experience led him, in this instance, to the commonsense solution. Nor did he show extravagant sympathy for the well-heeled who might expect to lose money as the result of going off gold. On 8 September he had told the House of Lords that, amid the financial crisis, 'The wealthy, it is true, may suffer very severely, but it does not touch their vital necessities of life. With the poor it effects the food that they can eat, the clothes that they can buy, and the coal that they can burn. It strikes at the very cost of living for them.'[22]

On 21 September, leading for the government in the Lords debate on the suspension of the gold standard, Reading pointed out that 'It is worthy of note that, as regards the Bill itself, there is no opposition.'[23] He went on, however, to criticize those who had undermined the work of the National government: 'Unfortunately there were statements made both outside the House of Commons and inside it which led to a renewal, not unnaturally, by foreign countries of a feeling of insecurity, of instability in this country.'[24]

Hand in hand with this essentially modest tinkering with sterling went certain national economies – far more unpopular because they were easier to understand and directly affected the ordinary man and woman. Snowden's emergency budget had been debated when Parliament reassembled on 8 September. The budget at least wiped out the £170,000,000 deficit which had been one of the causes of the downfall of MacDonald's Labour government. The cost of balancing the books was high: taxes, mainly income tax, were increased by £76,000,000; the payment into the sinking fund was reduced by £20,000,000; more uncomfortable were the economies imposed on all those paid by the state – a 10 per cent cut in pay affecting alike the salaries of Cabinet ministers and the dole for the unemployed. There were two exceptions to these 10 per cent cuts, both perhaps reflecting the mood of the times: the police escaped with a 5 per cent cut, but teachers suffered a 15 per cent reduction in pay.

Reading and the Liberal party supported the economy programme, though the vast bulk of the Parliamentary Labour party voted against it; the Conservatives were predictably enthusiastic for the economies. Opening for the National government in the House of Lords on 8 September 1931, Reading claimed that:

> In the present emergency, however, there are no divisions of opinion between Conservatives and Liberals, and, I trust, some representatives of Labour....
> We are united for the present purposes in the interests of the nation and as a national duty regardless of the political opinions which in normal times divide us.[25]

Where, Reading continued, the Labour government had 'failed – or at any rate, the reason that led to the downfall of the Government – was that they were not prepared to make economies that were adequate'.[26]

On 30 September, speaking for the government in the Lords debate on the National Economy Bill, Reading reiterated the patriotic call to defend the national interest, claiming that the government was motivated by the 'sole desire to benefit the nation and to do what we can, to restore the position which, for a time, we have lost'.[27]

He went on to talk, not particularly convincingly, of the need to share the burden of the economy measures: 'You cannot have strict equality, but what you can have is a spreading of the burden, so that it may be felt not too much by those who must be included, and a fair proportion is put upon the shoulders of those who already in the same interest have borne very heavy burdens.'[28]

The main achievement of the National government of August to November 1931 was to convince the public that something constructive had actually been done. In reality, the pound had not been 'saved' – indeed, the gold standard had been abandoned with unseemly haste. The national economies proposed in Snowden's budget of early September had not prevented a disastrous run on Britain's gold reserves. The National government ministers were united on very little, except the essentials of survival and a sentimental view of their patriotic duty.

Could the National government legitimately continue in office, once it had balanced the budget and apparently saved the pound? Most political leaders assumed that a general election would be necessary in the autumn, though MacDonald initially hoped to avoid this. Certainly the Conservatives stood to benefit from an election campaign that emphasized the cause of national unity, especially if enough Labour and Liberal politicians were prepared to fight on the same platform. The Tories, moreover, saw a chance of introducing protection, or tariff reform, in a House of Commons dominated by their party.

The protection of British industry, passionately espoused by Joseph Chamberlain in his last great campaign between 1903 and 1906, seemed to promise a remedy to the world depression by strengthening domestic industry against foreign imports. It also provided a non-socialist way of raising revenue through customs duties and indirect taxes as opposed to direct personal taxation. The only problem was that every party that had advocated protection since 1900 had suffered defeat at the polls: the Unionists in 1906 and 1910, and Baldwin's Conservative govern-ment in 1923. Camouflaged by an appeal to a lofty national purpose, protection at least stood a chance of avoiding rejection by an electorate largely raised on the assumption that free trade equalled prosperity.

Traditionally the Liberal party was the party of free trade, as was Labour. By 1931, however, things had changed: whereas Joseph Chamberlain's tariff reform campaign had united the Liberals before the 1906 general election, the movement for protection in 1931 divided them. A group of some twenty Liberal MPs led by Sir John Simon favoured protection, whereas the Liberals loyal to Samuel, Reading and Lloyd George stuck to free trade principles. The Liberal party were nastily trapped over this issue: if they supported the National govern-ment in an election campaign they were bound to underwrite protec-tion; if they dissociated themselves from the 'national' platform, they faced a further loss of seats. The answer was to oppose an early election.

Reading had no wish for an autumn election. Quite apart from the difficulties that this would pose for himself and the party leaders, he had received appeals from local Liberal organizations to oppose an early poll, including, on 4 September 1931, a message from the influential Manchester Liberal Federation asserting that: 'There is strong feeling here that the Government should remain in office for a longer period than is at present expected, and that the stability of the country should not be jeopardized by a General Election in the near future.'[29]

It is clear that Reading wanted to remain in the National govern-ment, more so than to stay rigidly loyal to free trade. When he had first spoken as government leader in the Lords on 8 September 1931 he had described himself as 'deeply sensible of the unexpected honour of leading this House', and had acknowledged that 'but for recent events, I could not have hoped to occupy this position'.[30] The financial crisis, therefore, had enabled him to realize once more his deep-seated ambition for high office and a place at the centre of events.

Reading, moreover, was fired by the idea of a National government, encompassing former political rivals and constituted for the nation's good. On 8 September he had told the Lords, 'I wish I could be quite sure that National Government is quite the correct term . . . since it only has a small representation of the Labour party so far as I am aware at present. . . .'[31]

Even after his exclusion from office after the general election of 27 October 1931, Reading told the Lords:

We sit opposite the Members of the Government in this House, but we are not in opposition. We are, indeed, a party of supporters of the Government. . . . I desire . . . to assure [the Leader of the House] that in whatever I may be able to do, whether in my personal capacity or in my association with the Party, he can always count upon me to do everything I can to assist the Government, because I believe it will act in the real interests of the nation.[32]

It is not surprising, therefore, to find Reading, at the end of September 1931, discussing with the Prime Minister the terms on which he would remain in the National government even after an early general election. None of Reading's earlier biographers seem to have been aware of these negotiations. The Second Marquess of Reading wrote, rather predictably, that 'Had he been consulted, he might well have come to the conclusion that he had performed the public service required of him by becoming a member of the National Government at the uncertain moment of its birth and that the time had now come when he would be well advised to free himself of the weight of cases and make room for a younger man'.[33] Montgomery Hyde, on the other hand, believes that there is evidence to show that 'Reading's retirement was voluntary and that he put his office at the Prime Minister's disposal'.[34] This is true in the direct aftermath of the general election, but it gives no indication of Reading's earlier willingness to stay in office.

Towards the end of September 1931, with MacDonald under pressure to ask for a dissolution of Parliament, Reading was subjected to a remarkable tug-of-war: the Prime Minister was asking him to stay with him, and Lloyd George was urging his old friend to disassociate himself from the National government and to fortify the Liberal party.

On 25 September Herbert Samuel wrote to Lloyd George, who was still convalescing after his operation the previous month, to say that MacDonald was 'on the point of surrender' over an early election. The same day Reading had visited Lloyd George at his country house at

Churt in Surrey, where he had been beseeched to stand firm against an immediate general election, to consider resignation and to help rally the party against the 'National' Liberals. Lloyd George said: 'I beg of you to come forward. You will do a great service and could bring the party together where no-one else can. They could never face your defection. You mean far more to the country than a party leader and they know it, that is why they are so anxious to keep you with them.'[35]

The next day, 26 September, Reading obediently met with MacDonald and told him his price for staying in the government – that an early general election must be based on nothing more specific than an appeal for a 'doctor's mandate' to complete the cure of the nation's ills. Reading did not give MacDonald the impression that he was eager to die in the last ditch for free trade principles. Nor did he appear over keen actually to leave the government. Reading left a record of the meeting:

I gave the PM a rough outline of my views and told him that I would be prepared to stand by him if his programme were one that asked the country to give him a mandate to do what was necessary leaving no door shut, and no avenue unexplored.

[I said that] in my opinion it was necessary to reconsider everything and that our main object should be to reinstate prosperity in industry and a revitalization of the whole of the industry of the country.

He asked me several times whether, in the event of his agreeing to go to the country as leader on this basis, I would remain and I told him I would.[36]

MacDonald was indeed to appeal to the country for a 'doctor's mandate' – the authority to undertake whatever measures the National government thought necessary to restore the country to full economic health. He was pushed into calling the election, however, by Baldwin and the Conservatives.

On 4 October 1931, while Lloyd George was still urging Herbert Samuel to stand firm against a general election, the Prime Minister unburdened himself to Reading over his difficulties with the Conservatives. Reading recorded that:

The PM was very apprehensive of the future and had endeavoured to get from Baldwin an undertaking that [during] the next eighteen months the Conservative majority would not, through their strength as [a] majority, try to force through any measure on which the Cabinet in general was not in agreement. I observed that even if Baldwin gave this promise he might not be in a position to deliver the keys.[37]

On 5 October MacDonald stopped havering, and on the seventh asked for a dissolution of Parliament. There was very little else he could do, given the Conservatives' desire for an early election. Herbert Samuel had been unable, and unwilling, much to Lloyd George's fury, to hold out against the election; Reading, as we have seen, had secured terms of the most general sort, before agreeing to the poll.

Not that the Liberal party's troubles ended there. It was plain that if, as was predictable, the Conservatives were returned in large numbers to the House of Commons, protection would follow as night follows day – no matter what reassurances were given about a full enquiry prior to taking so momentous a step.

The Liberals had consistently rejected successive calls for protection, or tariff reform. Could they continue to do so amid the shrunken markets and falling exports of 1931? Sir John Simon was prepared to sacrifice the sacred cow of free trade, and could count on over twenty Liberal MPs to support him. As early as March 1931 Simon was putting his case to Reading:

> I am becoming increasingly convinced that, much as many people will dislike it, and great as are the arguments against it, Free Traders will have to face the possibility of filling up the gap in revenue of this year and the next by some form of taxation which is not in accordance with their traditional fiscal principles. I do not see how direct taxation *can* be increased do you?[38]

Simon also wanted the Liberals to disentangle themselves from their long-standing flirtation with land taxes as an extra source of revenue. Reading had supported the proposed reform as a member of Asquith's pre-war government, and Simon felt obliged on 2 June 1931 to write to him telling him of 'the universal feeling' against land taxes, and to say, 'I . . . wish so much that you would express yourself. It seems to me quite impossible for a Liberal to support them, save for tactical reasons.'[39]

It was not Simon, however, but Samuel and Reading who, as members of the National government, had to tread most warily on the tariff reform issue as the election campaign began. As early as 1 October a Drafting Committee of the Cabinet had worked on a formula to be put out to the electorate. The next day Reading and Samuel tried to get part of the draft altered. In particular they objected to the sentence: 'We ask for powers to deal with and control imports whether by prohibition, tariffs or any other measures which may be necessary.'[40] Instead they proposed this wording: 'Strong efforts should be made to secure the lowering of Tariff barriers abroad. If it should be found necessary by the Government having regard to the conditions now prevailing to restrict imports, we ask for power to adopt any measures which the situation may require, whether by prohibition Tariffs, or otherwise.'[41]

Nothing came of this proposal, and neither side would give way. Samuel and Reading went on to record their objections to a general election, and to complain that they were being forced to agree, as in their proposed draft alteration, to an election programme that involved the possible restriction of imports. They went on to assert that:

Instead of the National Government going to the country to secure a mandate to complete its present work and to prevent the Opposition coming into power, the Election would be fought also on the Tariff issue, with the Liberal Leaders supporting that policy. They had not entered the National Government on any such understanding, and they felt strongly that they should not be put in the position of appearing to refuse to maintain unity for the reason that they objected to this policy.[42]

Although Reading associated himself with Samuel, it was the latter who proved the more obstinate. In attempts to resolve the deadlock there were many comings and goings in late September and early October between 10 Downing Street, Lloyd George's country house at Churt, and Baldwin's at Trent. Lloyd George was adamant that Samuel and Reading should leave the government and not agree to a general election. Reading, as we have observed, was able to find a way of more or less placating Lloyd George. Samuel, as acting party leader, was less lucky, and Lloyd George threatened to break with him and to withdraw the famous Fund. The Welshman had decided to have no truck with the National government, and told Samuel, 'If I am to die, I would rather die fighting on the Left.'[43]

With the unity of the National government in danger of being shattered upon the rock of the tariff controversy, the Cabinet struggled to find a formula that would satisfy Samuel. Eventually a solution was found: all three parties associated with the National government should be allowed to put forward their own election programme under a generalized appeal from the Prime Minister.

This still meant that Samuel and Reading would have to compromise on the tariff issue. MacDonald's electoral appeal included the formula: 'The Government must therefore be free to consider every proposal likely to help, such as tariffs, expansion of exports and contraction of imports, commercial treaties and mutual economic arrangements with the Dominions.' No true free trader could swallow this, and it is not surprising that the Liberals' draft election manifesto tried to revive the old 'free food' campaign by stating: 'The Liberal Party is opposed to and will resist any taxes upon the food of the people.'[44]

Reading, however, would have nothing to do with this echo from past tariff reform controversies. He bluntly told the compilers of the manifesto that unless they deleted this sentence he would not sign the document. Faced with this ultimatum they gave way and a bland rephrasing won Reading's approval and support.

By now the old Liberal united front on tariffs had been destroyed, and the party went into the election campaign divided into three factions: the Simonites who supported tariff reform, the followers of Lloyd George who still advocated free trade, and those who approved of Samuel's and Reading's middle path.

None of this did the Liberals much good at the polls. Voting took place on 27 October. Starved of funds by an enraged Lloyd George, the Liberals could only put up 122 candidates. Thus, despite the fact that in a good many seats Conservative candidates were not put up against Simonite and Samuelite Liberals, they polled 3,000,000 fewer votes than in 1929. As a whole the party ended up with seventy-two seats, thirteen more than in 1929, but split between the three factions: the Samuelites won thirty-three seats, Simon's National Liberals thirty-five and Lloyd George found himself the leader of a family party of four, himself, his son, his daughter and his son-in-law – thus, moralists might have noted, the controversial Lloyd George Fund had led directly to a blatant nepotism!

The only real winners of the 1931 election were the Conservatives, with 208 gained seats and a Commons representation of 471. Labour were swept aside everywhere except in Wales, the east end of London and South Yorkshire; they were reduced to fifty-two seats (six of them won by the Independent Labour Party) and saw their popular vote fall by one and three quarter million. The National Labour candidates, MacDonald, Thomas and the rest, won thirteen seats, often with huge majorities. The supporters of the National government, the Tories, the National Liberals and National Labour, received over 60 per cent of the poll, and won 521 seats. The 'doctor' had received an overwhelmingly convincing mandate – though whether he could make anything of it was not clear.

MacDonald set about restructuring the National government. Baldwin remained Lord President of the Council, Snowden, made a peer, became Lord Privy Seal, Neville Chamberlain took the Chancellorship of the Exchequer and with it the opportunity to give posthumous effect to his father's tariff reform campaign. The Liberals, apart from Lloyd George who resigned as party leader on 3 November, did well out of the reconstruction of the government: Sir Herbert Samuel, having made his stand on the tariff issue, stayed at the Home Office; Walter Runciman became President of the Board of Trade, with Hore-Belisha as his Parliamentary Secretary; Sir Archibald Sinclair was appointed Secretary of State for Scotland, and Sir Donald Maclean became Minister of Education; Sir John Simon was rewarded for his 'National' spirit with the Foreign Office, at Reading's expense.

Did Reading resign willingly or was he pushed? The evidence is confusing. Reading's son wrote, with a hint of bitterness, that 'he found himself superseded without any warning from the Prime Minister of his intentions'.[45] Reading himself told Arthur Murray in April 1932: 'I was sorry to leave the FO. I liked both the office and those officials with whom I was in closest contact very much indeed. I only gave up because I knew I was at breaking point.'[46]

Although Reading had indeed found his Foreign Office workload taxing, he had also been much stimulated by it. Certainly he was not 'superseded without any warning from the Prime Minister'. On 28 October as the result of the election became evident he had called on MacDonald and indicated his willingness to stand down. On 3 November 1931 he wrote to the Prime Minister putting the disposal of his office in his hands:

Ever since the results of the elections I have been impressed by the difficulties that must confront you on reconstructing the National Government. With the desire to be helpful I intimated to you on Oct. 28th, and again later, that I was willing to retire from the Government and I placed my office unreservedly in your hands.[47]

MacDonald was thus given a way out from what might have been an awkward piece of Cabinet-making. Reading had been a conspicuously loyal member of the first National government, and had even written a letter to his old constituency at Reading during the election campaign emphasizing the 'National' line that 'Party consideration must give way to national interests at this critical time in our country's history'.[48] He had proved far less obdurate than Samuel on the tariff issue, but it was Samuel who stayed in office not Reading. He had contributed much to the cause of Liberal unity whereas Simon had provoked dissent, but it was Simon who took his post at the Foreign Office.

Perhaps Reading's links with Lloyd George, though now tenuous, counted against him. After all, he had returned post haste from Churt and threatened MacDonald with his resignation on 26 September when the future of the first National government was delicately poised. MacDonald, moreover, had cause to fear Lloyd George's residual powers; indeed, when he had visited Lloyd George a day or two before announcing the date of the October general election 'He was not at all pleased to meet the "invalid" walking briskly into the house from the garden in his Tyrolean cloak, with his white mane blowing in the summer breeze. ("How Ramsay's face fell when he saw me!" said Lloyd George afterwards.)'[49] Although Lloyd George's political fortunes were at their lowest point as MacDonald reconstructed his Cabinet in early November 1931, there was no guarantee that they would remain so, and Reading had acted as a spokesman and negotiated for his friend on innumerable occasions in the past. Simon was both safely 'National' and safely anti-Lloyd George, and this may have weighed in MacDonald's calculations.

No hint of this, naturally enough, appeared in the Prime Minister's letter accepting Reading's sacrifice of his office. MacDonald wrote comfortingly and not altogether truthfully:

You came in to help us at a time of great crisis and accepted office because I urgently pressed you to do so and, as I know, much against your wish.

As you know the work of this Government will be very unusual and I may have to ask men of wide experience, who are not members of the administration, to come to our assistance.[50]

Simon hastened to make friendly contact, telling Lady Reading on 7 November: 'I shall be trotting round for council from time to time for I already appreciate how difficult and delicate beyond belief this tangle is. It would please you to hear how they speak of *him* and *his* views here [at the Foreign Office].'[51]

At any rate, Reading was out of power. He may have taken some comfort from a letter, written the day after MacDonald accepted his resignation, from a senior Foreign Office official to Lady Reading: 'We were all so hoping that Lord Reading would stay on with us here, and everywhere I go in the FO I hear the same story of regret and disappointment. In the brief space of ten weeks he has earned the complete confidence and affection of this office.'[52]

17 Out, But Not Down, 1931-5

[MacDonald] hoped that I would be ready to help him and now come into the Government.
Reading, September 1932

For myself, I still lead the Liberals in the House of Lords, and, to my surprise, still keep them united.
Reading, November 1934

These attacks are a horrid bore. I am afraid that when I am fit again, I shall have to give up some work, instead of taking on anything new.
Reading, on his death bed, December 1935

Reading's loss of the Foreign Secretaryship did not lead to a period of tranquil inactivity, enlivened by occasional contemplations of his navel. He was hardly out of office before the Second Round Table Conference on India opened in London on 7 November 1931.

As the leader of the Liberal delegation, and an ex-Viceroy, Reading was in as influential a position as at the First Round Table Conference of November 1930 to January 1931. He was in addition a member of the Cabinet Committee on the India Conference.

The Second Round Table Conference proved to be a bitter disappointment to those who hoped for further progress towards an independent federal India. There were several reasons for this: Hindu and Muslim delegates could not agree over the composition of the provincial legislatures under the proposed constitution; the Indian princes, having saved the First Round Table Conference by their willingness to consider federation, now backed away from the idea, fearing that they would be swamped and lose their influence in any future federal assembly; the Congress party delegates refused to accept that the Imperial government should hold the responsibility for defence and foreign affairs even for a transitional period; Gandhi, who attended the Conference, became unhelpful once the prospect of an all-India federation dimmed; moreover, the vast Conservative majority in the Commons, and the new Tory Secretary of State for India, Sir Samuel Hoare, were less inclined to make concessions than their Labour predecessors in 1930–1.

Having seized so eagerly upon the federal solution at the First Round Table Conference, Reading was unhappy at the deadlock and confusion of the Conference's second session. As early as June 1931 he had written gloomily to Lord Willingdon, now Viceroy, that he thought Gandhi would 'be a disturbing and not a conciliatory factor at the Conference'.[1] Three months later he had reinforced Willingdon's determination to rule firmly, saying, 'I agree absolutely with you and always have, as you know, in taking the stronger lines with regard to Civil Disobedience. It is the very essence of peace and good Government.'[2]

Although disliking Gandhi's spoiling tactics at the Second Round Table Conference, Reading was anxious that the opportunity for all-India federation should not be lost through the British government's refusal to compromise over certain issues. On 23 November, at the meeting of the Cabinet Committee on the Conference, he argued that Indians had been led to expect a finance minister of their own under the proposed constitution, and that if the British government 'proposed to concede no measure of authority over finance to the [central] legislature they might abandon hope of an agreed scheme of Reform'.[3] Hoare and Neville Chamberlain, Chancellor of the Exchequer, promptly declared that they 'were prepared to accept Lord Reading's suggestion that Indian Departmental Ministers (as agents of the new Legislature) should enjoy initiative and control over expenditure upon unreserved subjects provided that financial stability was not undermined'.[4]

Five days later Reading carried his liberal arguments further, writing a personal letter to the Prime Minister and urging him to reaffirm the British government's willingness 'to carry out its promises'. Reading told MacDonald:

On reviewing the situation as it presents itself on the eve of the final plenary session I am seriously perturbed at the possibility, indeed almost the certainty, that the Indian representatives on the Round Table Conference will return to India filled with distrust and suspicion of the intentions of the Government, unless you can dispel this atmosphere by your final statement of policy.[5]

Reading had a practical proposal as to how the Conference might be saved. He wanted MacDonald to reaffirm his end of Conference speech of 19 January 1931, and to implement it by introducing provincial autonomy as soon as possible, i.e. within a year or eighteen months, and at the same time proceeding with the policy of Federation, with responsibility and safeguards, on the broad lines laid down in the Federal Structure Committee's report, which must take a considerably longer period before completion.[6]

On 1 December 1931 MacDonald did indeed close the Second Round Table Conference with a reiteration of his policy statement of 19 January. He told the delegates, however, that if the communal antagonisms over the constitution continued the British government would themselves provide a provisional solution. A consultative committee was to be set up in India to thresh out, in time for a reconvened session of the Round Table Conference in 1932, the major outstanding questions involved in federation: the franchise, federal finance and the financial relationship between the states and the federation. Full provincial autonomy, as Reading had proposed, was to go ahead.

This end of Conference speech did not send the majority of Hindu delegates home with their spirits raised; they felt that the tide had turned, and that the Tory preponderance in Parliament was leading to a policy of placating and arousing the Muslims, and to a new era of repression.

Events were to prove the pessimists right. Civil disobedience was renewed in India, and Gandhi and thousands of his supporters were arrested and imprisoned.

Progress towards a new constitution was nevertheless made. Reading took part in the Third Round Table Conference of 17 November to 24 December 1932 where much time was devoted to the discussion of points of constitutional law. Agreement was finally reached on the principle of an all-India federation, though many details remained unsettled. The princes, moreover, had become even more wary of federation, which they now clearly realized would mean an essential surrender of their authority.

The British government was, however, now committed to putting a new Government of India Act on the statute books. Drafting this piece of legislation promised to be an arduous task, and a Joint Select Committee of Parliament was set up in the spring of 1933 to carry out the work. Reading was an obvious candidate for the Committee. His initial misgivings over the demands this work would make upon his time were overborne by appeals from leading statesmen of all three parties. On 7 March Herbert Samuel wrote, 'I think it would be a disaster if you were not to serve on the Committee. Indeed your membership seems to me almost indispensable.'[7] For the Tories, Lord Hailsham, Secretary of

State for War, said on 7 April, 'I am quite sure that [Hoare] will feel as I do that the importance of having you as a member far outweighs any difficulty resulting from occasional absence on other duties.'[8] For National Labour, Lord Sankey the next day urged Reading to serve on the Committee, and paid tribute to the 'consideration for others which makes you so well liked and trusted everywhere and by everybody'.[9]

Reading duly sat on the Committee which held 159 meetings between April 1933 and November 1934; 120 witnesses were examined by the Committee; Reading attended zealously, though the strain upon him was considerable.

In August 1935 the Government of India Act became law. Reading took an active part in the debates on the Bill, and made his last speech in Parliament on the subject, although so hoarse that his remarks were largely inaudible. His main contribution to the debates was once more to attack the phrase 'Dominion status' as being inappropriate for inclusion in the bill's preamble. He got his way on this, though he was not alone in making the point.

The passing of the 1935 Government of India Act gave Reading considerable pleasure, particularly since the day had been carried against Winston Churchill and the Tory die-hards. The Act did not, however, lead smoothly to a transfer of power. The princes shied away from federation, and Indian nationalists were divided in their response to the measure. Finally the outbreak of the Second World War distorted the British government's approach to Indian independence, and it was not until 1947 that the old Indian Empire, partitioned and awash with blood, achieved self-rule.

Reading had escaped after the ending of the Second Round Table Conference on a restorative holiday with his wife. They travelled to Palestine and Egypt. In Palestine, Reading, who had always steered clear of identification with Zionism, was warmly welcomed, and on 27 December 1931 delivered a public address in Haifa when he referred to Lord Melchett's influence upon him in support of the idea of a Jewish national homeland.

As we have seen, Reading, though sensitive to anti-semitic prejudice and horrified at the brutal excesses of the Nazis, preferred to think of himself as an Englishman first and a Jew second. He had refused to become the first chairman of the Jewish Agency for the Palestine mandate, and was content to give informal advice and help to such founder-members of the Jewish homeland as Chaim Weizmann.

Indeed, he hesitated before visiting Palestine in December 1931, although he could have justified his voyage simply as chairman of the

Palestine Electric Corporation. He was apparently aware 'that he was regarded with hero-worship throughout the Jewish world and that he would be enthusiastically received, and he feared that his presence might give rise to hopes of more active support on his part than he was prepared to give'.[10] Though impressed by what he saw, 'he did not change his views in the slightest degree or allow his emotions to outweigh his reason'.

Travelling into Egypt, Reading caught a chill at Luxor which developed into double pneumonia. For a while it seemed he might die, but the skill of a Swiss doctor and the nursing of his wife pulled him through. Oddly, for so gentle a man, 'In his delirium he reverted ... to the Lord Chief Justiceship and spent much of the time sternly sentencing his nurse to various periods of penal servitude.'[11]

By the following spring he was quite restored, and 'his spirits also regained much of their old effervescence, mounting at times to boisterousness. At the instigation of his grandchildren ... he would produce lurid anecdotes of his own very different youth, occasionally enriched with strange fragments of by-gone music-hall ditties, and snatches of sea-shanties learnt in remote "Blair Athole" days.'[12]

He was soon back in the boardroom and taking an active part in Liberal party politics. Although not competing for the leadership of the official, Samuelite, Liberals, Reading was closely involved in the formulation of certain aspects of policy through Samuel's frequent consultations with him.

The introduction of protection came in 1932 and was given its most comprehensive, and attractive, expression in the Ottawa agreements of July at the Imperial Conference. The Ottawa Conference produced several bilateral reciprocal trade agreements between different parts of the Empire, including Britain. The agreements were the final fulfilment of Joseph Chamberlain's tariff reform campaign three decades before. They did not create anything like an Imperial Common Market, but they were none the less nails in the coffin of free trade.

On 31 August 1932 Samuel wrote to Reading urgently requesting a meeting to discuss 'the serious position' that had arisen, and before 'any active movement takes place in the Liberal Party Organization'.[13] As a result of the meeting Reading, together with two other Liberal elder statesmen, Lords Grey and Crewe, published a letter in *The Times* on 29 September supporting Samuel's resignation, and that of Sinclair, over the principle of free trade versus protection (Philip Snowden had also resigned over the same issue). The letter to *The Times* emphasized that 'except as regards fiscal policy there has been no difference on main issues inside the Cabinet between Free Trade Members of it and their colleagues; we hope this degree of harmony may be found possible outside as it has been within the Cabinet'.[14] On 30 September Samuel warmly thanked Reading for his help and for signing the letter which 'has had considerable effect in steadying public opinion'.[15]

Reading was much more sympathetic than Samuel to the National government over the tariff issue. Just as Samuel had been a far more stubborn supporter of free trade in the attempts to draw up a National government election manifesto in late September and early October 1931, Reading was only lukewarm in his support of the Samuelite Liberal attitude in 1932 towards protection.

Far from pushing Samuel towards resignation on 28 September 1932, Reading had even been reluctant to sign the joint letter with Crewe and Grey until he 'had seen an account of the events of today [28 September] and the reasons given for resignation'.[16]

Such was Reading's reluctance to rock the National government boat, that the Prime Minister actually tried to entice him back into the Cabinet, as Lord Privy Seal, to fill the gap left by Samuel and Sinclair, and to help settle the American debt and advise on economic matters. According to Reading's notes, MacDonald told him that:

> [the National government] had been very seriously injured by the resignations and these would have a weakening effect upon the position of the British Government in Foreign Council. He hoped that I would be ready to help him and now come into the Government.
>
> I said that I was very sorry but I could not join the Government. Apart altogether from the fact that I had written a letter [of 28 September], I reminded him that the attitude I was now taking was the same as on the last occasion of our meeting seven or eight days back when I said I deeply regretted that the Liberal Ministers should go and that I thought I was probably the one who was most anxious and would go furthest to support the Government and keep the Ministers in. . . . I said I was very sorry indeed but I could not again join his Cabinet. . . . He was evidently disappointed.[17]

What were the reasons for Reading's flirtation with a National government committed to the introduction of protection? At one level, he still found the prospect of power very seductive; at another, his deeply felt, though undemonstrative, love for his country made him eager for the success of the economic remedies proposed by the National government. In Reading's case, patriotism was not the last refuge of scoundrels but of men of good will and some ambition.

Reading's misgivings over the Samuelite Liberals' hostility to the National government were once more demonstrated in November 1933.

From the resignations of September 1932, the thirty-odd Liberal MPs who followed Samuel were in a most peculiar position; in theory they were supporters of the National government on every issue except that of tariffs; in practice they were suspended in an ungainly, and at times ridiculous, posture between government and opposition. In November 1933 the Samuelites restored some self-respect by moving formally into opposition on the ground that the government was not promoting the cause of disarmament seriously enough.

Knowing Reading's ambivalence over the Samuelites' move, the Prime Minister had written to him on 16 November 1933 saying, 'I am very sorry that the section of the Liberals to which, I believe, you belong are crossing the floor. . . . I cannot do anything but deplore the decision you have come to.'[18]

The next day, 17 November, a Liberal peer, Lord Elgin, wrote to Reading reminding him of his earlier assurance that there was no intention of 'withdrawing support from the National government', and stating that he would not follow, in the Lords, 'the same course as that adopted by Sir Herbert Samuel in the House of Commons'.[19] In fact, Reading swallowed his anxieties over the wisdom of Samuel's moving into opposition and continued to lead the Liberals in the House of Lords. Perhaps it did not much matter whether the Liberal Lords supported the National government or not. Reading kept them together at any rate, writing on 2 November 1934, 'For myself, I still lead the Liberals in the House of Lords, and, to my surprise, still keep them united. . . .'[20]

Privately, however, Reading deplored Samuel's more militant approach, even to the extent of criticizing in November 1933 his attacks on the Simonite National Liberals and other National government supporters: 'I, for one, cannot approve either of [Samuel's] repeated attacks on life-long Liberals such as Mr Runciman and Sir John Simon and other members or supporters of the National Government, or his present active opposition to that Government both in Parliament and at elections.'[21]

Despite these misgivings over tactics, Reading continued to be associated with the Samuelite brand of Liberalism. He vetted the draft Liberal manifesto of January 1933, though largely contenting himself with underlining the free trading proposals that the party should push '*on more vigorously* than ever with the endeavour *to secure* real *political appeasement*', should strive for 'the *bold reversal* of *recent tendencies* in Economic *policy*', and that nations, including Britain, should '*Frankly abandon the attempt to make themselves self-sufficient* and recognize that it is in their own interests to *assist the prosperity of other nations as well as that of ourselves.*'[22]

Reading also expressed tentative support for House of Lords reform when the subject briefly re-emerged in 1934 in the form of a bill presented by Lord Salisbury. Lords reform had not been the prerogative of Liberal or Labour governments since the Parliament Act of 1911 and Lord Salisbury had advocated certain reforms during Baldwin's Conservative government of 1924-9. Admittedly Reading was a very moderate reformer of the upper house, telling Lord Crewe on 1 May 1934: 'Like you I am not opposed to all reform of the Lords. I recall the Preamble of the Parliament Act and Asquith's view etc., and am disposed to take this line in Debate, while offering [the] strongest opposition to the Bill as it stands.'[23]

There was no need for great anxiety: Lords reform came to nothing during Reading's lifetime.

In June 1934 Reading was installed in his last public office, although not one to rank with the Lord Chief Justiceship, the Viceroyalty or the Foreign Secretaryship. Earlier in the year MacDonald had offered him the post of Lord Warden and Admiral of the Cinque Ports on Lord Beauchamp's resignation. Reading was the 156th man to hold the office, and the first Jew – something which pleased him when set against the background of Hitler's ruthless harrying of German Jewry.

Reading was delighted with his historic, though unsalaried, post, and enjoyed showing friends round Walmer Castle where he and Lady Reading spent a good deal of their remaining eighteen months together. At Christmas 1934 he had a large family party at Walmer:

He was in exuberant spirits and enjoyed every moment, and his examination of the contents of his stocking was as excited as it might have been if stockings had come his way seventy years before. His only trouble was his voice. The hoarseness which had descended upon him some months earlier refused to yield to any treatment and he was difficult to hear, except in an otherwise silent room. This disability worried him greatly for he realized it might be permanent and that, if so, he would have to some degree to re-orient a life which still involved much making of speeches.[24]

In May 1935 he was happy to attend the service in honour of King George v's Silver Jubilee. A few weeks later he received Sir Herbert Samuel, still Liberal leader, at Walmer Castle. Both men thought the government should now rearm to contain Nazi Germany's growing strength in the air. They also discussed their old chief Lloyd George's latest political initiative, which was to call for a Council of Action for

Peace and Reconstruction to wage a 'non-political campaign for peace and prosperity'. Reading advised cautious support for Lloyd George's proposals.

Reading was concerned lest he should suffer a steady and embarrassing diminution in his physical and mental powers. He remarked poignantly to his son, after seeing a news poster announcing the death of Lord Buckmaster, a former Liberal Lord Chancellor:

That is the real tragedy of growing old, that your friends keep dropping off one by one. I sometimes look round in the House of Lords at my contemporaries and I notice this one failing in that and that one in another, and I wonder whether they themselves are conscious of it. And I wonder whether it is all the time happening to me without my knowing it. I should hate above all things to lose my faculties and linger on.[25]

He need not have worried. He had been fortunate during his life, and he was fortunate in his death. At the end of September he suffered a violent attack of cardiac asthma after playing some practice shots of golf, and had to stay in bed for several weeks watching through the window ships passing by and enjoying John Masefield's sea stories.

Reading made a good recovery from his illness. He was back in London for the results of the general election of November 1935 which saw the Samuelite Liberals reduced to sixteen MPs – a far cry from the great Liberal majority of 1906 a few years before Reading first took office. Baldwin, who had succeeded MacDonald as Prime Minister five months before the 1935 poll, was confirmed in office with a huge majority, including the National Liberals.

The Abyssinian crisis had been one issue in the election campaign, and Reading approved of the application of League of Nations' sanctions against Italy, although not to the closing of the Suez Canal to Italy as a means of enforcing them. He later heard with some distaste of the Hoare–Laval pact to partition Abyssinia, believing that this piece of undercover diplomacy was a death blow to the League of Nations.

In early December Reading was well enough to hold board meetings at 32 Curzon Street, and to spend some time in his offices at Imperial Chemical House.

In the middle of the month, however, he was stricken with another serious attack of cardiac asthma. His condition now steadily deteriorated. By 27 December the press was informed that his condition was giving some anxiety.

His wife and son stayed at his bedside as his life came slowly to a close.

For his part, he seemed to feel no pessimism, remarking to Gerald Isaacs, 'These attacks are a horrid bore. I am afraid that when I am fit again, I shall have to give up some work, instead of taking on anything new.'

On the night of 29 December 1935 he finally lapsed into unconsciousness, and died peacefully the following afternoon as the street lights were being turned on in the winter gloom.

Lord Reading's death prompted countless messages of sympathy and a deluge of press obituary notices, a reaction that was uncannily like a dress rehearsal for the public response to King George v's death which was to follow within a month. The King himself wrote simply, 'His services to the State will always be remembered by the nation.' Among Reading's friends, colleagues and even opponents, tributes came from Lloyd George, Herbert Samuel, Ramsay MacDonald, Anthony Eden, Lady Oxford and Asquith, Colonel House, the Prince of Wales, Pierre Laval, Mahatma Gandhi, Mackenzie King, John Simon and Philip Snowden.

The press obituaries were almost universally favourable, although the *Daily Herald*, as well as making several errors of fact, referred to him rather ambivalently as 'the tireless Jew', and remarked that his 'attempt to crush "Gandhism" proved a clumsy failure'. The *Herald* drew some predictable comfort, however, from Reading's humble beginnings: 'Faced with all the handicaps that confront boys born to uncongenial jobs, he set out to make his name, his chief assets being an unlimited fund of patience, a capacity for hard work, and a brain of remarkable capacity.'[26] The *Belfast Telegraph* referred to the 'Close of a Unique Career',[27] and the *Gloucester Citizen* spoke of his 'Example to Youth'.[28] The *Scotsman* mourned a 'Brilliant Lawyer and Able Administrator',[29] while the *Western Mail* claimed that his life, if traced step by step, 'was like a magic ladder of the Arabian fables'.[30] The *Yorkshire Observer* paid tribute to the 'Greatest Jewish Statesman Since Disraeli'.[31]

Of the great British daily papers, the *Daily Express* put a new slant on things by claiming that 'He was born "comfortable" but chose to live hard';[32] the *Daily Mail* announced its deep regret for the death of a 'Man Who Rose from Ship's Boy to be Lord Chief Justice and Viceroy';[33] the *News Chronicle* believed that he 'will live in history as the most romantic and stately figure, with the dubious exception of Disraeli, that British Jewry has produced'.[34] The *Daily Telegraph*, having paid tribute on 31 December, the next day ran a column wondering who would be the next Lord Warden of the Cinque Ports.[35] *The Times* printed an appreciation by Lady Oxford, Asquith's widow, who wrote that Reading 'was born with the advantage of a beautiful face and a resonant enunciation – as clear in the Courts of Law as it was in private conversation. ... My husband always said that Lord Crewe and Lord Reading were the two men whose advice he most valued.'[36] The *Manchester Guardian* hailed a 'Liberal Statesman's Career', and approvingly quoted Reading's remarks in February 1929 when he declared, 'I have been a Liberal all my life. ... I deny that there is no room for Liberalism and that we cannot have a really effective third party.'[37] The *Morning Post* recalled that 'His powerful brain kept a sharp rein on his tongue which was seldom, even on the most harmless occasions, allowed a free run.'[38]

The *Jewish Chronicle* printed a statement by the Zionist Federation of Great Britain and Ireland which said, among other things, 'The whole of the Jewish world mourns in the death of Lord Reading, a leader who, in his own life symbolized the traditional Jewish ideal of the highest conception of citizenship and national service in perfect union with unwavering loyalty to the faith and fellowship of Israel.'[39] The London *Evening Standard* robustly pointed out that 'Rufus Isaacs was a Jew. In modern Germany he would have been persecuted or driven into exile. ... England, not interested in Aryan legends but deeply interested in using the best brains available to advance the power and prestige of the British Empire, opened the gates of opportunity to him. ... It takes brains to USE brains. England has "what it takes".'[40]

United States newspapers vied with their British counterparts in praising Reading's career. The *New York Times* quoted Lord Birkenhead's view that 'Compared with the romance of Lord Reading, the story of Richard Whittington fades into pale ineffectiveness,' and went on to remark, 'He was beloved for his wit and fairness, his tact and patience and never failing courage.'[41] The New York *Herald Tribune* claimed that his life 'has been one of the most dazzling stories of [a] successful personal career in recent history. It was the rise of a handsome stripling, tactful, acquisitive and shrewd who worked prodigiously and relied considerably on the judgement of the woman who was his wife for forty-three years.'[42] 'America is traditionally the home of self-made men', declared the Baltimore *Sun*, 'yet it is unlikely that any American ever made for himself a more brilliant career sheerly on merit and will than Rufus Daniel Isaacs born the son of a London fruit merchant ... who died on Monday as the Marquess of Reading.'[43]

Thus garlanded, Lord Reading was laid to rest. The body, in accordance with his wishes, was cremated at the Golders Green crematorium on New Year's Day 1936. Despite heavy rain and dull skies a huge crowd had gathered outside the crematorium. Reading's coffin was covered with the flag of the Warden of the Cinque Ports, and piled high with 'masses of beautiful wreaths'.[44]

The service in the crematorium chapel was conducted, partly in English and partly in Hebrew, by two rabbis, one from the Liberal Jewish Synagogue and one from the West Ham Reform Synagogue: 'Few of the austere rites of Judaism were observed.'[45] After the cremation his ashes were buried near the remains of his first wife in the Golders Green Jewish cemetery.

On 2 January a memorial service was held at the Synagogue in Upper Berkeley Street, not far from Reading's Curzon Street home. The hymn 'I vow to thee, my country' was sung at this service: it was an appropriate choice given Reading's steadfast patriotism, although perhaps less appropriate as the composition of the man whom he had rather abruptly replaced as British Ambassador in Washington in 1918.

Reading's life had a beautiful symmetry about it. It represented glittering achievements won at the cost of great endeavour and after a very ordinary start in life; it included a rakish youth, and a sober and stately maturity; it was the triumph of an outsider against the prejudices of the establishment; it comprised a happy family life and a rebellious childhood; it combined moments of rashness with the most measured and balanced judgement; it was immensely varied, yet finally fell into place like a rich and challenging jigsaw puzzle.

Even Reading's death had a curious symmetry about it: he died as one year was closing, and his ashes were buried on the first day of the New Year. Such a tidy and comely ending was wholly in character.

Notes

Introduction: Rufus Isaacs and Lord Reading

1. Quoted in *New York Times* (31 December 1935)
2. Reading papers, Eur F 118/636/112, Lady Oxford to Reading
3. Derek Walker-Smith, *Lord Reading and His Cases* (1934), pp. 2–3
4. Frances Donaldson, *The Marconi Scandal* (1962), p. 251
5. *The Times* (1 January 1936)
6. Quoted in Lord Beaverbrook, *Men and Power, 1917–18* (1956), p. 97
7. Beaverbrook, p. 96
8. New York *Herald Tribune* (1 January 1936)

Chapter 1: Origins and Schooldays, 1860–75

1. Second Marquess of Reading, *Rufus Isaacs: First Marquess of Reading*, 2 vols. (1942 and 1945), I, p. 11
2. Reading, I, p. 12
3. Reading, I, p. 17
4. Reading, I, p. 18
5. Reading, I, pp. 17–18
6. Reading, I, p. 19
7. Reading, I, p. 11
8. Syed Sirdar Ali Khan, *The Earl of Reading* (1924), p. 3
9. Reading, I, p. 15

Chapter 2: Some False Starts, 1876–85

1. Reading, I, p. 23
2. Reading, I, p. 24
3. Reading, I, p. 25
4. Speech at the Pilgrim's Dinner, London, 28 April 1926, quoted in Montgomery Hyde, *Lord Reading* (1967), p. 13
5. Reading, I, p. 27
6. Hyde, p. 15: Isaacs to Asquith, 30 July 1913
7. *The Times* (15 August 1884)

Chapter 3: Barrister: Called to the Bar, 1886–97

1. Reading, 1, p. 36
2. Reading, 1, p. 37
3. Quoted in Reading, 1, p. 38
4. Reading, 1, p. 41
5. India Office Library, Reading papers, Eur F 118/95, Lloyd George to Reading, 1 January 1925
6. Lady Cynthia Asquith, *Diaries 1915–18* (1968), p. 152
7. Lloyd George papers, F/43/1/32, Reading to Lloyd George, 22 May 1919
8. Lloyd George papers, F/43/1/35, Reading to Lloyd George, 25 June 1919
9. Reading, 1, p. 112
10. Reading, 1, p. 112
11. Reading, 1, p. 113
12. Reading, 1, p. 54
13. Francis Oppenheimer, *Stranger Within* (1960), p. 103
14. Oppenheimer, p. 99
15. Oppenheimer, p. 99
16. Reading, 1, pp. 58–9
17. Reading, 1, pp. 57–8
18. Lord Riddell, *Diaries*, 1, p. 107

Chapter 4: Rufus Isaacs, QC, 1897–1904

1. Reading, 1, p. 65
2. Reading, 1, p. 69
3. Walker-Smith, p. 391
4. Walker-Smith, p. 391
5. Stanley Jackson, *Rufus Isaacs* (1936), p. 53
6. Lewis Broad, *Advocates of the Golden Age* (1958)
7. IOL, Reading papers, Eur F 118/134, *Daily Graphic* (January 1902)
8. *Illustrated News* (30 August 1904)
9. *Daily Mirror* (2 March 1910)
10. *Lancashire Post* (7 March 1910)
11. *Star* (28 March 1901)
12. Letters of 6 August 1901, quoted in Reading, 1, p. 84
13. Reading, 1, p. 120
14. Reading, 1, pp. 126–7

Chapter 5: Member of Parliament and King's Counsel, 1904–10

1. Reading, 1, p. 70
2. Reading papers, Eur F 118/58/151, Morgan (miners' secretary) to Isaacs, 15 August 1902
3. Reading papers, Eur F 118/26/14, Godfrey to Isaacs, 20 August 1902
4. Denis Judd, *Radical Joe: a Life of Joseph Chamberlain* (1977), p. 246
5. Roy Jenkins, *Asquith* (1964), p. 137
6. See Denis Judd, *Balfour and the British Empire* (1968), chapters 6–9
7. Quoted in Hyde, p. 57
8. Reading, 1, p. 131
9. *Morning Post* (3 August 1904)
10. *Daily Chronicle* (1 August 1904)
11. *Daily News* (4 August 1904)
12. *Pelican* (6 August 1904)
13. *Morning Post* (8 August 1904)
14. Walker-Smith, p. 3
15. Reading, 1, p. 5
16. *Saturday News* (15 February 1908)
17. Walker-Smith, pp. 8–9
18. Hansard, 4th series, vol. 148 (July 1905)
19. Reading, 1, p. 73
20. Reading, 1, p. 156
21. Reading papers, Eur F 118/109
22. British Library, Add. Mss. 46304, Burns to Isaacs, 21 December 1908
23. BL, Add. Mss. 46304, Reading to Burns, 19 July 1922
24. *Reading Standard* (20 January 1906)
25. *Reading Standard* (2 February 1907)
26. *Saturday News* (15 February 1908)
27. *Reading Standard* (5 January 1910)

Chapter 6: Solicitor-General, 1910

1. Reading, 1, p. 185
2. *Lancashire Post* (7 March 1910)
3. *Manchester Evening Chronicle* (7 March 1910)
4. *Evening Standard* (7 March 1910)
5. *Daily Mail* (7 March 1910)
6. *Daily Mirror* (2 March 1910)
7. Edward David (ed.), *Inside Asquith's Cabinet: from the Diaries of Charles Hobhouse* (1977), p. 88. NB, in his endnotes Dr David wrongly

describes Sir Arthur Bigge as private secretary to Lloyd George at this time

8. Reading, 1, p. 191
9. Reading, 1, p. 196
10. Reading, 1, p. 111
11. Reading, 1, p. 110

Chapter 7: Attorney-General, 1910–13

1. Lucy Masterman, *C. F. G. Masterman* (1939), pp. 179–83
2. Masterman, pp. 179–83
3. Masterman, pp. 179–83
4. Reading, 1, p. 207
5. Reading, 1, p. 207
6. Reading, 1, p. 204
7. William J. Braithwaite's memoirs (ed. Bunbury), *Lloyd George's Ambulance Wagon* (1957), p. 192, quoted in John Grigg, *Lloyd George: the People's Champion, 1902–11* (1978), p. 336
8. Quoted in Donald Read, *Edwardian England* (1972), p. 191
9. Reading papers, Eur F 118/109, Notes by Rufus Isaacs, 1909
10. Reading papers, Eur F 118/110, Cabinet paper on Land Question, October 1913
11. Read, p. 217
12. *Manchester Guardian* (18 December 1911)
13. Second Viscount Esher (ed.), *The Captains and the Kings Depart: Journals and Letters of First Viscount Esher* (1938), p. 95, entry for 12 June 1912
14. David (ed.), p. 124
15. Hyde, p. 117
16. Viscount Simon, *Retrospect* (1952), pp. 88–9
17. Jenkins, p. 242
18. Reading, 1, p. 224
19. John Wilson, *C. B., a Life of Sir Henry Campbell-Bannerman* (1973), p. 454
20. Reading, 1, p. 224
21. Simon, p. 89
22. *The Liberator* (November 1910)
23. Quoted in Hyde, p. 96
24. Quoted in Hyde, p. 97
25. Reading, 1, p. 217

Chapter 8: The Marconi Scandal, 1912–13

1. Hyde, p. 133
2. For a detailed and perceptive account of the controversy see Frances Donaldson, *The Marconi Scandal* (1962)
3. Hansard, 5th series, vol. 42 (11 October 1912)
4. Minority (Cecil) Report from the Select Committee on Marconi's Wireless Telegraph Company Limited, Agreement
5. Donaldson, p. 196
6. Donaldson, p. 135
7. Lloyd George papers, C/7/2/7, Isaacs to Lloyd George, 27 December 1913
8. Masterman, p. 255
9. Samuel papers, A/38, Samuel to Isaacs, 8 August 1912
10. Samuel papers, A/38, Isaacs to Samuel, 14 August 1912
11. Reading, 1, p. 242
12. Samuel papers, A/38, Isaacs to Samuel, 31 August 1912
13. Samuel papers, A/38, Godfrey Isaacs to Samuel, 27 August 1912
14. Samuel papers, A/38, 9 September 1912
15. Hansard, 5th series, vol. 42 (11 October 1912)
16. Quoted in Hansard, 5th series, vol. 42 (11 October 1912)
17. Hansard, 5th series, vol. 42 (11 October 1912)
18. Jenkins, p. 253
19. Viscount Samuel, *Memoirs* (1945), p. 75
20. Report from the Select Committee of Inquiry
21. Hyde, p. 129
22. Jenkins, p. 253
23. Jenkins, p. 254
24. David (ed.), p. 139
25. Reading papers, Eur F 118/636/169, Lady Oxford to Reading, 22 June 1931
26. Reading papers, Eur F 118/636/112, Lady Oxford to Reading (no date)
27. Reading papers, Eur F 118/636/225, Lady Oxford to Reading (no date)
28. Lloyd George papers, C/6/11/13, Asquith to Lloyd George, 16 June 1913
29. Reading papers, Eur F 118/1/42, Asquith to Isaacs, 16 June 1913
30. David (ed.), p. 138, entry for 13 June 1913
31. David (ed.), p. 138, entry for 13 June 1913
32. David (ed.), p. 139, entry for 22 June 1913
33. Lloyd George papers, C/3/15/20, Northcliffe to Churchill, spring 1913

34. Lloyd George papers, C/3/15/20, Northcliffe to Churchill, spring 1913
35. Duff Cooper, *Old Men Forget* (1953), p. 46
36. Donaldson, p. 250
37. Colin Holmes, *Anti-Semitism in British Society 1876-1939* (1979), p. 79
38. *National Review* (April 1912), p. 189
39. Leonard Woolf, *Sowing* (1960), p. 92
40. *The Times* (18 April 1925)
41. See David (ed.), pp. 216-19
42. A.K. Chesterton, *Oswald Mosley: Portrait of a Leader* (1937), p. 126
43. Holmes, p. 218
44. Lord Winterton, *Orders of the Day* (1953), pp. 41-2
45. Reading, 1, p. 273
46. Lloyd George papers, F/43/1/37, Reading to Lloyd George, 30 August 1919
47. Lloyd George papers, F/43/2/2, Reading to Lloyd George, 5 July 1922
48. Lloyd George papers, F/94/3/11, Ellis T. Powell to Lloyd George, 24 January 1918
49. Donaldson, p. 252

Chapter 9: Lord Chief Justice, 1913-19

1. Reading, 1, p. 274
2. Reading, 1, p. 274
3. Jenkins, p. 254
4. Hyde, p. 162
5. *Daily Express*, quoted in Reading, 1, p. 275
6. Papers lent to the author by the Third Marquess of Reading: notes made by Edgar Davis for the Second Marquess of Reading
7. Reading papers, Eur F 118/2, Asquith to Isaacs, 16 October 1913
8. Reading, 1, p. 276
9. Reading, 1, p. 276
10. *Definitive Edition of Rudyard Kipling's Verse* (1940), pp. 242-3
11. Reading, 1, p. 279
12. *The Times*, quoted in Hyde, p. 163
13. Eva Erleigh, *In the Beginning* (1926), and *Little One's Log* (1927)
14. Reading, 1, p. 281
15. Lord Riddell's diaries, quoted in Hyde, p. 166
16. See Montgomery Hyde (ed.), *The Trial of Sir Roger Casement* (1960)
17. Quoted in Hyde, *Lord Reading*, p. 169
18. Holmes, pp. 122-3

Chapter 10: Wartime Duties, 1914–18

1. Reading, 2, pp. 8–9
2. David (ed.), pp. 179–80
3. Hyde, *Lord Reading*, p. 166
4. Reading, 2, p. 9
5. David Lloyd George, *War Memoirs*, 1, p. 69
6. Tom Jones, quoted in Hyde, *Lord Reading*, p. 176
7. A.J.P. Taylor, *English History, 1914–45* (1965), p. 5
8. Lloyd George papers, Reading to Lloyd George, 2 January 1915
9. Lord Beaverbrook, *Politicians and the War* (1960), p. 154
10. Public Record Office, Foreign Office papers, American (War) FO 371/2589–90
11. PRO, Foreign Office papers, American (War) FO 371/2589–90
12. Hyde, *Lord Reading*, p. 191
13. Diaries of Colonel House, quoted in Hyde, *Lord Reading*, p. 193
14. Quoted in Hyde, *Lord Reading*, p. 195
15. Hyde, *Lord Reading*, p. 196
16. Hyde, *Lord Reading*, p. 196
17. Hyde, *Lord Reading*, p. 199
18. Reading, 2, p. 52
19. Reading papers, Eur F 118/63b/72, Lady Oxford to Reading, 8 January 1921
20. See Taylor, p. 68
21. S.D. Waley, *Edwin Montagu* (1964), p. 104
22. Taylor, p. 68
23. Asquith papers, quoted in Hyde, *Lord Reading*, pp. 206–7
24. Lloyd George papers, F/43/1/7, Reading to Lloyd George, 18 August 1917
25. House's diaries, 16 July 1917, quoted in Hyde, *Lord Reading*, p. 212
26. House's diaries, 22 September 1917, quoted in Hyde, *Lord Reading*, pp. 220–1
27. Hyde, *Lord Reading*, p. 227
28. Sir Arthur Willert, *The Road to Safety* (1952), p. 123
29. Reginald Pound and Geoffrey Harmsworth, *Northcliffe* (1959), p. 590
30. Hyde, *Lord Reading*, p. 221

Chapter 11: Ambassador to the United States, 1918–19

1. Lloyd George papers, F/23/1/25, Murray to Davidson, 20 October 1917

2. Holmes, pp. 85-6
3. Lloyd George papers, F/94/3/1, Ellis T. Powell to Lloyd George, 24 January 1918
4. Lloyd George papers, F/94/3/1, Powell to Lloyd George, 24 January 1918
5. Lloyd George papers, F/94/3/1, Powell to Lloyd George, 24 January 1918
6. Hyde, *Lord Reading*, pp. 236-7; from the Page Hines papers, Harvard University
7. Reading papers, Eur F 118/50/7, Sir Henry Lucy to Reading, 8 January 1918
8. Beaverbrook, *Men and Power*, pp. 95-6
9. Beaverbrook, *Men and Power*, pp. 95-6
10. J.M. Keynes, *Two Memoirs* (1949), p. 23
11. Lloyd George papers, F/10/5/3, Lord Finlay to Lloyd George, 9 January 1918
12. Reading Papers, Eur F 118/1 and 2, Reading to Balfour, 29 January 1918
13. Lloyd George papers, F/43/1/27, Reading to Lloyd George, 21 January 1919
14. Reading papers, Eur F 118/1 and 2, Reading to Balfour, 29 January 1919
15. Reading papers, Eur F 118/1 and 2, Balfour to Reading, 24 December 1917
16. Reading papers, Eur F 118/1 and 2, Balfour to Reading, 24 May 1919
17. Balfour papers, BL Add. Mss. 49741, Wiseman to Balfour, 25 January 1918
18. Balfour papers, BL Add. Mss. 49741, Wiseman to Drummond, 25 January 1918
19. Balfour papers, BL Add. Mss. 49741, Wiseman to Drummond, 14 March 1918
20. Reading, 2, pp. 94-5
21. Quoted in Hyde, *Lord Reading*, p. 249
22. House's diaries, 28 March 1918, quoted in Hyde, *Lord Reading*, pp. 250-1
23. Hyde, *Lord Reading*, pp. 254-5
24. Balfour papers, BL Add. Mss. 49741, Balfour to Wiseman, 27 February 1918
25. Balfour papers, BL Add. Mss. 49741, FO cypher to Reading, 19 April 1918

26. Balfour papers, BL Add. Mss. 49741, Reading to Balfour, 5 May 1918
27. Balfour papers, BL Add. Mss. 49741, Reading to Balfour, 24 June 1918
28. Reading, 2, pp. 119–20
29. Balfour papers, BL Add. Mss. 49741, Reading to Foreign Office, 14 July 1918
30. Balfour papers, BL Add. Mss. 49741, Wiseman to Drummond, 30 June 1918
31. Balfour papers, BL Add. Mss. 49741, Barclay to Reading, 3 September 1918
32. Balfour papers, BL Add. Mss. 49741, Reading to Barclay, 19 September 1918
33. Lloyd George papers, F/3/3/6, Reading to Drummond, 4 April 1918
34. Balfour papers, BL Add. Mss. 49741, Reading to Balfour, 4 June 1918
35. Hyde, *Lord Reading*, p. 278
36. Balfour papers, BL Add. Mss. 49741, Reading to Drummond, 14 May 1918
37. Balfour papers, BL Add. Mss. 49741, Long to Reading, 17 May 1918
38. Willert, p. 123
39. Reading papers, Eur F 118/1/11, Serbian Chief Rabbi to Reading, 10 February 1915
40. Reading papers, Eur F 118/10/5, Cohen to Reading, 9 October 1918
41. Lloyd George papers, F/38/2/6, Milner to Lloyd George, 31 May 1917
42. Reading papers, Eur F 118/99, Samuel to Reading, 12 January 1921 and 9 August 1923
43. Reading papers, Eur F 118/95, Reading to Montagu, 19 March 1916
44. Hansard, 5th series, vol. 79 (3 December 1930)
45. Reading papers, Eur F 118/88/104, Reading to Wauchcope, 18 March 1934
46. Reading papers, Eur F 118/88/110, Reading to Wauchcope, 28 November 1934
47. Stanley Jackson, *Rufus Isaacs* (1936), pp. 52–3
48. Reading papers, Balfour to Reading, 5 June 1918
49. Balfour papers, BL Add. Mss. 49741, Reading to Balfour and Lloyd George, 11 June 1918

50. Balfour papers, BL Add. Mss. 49741, Wiseman to Drummond, 19 July 1918
51. Arthur C. Murray, *At Close Quarters* (1946), p. 29
52. Balfour papers, BL Add. Mss. 49741, Wiseman to Drummond, 19 July 1918
53. Hyde, *Lord Reading*, p. 286

Chapter 12: Peacemaking 1918–19

1. Reading, 2, pp. 142–3
2. Reading, 2, p. 144
3. *The Times* (14 February 1919)
4. *The Times* (14 August 1918)
5. *The Times* (14 August 1918)
6. Hyde, *Lord Reading*, p. 287
7. Lloyd George papers, F/43/1/18, Reading to Lloyd George, 9 September 1918
8. Lloyd George papers, F/43/1/15, Lloyd George to Reading, 26 August 1918
9. Lloyd George papers, F/43/1/15, Lloyd George to Reading, 26 August 1918
10. David Lloyd George, *War Memoirs*, vol. 2 (1938), p. 1605
11. Lloyd George papers, F/43/1/17, Lloyd George to Reading, 9 September 1919
12. Hyde, *Lord Reading*, pp. 289–90
13. Hyde, *Lord Reading*, p. 291
14. Reading to Wiseman, quoted in Hyde, *Lord Reading*, p. 290
15. C.A. Repington, *The First World War* (1920), 2, p. 378
16. Reading, 2, p. 142
17. Balfour papers, BL Add. Mss. 49741, Barclay to Reading, 9 September 1918
18. Lloyd George papers, F/43/1/14, Reading to Lloyd George, 18 August 1918
19. Lloyd George papers, F/43/1/14, Reading to Lloyd George, 18 August 1918
20. Reading papers, Note by Reading, 28 July 1918
21. Balfour papers, BL Add. Mss. 49741, Wiseman to Reading, 18 August 1918
22. Hyde, *Lord Reading*, p. 297
23. Balfour papers, BL Add. Mss. 49741, Wiseman to Reading, 3 October 1918
24. Balfour papers, BL Add. Mss. 49741, Barclay to Reading, 10 October 1918

25. Lloyd George papers, F/43/1/7, Reading to Lloyd George, 7 January 1918
26. Reading, 2, p. 143
27. Open letter by G.K. Chesterton, quoted in Donaldson, pp. 256–9
28. Hyde, *Lord Reading*, p. 308
29. Keynes, p. 7
30. Reading, 2, p. 149
31. Reading papers, Eur F 118/19/1, Viscount Erleigh to Reading, 7 October 1918
32. Reading, 2, p. 145

Chapter 13: Unwillingly Back to the Law, 1919–21

1. Reading, 2, p. 148
2. Reading, 2, p. 148
3. Reading, 2, p. 149
4. Reading, 2, p. 150
5. Lloyd George papers, F/43/1/35, Reading to Lloyd George, 26 June 1919
6. Lloyd George papers, F/43/1/35, Reading to Lloyd George, 7 August 1919
7. Lloyd George papers, F/43/1/37, Reading to Lloyd George, 30 August 1919
8. Lloyd George papers, F/43/1/44, Reading to Lloyd George, 19 November 1919
9. Lloyd George papers, F/43/1/18, Lloyd George to Reading, 29 October 1919
10. Lloyd George papers, F/43/1/44, Reading to Lloyd George, 19 November 1919
11. Lloyd George papers, F/43/1/48, Reading to Lloyd George, 18 July 1920
12. Quoted in Hyde, *Lord Reading*, p. 315
13. Reading, 2, p. 151
14. Reading 2, p. 147
15. Reading, 2, p. 152
16. Reading papers, Eur F 118/37/87, *Bristol Times and Mirror* (31 January 1923)
17. Hyde, *Lord Reading*, p. 318, and Robert Jackson, *The Chief: the Biography of Gordon Hewart* (1959)
18. Hyde, *Lord Reading*, p. 320
19. Hyde, *Lord Reading*, p. 320
20. Hyde, *Lord Reading*, pp. 321–4
21. Hyde, *Lord Reading*, p. 324

22. Lloyd George papers, F/43/1/55, Reading to Lloyd George, 17 January 1921
23. Lloyd George papers, F/13/1/44, Curzon to Lloyd George, 13 December 1920
24. Lloyd George papers, F/13/1/44, Curzon to Lloyd George, 13 December 1920

Chapter 14: Viceroy of India, 1921–6

1. Reading, 2, p. 154
2. Waley, p. 253
3. Reading, 2, p. 154
4. R.J. Moore, *The Crisis of Indian Unity, 1917–40* (1974), p. 1
5. Reading, 2, p. 158
6. Hyde, *Lord Reading*, p. 337
7. Reading, 2, pp. 173–4
8. Reading papers, Eur F 118/103/20, Lady Reading to Gerald Isaacs and family, 17 May 1921
9. Reading papers, Eur E 316/2/7, Lady Reading to family, 8 February 1922
10. Reading papers, Eur F 118/103/42, Lady Reading to family, 24 August 1921
11. Reading papers, Eur E 316/1/9, Lady Reading to family, May 1921
12. Reading papers, Eur F 118/103/45, Lady Reading to family, 7 September 1921
13. Reading papers, Eur F 118/103/55, Lady Reading to family, 1921
14. Reading papers, Eur E 116/8/10, Diary of Lady Fitzroy, 18 April 1921
15. Earl of Birkenhead, *Halifax* (1965), p. 186
16. Reading, 2, p. 171
17. Reading, 2, p. 171
18. Sir Almeric Fitzroy, *Memoirs* (1925), 2, p. 796
19. Reading papers, Eur F 116/56/117, Reading to Buller, 1 March 1924
20. Lloyd George papers, F/43/1/60, Reading to Lloyd George, 21 February 1921
21. Reading, 2, pp. 195–7
22. Lloyd George papers, F/43/2/1, Reading to Lloyd George, 4 May 1922. Note, Reading wrote this account of his meeting with Gandhi a year after it had taken place.
23. Hyde, *Lord Reading*, p. 353
24. Reading papers, Eur E 238/3/17, Reading to Montagu, 28 July 1921

25. Reading papers, Eur E 238/3/24, Reading to Montagu, 22 September 1921
26. S.R. Mehrotra, *India and the Commonwealth, 1885-1929* (1965), p. 198
27. Moore, p. 23
28. Reading papers, Eur E 238/10/1077, Reading to Montagu, 2 November 1921
29. Reading, 2, p. 227
30. Hansard, 5th series, vol. 65 (28 July 1926)
31. PRO, Cab. 37/79/154, Balfour 1904
32. Reading papers, Eur E 238, 63 (a) i/206, Montagu to Reading, 10 March 1922
33. Reading papers, Eur F 112/226 a/16, Sir Walter Lawrence to Curzon, 14 March 1922
34. Reading papers, Eur F 118/58/69, Montagu to Reading, 15 March 1922
35. Austen Chamberlain papers, AC 23/7/26, Reading to Secretary of State for India, 11 March 1922
36. Austen Chamberlain papers, AC 23/7/31, Chamberlain to Reading, 13 March 1922
37. *The Times* (13 March 1922)
38. Austen Chamberlain papers, AC 23/7/65, Chamberlain to Lloyd George, 15 March 1922
39. Hyde, *Lord Reading*, pp. 370-1
40. Reading, 2, p. 230
41. Reading, 2, p. 231
42. Hyde, *Lord Reading*, p. 343
43. Hyde, *Lord Reading*, p. 343
44. Waley, p. 235
45. Reading, 2, p. 217
46. Reading, 2, p. 334
47. C.H. Philips (ed.), *The Evolution of India and Pakistan, 1858-1947* (1962), p. 530
48. Quoted in Hyde, *Lord Reading*, p. 382
49. Hyde, *Lord Reading*, pp. 382-3
50. Reading papers, Eur 238/63 611/201, Reading to Chelmsford, 22 May 1924
51. Moore, p. 4
52. Reading papers, Eur E 238/10/311, Reading to Montagu, 9 June 1921
53. Reading papers, Eur E 238/3/6, Reading to Montagu, 19 May 1921

54. Reading papers, Eur E 238/3/18, Reading to Montagu, 4 August 1921
55. Reading papers, Eur E 238/3/33, Reading to Montagu, 24 November 1921
56. Reading papers, Eur E 238/4/1, Reading to Montagu, 5 January 1922
57. Reading papers, Eur E 238/16/37, Montagu to Reading, 26 January 1922
58. Reading papers, Eur E 238/16/62, Montagu to Reading, 11 February 1922
59. Reading papers, Eur F 118/56/33, Mears to Reading, 14 April 1921
60. Reading papers, Eur E 238/11/55, Reading to Peel, 17 October 1922
61. Reading papers, Eur D 703/1/5, Reading to Birkenhead, 20 November 1924
62. Reading papers, Eur D 703/1/20, Reading to Birkenhead, 1 January 1925
63. K.M. Panikkar, *His Highness the Maharajah of Bikaner* (1937), p. 243
64. Reading, 2, pp. 190 and 182-3
65. From programme of Reading's visit to Alwar, in the possession of the Fourth Marquess of Reading
66. From programme of Reading's visit to Alwar
67. Marchioness Curzon, *Reminiscences* (1955), p. 182
68. Moore, p. 31
69. Reading papers, Eur D 595/4, Reading to Goschen, 15 February 1925
70. Reading papers, Eur E 238/3/14, Reading to Montagu, 7 July 1921

Chapter 15: Elder Statesman, 1926-31

1. Reading, 2, p. 344
2. Reading, 2, p. 346
3. Conversation between the author and the Fourth Marquess of Reading
4. Frank Owen, *Tempestuous Journey: Lloyd George his Life and Times* (1954), p. 694
5. A.J.P. Taylor, *Beaverbrook* (1974), p. 369
6. Reading, 2, p. 345
7. Jenkins, p. 514
8. Lloyd George papers, F/43/1/12, Reading to Lloyd George, 1 February 1918

9. Taylor, *Beaverbrook*, p. 313
10. Reading papers, Eur F 118/97, Crosfield to Beauchamp, 3 September 1926
11. Reading papers, Eur F 118/97, Beauchamp to Crosfield, 4 September 1926
12. Reading papers, Eur F 118/97, Crosfield to Reading, 7 September 1926
13. Reading papers, Eur F 118/97, Reading to Crosfield, 12 September 1926
14. Reading papers, Eur F 118/97, Crosfield to Simon, 13 September 1926
15. Reading papers, Eur F 118/97, Crosfield to Reading, 17 September 1926
16. Reading papers, Eur F 118/97, Crosfield to Simon, 17 September 1926
17. Taylor, *English History, 1914–45*, p. 253
18. Keith Robbins, *Sir Edward Grey* (1971), pp. 360–1
19. Reading papers, Eur F 118/127, Lloyd George to Reading, 14 August 1929
20. Reading papers, Eur F 118/127, Reading to Lloyd George, 2 September 1929
21. Reading papers, Eur F 118/127, Reading to Grey, 10 October 1929
22. Reading papers, Eur F 118/98, Seely to Reading, 8 October 1930
23. Hansard, 5th series, vol. 66 (30 March 1927)
24. Reading papers, Reading to Wedgwood Benn, 27 October 1929
25. Hansard, 5th series, vol. 75 (5 November 1929)
26. See Judd, *Balfour and the British Empire*, chapter 20
27. PRO, PP 1926, Cmd. 2768
28. Hansard, 5th series, vol. 77 (28 May 1930)
29. Reading papers, Eur F 118/101, Simon to Reading, 26 July 1929
30. Reading papers, Eur F 118/101, 4 June 1930
31. Reading papers, Eur F 118/101, Reading to Collins, 8 July 1930
32. Minutes of Liberal and Conservative delegations' meeting, 10 November 1930, quoted in Moore, p. 120
33. Moore, p. 120
34. Moore, p. 153
35. Moore, p. 153
36. See chapter 11
37. Osbert Sitwell, *Laughter in the Next Room* (1949), p. 224
38. Lord Citrine, *Men and Work* (1964), p. 157; see also Margaret Morris, *The General Strike* (1976), p. 258

39. Letter in possession of Fourth Marquess of Reading
40. Reading, 2, p. 362
41. Conversation of author with Fourth Marquess of Reading and his brothers
42. Conversation of author with Fourth Marquess of Reading
43. Conversation of author with Lady Joan Zuckerman
44. Dunbar (ed.), *It's the Job that Counts* (1973)

Chapter 16: Foreign Secretary, 1931

1. Taylor, *English History, 1914–45*, p. 290
2. Keith Feiling, *Neville Chamberlain* (1946), p. 191
3. Owen, *Tempestuous Journey*, p. 717
4. Reading papers, Eur F 118/106, Reading to Willingdon, 20 May 1931
5. Hyde, *Lord Reading*, p. 407
6. Reading papers, Eur F 118/131, MacDonald to Reading, 5 November 1931
7. Reading, 2, p. 362
8. Reading papers, Eur F 118/24/23, Garvin to Reading, 26 August 1931
9. Reading papers, Eur F 118/27/171, Guedalla to Reading, 26 August 1931
10. Reading papers, Eur F 118/18/6, Eden to Reading, (undated) 1934
11. Conversation of author with Dr David Carlton, author of *Anthony Eden* (1981)
12. PRO, Cab. 48/31/3, Cabinet Minutes for 26 August 1931
13. PRO, Cab. 57/31/3, 16 September 1931
14. PRO, Cab. 51/31/2, 2 September 1931
15. Reading papers, Eur F 118/131, Reading to MacDonald, 11 September 1931
16. Reading papers, Eur F 118/131, Reading to Snowden, 11 September 1931
17. PRO, Cab. 27/462, Minutes of the Cabinet Committee on the Financial Situation, 14 September 1931
18. PRO, Cab. 27/462, 14 September 1931
19. PRO, Cab. 27/462, Meeting of 17 September 1931
20. Quoted in Hyde, *Lord Reading*, p. 411
21. Taylor, *English History, 1914–45*, p. 297
22. Hansard, 5th series, vol. 80 (8 September 1931)
23. Hansard, 5th series, vol. 80 (21 September 1931)
24. Hansard, 5th series, vol. 80 (21 September 1931)
25. Hansard, 5th series, vol. 80 (8 September 1931)

26. Hansard, 5th series, vol. 80 (8 September 1931)
27. Hansard, 5th series, vol. 80 (30 September 1931)
28. Hansard, 5th series, vol. 80 (30 September 1931)
29. Reading papers, Eur F 118/131, Manchester Liberal Federation to Reading, 4 September 1931
30. Hansard, 5th series, vol. 80 (8 September 1931)
31. Hansard, 5th series, vol. 80 (8 September 1931)
32. Hansard, 5th series, vol. 83 (10 November 1931)
33. Reading, 2, p. 365
34. Hyde, *Lord Reading*, p. 415
35. Reading papers, Eur F 118/131, Record of a conversation between Lloyd George and Reading, 25 September 1931
36. Reading papers, Eur F 118/131, Record of a conversation between Reading and MacDonald, 26 September 1931
37. Reading papers, Eur F 118/131, Record of a conversation between Reading and MacDonald, 4 October 1931
38. Reading papers, Eur F 118/101, Simon to Reading, 2 March 1931
39. Reading papers, Eur F 118/101, Simon to Reading, 2 June 1931
40. PRO, Cab. 69/31/7, 2 October 1931
41. PRO, Cab. 69/31/7, 2 October 1931
42. PRO, Cab. 69/31/7, 2 October 1931
43. Keith Middlemas and John Barnes, *Baldwin* (1969), p. 647
44. Reading papers, Eur F 118/131, Record of discussion between Reading and the authors of the Liberal manifesto, 10 October 1931
45. Reading, 2, p. 365
46. Reading, 2, p. 367
47. Reading papers, Eur F 118/131, Reading to MacDonald, 3 November 1931
48. Reading papers, Eur F 118/131, Reading to the voters of Reading, September 1931
49. Owen, *Tempestuous Journey*, p. 720
50. Reading papers, Eur F 118/131, MacDonald to Reading, 5 November 1931
51. Reading papers, Eur F 118/131, Simon to Lady Reading, 7 November 1931
52. Reading papers, Eur F 118/131, R.G. Leigh to Lady Reading, 6 November 1931

Chapter 17: Out, But Not Down, 1931–5

1. Reading papers, Eur F 118/106, Reading to Willingdon, 12 June 1931

2. Reading papers, Eur F 118/106, Reading to Willingdon, 9 September 1931

3. PRO, Cab. 27/469, Cabinet Committee on the Indian Round Table Conference, Minutes of 23 November 1931

4. PRO, Cab. 27/469, Minutes of 23 November 1931

5. Samuel papers, A/86, Reading to MacDonald, 28 November 1931

6. Samuel papers, A/86, Reading to MacDonald, 28 November 1931

7. Reading papers, Eur F 118/133, Samuel to Reading, 7 March 1933

8. Reading papers, Eur F 118/133, Hailsham to Reading, 7 April 1933

9. Reading papers, Eur F 118/133, Sankey to Reading, 8 April 1933

10. Reading, 2, p. 66

11. Reading, 2, p. 367

12. Reading, 2, p. 367

13. Reading papers, Eur F 118/99, Samuel to Reading, 31 August 1932

14. Samuel papers, A 89/85, Copy of letter to *The Times* of 28 September 1932, signed by Crewe, Reading and Grey of Fallodon

15. Reading papers, Eur F 118/99, Samuel to Reading, 30 September 1932

16. Reading papers, Eur F 118/104, Reading's record of meetings with Crewe, Grey and MacDonald, 28 September 1932

17. Reading papers, Eur F 118/104, Reading's record of meetings with Crewe, Grey and MacDonald, 28 September 1932

18. Reading papers, Eur F 118/116 L, MacDonald to Reading, 16 November 1933

19. Reading papers, Eur F 118/18/12, Elgin to Reading, 17 November 1933

20. Reading papers, Eur F 118/14/145, Reading to Dawes, 2 November 1934

21. Reading papers, Eur F 118/83/24, Reading to Stanmore, 27 November 1933

22. Reading papers, Eur F 118/99, Layton's draft of the Liberal manifesto, 12 January 1933

23. Reading papers, Eur F 118/104, Reading to Crewe, 1 May 1934

24. Reading, 2, p. 271

25. Reading, 2, p. 271

26. *Daily Herald* (31 December 1935)

27. *Belfast Telegraph* (31 December 1935)

28. *Gloucester Citizen* (31 December 1935)

29. *Scotsman* (31 December 1935)

30. *Western Mail* (31 December 1935)

31. *Yorkshire Observer* (31 December 1935)

32. *Daily Express* (31 December 1935)
33. *Daily Mail* (31 December 1935)
34. *News Chronicle* (31 December 1935)
35. *Daily Telegraph* (1 January 1936)
36. *The Times* (1 January 1936)
37. *Manchester Guardian* (31 December 1935)
38. *Morning Post* (1 January 1936)
39. *Jewish Chronicle* (10 January 1936)
40. *Evening Standard* (30 December 1935)
41. *New York Times* (31 December 1935)
42. New York *Herald Tribune* (31 December 1935)
43. Baltimore *Sun* (1 January 1936)
44. *Birmingham Gazette* (2 January 1936)
45. *Daily Mail* (2 January 1936)

on first opportunity

of first introduced matter to the Ch. of E. & Elibank

I intervene in this debate at the earliest

moment/because I take the first place in the historical

order and have played the chief part in the matters under

discussion. ⎯ I have already stated on more than one

occasion, and take this opportunity of repeating, that

any criticism to be made should be directed in the main

to my action, and any blame to be attached should in the

main fall upon me, ~~and~~ for the reason that I was

responsible for the introduction of the American shares

to the Chancellor of the Exchequer and the Master of

Elibank. I do not intend to trouble the House

with a recital of the facts. They are well known.

I am glad however to allow *Ch. of Matin*

~~But I am entitled~~ to say that in making my offer to ~~them~~

I was solely actuated by a desire to befriend those to

whom I was much attached.

Before I proceed to deal, ~~as I shall quite~~

~~shortly,~~ with the transactions in American shares, let

me assure the House that nothing ~~that has transpired~~

during the whole of the public discussion in this

w *myself am*

controversy has given ~~me~~ greater pain than the ~~contention~~

that we displayed a want of frankness ~~in respect~~ to the

let me say at once looking back upon all that has happened and the time that elapsed from the appointment of the Committee to the day to the date of our being called to give evidence that it would have been better had we told the House of the purchase of American shares during the debate

The opening page of the first draft of Isaacs's Commons' statement, delivered on 18 June 1913, explaining the true nature of his involvement in the Marconi scandal. The draft had in fact been drawn up two days earlier by Asquith, who prudently did the same thing for Lloyd George. The text has been heavily altered in Isaacs's hand, and is a testament to the desperate need to make a final, watertight defence of his actions. As it happened, not all parts of the revised draft were included in the Commons statement (see Hansard, 5th series, vol. 5A, 18 June 1913, cols. 420–38).

Bibliography

I Manuscript Sources

The Reading papers deposited in the India Office Library, London
Other private papers lent to the author by the Marquess of Reading
Balfour papers, British Library
Burns papers, British Library
Campbell-Bannerman papers, British Library
Austen Chamberlain papers, Birmingham University Library
Lloyd George papers, House of Lords' Record Office
Samuel papers, House of Lords' Record Office
Asquith papers, Bodleian Library, Oxford
Montagu papers, India Office Library
Simon papers, India Office Library

II Parliamentary Papers and Official Documents

The Public Record Office's collection of Cabinet papers
Hansard's Parliamentary Debates
Reports from the Select Committee on Marconi's Wireless Telegraph
Company Limited, Agreement, together with Proceedings, Minutes of
Evidence, and Appendices, 1912 and 1913

III Journals and Newspapers

Manchester Guardian
The Times
Daily Mail
Daily Herald
News Chronicle
Morning Post
Scotsman
Daily Express
Evening Standard

Jewish Chronicle
Western Mail
Belfast Telegraph
Gloucester Citizen
Yorkshire Observer
Daily Graphic
Illustrated News
Daily News
Daily Mirror
Lancashire Post
Star
Pelican
Saturday News
Reading Standard
Manchester Evening Chronicle
The Liberator
National Review
The Eye-Witness
New York Times
New York *Herald Tribune*
Baltimore *Sun*
Birmingham Gazette

IV Biographies and Studies of Lord Reading's Life and Career

Broad, Charlie L., *Advocates of the Golden Age* (1958)
Goodhart, Arthur L., *Five Jewish Lawyers of the Common Law* (1949)
Hyde, Montgomery, *Lord Reading* (1967)
Jackson, Stanley, *Rufus Isaacs* (1936)
Khan, Syed Sirdar Ali, *The Earl of Reading* (1924)
Reading, Second Marquess of, *Rufus Isaacs: First Marquess of Reading*, vol. 1 (1942), vol. 2 (1945)
Street, Cecil J.C., *Lord Reading* (1928)
Walker-Smith, Derek, *Lord Reading and His Cases* (1934)

V Books

(Below are the books that the author has found particularly useful in writing this biography. The list is not a full bibliography of the period. Books acknowledged in the endnotes have not necessarily been included in the bibliography.)

Amery, L.S., *My Political Life*, vols. 1 and 2 (1953)

Asquith, Lady Cynthia, *Diaries 1915–18* (1968)

Asquith, Lady Margot, *Autobiography*, 2 vols. (1920 and 1922)

Aubyn, G. St, *Edward VII* (1979)

Beaverbrook, Lord, *Men and Power 1917–18* (1956)

Beaverbrook, Lord, *Politicians and the War* (1960)

Birkenhead, Earl of, '*F.E.': The Life of F.E. Smith, First Earl of Birkenhead* (1959)

Blake, Robert, *The Unknown Prime Minister* (1955)

Blewitt, N., *The Peers, the Parties and the People: the General Elections of 1910* (1972)

Bowle, John, *Viscount Samuel* (1957)

Brown, Judith, *Gandhi's Rise to Power: Indian Politics 1915–22* (1972)

Butler, Iris (ed.), *The Viceroy's Wife: Letters of Alice, Countess of Reading, from India 1921–6* (1969)

Camplin, Jamie, *The Rise of the Plutocrats* (1978)

Carlton, David, *Anthony Eden* (1981)

Chamberlain, Austen, *Down the Years* (1935)

Chamberlain, Austen, *Politics from the Inside* (1936)

Chesterton, A.K., *Oswald Mosley: Portrait of a Leader* (1937)

Churchill, Randolph S., *Winston S. Churchill*, vol. 1 (1966), vol. 2 (1967)

Citrine, Lord, *Men and Work* (1964)

Clarke, P.F., *Lancashire and the New Liberalism* (1971)

Cooper, Duff, *Old Men Forget* (1953)

Curzon, Marchioness, *Reminiscences* (1955)

Dangerfield, George, *The Strange Death of Liberal England* (1935)

David, Edward (ed.), *Inside Asquith's Cabinet: from the Diaries of Charles Hobhouse* (1977)

Donaldson, Frances, *The Marconi Scandal* (1962)

Dugdale, Blanche, *Arthur James Balfour*, vols. 1 and 2 (1936)

Esher, Second Viscount (ed.), *The Captains and the Kings Depart: Journals and Letters of First Viscount Esher* (1938)

Feiling, Keith, *Neville Chamberlain* (1946)

Fitzroy, Sir A., *Memoirs* (1925)

Fraser, Peter, *Joseph Chamberlain* (1966)

Fowler, W.B., *British American Relations 1917–18: the Role of Sir William Wiseman* (1969)

George, David Lloyd, *War Memoirs*, vols. 1–6 (1933–6)

Gilbert, Martin, *Winston S. Churchill*, vol. 3 (1971), vol. 4 (1975)

Grey of Fallodon, Viscount, *Twenty-Five Years, 1892–1916*, 2 vols. (1925)

Grigg, John, *Lloyd George: the People's Champion, 1902–11* (1978)

Gwynn, S. (ed.), *The Letters and Friendships of Sir Cecil Spring Rice* (1929)

Haldane, Viscount, *An Autobiography* (1929)

Hamer, D.A., *John Morley: Liberal Intellectual in Politics* (1968)

Hankey, Lord, *The Supreme Command*, 2 vols. (1961)
Holmes, Colin, *Anti-Semitism in British Society 1876–1939* (1979)
House, Edward M., *The Intimate Papers of Colonel House* (ed. Seymour), 4 vols. (1926–8)
Hyde, Montgomery, *Carson: the Life of Sir Edward Carson* (1953)
Jackson, Robert, *The Chief: the Biography of Gordon Hewart* (1959)
James, Robert Rhodes, *Rosebery* (1963)
Jay, Richard, *Joseph Chamberlain* (1981)
Jenkins, Roy, *Asquith* (1964)
Jones, Tom, *Lloyd George* (1951)
Judd, Denis, *Balfour and the British Empire* (1968)
Judd, Denis, *Radical Joe: a Life of Joseph Chamberlain* (1977)
Keynes, J.M., *Two Memoirs* (1949)
Koss, Stephen, *Lord Haldane, Scapegoat for Liberalism* (1969)
Koss, Stephen, *Asquith* (1976)
Marquand, David, *Ramsay MacDonald* (1977)
Masterman, Lucy, *C.F.G. Masterman* (1939)
May, E.R., *The World War and American Isolation, 1914–17* (1959)
McKenna, Stephen, *Reginald McKenna* (1948)
Mehrotra, S.R., *India and the Commonwealth, 1885–1929* (1965)
Middlemas, Keith and Barnes, John, *Baldwin* (1969)
Moore, R.J., *The Crisis of Indian Unity, 1917–40* (1974)
Morgan, K., *Lloyd George* (1974)
Morley, J., *Recollections*, 2 vols. (1917)
Morris, Margaret, *The General Strike* (1976)
Murray, Arthur C., *At Close Quarters* (1946)
Nicolson, Sir Harold, *King George V* (1952)
O'Brien, Terence H., *Milner* (1979)
Oppenheimer, Francis, *Stranger Within* (1960)
Owen, Frank, *Tempestuous Journey: Lloyd George his Life and Times* (1954)
Oxford and Asquith, Earl of, *Memories and Reflections*, 2 vols. (1928)
Pershing, J.J., *My Experiences in the World War* (1931)
Petrie, Sir Charles, *Life and Letters of Sir Austen Chamberlain*, 2 vols. (1940)
Philips, C.H. (ed.), *The Evolution of India and Pakistan, 1858–1947* (1962)
Pound, Reginald and Harmsworth, Geoffrey, *Northcliffe* (1959)
Read, Donald, *Edwardian England* (1972)
Riddell, Lord, *Diaries*, vols. 1–3 (1933–4)
Robbins, Keith, *Sir Edward Grey* (1971)
Rose, Kenneth, *Superior Person: a Portrait of Curzon and his Circle* (1969)
Roskill, Stephen, *Hankey: Man of Secrets*, 3 vols. (1970–4)
Russell, A.K., *Liberal Landslide: the General Election of 1906* (1973)
Samuel, Viscount, *Memoirs* (1945)

Searle, G.R., *The Quest for National Efficiency* (1971)

Seymour, C., *The Intimate Papers of Colonel House* (1926)

Shannon, R., *The Crisis of Imperialism* (1974)

Simon, Viscount, *Retrospect* (1952)

Sitwell, Osbert, *Laughter in the Next Room* (1949)

Skidelsky, Robert, *Mosley* (1975)

Snowden, Philip, *An Autobiography* (1934)

Speaight, R., *The Life of Hilaire Belloc* (1957)

Stevenson, John and Cook, Chris, *The Slump* (1977)

Sutro, Alfred, *Celebrities and Simple Souls* (1933)

Sykes, Alan, *Tariff Reform in British Politics, 1903–13* (1979)

Taylor, A.J.P., *English History, 1914–45* (1965)

Taylor, A.J.P., *Beaverbrook* (1974)

Waley, S.D., *Edwin Montagu* (1964)

Ward, A.J., *Ireland and Anglo-American Relations, 1899–1921* (1963)

Willert, Arthur, *The Road to Safety* (1952)

Wilson, John, *C.B., a Life of Sir Henry Campbell-Bannerman* (1973)

Wilson, T., *The Downfall of the Liberal Party, 1914–35* (1968)

Windsor, H.R.H. Duke of, *A King's Story* (1951)

Winterton, Lord, *Orders of the Day* (1953)

Woolf, Leonard, *Sowing* (1960)

Young, Kenneth, *Arthur James Balfour* (1965)

Zebel, S.H., *Balfour* (1973)

Index